This book is to be returned on or before
the last date stamped below

THE ASSOCIATION FOR SCOTTISH LITERARY STUDIES

NUMBER TWENTY-NINE

THE SCOTSWOMAN AT HOME AND ABROAD

THE ASSOCIATION FOR SCOTTISH LITERARY STUDIES

The Association for Scottish Literary Studies aims to promote the study, teaching and writing of Scottish literature, and to further the study of the languages of Scotland.

To these ends, the ASLS publishes works of Scottish literature (of which this volume is an example), literary criticism in *Scottish Literary Journal*, scholarly studies of language in *Scottish Language*, and in-depth reviews of Scottish books in *SLJ Supplements*. It also publishes *New Writing Scotland*, an annual anthology of new poetry, drama and short fiction, in Scots, English and Gaelic, by Scottish writers. ASLS has also prepared a range of teaching materials covering Scottish language and literature for use in schools.

All the above publications, except for the teaching materials, are available as a single 'package', in return for an annual subscription. Enquiries should be sent to: ASLS, c/o Department of Scottish History, University of Glasgow, 9 University Gardens, Glasgow G12 8QH. Telephone 0141 330 5309.

A list of Annual Volumes published by ASLS can be found at the end of this book.

THE ASSOCIATION FOR SCOTTISH LITERARY STUDIES

GENERAL EDITOR – C. J. M. MACLACHLAN

THE SCOTSWOMAN AT HOME AND ABROAD

Non-Fictional Writing
1700–1900

Edited by

Dorothy McMillan

GLASGOW
1999

First published in Great Britain, 1999
by The Association for Scottish Literary Studies
c/o Department of Scottish History
University of Glasgow
9 University Gardens
Glasgow G12 8QH

ISBN: 0 948877 42 1

This edition © Dorothy McMillan, 1999.

A catalogue record for this book is available from the British Library.

The Association for Scottish Literary Studies acknowledges subsidy from the
Scottish Arts Council towards the publication of this book.

Typeset by Roger Booth Associates, Hassocks, West Sussex

Contents

Acknowledgements

My grateful thanks are due to Lord Crawford, the Earl of Crawford and Balcarres, for permission to include letters from Sophy Johnston to Lady Anne Lindsay Barnard and to extract passages from *The Lives of the Lindsays*. Joanna Baillie's 'Reminiscences Written at the Request of Miss Berry' are reproduced by kind permission of the President and Council of the Royal College of Surgeons of England; Baillie's 'Memoirs Written to Please My Nephew, William Baillie' from the Wellcome Institute for the History of Medicine Library, are reproduced by kind permission of the Wellcome Trust. I should like to thank the librarians of the Royal College of Surgeons and the Wellcome Institute for their kind helpfulness and to thank also the staff of Glasgow University Library in Special Collections and elsewhere, the staff of the Special Collections in the North Reading Room of the National Library of Scotland and the staff of the Arts section of the Mitchell Library, Glasgow. My colleagues in the Departments of English and Scottish Literature at the University of Glasgow have been helpful to me in many ways; particularly Robert Cummings, who almost always tracks down a quotation, and Douglas Gifford who in co-editing with me *A History of Scottish Women's Writing* for Edinburgh University Press helped to confirm my interest in the women in this volume. Some specific debts to other scholars are mentioned in the notes. My family, as usual, have put up with my preoccupations with good humour.

I am grateful to the Association for Scottish Literary Studies for providing the opportunity to put this anthology together and especially I must thank the General Editor, Christopher MacLachlan, for waiting patiently for the manuscript to arrive and for working so helpfully with it. And I want to pay tribute to the late John Blackburn, former President of the Association, for suggesting that this would be a worthwhile project.

Abbreviations

Anderson   William Anderson, *The Scottish Nation* (Edinburgh: Fullarton, 1863)

Chambers   Robert Chambers, *A Biographical Dictionary of Eminent Scotsmen*, rev. Thomas Thomson (London & Edinburgh: Blackie, 1875)

DNB   *The Dictionary of National Biography* (London: 1885-1901; supplements, 1901-60)

DLB   *The Dictionary of Literary Biography* (Detroit: Gale Research Company, 1978-)

Elwood   Anne Katharine Curteis Elwood, *Memoirs of the Literary Ladies of England, from the Commencement of the Last Century*, 2 vols. (London: H. Colburn, 1843)

Fyfe   J. G. Fyfe, ed., *Scottish Diaries and Memoirs, 1746-1843*, with an Introduction by J. D. Mackie (Stirling: Eneas Mackay, 1942)

HSWW   Douglas Gifford & Dorothy McMillan, eds, *A History of Scottish Women's Writing* (Edinburgh: Edinburgh University Press, 1997)

Irving   Joseph Irving, *The Book of Scotsmen Eminent for Achievements in Arms and Arts etc.* (Paisley: A. Gardner, 1881)

Lonsdale   Roger Lonsdale, ed., *Eighteenth-Century Women Poets* (Oxford: Oxford University Press, 1989)

Todd 1   Janet Todd, ed., *Dictionary of British and American Women Writers, 1660-1800* (London: Methuen, 1985)

Todd 2   Janet Todd, ed., *Dictionary of British Women Writers* (London: Routledge, 1989)

Introduction

This book could have been two or three or four times as long as it is. Encountering the wealth of uncollected, unpublished and out of print writing by women within the period I have chosen for this collection has been an exhilarating experience. Obviously, of course, it would have been possible for me to make my selection in a completely different way: I could have limited myself to diaries and memoirs on the one hand, or travel writing on the other. But as I looked around for material, I came increasingly to feel that women's writing in all its variousness was best represented by an almost wild promiscuity of choice rather than generic limitation. The test came for me with the 'writing' of Lady Grisell Baillie. In 1992 I wrote briefly about Lady Grisell Baillie in a chapter, 'Heroines and Writers', about the preoccupations of Scottish women's writing in *Tea and Leg-Irons*, a volume of gently feminist readings from Scotland. My argument then was that writing by Scottish women followed a pattern over about two hundred years (the period of this anthology) which could be characterised by the opposite but linked notions of the 'heroine as writer' and the 'writer as heroine'. At that point I registered that Grisell Baillie had sacrificed her writing of songs to the duties that she willingly recognised to her family, to her father at first and to her children after her marriage. Her acceptance of these duties made it possible for Lady Grisell Baillie to be celebrated subsequently as a heroine rather than as a writer. When I wrote that, I was making a fairly obvious feminist point about the place of writing in the life of even quite strong and independent women at the time, and so I registered with a tone of regret that Lady Grisell Baillie's most enduring monument was her *Household Book* and not her songs. I remarked too that although the *Household Book* spoke the woman, it never became in any way personal. As I contemplated the anthology I considered how I would include my own earlier heroine and it was at this point that I understood how limited and limiting my notion of women's writing had been when I first admired Grisell Baillie. I have now come to feel that it may well have been more propitious for women, for writing and for an understanding of the social and political context of Scottish life in the first part of the eighteenth century that Grisell Baillie wrote a meticulous series of accounts and advices for her family and friends. In discovering for myself the importance of Grisell Baillie's *Household Book*, I found a wholly new way of thinking about the significances of women's writing and not merely for social historians.

Lady Grisell Baillie's writing was largely functional, of course, but we have to ask nonetheless why she *wrote* down what she wanted to convey. As far as the servants were concerned, they could not all be assumed to be able to read those things that concerned them. But when Lady Grisell was not herself present, her instructions would take her place. Similarly, she must have felt some need to register her feelings about the places she visited for more than the friends she was advising. The compulsion to record, to put the stamp of self on experiences, seems as strong as the obligation to be helpful to friends. And so if Lady Grisell Baillie sacrificed her art to her family and friends, she also used her authoritative situation within the family and with her friends to authorise them to behave in particular ways prescribed by her. In the end Lady Grisell Baillie's household writings may have made things happen, to steal a phrase from Auden, in a manner that no amount of song writing could do. Here then is a case that I once read as the domestic inhibiting writing, which, differently conceived, turns out to be the domestic revealing one source of writing's power.

Similarly the writing shows how the control of household affairs is itself a source of power and goes some way to explaining why the separate spheres ideology of the later eighteenth and nineteenth centuries was in many ways as attractive to women as to men. And this is, of course, the argument of Margaret Oliphant, who points out that to rule a household is to rule something at the very foundation of our daily life and values.

But most of the women in this book, including Mrs Oliphant herself, were not content to rule at home, or if they did, they wished, like Elizabeth Mure, or Janet Hamilton, to place the nature of their activities and show what was to be learned from them. The process of self-construction and self-comprehension for these women is one which insists on placing selves within the larger context of their times. Self-illumination is always more than mere introspection.

Similarly the travelling women seek to comprehend home from abroad and vice versa: we will feel them to be more or less 'advanced' according to our estimation of our own level of advancement but we should not rush to feel superior to these woman who travelled under conditions that we can only imagine through their intelligent reconstruction of them.

Of course, some of the women writers were professional and some not, some sought print and some not, although in one way or another all sought publication. It is most important, especially for women's writing of the eighteenth century, to make this distinction. Both Alison Cockburn and Lady Anne Lindsay Barnard make it quite clear that they deliberately eschew print but they clearly seek to be read by more than the immediate recipients of their letters. The same is true for that other great aristocratic writer who might have been included in the volume, Lady Louisa Stuart, who felt that print was beneath her. Other women, like Anne Grant, were forced into the marketplace to keep their families, although it seems generally true that motives other than economic produced their works.

Some very famous women writers are omitted from this volume. I felt they were disqualified precisely by their already being easily available. Elizabeth Grant and Jane Welsh Carlyle fall into this category. Those who know the field may be surprised that Janet Schaw's *Journal of a Lady of Quality, 1774-1776*, which had three Yale editions in 1921, 1934 and 1939, is not represented, but I have come to feel that Schaw's actual existence is so open to question that I do not feel secure in writing about her or her alleged journal. I am sorry that reasons of space have meant that I have not been able to include a number of other pieces: the Testamentary Letter of Anne Stewart, Lady Caldwell, to her son, the devotional diary of Lady Henrietta Campbell, the biographical work of Lady Louisa Stuart, the letters of Margaret Balfour Stevenson; other names will, of course, occur to readers.

The volume is called *The Scotswoman at Home and Abroad* and perhaps some readers will feel that I have paid too little attention to issues of nationality in my selections but my defence is that I have tried to pay the attention of the times rather than of our time, that is I have tried to show the degree of awareness of national difference that was felt by my women as they wrote. And the results are open to numerous interpretations. Thus Eliza Fletcher is included, although she was an Englishwoman by birth. But the most interesting thing is how many of the women included can call themselves Englishwomen without for a moment forgetting that they are Scots. Thus Charlotte Waldie describes herself as an Englishwoman, while clearly identifying particularly with the soldiers of the Highland Regiments as her gallant countrymen. Henrietta Keddie points out the British sentiment (during war, of course) felt in local Scottish communities. Fanny Wright describes herself as an Englishwoman, while clearly identifying herself with a Scottish radical tradition. But when reviewers of her work thought that the description 'Englishwoman' must be a lie, it was not because they thought she was Scottish, but because they thought she was a man. A large number of the women in this anthology are what we must call border-crossing Scots, who play at home and away. Joanna Baillie and Mary Somerville are good examples and both retained their Scottish accents throughout their lives; Henrietta Keddie, another border-crosser, makes the point that Margaret Oliphant had a pleasant Scottish voice.

I have tried then to explain how I came to devise this anthology but perhaps all my justifications may seem to leave unaddressed the fundamental issue of the anthology as *ipso facto* unsatisfying, the *coitus interruptus* of the reading experience. Nor would it be quite true to say that I hope that these selections will whet the appetite for further reprints so that whole texts are available. This would be a Utopian expectation and in any case whole texts would not always sustain interest. But some of the memoirs and travel writing that I have extracted are clearly overdue for republication: Christian Isobel Johnstone will stand further reading as will Henrietta Keddie; Mary Somerville's *Recollections* call out for a modern edition as do Fanny Wright's 'Lectures and Addresses'.

As I have prepared this volume I have often found myself moved and inspired. In many ways the Books of Heroines which constituted some of the intenser reading of my childhood seem not to have got things so very wrong: many of these women may still stand as role models for our children, and what is most distressing, perhaps, is that after reading through Mary Somerville's sheer intelligent goodness or Fanny Wright's ringing oratory, I am conscious how much they got it right and how much there still is to do. Obviously there are local and homely virtues also celebrated in this book; some of the heroines are, if not quite obscure, at least temporarily obscured, and of course, wealth and position are as likely to secure a place in posterity's regard as merit. But in no case in this book will the women be felt, I believe, to be unmeritorious, whatever their social rank or personal fortune. I have found myself moved also by the inter-generational love and respect which the anthology has demonstrated. The careful editing of parents' work by their children, the tributes made, usually but not exclusively, by daughters to their mothers, have demonstrated a continuity of thought and belief which undermines any simplistic notions of progress.

The claim that I would finally like to make for the writing in this volume is that the private and public life of the times may be read out of it in ways that would probably not be possible from selections from male writing of the period. This may seem hyperbolic at first but I hope that the experience of reading it will gradually substantiate the claim. The experience of reading should first of all give a sense of interconnectedness and I must insist that some of this was simply serendipitous. Often when I began looking at memoirs, for example, with a view to selection I found that relationships more and more established themselves; either the writers discussed the same public figures, or knew the same public figures, or knew each other, or each other's families. Now obviously as far as aristocratic families are concerned, this is unsurprising, but it does not stop there. The middle classes too show networks of acquaintances and concerns; even two such apparently different working class figures as Ellen Johnston and Janet Hamilton are united through their celebration of Garibaldi as people's hero, a kind of nineteenth-century William Wallace (whom the nineteenth century also made its own). Of course, such public figures as Garibaldi were not a female preserve, but I would still want to contend that the balance of interest between the public and private spheres is peculiarly female. Women almost always take an interest, even if not a part, in public life and they write about that interest, while at the same time they are almost always committed to creating stable private environments in which the public figures may relax and develop more complete senses of self: women provide the fabric of social cohesion. Even Isabella Bird Bishop, who was seldom at home, insists that a woman's mission is to create loving homes or to take home abroad with her when she travels. Of course, there are exceptions, and I have tried to allow for those too. Fanny Wright's success as a public figure was not balanced by a personal investment in private life: the emotional deprivations of her own childhood may simply have left her more able to love the world than to love a few special people. Some varieties of feminist thought have asked women to deplore the juggling acts they must perform in order to preserve a foot in both private and public camps but my aim in this anthology has been rather to celebrate the skill of the jugglers and to bring to light the loving energies and breadth of interest of a group of remarkable women.

And, of course, the distinctions that we make between private and public spheres are themselves shown to be simplifications of the way we live. Clearly certain concerns repeat themselves throughout the pieces in this volume, and the most significant is probably the one that ties the private and the public spheres inextricably together – the question of education. None of the writers in this volume neglects to consider the meaning and value of female education for every aspect of the life of young and old, men and women. Similarly my promiscuity of selection is, I think, vindicated by the inevitable conclusion to which a reader of this volume will be forced: there is no writing that is not self-writing and no writing that is not more than that. In other words autobiography and reminiscence surely do involve processes of self-construction or self-invention, but they are never exclusively focused on self; polemic or didactic or travel writing have public and explicit aims, but they seldom fail to reveal a version or versions of the self. The relationships among these journeys into the self and others are often complex and that is why we continue to be interested by them. I hope this is a volume that will constantly invite interpretation, while refusing the security of final definition.

Dorothy McMillan, Glasgow, 1999

Lady Grisell (variously Grizel, Grizeld etc.) Baillie (1665–1746)

Grisell Baillie was the daughter of Sir Patrick Hume of Polwarth, afterwards Earl of Marchmont. She was born at Redbraes Castle in Berwickshire. When she was only twelve years old she acted as go-between for her father, who was in hiding in Polwarth Church, and Robert Baillie of Jerviswood, then imprisoned in Edinburgh for 'opposing popery and arbitrary power' as Lady Grisell herself puts it in her memoir of Robert Baillie (which is included in the Scottish History Society edition of her 'Household Book'). She married Robert Baillie's son, George, in September, 1692. The marriage seems to have been supremely happy and her relationship with her two daughters exceptionally close. Lady Grisell is primarily remembered for her songs: she wrote several ballads which were included in Ramsay's *The Tea Table Miscellany*, the most famous of which is 'Werena my heart licht I wad dee'.[1] An account of her life was written by her daughter, Lady Murray of Stanhope, edited and published in Edinburgh in 1822: I have given a substantial portion of this life in the entry for Lady Murray of Stanhope. Joanna Baillie, who was probably distantly related to Lady Grisell, wrote a Metrical Legend about her, based on Lady Murray's biography. Her 'Household Book' was edited by R. Scott-Moncrieff for the Scottish History Society in 1911. I have given those extracts from the 'Household Book' that seem to reveal something of herself as well as the life of her times. In addition to the directions which I have extracted, Scott-Moncrieff's volume contains her detailed household accounts and accounts for travelling expenses and a number of bills of fare for family and special dinners. Readers will see that Lady Grisell Baillie should not be sentimentalised: she may have been a Scottish heroine but she was also clearly an exacting mistress of her household and the unleisured life of the lower servant comes over in all its unremitting toil from her directions to the House Keeper. But, as her daughter's account shows, Lady Grisell was quite as exacting upon herself.

Lady Grisell Baillie, *The Household Book of Lady Grisell Baillie*, ed. R. Scott-Moncrieff, Scottish History Society Publications ser.2, vol.1 (Edinburgh: EUP for Scottish History Society, 1911). All extracts are from this edition but with spelling and punctuation largely modernised.

Further Reading

Grisell Baillie, Lady Murray of Stanhope, 1693-1759, *Memoirs of the Lives and Characters of the Right Honourable George Baillie of Jerviswood, and of Lady Grisell Baillie by their daughter Lady Murray of Stanhope* (Edinburgh: Printed by John Pillans, 1822)

Joanna Baillie, 'Lady Grisell Baillie', *Metrical Legends* (London: Longman, Hurst etc., 1821)

Anne Grant, *Memoir and Correspondence of Mrs Grant of Laggan*, edited by J. P. Grant, 3 vols (London: Longman, Brown, Green and Longmans, 1844) vol.III, p.41

Dorothy McMillan, 'Heroines and Writers', in Caroline Gonda, ed., *Tea and Legirons: New Feminist Readings from Scotland* (London: Open Letters, 1992)

DNB; *HSWW*; Irving; Royle; Todd 1 & 2

From *The Household Book*. Spelling and punctuation are modernised where possible for ease of reading. But this means that some of the flavour of the original is lost since neither spelling nor punctuation is as formally standardised as here.

The following Memorandums and Directions to Servants with rules laid down for their diet and work were made by her in December 1743 and copied and collected by her daughter in 1752.

TO THE BUTLER

1. You must rise early in the morning which will make your whole business and household accounts easy.

2. Two bells are to be rung for every meal; for breakfast half an hour after 8 and at 9; for dinner half an hour after 1 and at 2; for supper half an hour after 8 and at 9. At the first bell for supper lay the bible and cushions for prayers.

3. Have bread toasted, buttered toast and whatever is ordered for breakfast all set ready by the second bell.

4. Consider your business and have a little forethought that you may never be in a hurry or have anything to seek, to which nothing will contribute more than having fixed and regular places for setting everything in your custody in order, and never fail setting everything in its own place, which will prevent much trouble and confusion, and soon make every thing easy, when you know where to go directly for what you want.

5. See that the back doors of the porch be shut as soon as the last bell rings for dinner and supper. *N.B.*

6. That all the servants that are to wait at table be ready *in the room before we come.*

7. That you may never have occasion to run out of the room for what is wanted have always at the sideboard what follows or anything else you can foresee there can be occasion for

bread	water	pepper	vinegar
ale	wines	mustard	shalott
small beer	sugar	oil	salad

8. Stand at the sideboard and fill what is called for to the other servants that come for it, and never fill, nor let any other do it in a dirty glass, but as soon as a glass is drunk out of, range [rinse] it directly in the brass pail which you must have there with water for that purpose, then wipe it.

9. Never let the dirty knives forks and spoons go out of the dining room, but put them all in the box that stands for that use under the table.

10. When a sign is made to you, go and see if the second course is ready, then come and take away all the first course before you set down any of the second.

11. In like manner when a sign is made take away the second course.

12. Take the napkin off the middle of the table and sweep all the bread and crumbs, clean off all round the table into a plate.

13. Have any dessert that there is ready to set down, always have butter and cheese, and set plates and knives round.

14. When all that is taken away, set down water to wash.

15. Then take away the cloth and set down what wine is called for, with the silver marks upon them, in bottle boards, and a decanter of water, and glasses to every one round.

16. When dinner and supper is over, carry what leaves of small beer and bread into the Pantry your self, and the cheese, that nothing may go to waste.

17. As soon as the company leaves the dining room after dinner and supper, come immediately and lock up what liquors are left, clean your glasses, and set everything in its place and in order.

18. Always take care to keep your doors and your cupboards locked where you have any charge.

N.B.[2] 19. The Plate must always be clean and bright, which a little wiping every day will do, when once it is made perfectly clean, which must not be by whitening but a little soap suds to wash it, or spirit of wine if it has got any spots, and wiping and rubbing with a brush and then a piece shambo [chamois] leather.

20. The pantry, cellar and larder and every thing that is under your care must be kept perfectly clean and sweet, which will require constant attention, but if things are allowed to run into dirt and confusion, double the time and pains will not set it right, and everything that stands in dirty places will soon grow musty and stinking and unfit to be used.

21. Let not the dirty china go into the kitchen till the cook be ready to clean it and empty the meat off them into pewter dishes before it goes to the second table, and see that none of them is broken when you put them by.

22. Who ever breaks china, glasses or bottles let me know that day, otherwise they will be laid to your charge.

23. Be exact in giving your pantry cloths to wash, and in getting them back and keeping them together.

24. Clean everything without delay and put all your things in order after every meal and after tea.

25. Have tea, water and what may be usually called for in the afternoon ready, that it may not be to wait for.

26. Every morning clean all the bottles that have been emptied the day before, and set them up in the bottle rack, this will save much trouble and make cleaner bottles, than when the dirt is allowed to dry in them. To make them as sweet and clean as new, boil some wood ashes in water and make a strong lee,[3] put the bottles into it before it is cold, let them soak in it all night, next day wash them well in it, then in clean water. A few hours standing in the lee may do for those not very dirty, and hang them in the bottle rack with their heads down. The most necessary thing for having good wine and ale is clean bottles and good corking, every bottle must be rinsed with a little of the liquor that is bottling, and one bottle of it will do the whole.

27. Be constantly attentive in looking about to see what any one wants at table and when you take away a dirty plate take also the dirty knife and fork and give all clean.

28. You must keep yourself very clean.

29. At one o'clock in the summer when the servants are at out work all the stable people, carters and maids go to dinner, in the winter they dine at the hour with the rest of the family altogether after we have dined, but in the summer you and those that wait at table must dine after us, both second table and later meat are allowed a clean table cloth every other day, and you must see that all get their victuals warm and in order without confusion or waste.

N.B. 30. You must see that all the servants about the stables and out works be out of the kitchen before ten a clock, except when any of them is obliged to wait at supper.

N.B. 31. The under butler puts on the gentlemen's fires, cleans their boots and shoes, helps you to clean everything, and to get breakfast and to cover the table, etc.

32. If any of the family is indisposed and eat in their room, require back from the person you gave it to any thing that is under your charge, such as knives, forks, spoons, glasses, linen, etc., and never allow any thing of that sort to go about the house or to be out of its proper place.

33. Deliver carefully back to the house keeper whatever table linen you get from her and upon no account make any other use of them, nor dirty them by wiping any thing as you have cloths for every use you can want.

34. *N.B.* If a glass of wine is called for to company bring as many glasses on a salver as there is people, and *fill it before you come* into the room, and leave the bottle at the door in case more is wanted, and have a clean napkin hung over your arm.

THE SERVANTS' DIET

There is to be brewed out of every Lothian boll of malt 20 gallons of small beer, our copper and looms brews 2½ bolls at a time which is 50 gallons, that is 400 Scots pints. From 6 furlets of malt that is a Lothian boll and half there is 240 Scots pints of beer.[4]

	pints
17 servants 3 mutchkins a day each is about 13 pints a day which in 14 days is	182
For the table 2 pints a day in 14 days is . . .	28
For second table 2 pints a day is and 2 more . .	30
	240

This calculation is when all the servants get beer.

8 stone of meal or brown flour should fully serve 17 servants eight days.

There is 30 loaves out of the stone of oatmeal, the same reckoning to be made of brown flour or rye, baked in half peck[5] loaves. Beef salted for the servants is cut in pieces of as many pounds as there are common servants, if 15, every piece is 15 pounds, no allowance in that for the second table, they getting what comes from the first table.

Sunday they have boiled beef and broth made in the great pot, and always the broth made to serve two days.

Monday broth made on Sunday and a herring.

Tuesday broth and beef.

Wednesday broth and 2 eggs each.

Thursday broth and beef.

Friday broth and herring.

Saturday broth without meat, and cheese, or a pudding or blood pudding, or a haggis, or what is most convenient.

In the big pot for the 2 days broth is allowed 2 pound of barley or groats, or half and half.

Breakfast and supper half an oat loaf or a proportion of brown bread, but better set down the loaf, and see none is taken or wasted, and a mutchkin of beer or milk when ever there is any. At dinner a mutchkin of beer for each.

DIRECTIONS FOR THE HOUSE KEEPER

The servants' diet belongs to her charge but I choose to put it altogether.

To get up early is most necessary to see that all the maids and other servants be about their proper business. A constant care and attention is required to every thing that there be no waste nor any thing neglected that should be done.

The dairy carefully looked after, you keep the key of the inner milk house where the butter and milk is, see the butter weighed when churned, and salt what is not wanted fresh, to help to make the cheese and every now and then as often as you have time to be at the milking of the cows.

Keep the maids close at their spinning till 9 at night when they are not washing or at other necessary work, weigh out to them exactly the soap, and often go to the wash house to see it is not wasted but made the proper use of, and that there be no linen washed there but those of the family that are allowed to do it. Often see that they waste not fire either in the wash house or Laundry and that the Laundry be kept clean.

Take care that the Cooks waste not butter, spices, nor anything amongst their hands, nor embezzle it, and that the kitchen fire be carefully looked after and no waste, let it be gathered after dinner and the cinders thrown up that none be thrown out, neither from that nor by the chambermaid.

Make the kitchen maid keep all the places you have locked up very clean, also the kitchen, hall and passages, and see the Cook feed the fowls that are put up right and keep them clean or they can never be fat nor good.

To take care the house be kept clean and in order, help to sheet and make the strangers' beds, that the beds and sheets be dry and well aired. Get account from the chambermaid of what candles she gets from you for the rooms and see there be no waste of candle nor fire any where.

Keep the key of the coal house but when it is wanted to get out coals, but be sure it be always locked at night, that the turf stack be not trod down but burnt even forward. Let them fill all their places with coals at once, that the key be not left in the door.

To make skimmed milk cheese for the use of the family when ever there is milk enough for it. When there are more cows then the dairy maid can milk so soon as they should be, let Grisell Wait or any other in the town I shall name help her and get for doing it a pint of skimmed milk a day.

As everything is weighed to you, give out nothing but by weight.

6 ounces prunes for Cockaleekie or stove.[6]

6 oun. Macaroni for a small dish, 8 oun. larger.

6 oun. Vermicelli for a soup.

A pound peas for a pudding or soup.

For best short bread: 8 lb. flour 3 lb. butter; second short bread: 8 lb. flour 2 lb. butter.

For a bun of 5 lb.: flour 1 lb., butter, 2 lb. raisins, 1 lb. currants, 4 ounces caraway seed, 4 ounces sugar and barm.

The servants' sheets is changed once a month.

One week the body linen is washed, the second week table and bed linen and always bouckt [steeped in lye and bleached] when the weather will allow of it, the third week the laundry maids must be kept close at spinning and at all times when they have not other necessary business, such as hay and harvest and the barn which the dairy maid always goes to when she has a moment's time for it, and always to the mill with any melder.[7] The dairy maid, house maid and kitchen maid always to spin when they are not otherwise necessarily employed which they will often pretend to be if they are not diligently looked after and kept to it.

Thomas Yule, George Carter and postilion do not wash in the house nor John Hume the Carter.

The other men servants wash in the house or out of the house as I can agree for them, but not at a certainty. When washed out I give 10s. a year for each of them.

All the skimmed milk that can be spared after serving the family or when cheese is not made of it, to be measured and sent to Grisell Wait who sells it and accounts for it, or gives it away to such poor people in the town as I give her a note of. But none of them to come about the doors for it.

Take care there be no hangers on, nor sauntering odd people come about the house, but those that have business and that not at meal time, which they will always do if not hindered.

See that all the maids keep their dusters and washing clouts dry and in order, and not let them lie about in holes wet, which soon rots and makes an end of them.

See that every one keeps what is in their charge in their proper stated places, then nothing will be out of order, or to seek when wanted, nor any hurry.

In general to keep all the servants in order, with some authority and make them obey you and do their duty without feed or favour to any, and to look after everything with the same care and faithfulness as if it was your own, then few things can go wrong. If diffident or ignorant of any thing, ask directions from me or Mrs Menzies or any that can inform you.

The following Memorandums were provided for the travels of the Earl of Haddington and Mr Baillie, Oxford, March 10th, 1740. They 'are contained in a note-book of 120 pages and are not in Lady Grisell's handwriting, though evidently of her composition' (HB, p.384). The Directions are preceded by a list of Inns in France, Italy and Germany.

Directions for Holland

In general avoid lodging at any English or Dutch house, they being the most imposing,[8] the French the best. A rule never to be departed from through all Holland is constantly to make an agreement first for every thing you get, or in employing anybody if but for a message, or you will be greatly imposed upon and pay double. If you use them with civility and show them you will not be bubbled they will use you well, but in no way will bear rough treatment, and are ever ready to impose upon any they see ignorant and careless.

At Rotterdam

Avoid the English house the most impertinently imposing of any we met with. If Mr Baillie the banker be alive send for him, or for Mr Knaghten a banker, both Scots men, either of them will be useful to you, when they know who you are.

Directions follow for The Hague and Amsterdam; a route for seeing North Holland is given. There is a section on the difference of money in Holland and Flanders, France, Italy and Germany. The instructions continue:

Going into Italy over the Alps

[…] You are carried over Mount Cenis in chairs by men, for which you give a pistole a piece,[9] and your chaises and baggage by mules for which you must make the best bargain you can, there will be fifty people tearing you to pieces to be employed.

Directions follow for Turin, Milan, Bologna, Rome, where 'so many things are to be seen that it will take you up some months and you must have an antiquary to conduct and show you everything', then Naples to Florence where:

A French house in the Via Maggia is the best to lodge at, where we were well used, Collins's, an English house there is generally full and not the most reasonable. All English houses or any English body you employ abroad for any thing are generally the first and readiest to impose upon you, therefore to be avoided, or at least be much upon your guard. […]

Boboli the Duke's garden is very fine, desire to see the Menagerie there, where George will be delighted with great variety of all kinds of strange birds and beasts, if you have any brass money in your pockets it will be very good food for the Ostrich, in the upper part of the garden where the citronades grow there is a good statue of Adam and Eve by Michelangelo. You will have good luck if you escape without being wet when the water work plays, they are very pretty.

From Florence the traveller is taken to Bologna then Venice.

At Venice

Lodge at Monsieur D'Henry's on the Great Canal where we were well used and cheap. See the Church and Procuratories of St Mark. The small church dedicated to St Geminiano, which stands at one end of the Place of St Mark's, was built by Sansovino. Mr Law[10] that made such a figure in France in the Messasipie [Mississippi] year, your country man is buried there. If Mr Consul Brown be alive who is a worthy honest Scots man send to him and he will do every thing for you when he knows who you are. Your hired servant will carry you to all the churches worth seeing. In the Church and Convent of St Giorgio Maggiore are fine paintings by Titian, Tintoret and other masters of the Venetian school, in the refectory is the famous Marriage of Cana by Paul Veronese. There is good paintings in the schools of St Rocco and St Marco. The Palaces best worth seeing are Grinani – Maniani – Grassi – Delphino – Pisani – Barberigo. The Doge's Palace and the Courts of Justice are adorned with fine paintings of Titian, Tintoret, Paul Veronese, Bassanio, etc. Observe in going into the Palace the statues of Adam and Eve much esteemed. The Arsenal is well worth seeing and the Treasury and Tower of St Mark. The Library of St Mark contains several fine busts, statues and other remains of antiquity, the roof is finely painted. The Rialto, a bridge over the great Canal, is very fine and many fine buildings by Paladio. Eat Sebetti at a house near St Mark's famous for making every thing in ice the best of any place, it is like a Coffee house.[11]

From Venice to Padua, Vicenza and Verona; to Trent, Innsbruck, and Munich, where the traveller is advised:

Lodge at the Daler and not at the Soleil d'Or; it is an imposing house. See the Elector of Bavaria's 3 houses, that in the town, Slyskam about 4 miles out of town, and as you go on your way to Auxburg see Nymphenberg, it is in the post road. The Jesuits' Church is fine; the whole town very pretty. The Elector has many fine houses.

Back at the Channel:

Here if you do not think it worth while to bring your Chaises home and they are but unwieldy and troublesome in our country, sell them for what you can get. Some times it happens people just come there wanting to go to Paris or Italy will give you their value and be glad to get them. If that does not happen, the people there who make it their business to buy chaises to sell them again, will give you very little for them, but take it rather then leave them there to be sold. It will perhaps cost double their price for the hire of their standing and not to be sold at last, as we found by two we left there.[12]

From Calais to Dover we hired a little ship, one of Mr Minet's, 3 guineas is the common hire for the whole ship, if others are going you may get passage cheaper, either in those boats or in the King's packet boats that go constantly. Lie at Dover at the Ship. Your trunks and baggage.[13]

NOTES

1. Allan Ramsay (1686-1758) Edinburgh wig-maker, poet and bookseller, published *The Tea-table Miscellany* 1724-32 and these volumes together with *The Evergreen* in 1724 were significant in the revival of vernacular Scottish poetry.

2. The original book has marginal 'N.B.s' here and at 30 and 31.

3. Lee or more commonly now, lye, is alkalized water, usually as here, made by percolating water as salts from wood ash. Later in her instructions Lady Grisell insists that linen be steeped in lye.

4. A boll is a measure of grain: in Scotland, 6 imperial bushels. A mutchkin is about a fourth of a pint, old Scots; three-quarters of an imperial pint (see also Mure, p.41). A furlet is $^1/_4$ boll.

5. 'This should surely be half pound; a peck is a measure of capacity containing about two stones': note from Scott-Moncrieff edition.

6. Cockaleekie soup is made with a whole boiling fowl and the best recipes still include prunes. 'Stove' I am not sure about but my family used to eat 'stoved potatoes' or 'stovies' which were savoury potatoes baked with lard; prunes would have been a possible addition.

7. Melder is the quantity of one person's corn taken to the mill to be ground at any one time.

8. Most likely to impose upon the traveller by overcharging, or in other ways not giving good value.

9. A pistole was a 12 pound piece Scots = £1 or an old Spanish gold coin = 17s.

10. John Law, the famous writer on finance, was born in Edinburgh in 1681 and died in poverty in Venice in 1729.

11. Sebetti is sherbet or sorbet; the café is probably Florian's which is still there (and is very 'imposing').

12. 'They ask me here [Calais, 27 July 1739] extravagant prices for chaises, of which there are great choice, both French and Italian: I have at last bought one for fourteen guineas of a man whom Mr. Hall recommended me.' – *Lady Mary Wortley Montagu's Letters* : note by Scott-Moncrieff.

13. The text ends rather abruptly – Lady Grisell may have intended to add more specific instructions.

Griseld Baillie, Lady Murray of Stanhope (1693–1759)

Griseld Baillie was the eldest daughter of George Baillie of Jerviswood, Lanarkshire, and Griseld Hume, daughter of Patrick, first Earl of Marchmont. Griseld Hume appears in this volume as Lady Grisell Baillie, with extracts from her Household Book. Lady Murray's memoir of her parents is a chief biographical source for Lady Grisell's life and it is her own claim to literary fame. Lady Murray's only brother died in early infancy and the family estates ultimately passed to the second son of her younger sister, Rachel, who married Lord Binning, the eldest son of the Earl of Haddington, after Lady Murray's death in 1759.

Lady Murray's own life was less dangerous than that of her mother but also less happy. When she was only 17 she married against her parents' advice, although with their unwilling consent, the son and heir of Sir David Murray of Stanhope. Murray displayed completely irrational and most alarming jealousy of his wife on the day of their marriage, believing that she had transferred her affections to one of his friends, Hamilton, whom she had only just met. Although he remained passionately attached to his wife, he could not be persuaded that he had not lost her love. His increasingly worrying behaviour eventually resulted in a formal separation and his wife subsequently went to live with her parents. Murray succeeded to his title in 1724 but his conduct remaining erratic, his wife did not return. According to Elwood when Lady Murray sat for her portrait in London, 'the painter told her, a gentleman came frequently to his house, and would stand for an hour with his arms folded, gazing on her likeness. This individual afterwards proved to be her eccentric and unfortunate husband' (Elwood, I, 53).

The Baillies spent much of their time in London and Mrs Murray, as she then was, became one of the celebrated beauties of the Augustan court, although without any scandal ever attaching to her name. Her friendship with Lady Mary Wortley Montagu was broken when Lady Mary could not resist penning a ballad at her expense but her friendship with Mary (Molly) Lepell, Lady Hervey, continued until her death

Lady Murray was already over fifty when, on her mother's death, she came into the full possession of the family property. She continued to live with her widowed sister, to whose second son the family property was bequeathed. Lady Murray died in June 1759 aged 67 and mourned by a large number of friends. Elwood quotes Lady Hervey on her friend:

> Never in my life did I ever meet with a creature in all respects like her; many have excelled her, perhaps in particular qualities, but none that I ever met with have equalled her in all. Sound good sense, strong judgement, great sagacity, strict honour, truth and sincerity, a most affectionate disposition of mind, constant and steady, not obstinate; great indulgence to others, a most sweet and cheerful temper, and a sort of liveliness and good humour that promoted mirth wherever she came; and with all this, her nature, or her understanding, or both, gave her

such an attention to every thing and everybody, that neither when she was most vexed, (and many vexations she had,) nor when in her highest spirits, did she ever say or do a thing that could offend or hurt me. (Elwood, 59-60)

And in her biography, *Molly Lepell, Lady Hervey*, Dorothy Margaret Stuart quotes Lepell continuing more personally:

In forty years, and much as we lived together, she never said or did the least thing to me that, from any reason in the world, I could have wished undone or unsaid. Of no other person that I ever had any connection with can I say the same. Inadvertence, ill-humour, or too much spirits, will in most people, at some time or other, make them do or say what may hurt, at least for a time, their best friends. But she had a kind of delicacy in her way of thinking, accompanied by a reflection so quick, that though she seemed to speak without considering beforehand, she could not, had she considered ever so long, have more dextrously and more effectually avoided the least thing that could either directly or obliquely have made any one uneasy or out of countenance. Oh, she was – what was she not? but 'tis all over.

A summary of Lady Grisell Baillie's life is given under her entry and I have included here a substantial portion of Lady Murray's memoir of her mother.

Lady Murray of Stanhope, *Memoirs of the Lives and Characters of the Right Honourable George Baillie of Jerviswood and of Lady Grisell Baillie* (Edinburgh: printed by J. Pillans, 1822)

Further Reading:
Dorothy Margaret Stuart, *Molly Lepell, Lady Hervey* (London: Harrap & co., 1936)

Elwood

From *Memoirs of the Lives and Characters of the Right Honourable George Baillie of Jerviswood and of Lady Grisell Baillie*. The text is from the second edition, 1824.

FACTS RELATING TO MY MOTHER'S LIFE AND CHARACTER
Mellerstain, December 12, 1749
I am desirous of nothing so much as to preserve, and make known to her family, what I have observed in my dear mother's life and character; and also those things I well remember to have often heard her tell of, which passed in her younger years. Though it has often been in my thoughts, my unfitness to do it has hindered my setting about it. My affection to the best and tenderest of mothers possibly may bias and blind me; I will therefore set a guard upon myself, to keep strictly to truth, and relate facts which will speak for themselves. Happy for me, were her whole actions imprinted on my mind, that none of them were forgot! but so far from that, all I can remember must be trifling, compared to what a judicious observer might relate, that had access to know her well.

LADY GRISELL BAILLIE was born at Redbraes Castle, [in Berwickshire] December 25, 1665; was married there, September 17, 1692; and died at London, December 6, 1746. She was buried close by my father's side, in the monument of Mellerstain, on her birth-day, Christmas, 25th of December, in the same manner she had directed my father's funeral, according to his own orders; near relations, near neighbours, and her own tenants only being present; – a day never to be forgot by her family; as it brought *her* into the world, who was so great a blessing to it, and also hid and buried her from us.

She was the eldest of eighteen children my grandmother bore, except two, that died infants. My Lady Torphichen, the youngest, is now the only one alive, and sixteen years younger than my mother. She was called after her mother, and from her infancy, was the darling and comfort of her parents, having early occasion to be trusted and tried by them. In the troubles of King Charles the Second's time, she began her life with many afflicting, terrifying hardships; though I have often heard her say, she never thought them any. At the age of twelve, she was sent by her father from their country-house to Edinburgh, a long journey, when my grandfather Baillie was first imprisoned, (my grandfathers being early and intimate friends, connected by the same way of thinking in religion and politics) to try if, by her age, she could get admittance into the prison unsuspected, and slip a letter into his hand, of advice and information, and bring back what intelligence she could. She succeeded so well in both, that from that time I reckon her hardships began, from the confidence was put in her, and the activity she naturally had far beyond her age, in executing whatever she was entrusted with.

Soon after that, her father was confined fifteen months in Dumbarton Castle, and was then set at liberty, without ever being told for what he was put up all that time; and till he went to Holland, she was the active person that did all, by my grandmother's directions; whose affliction, and care of her little ones, kept at home, besides being less able to make journeys, and would have been more narrowly watched, and sooner suspected, than any one of my mother's age.

After persecution began afresh, and my grandfather Baillie again in prison, her father thought it necessary to keep concealed; and soon found he had too good reason for so doing; parties being continually sent out in search of him, and often to his own house, to the terror of all in it; though not from any fear for his safety, whom they imagined at a great distance from home; for no soul knew where he was, but my grandmother and my mother, except one man, a carpenter called Jamie Winter, who used to work in the house, and lived a mile off, on whose fidelity they thought they could depend, and were not deceived. The frequent examinations and oaths put to servants, in order to make discoveries, were so strict, they durst not run the risk of trusting any of them. By the assistance of this man, they got a bed and bed-clothes carried in the night to the burying-place, a vault under ground at Polwarth Church, a mile from the house; where he was concealed a month, and had only for light an open slit at one end, through which nobody could see what was below. She went every night by herself, at midnight, to carry him victuals and drink, and stayed with him as long as she could to get home before day. In all this time, my grandfather showed the same constant composure, and cheerfulness of mind, that he continued to possess to his death, which was at the age of eighty-four; all which good qualities she inherited from him in a high degree. Often did they laugh heartily, in that doleful habitation, at different accidents that happened. She at that time had a terror for a church-yard, especially in the dark, as is not uncommon at her age, by idle nursery stories; but when engaged by concern for her father, she stumbled over the graves every night alone, without fear of any kind entering her thoughts, but for soldiers, and parties in search of him, which the least noise or motion of a leaf put her in terror for. The minister's house was near the church; the first night she went, his dogs kept such a barking, as put her in the utmost fear of a discovery; my grandmother sent for the minister next day, and upon pretence of a mad dog, got him to hang all his dogs. There was also difficulty of getting victuals to carry him without the servants suspecting: the only way it was done, was by stealing it off her plate at dinner into her lap. Many a diverting story she has told about this, and other things of a like nature. Her father liked sheep's head; and while the children were eating their broth, she had conveyed most of one into her lap; when her brother Sandy, the late Lord Marchmont, had done, he looked up with astonishment, and said, 'Mother, will ye look at Grisell; while we have been eating our broth, she has eat up the whole sheep's head.' This occasioned so much mirth amongst them, that her father at night was greatly entertained by it, and desired Sandy might have a share of the next. I need not multiply stories of this kind, of which I know many. His great comfort, and constant entertainment, (for he had no light to read by), was repeating Buchanan's Psalms, which he had by heart from beginning to end, and retained them to his dying day.¹ Two years before he died, which was in the year 1724, I was witness to his desiring my mother to take up that book, which amongst others always lay upon his table, and bid her try if he had forgot his Psalms, by naming any one she would have him repeat; and by casting her eye over it, she would know if he was right, though she did not understand it; and he missed not a word in any place she named to him, and said, they had been the great comfort of his life, by night and day, on all occasions.

As the gloomy habitation my grandfather was in, was not to be long endured but from necessity, they were contriving other places of safety for him; amongst others, particularly one under a bed that drew out in a ground floor, in a room of which my mother kept the key. She and the same man worked in the night, making a hole in the earth, after lifting the boards; which they did by scratching it up with their hands, not to make any noise, till she left not a nail upon her fingers; she helping the man to carry the earth, as they dug it, in a sheet on his back, out at the window into the garden. He then made a box at his own house, large enough for her father to lie in, with bed and bed-clothes, and bored holes in the boards for air. When all this was finished, for it was long about, she thought herself the most secure, happy creature alive. When it had stood the trial, for a month, of no water coming into it, which was feared, from being so low; and every day examined by my mother, and the holes for air made clear, and kept clean picked, her father ventured home having that to trust to. After being at home a week or two, the bed examined as usual, one day, in lifting the boards, the bed bounced to the top, the box being full of water. In her life she was never so struck, and had near dropped down, it being at that time their only refuge. Her father, with great composure, said to his wife and her, he saw they must tempt Providence no longer, and that it was now fit and necessary for him to go off and leave them; in which he was confirmed by the carrier telling for news he had brought from Edinburgh, that the day before, Mr Baillie of Jerviswood had his life taken from him at the Cross, and that every body was sorry, though they durst not show it. As all intercourse by letters was dangerous, it was the first notice they had of it; and the more shocking, that it was not expected. They immediately set about preparing for my grandfather's going away. My mother worked night and day, in making some alteration in his clothes for disguise. They were then obliged to trust John Allan, their grieve [farm overseer], who fainted away when he was told his master was in the house, and that he was to set out with him on horseback before the day, and pretend to the rest of the servants, that he had orders to sell some horses at Morpeth Fair. Accordingly, my grandfather getting out at a window to the stables, they set out in the dark. Though, with good reason, it was a sorrowful parting, yet after he was fairly gone, they rejoiced, and thought themselves happy that he was in a way of being safe; though they were deprived of him, and little knew what was to be either his fate or their own.

My grandfather, whose thoughts were much employed, and went on as his horse carried him without thinking of his way, found himself at Tweedside, out of his road, and at a place not fordable, and no servant. After pausing, and stopping a good while, he found the means to get over, and get into the roads on the other side, where after some time, he met his servant, who showed inexpressible joy at meeting him, and told him, as he rode first, he thought he was always following him, till upon a great noise of the galloping of horses after him, he looked about, and missed him. This was a party sent to the house to take him up; where they searched very narrowly, and possibly hearing horses were gone from the house, suspected the truth, and followed. They examined this man, who, to his great joy and astonishment missed his master, and was too cunning for them, and they were gone back before my grandfather came up with him. He immediately quitted the high road, after a warning by so miraculous an escape; in two days sent back the servant, which was the first notice they had at home of his not having fallen into their hands. He got to London through bye-ways, passing for a surgeon; he could bleed, and always carried lancets. From that he went to Holland on foot; where he sent for his wife and ten children.

He was then forfeited, and his estate given to Lord Seaforth. My grandmother and mother went to London by sea, to solicit an allowance for her and her ten children, where they long attended; and even though assisted by many good friends, from whom they met with much kindness and civility, Lord Russell's family, Lord Wharton's, and others, all she could obtain for herself and them was about £150 a year. They then returned to Scotland, to carry over the children; and found my aunt Julian so ill, she could not go with them. My mother returned from Holland by herself, to bring her over, and to negotiate business, and try if she could pick up any money of some that was owing to her father. Her sister was still very weak, so had the attendance of a nurse all the voyage, which happened to be very long. She had agreed for the cabin-bed, and was very well provided in victuals and other necessaries; she found three or four more in the ship, with whom the captain had also agreed for the same bed: a gentleman who was in the cabin, as they all were, said to her, 'Let them be doing,' when a dispute arose who should have the bed, for she made none, 'you will see how it will end.' Two of the gentlewomen went to bed; the rest lay down as they could best, my mother and her sister upon the floor, with a clogbag of books she was carrying to her father, for their pillow. Then in came the captain, and first eat up their whole provisions with a gluttony incredible; then said to the women in the bed, 'Turn out, turn out;' and stripped before them, and lay down in the bed himself. But he did not long enjoy the effects of his brutality; for a terrible storm came on, so that his attendance and labour was necessary to save the ship; they never saw more of him till they landed at the Brill. From that they set out at night on foot for Rotterdam, with a gentleman who was of great use to them, that came over at the same time to take refuge in Holland. It was a cold, wet, dirty night; my aunt, a girl not well able to walk, soon lost her shoes in the dirt; my mother took her upon her back and carried her the rest of the way, the gentleman carrying their small baggage. At Rotterdam they found their eldest brother and their father, waiting for their arrival to conduct them to Utrecht, where their house was; and no sooner were they all met, than she forgot everything, and felt nothing but happiness and contentment.

They lived three years and a half in Holland, and in that time she made a second voyage to Scotland about business. Her father went by the borrowed name of Doctor Wallace, and did not stir out, for fear of being discovered; though who he was, was no secret to the well-wishers to the Revolution. Their great desire was, to have a good house, as their greatest comfort was at home; and all the people of the same way of thinking, of which there was great numbers, were continually with them. They paid for their house, what was very extravagant for their income, near a fourth part: they could not afford keeping any servant, but a little girl to wash the dishes. All the time they were there, there was not a week my mother did not sit up two nights, to do the business that was necessary. She went to the market, went to the mill to have their corn ground, which it seems is the way with good managers there, dressed the linen, cleaned the house, made ready the dinner, mended the children's stockings and other clothes, made what she could for them, and in short did everything. Her sister Christian, who was a year or two younger, diverted her father and mother, and the rest, who were fond of music. Out of their small income they bought a harpsichord, for little money, but it is a *Ru-ar*,[2] now in my custody, and most valuable. My aunt played and sung well, and had no turn to business. Though my mother had the same qualifications, and liked it as well as she did, she was forced to drudge; and many jokes used to pass betwixt the sisters, about their different occupations. Every morning before six, my mother lighted her father's fire in his study, then waked him; (he was ever a good sleeper, which blessing, among many others, she inherited from him); then got him, what he usually took as soon as he got up, warm small beer with a spoonful of bitters in it, which he continued his whole life, and of which I have the receipt. Then she took up the children, and brought them all to his room, where he taught them every thing that was fit for their age; some Latin, others French, Dutch, geography, writing, reading, English, &c.; and my grandmother taught them what was necessary on her part. Thus he employed and diverted himself all the time he was there, not being able to afford putting them to school; and my mother, when she had a moment's time, took a lesson with the rest, in French and Dutch, and also diverted herself with music. I have now a book of songs of her writing when there; many of them interrupted, half writ, some broke off in the middle of a sentence. She had no less a turn for mirth and society than any of the family, when she could come at it, without neglecting what she thought more necessary.

Her eldest brother Patrick, who was nearest her age, and bred up together, was her most beloved. My father was there, forfeited and exiled, in the same situation with themselves. She had seen him for the first time in the prison with his father, not long before he suffered; and from that time their hearts were engaged. Her brother and my father were soon got in to ride in the Prince of Orange's guards, till they were better provided for in the army; which they were before the Revolution. They took their turn in standing sentry at the Prince's gate, but always contrived to do it together; and the strict friendship and intimacy that then began, continued to the last. Though their station was then low, they kept up their spirits: the Prince often dined in public; then all were admitted to see him; when any pretty girl wanted to go in, they set their halberds across the door and would not let her pass till she gave each of them a kiss, which made them think and call them very pert soldiers. I could relate many stories on that subject; my mother could talk for hours, and never tire of it; always saying it was the happiest and most delightful part of her life. Her constant attention was, to have her brother appear right in his linen and dress: they wore little point [lace] cravats and cuffs, which many a night she sat up to have in as good order for him as any in the place; and one of their greatest expenses was in dressing him as he ought to be.

As their house was always full of the unfortunate banished people like themselves, they seldom went to dinner, without three, or four, or five of them, to share with them: and many a hundred times I have heard her say, she could never look back upon their manner of living there, without thinking it a miracle: they had no want, but plenty of every thing they desired, and much contentment, and always declared it the most pleasing part of her life; though they were not without their little distresses; but to them they were rather jokes than grievances. The professors and men of learning in the place came often to see my grandfather: the best entertainment he could give them was a glass of allerbest beer, which was a better kind of ale than the common. He sent his son Andrew, the late Lord Kimmerghame, a boy, to draw some for them in the cellar; he brought it up with great diligence, but in the other hand the spigot of the barrel. My grandfather said, 'Andrew, what is that in your hand?' When he saw it he run down with speed, but the beer was all run out before he got there: this occasioned much mirth, though perhaps they did not well know where to get more.

It is the custom there to gather money for the poor, from house to house, with a bell to warn people to give it. One night the bell came, and no money was there in the house, but an orkey, which is a doit, the smallest of all coin: everybody was so ashamed, no one would go to give it, it was so little, and put it from one to the other: at last my grandfather said, 'Well then, I'll go with it; we can do no more than give all we have.' They were often reduced to this, by the delay of the ships coming from Scotland with their small remittance; then they put the little plate they had (all of which was carried with them) in the Lumber, which is pawning it, till the ships came: and that very plate they brought with them again to Scotland, and left no debt behind them.

When the long expected happiness of the Prince going to England took place, her father and brother, and my father, went with him.³ They soon heard the melancholy report of the whole fleet being cast away or dispersed, and immediately came from Utrecht to Helvoetsluys, to get what information they could. The place was so crowded by people from all quarters, come for the same purpose, that her mother, she, and her sister, were forced to lie in the boat they came in; and for three days continually to see come floating in beds, chests, horses, &c. that had been thrown over-board in their distress. At the end of the third day, the Prince, and some other ships, came in; but no account of the ship their friends were in. Their despair was great; but in a few days was relieved by their coming in safe, but with the loss of all their baggage, which at that time was no small distress to them.

When they set out again, the eagerness of their expectation was augmented; to hear they were all safe landed, was the greatest joy they could figure to themselves; yet, when that happy news came, it was no more to my mother than any occurrence she had not the least concern in; for that very day, her sister Christian died of a sore throat, which was so heavy an affliction to both her mother and her, that they had no feeling for anything else: and often have I heard her say, she had no notion of any cause of sorrow, but the death and affliction of those she loved; and of that she was sensible to her last, in the most tender manner. She had tried many hardships, without being depressed by them: on the contrary, her spirits and activity increased, the more she had occasion for it; but the death of her friends was always a load too heavy for her. She had strong and tender passions, though she never gave way to them, but in what was commendable and praiseworthy.

When all was settled in England, the children were sent to Scotland, and my grandmother and she came over with the Princess. She was offered to be made one of the maids of honour, and was well qualified for it: her actions show what her mind was, and her outward appearance was no less singular. She was middle-sized, well made, clever in her person, very handsome, with a life and sweetness in her eyes very uncommon, and great delicacy in all her features; her hair was chestnut, and to her last had the finest complexion, with the clearest red in her cheeks and lips, that could be seen in one of fifteen; which, added to her natural constitution, might be owing to the great moderation she had in her diet, throughout her whole life. Pottage and milk was her greatest feast, and by choice preferred them to every thing; though nothing came wrong to her that others could eat. Water she preferred to any liquor; though often obliged to take a glass of wine, always did it unwillingly, thinking it hurt her, and did not like it.

She declined being maid of honour, and chose going home with the rest of her family. Having had her union with my father always in view, their affection for one another increased in their exile; though they well knew it was no time to declare it, neither of them having a shilling; and were at no small trouble to conceal it from her parents, who could not but think such an engagement ruinous to them both; especially when, in the midst of their distress, there were offers pressed upon her by them, from two gentlemen, in their neighbourhood at home, of fortune and character, who had done nothing to forfeit either, and with whom they thought it would have been happy to settle their daughter at any time. She earnestly rejected both, but without giving any reason for it, though her parents suspected it; and it was the only thing she ever displeased or disobeyed them in. These gentlemen I have mentioned, were intimate and sincere friends to my father and her to the day of their death, and often said to them both, she had made a much better choice in him; for they made no secret of having made their addresses to her. Her parents were ever fond of my father, and he was always with them: so great an opinion had they of him, that he was generally preferred to any other, and trusted to go out with my mother and take care of her, when she had any business to do. They had no objection but the circumstances he was in; which had no weight with my mother, who always hoped things would turn out at last as they really did; and if they did not, was resolved never to marry at all.

When he was put in possession of his estate by King William, (which had been given to the Duke of Gordon) he made their engagements known; and they were married about two years after the Revolution. Then my grandfather was in high favour, as he well deserved from his great sufferings; and was made Chancellor of Scotland, and afterwards made the King's High Commissioner to the Parliament, which was the greatest office in this country.

I have heard my mother and many others say, that the great sweetness, composure, and evenness of temper my grandmother showed in all her high propriety, was most singular: that from the highest to the lowest of her acquaintance, none ever found a difference from the great difference in her situation. I was but ten years old when she died; and though tenderly caressed by her, lived much with her, and was her darling, being her first grandchild, I can only remember, which I do now in a lively manner, the sorrow I was in when she died; and cannot give, from what I have heard, so good a description of her, as what my grandfather writ in her Bible, which he gave my mother, and is now in my possession.

Grisell Lady Marchmont, her book. To Grisell Hume, Lady Jerviswood, my beloved daughter.– My Heart, in remembrance of your mother, keep this Bible, which is what she ordinarily made use of. She had been happy of a religious and virtuous education, by the care of virtuous and religious parents. She was of a middle stature, of a plump, full body, a clear countenance, a composed, steady, and mild spirit, of a most firm and equal mind, never elevated by prosperity, nor debased or daunted by adversity. She was a wonderful stay and support to me in our exile and trouble, and a humble and thankful partner with me in our more prosperous condition; in both which, by the blessing of God, she helped much to keep the balance of our deportment even. She was constant and diligent in the practice of religion and virtue, a careful observer of worship to God, and of her duties to her husband, her children, her friends, her neighbours, her tenants, and her servants; so that it may be justly said, her piety, probity, virtue, and prudence, were without a blot or stain, and beyond reproach. As, by the blessing of God, she had lived well, so by his mercy, in the time of her sickness, and at her death, there appeared many convincing evidences, that the Lord took her to the enjoyment of endless happiness and bliss. She died the 11th of October 1703, at Edinburgh, and was buried in my burying-place near the Canongate Church, where I have caused mark out a grave for myself close by hers, upon the left side, in the middle of the ground.   MARCHMONT

The sorrow her whole family and friends were in at losing her, was very great. She had her judgment to the last; her children were all around her bed; my mother was in such agonies of grief, she had hid herself behind the curtain of the bed, that my grandmother, in looking round to them all, did not see her, and said, 'Where is Grisell?' upon which she came near her: she, taking her by the hand, said, 'My dear Grisell, blessed be you above all, for a helpful child have you been to me.' I have often heard my mother tell this in floods of tears, which she was always in when she spoke of her mother at all, or of her eldest brother.

My grandfather, while in high station, had frequent opportunities of showing his natural humanity to those in distress, always remembering he had been so himself. Amongst many, one captain Burd had a process before the Privy Council, of which my grandfather was President as Chancellor, for something that imported no less than his life. The moment he appeared before him, though he had not recollected him by his name, he knew him to be the same Captain Burd with whom he had been intimately acquainted in France, and had made part of the journey on foot from that together to Holland: but the Captain little suspected to find his old friend Dr Wallace sitting there as his judge, and had not the least knowledge of his ever having been other than what he then appeared. My grandfather examined him pretty strictly, and with some severity; so that he was dismissed with the utmost apprehension of no favour. My grandfather ordered his son, Sir Andrew Hume, who was then a lawyer, to get acquainted with him, and bring him one day to tell his own case; which he did in fear and trembling, dreading the severity he had already experienced. When they were alone, he was telling his story without lifting his eyes from the ground; when he had done, my grandfather said smiling, 'Do you not know me?' upon which he looked up, cried out, 'God's wounds, Doctor Wallace!' run to him, and hung about his neck with tears of joy. One may judge what succeeded, and the pleasure they had to see one another. The cause was given for him, which indeed was but just, though he feared the consequence, from the first appearance of severity he met with.

I should never have done if I related or could remember, all the particulars I have heard my mother tell of those times, – a subject she never tired of; but must now come to what more nearly concerns herself, though most incapable am I of giving but very imperfect hints. She deserved so much, and from me in particular, I never can say enough; and yet certain I am, no one that knew her well will be satisfied with any thing I can say. I shall mention facts as they daily appeared to me, as I was never in my life from her above two months at a time, and that very seldom, and always unwillingly; she having from our infancy treated my sister and me like friends, as well as children, and with an indulgence that we never had a wish to make she could prevent; always used us with an openness and confidence which begat the same in us, that there never was any reserve amongst us, nor any thing kept secret from one another, to which she had used us from our early years. We were always with her at home and abroad, but when it was necessary we should learn what was fit for us; and for that end she got Mrs May Menzies, a daughter of Mr Menzies of Raws, writer to the signet, to be our governess, who was well qualified in all respects for it, and whose faithful care and capacity my mother depended so much upon, that she was easy when we were with her. She was always with us when our masters came, and had no other thought or business but the care and instruction of us; which I must here acknowledge with gratitude; having been an indulgent though exact mistress to us when young; and to this time, it being now forty-five years that she has lived with us, a faithful disinterested friend, with good sense, good temper, entirely in our interest, and that with so much honesty, that she always spoke her mind sincerely, without the least sycophancy. She has a solid judgment and advice to give upon any occasion, and an integrity in all her actions even to a scruple. As such she always has been, and still is regarded by us all; nor has she been less diligent in the care of Lady Binning's children, than she was of us.

When we were more advanced, my mother was pleased to hear whatever we could inform her of; and to whatever company or diversion we went, never thought ourselves so happy as in the relating it all to her; in which she would either approve, or tell us how to do otherwise another time. Nor did we think any thing right done, to the smallest trifle, in which we had not her advice and approbation; and she always condescended to ask ours, though none could better judge than herself what was most proper to be done upon any occasion; of which my father was so convinced, that I have good reason to believe, he never did any thing of consequence, throughout his whole life, without asking her advice.

Lady Grisell Baillie subsequently lived a wholly domestic life, although she travelled considerably on the continent. Her daughter's praise of her mother clearly proceeds from very deep love but it is utterly convincing: if we want a Scottish heroine, Lady Grisell Baillie is as good as we are likely to get. Her death is typically wholly ordinary and wholly moving:

She had been ill of a cold that was epidemical, but was down stairs the week before she died; was confined to her bed but a few days, and had her senses entire to the last. Two days before she died, we were all in the room: she said, 'My dear, read the last chapter of the Proverbs; you know what it is.' To have her grandsons happily married, lay near her heart; and I imagine it was with regard to that, she said it. I think it a very strong picture of herself; and if any deserved to have it said of them, she does. The next day, she called me; gave directions about some few things; said she wished to be carried home to lie by my father, but that perhaps it might be too much trouble and inconvenience to us at that season, therefore left it to me to do as I pleased; but that, in a black purse in her cabinet, I would find money sufficient to do it, which she had kept by her for that use, that whenever it happened, it might not straiten us. She added, 'I have now no more to say or do;' tenderly embraced me, and laid down her head upon the pillow, and spoke little after that.

Can my sorrow be utterable after such a loss? I am certain no number of years allotted me to live, can ever make me feel less, either of grief or wonder, when I reflect on her whole conduct. Her whole family was round her bed, and showed a lively sense of what they lost, when she breathed her last. My sister, who had been long ill, was carried out of her bed to attend her; but we were both almost incapable of doing the last duties to her; but *that*, Lady Stanhope supplied, with the same tender dutifulness she had ever behaved to her; and, with a fortitude uncommon at her age, stretched and dressed her in the manner she had always directed; which was in her ordinary night clothes, and then rolled in a sheet; all which she did, without letting another hand touch her; for which, and her tender care and concern for her mother and me, I doubt not God will reward her by the dutifulness of her own child. My mother had always expressed a dislike of the method in London, of delivering over to the undertakers for funerals, any one that died, to be ordered by them as they thought proper; therefore we were desirous that none should come about her, or touch her; nor was she ever left by some of her family, till they saw the lead coffin soldered down. Though it rent the heart to be witness to it, we were all there, to see the last thing done that was in our power.

The concern and agitation of mind I have been under, the whole time of my writing of this, and whenever I set about it, makes me very unfit to do it at all; but my desire of putting in writing so many surprising and uncommon truths, which nobody else had the same access to know, made me undertake it. I here declare, whatever I have said, to the best of my knowledge, to be strictly just and true; but far less than I think the subject deserves.

GRISELL BAILLIE

NOTES

1. George Buchanan (1506-82) was in the course of his chequered career tutor to one of the bastard sons of James V, tutor to Mary Queen of Scots and finally, after a break with Mary, tutor to the young James VI. During the last tutorship he spent much of his time pamphleteering against Mary. He translated the Psalms into Latin while imprisoned in Portugal by the Inquisition. His *Rerum scoticarum historia*, a twenty volume history of Scotland, was completed just before his death.

2. I think this must be a misprint for one of the versions of the name Ruckers (Ruckaert, Ruckaerts, Rucqueer etc.). They were a Flemish family of harpsichord and virginal makers whose instruments from the sixteenth to the eighteenth century influenced the manufacture of stringed keyboard instruments throughout Europe. The instrument in Vermeer's *The Music Lesson* is probably a Ruckers.

3. The 'Glorious Revolution' which overthrew James II and placed his sister, Mary, and her consort, William of Orange, on the British throne took place in 1688. William of Orange landed at Torbay on 5 November and proceeded to London while James's supporters, including his daughter, Anne, steadily deserted him. As William III and Mary II the couple accepted the Bill of Rights which established constitutional monarchy in England and secured the Protestant succession.

Alison (Alicia) Cockburn (1713–1794)

Alicia or Alison Cockburn was born Alison Rutherford, daughter of Robert Rutherford of Fairnilee, Selkirkshire, in 1713. Her mother, Alison Ker Cockburn, died when she was ten, but her sisters loved and taught her well. She married the advocate, Patrick Cockburn, in 1731; Cockburn became Commissioner for the estates of the Duke of Hamilton. Her only son, Adam, was born in 1732. He became a captain of dragoons and died in 1780. Patrick Cockburn died in 1753 after which his widow lived mainly in Edinburgh.

She is perhaps most famous for her song, 'I've Seen the Smiling of Fortune Beguiling', one version of 'The Flowers of the Forest', first printed in *The Lark,* Edinburgh 1765. She also wrote several songs concerning the Jacobite Rising of 1745 but, like other upper class women of her period, she feared the indignity of print. Distantly related to Sir Walter Scott, she was for many years the centre of a distinguished social circle in Edinburgh. She was celebrated for her wit and her beauty: her auburn hair apparently survived without artificial aid into old age. She died on 22 November 1794.

I have given her own account of her life, written 10 May 1784 when she was already over seventy, and dedicated to the Rev. Mr Douglas of Galashiels, her usual correspondent, and also some letters which give a notion of her social circle, which included David Hume and Lord Monboddo,[1] and her intellectual interests, as well as indicating how circulating letters was a form of publication which avoided the indignity of print. Although it is customary to deprecate the self-effacement of women writers of the period, the moving directness of Alison Cockburn's autobiography is made possible by private rather than public circulation: I know of no more convincing, because unembellished, expression of the physical and emotional ties of married love than is contained in Alison Cockburn's account of her comforting of her dying husband.

Alison Rutherford or Cockburn, *Letters and Memoir of Her Own Life; also 'Felix', a Biographical Sketch and Various Songs;* notes by T. Craig-Brown (Edinburgh: printed for David Douglas, 1900). All extracts are from this edition as is some of the biographical information. I have modernised most spelling, although I have retained period expressions.

Further Reading:
Chambers; *DNB*; *HSWW*; Irving; Lonsdale

From *Letters and Memoir of Her Own Life*:

A SHORT ACCOUNT OF A LONG LIFE
A short account of a long life full of vicissitudes! Human life is ever interesting to human creatures, for we are all subject to the same joys, passions, griefs, pains, and dissolution!

Born in the year 1713, 29th September, old style, the youngest of a numerous family, and coming unexpectedly seven years after my mother had bore children, I was the little favourite of all the family. My mother died when I was ten years old. My father and sisters doated on me. I was caressed in childhood, and indulged in youth. My eldest sister became my mother, she was fourteen years older than me; she it was who formed my taste for reading, which has ever since been my greatest amusement. I cannot recollect ever being taught to read, I suppose I was begun so early and so easily that I never got a formal lesson; and my father taught me arithmetic the same way.

My education was with the politest lady of the age, who had me as a boarder; and I had dancing, French, etc., in the common course. Music I would not go to, as I was disgusted with hearing some misses who had been taught to squall horribly. As my preceptress (for whose memory I retain the utmost veneration) found me averse to the needle, she made me read to the family, and her sensible remarks has been of use to me through life. She always said girls sewed naturally, and as she saw I never loved to be idle a moment, and would not have patience to do *nothing*, she was sure I would work enough, which is true. As I grew up I was thought handsome; my chief beauty was fair hair (then in fashion), fine teeth, a fresh complexion, a good dancer, and very agile; apt to blush (which fair people always are), and these were all my personal perfections. I was early connected with the best families by intimacy at school, and some of my most steady friends through life were my childhood companions. At seventeen years a beloved brother died: my first grief was violent, as nature never afforded me the relief of tears. It cost me a fever and a quinsy, to which I was subject ever after. In that year I had several matrimonial as well as dancing lovers: – to *one* I gave my hand and heart. We lived loving and beloved for twenty-two years. No body kept a house of more resort. No body more in the gay world. Our whole income was £150 a year, and we never owed a shilling. An only beloved son was educated to be a physician – went through all the colleges. A young nobleman took a most uncommon attachment to my husband, and entreated him to take charge of his estate of £10,000 a year, and would have no cautioner. We accordingly went to his palace, where my husband proved a blessing to many.² £200 a year salary, with free house and coal, made us to send our son abroad, though my heart died within me to part with him. I acquiesced indeed, as I was fully assured of his father's tenderness being equal to mine, and his understanding much superior. I never in my life disputed a point but in sport, and to display my powers of argument on the wrong side of the question, a sort of sport he often led me into for his amusement. I almost forget to mention a memorable part of my life: we lived four years with his venerable father, during which time I was as much married to a man of four score as to one of twenty-three, for it was my highest ambition to gain the heart and approbation of the father, as to secure the affections of the son. And indeed I found the one was the most essential means of doing the other: my husband adored me for my unremitting attention to his father, and I was fully rewarded for entirely quitting the scenes of public admiration by being truly beloved and admired at home. The good old man's affection for me was infinitely more pleasing than all the adulation I ever met with, and I still remember it with pleasure.³

I was married March 25 1730; bore my son 15 May 1732.⁴ When he was fit for school, we gave up living in Edinburgh and lived five years in a country town, where there was a good master. We lived in family with my beloved mother-sister; at the removal of the master, we boarded our son with him at Edinburgh. Let me with pride record an uncommon bit of friendship my husband performed. He had a near relation who had been long his intimate friend: his affairs were in great disorder, and was in hazard of being obliged to sell his estate, which had been many hundred years in the family. Mr Cockburn lifted all his stock, prevented the sale; and as he knew *he* only could check the bad management of his friend, we went and lived with him till affairs were in a proper train. With some difficulty he recovered his money, and we then settled in Edinburgh to attend our son at colleges; there we remained as happy as human beings can be. I can only remember one deep grief I sustained in these happy years, it was the death of my brother's lamented and beloved wife, who died in child-bed, December 18th, 1737. The only vent I had was a violent bleeding of the nose.

It was in the year 1750 we went to the charge of the ducal estate: it would look like vanity to say how much we were beloved in a country where we were strangers. The Duke engaged to live abroad five years, and restrict his expenses to £4000 a year. This both his health worn out with *dissipation*, and his estate by *extravagance*, required: and Mr Cockburn would not undertake the management without an absolute promise (upon honour), that he would do so. Just as things were in a train, and a load of debt clearing, in less than two years the Duke returned; and with three guineas in his pocket, and not credit to raise £20, he married a young beauty without a shilling. He wrote to his friend begging credit and pardon! What was to be done? Mr Cockburn and Mr Stewart sent a credit for £30,000: no less would do; and they became bound for that sum (for the heir of an entailed estate). The Duke, intoxicated with beauty, forgot friendship, and let the man who saved his life by sending him abroad, for he went to London on purpose and saw him shipped off; who also saved his forfeiture of titles and estates by preventing his joining the rebels in the 1745; and by whose credit alone he could come home to his own house, shift for himself to find a place to live in, though often wrote to about it. We must have taken some paltry house in the village, or left the affairs altogether, if a worthy and excellent old bachelor had not taken us and our domestics into his house in the neighbourhood, where we boarded: and the old man said, had we always stayed with him gratis, he had been a rich man; for he added that, by living gratis himself most of his life in the family of Hamilton, he had contracted forty thousand marks of debt. Indeed I found him, as most single men are, most immoderately cheated by his domestics. Young men! trust no nobles! Marry, be rich, be happy!

Here ends the First Chapter

Now the scene changes, and after twenty-two years of uncommon happiness, I have to recount the sad reverse. But first! let me bow in grateful thanks to the unerring Disposer of all events, who sent the staff along with the rod, who preserved my reason and the best use of it – resignation to his Will! In the year 1753, my beloved husband was seized with a bowel complaint, for which all medicine proved vain: exercise, minerals – all was tried. A medicine he could not endure any one but myself to administer, I have given at all hours of the night: and as his fondness for me increased to such a pitch that I saw any other attendant than myself give him pain, I never allowed any to come near him. From a weak habit of body I grew strong and healthy by constant watching and perpetual anxiety. His disease was dreadfully painful, but his fortitude and patience were equal to it. He once told me he was going to a mineral [a spa] in a foreign country; I asked when I should get ready. 'You are not to go with me now,' says he, 'it is too expensive – I must go by myself.' – I vowed I would not stay behind. – 'Well, well, we shall see,' and smiled. I afterwards knew his meaning: he wished to arm me for his death. A niece of mine who had been educated with us, was too full of sensibility; and in a violent fit of pain (*I* of despair), she fell into an hysteric fit; and from that time till the day of her death never retained a bit of meat or medicine on her stomach. She was worn so weak as to be confined to bed; so that my toils and cares were doubled. On the 10th of March 1753, we left our excellent landlord with tears streaming from his venerable eyes. My niece's father came for her; she was carried in a litter, laid round with hot bottles of water to keep her alive, which were renewed every stage. My spouse and me in a carriage: slow and dismal was our journey; and, to complete it, we were covered with snow. We went to a house we had ordered to be hired and furnished at Musselburgh; which, in spite of much cleaning, was so full of fleas there was no sleeping. My niece was carried to a country house, where her mother and sisters came to attend her. Judge the state of my mind. But despair gave strength, and the desire of cheering my husband kept really up my own heart: he had a horse and chair in which he aired every day. The day before his death, he went to Edinburgh by himself, and told me he would bring me a female companion, as I needed one. Surely he knew what happened; he brought me Miss Violet Pringle. We had Rae the surgeon and Dr Rutherford every day, and found there Mr Wood, a young man Mr Cockburn took a fancy to. That very night the violence of the disease increased. Wood stayed in the house. Mr Cockburn, on whom were the sweats of death, begged me to lie down with him. Wood was in the room, but I stripped instantly and was embraced in his cold wet arms with such affection, dearer than the first embrace. Nature was worn out, and I fell asleep. He watched some minutes, and then bade me go to my own bed: I did so, and sleep was allowed me. About 8 o'clock I got up and applied the usual remedy. He found all was over. He looked to me and said, 'Alice! it has seized my heart, while I can speak, I will pray.' His words were – 'O my God! preserve the dearest and best of wives, and my dear Son! – help me, Alice! – Adam will be kind to you – go away'. He then thanked Violet Pringle and bid Mr Wood do the last offices, as he knew I was incapable. Those moments are as fresh before me as on the 23rd of April, 1753. As his disease was never perfectly understood, I determined for the sake of his son to have the body opened. The mad impatience I had to have it performed was ridiculous; and certainly I had a secret hope he might come alive. The next folly was that I should have no mournings, thinking I was immediately to follow; besides, having seen joyful hearts in weeds, I thought the form below the sacredness of sorrow. My son arrived from France in a very short time. The pangs I felt when I saw him was unutterable. Beautiful he was in his dress, and sad it made him for he adored his father:– he lost in him father, friend and conductor. As it was terrible to live in that house, I determined to board with a much beloved brother whose wife was sister to my spouse. My son to perfect his medical studies went to Holland. I remained a year in a sedate state of stupidity. As sleep had forsaken me, I endeavoured to bring it back by fatigue, so got a heavy wheel to spin on: and if it was fair, walked on one hidden walk two hours every day. If I could not go out, I performed the same task in the house. I succeeded at last. I let my small house furnished, and after a year, a house which was our property in Edinburgh being ill-used by one who rented it for some years, I went to it and had it almost new to furnish and to repair. My son returned and lived with me:– both he and his friends thought our finances too straitened to pursue his business; and the offer of the present of a Cornetsy of Dragoons, which was worth £1000, made him determine to go into the Army. A severe present it was to me; but I was obliged to go and thank the then President of the Session, who gave it, and who told me he was happy it was in his power to return obligations he owed to my son's Grandfather, who made his fortune. He went into the 11th regiment of Dragoons in the 1756 year of God. The clearing him out and paying all extraordinary expenses made it necessary to lift £500. Before he joined his regiment he made a will in my favour writ by his own hand, and, this instance as well as every other of his life, behaved to me as a son and friend. Alas! that I should be *his* heir! He went to join his regiment, and our house being too large, I sold it, and rented a house in the Castlehill twelve years. At my going there, my sister-mother's only son who was to be bred to the law, came to be my boarder. I had him several years at £18 a year. A pleasanter boy never was: a temper gentle as a female and very good sense; happy for me to have a companion I was so fond of. Another resource from sorrow in my lot was a family (to whom I was obliged, and with whom we had lived many years in the most intimate friendship) attached me to them by every act of kindness in my deep distress; so that I became in a manner one of the family. The mother, a most superior woman, was my model for wife and mother: the eldest son known and esteemed not only as the most agreeable man of the age, but of a larger share of genius than is common. As he was often for months afflicted with the gout, it became my pleasure and my business to amuse him; and it pleased both my heart and my vanity to see I succeeded: so that I may say I lived with that family.⁵ No man had a greater taste for *belles lettres*, so that this amusement in instruction went hand in hand. In the year 1755 or 56, my dear sister was seized with a strange illness. Her ideas were darkened with the blackest melancholy. Though her understanding was not overturned it was overwhelmed. She blamed herself for all the miseries of human life, as if she had been the Tempter that caused the fall of man. Her reveries were full of horror: she saw war and blood-shed, shipwrecks and earthquakes, and moaned over the miseries of mankind. If we interrupted her with any common question or discourse, she spoke with the same sense she always did, and slept sometimes ten hours at a time as sound as an infant. She retained no food; and never had a natural passage. I let my house in town and came to take care of her. In this melancholy period my son's regiment was ordered to Germany, and I lifted £200 I had of a legacy from my dear brother, whose death a year before was a second widowhood. I lent my son the money for field equipage, etc. How I was supported in this melancholy scene, my heart torn with anxiety for my son, and my nephew sent to Holland, so miserable and beloved an object forever in my sight, that I look back with astonishment I outlived it; but the constant endeavour to comfort as to cure my dear sister gave my mind occupation, and internal prayer strengthened my spirit. A year passed in this way; with a terror for every newspaper and for every battle. At last I was advised to change the scene with her, and she was brought near to Edinburgh, and I went to my own house, where her son joined me and passed lawyer, after which we were equal expenses in house-keeping, which seldom exceeded £60 the piece. I was three years without seeing my son, though he was sent over to England to buy horses, and return again with them to Germany. During my sister's illness, she had many times told us she was to live in misery 15 years;– it was so, for she fell first ill in the 1755, and died in the year 1770, just in her seventieth year of her age. When her body was opened, they found the guts turned the wrong way; so that her torture was immense. But by her illness she escaped a more poignant pain than the body can feel. In the 1768 or 69, my nephew began to grow discontent with his business. He did not come on in the law; and his uncle and he projected buying an uncultivated estate, so as to give him occupation of mind and body. As I was sure they must borrow money for the purchase, and more for a precarious improvement, I opposed it as much as possible, to no effect. The purchase was made. In a year's time they found the ruin that was to ensue. A deep melancholy seized him; and the agonies I suffered by daily witnessing deep despair is inexpressible! One night he showed me an opium bottle, and asked me if drinking that would not cure all heartaches. I assured him that it would not, and took it from him, though really I was not so much alarmed as I had cause to be the very next morning, being the King's birth, month of June. We had just removed to a house not half ready; and in the utmost confusion. He got up by five in the morning, took a pistol he had ready, and lodged a ball in his head. As he found it had not the effect, he fired another which went deeper, but did not kill. How I did not hear the report I know not, but I had lain in an agony of horror without knowing why: so that when the dreadful deed was told me, I only asked if he was dead. When I found he was not, I went to him directly; but trembled so I could scarce walk. He asked my pardon, embraced me, and cried in my arms – dreadful was the scene altogether; and I thought I should have died of the pain he suffered in extracting the balls. In spite of his numerous relations and my wide connections the unhappy affair was never heard of. For 40 days he was confined to bed and I to the house; it passed for a fever: and were both together visiting our friends in the town without the least suspicion.[6] His mind seemed placid, felt more for me than for himself. Much discourse we had, and I endeavoured to prevent his looking on that fatal action as so very disgraceful as it seemed to him. Such is the power of custom: what a Roman gloried in, a Briton thought most contemptible. I must mention a circumstance so strange that it deserves remark: on the very hour on which he shot himself, his mother, who always slept with the gentlewoman who had the care of her, fell a trembling and crying through her sleep, crying out, 'my son, Oh horror, blood, blood!' Her woman had much ado to wake her. She would not tell her dream, but repeated, 'horror, horror,' and sent her in next day to enquire after her son and me. She was told he was in a fever – his mother seemed not distressed with it. After he was well and had a wig, she came and saw him: and he frequently saw her. She got out of her miserable body much about her birthday, and I observed his spirits did not stand any sort of shock: he was confused and perturbed. He had fitted up a room at his country place, and after burying his mother, went frequently there.

   Whilst I was mostly with my friends in the country, a curious affair happened me, which might have excited vanity, had I not foreseen that by finding a lover I should lose a friend. Happening to be more than commonly residing near an old and intimate friend I had known from my earliest years, and lived in intimacy with all my married life, he grew uncommonly fond of me. I was not surprised, as we had been always on an intimate and friendly footing. For 12 years the fondness increased; and at last produced what I had always foreseen, though I endeavoured all I could to turn passion back to friendship, and thought (vainly) I had address enough to make it good. This was one additional vexation unknown to many well-known, and severely felt – let me drop a veil over the foibles of a friend and my own presumption. I was in my 57th year when this affair commenced. My poor nephew's melancholy began to return; and the year after the first attempt on his life, he ended it in the same manner. Luckily for me, my son was here with his regiment. He managed me with tenderness : burned a long letter my nephew had wrote to me the night before his death. He said it served no purpose, but to wound me deeper which was needless. He carried me out to Ayr, to my most beloved and intimate friends, where I gathered some strength of body and mind. I had a year before my nephew's death, purchased, by my son's consent, the house I now reside in, and got it fitted up for him to live with me, which greatly contributed to recover my health.[7] He was ordered to his regiment, and I passed much of my time amongst my friends, of whom were a few intimates in youth and sincere friends though life – heaven blest me with a few remaining. On his return home, he was seized with a violent stomatic illness, which confined him long; and though he was remarkable for fortitude, at last confined him to bed. Though he partly lost the power of both hands and feet, his spirits never sank; and he enjoyed a book as his friend, in that situation without fretfulness or impatience. Though always a plain dresser, he was finical in cleanliness, and was shifted, shaved and dressed every day in bed. A melancholy prospect it was to me to think my son at middle life should be cut off from action, and must no longer be a member of society. But his spirit kept up mine, and I only begged God to continue that blessing, while I should be content to employ all the rest of my life in attending and amusing him. He took a resolution to go to Harrowgate,[8] and though very lame, went by himself and there perfectly recovered. But, alarmed for fear of the return of his malady, he sold his commission, and came home. A strong and early attachment to a family where his cousin (almost his sister by habitude) had been the wife and mother, made him from their infancy doat upon her children. My intimacy with the father lasted many years, nor did the death of my niece alter, but rather increased it.[9] He was fond of my son from a boy, and he again loved no man so well. The intimacy betwixt the families brought about an event which proved fatal to me. The kindness my son had for the children of his beloved cousin softened into the stronger passion for her daughter; and *she* loved him with the utmost sincerity and tenderest affection: there could be no reserve where habitual intimacy dwelt. I was quite a stranger to this, and never imagined she had seen him in any other light than an uncle: they never told me till they should try her father; and she gave a proof of her affection stronger than could be expected from youth and timidity. She would not let him speak to her father, but took it on herself to assure him the happiness of her life depended on his consent. He had been a most indulgent father: so much more severe was it on her to receive the utmost abuse, with orders never to see or think of her cousin more. I was in the country at this time, and when I came in I found my son thoughtful – not melancholy. He soon told me all that had passed; but her love for him was a comfort. Though our finances were not great, yet our capital was rather increased than when his father and I were married; and as her mother's portion was £2000, and she the only younger child of the marriage, I saw no distress in the affair. I wrote to my old friend to tell him so; as also that the lives of them depended on their union. Indeed he had reason to see it, for his daughter grew very ill, so as to alarm him, and to call a physician. His answer was such as to rouse my resentment and contempt; so that I hardly felt a pang for determining never more to see, to speak to, nor think of a man whom I had loved for thirty years with sincere affection, and whose life I had saved by my care and attention. Mean time I did all I could to encourage the lovers: and many happy hours they had walking by themselves, planning schemes of life; but she was still firm not to marry without her father's consent. I saw they were both to be miserable and separated; I therefore offered everything in my power to join them. At last a day was set; and I was prepared to see them wedded. She came dressed in black; he challenged it; and she desired to speak with him alone: they were two hours together. She came to me all in tears, and bid me go and comfort my son. He needed it indeed! They had bid a final adieu. After this he plunged into dissipation. He did everything to recover his spirits, to no purpose. To be affronted and ill used by the man on earth he loved most, to see his dear girl miserable, was too much; and the distress I was in made it worse. His health got a shock. A violent bleeding at the nose, for which he would do nothing, was succeeded by a cough so violent as to make him throw up blood; yet he would not draw blood.[10] I cannot recollect the time of this dismal period. My constant apprehensions took up my mind so much, I forgot all times and seasons. Yet he kept up spirits, tried goat's whey, grew weaker every day – but I sicken and can go no farther now. The death-bed scene was severe; and the very day before he died he sent for me and ordered his funerals; also he was shaved and dressed. How I am alive I know not, after losing the care and comfort of my whole life. After the last parting with his cousin, he never spoke of her but once, which was to say he esteemed her more than ever. She was in town after he was wasting, and asked to see him; but he shunned her; and when he made a will in her brother's favour, I knew it meant her – the delicacy prevented. Fain would I have asked him if he had anything to say to her, but fear of agitating him prevented me.

When her father's affairs came out, he said that it explained to him all his behaviour; that concealing the circumstances was the reason of it, and pitied him most sincerely.[11]

I have thus marked the chief occurrences of my various life. Nothing remains but to thank, with a grateful heart, the Merciful Disposer of all events for preserving my reason under such acute feelings as he formed me with; and to pray that the closing scene may be rendered serene, through the influence and intercession of the blessed Saviour.

To you, my young friend, I dedicate these sheets which are improper for any eye but those of a partial friend. May God reward you for your exact and kind attention to me and my affairs. Amen. 10th May 1784.

A selection from Letters to David Hume:
The affectionate teasing tone is characteristic of all her letters to Hume.

20th August 1764: to Hume in Paris where he went with Lord Hertford then British Ambassador:
From the bleak hills of the north – from the uncultured daughter of Caledon – will the adored sage of France deign to receive a few lines? […] Idol of Gaul, I worship thee not. The very cloven foot for which thou art worshipped I despise, yet I remember thee with affection. I remember that, in spite of vain philosophy, of drab doubts, of toilsome learning, God had stamped his image of benignity so strong upon thy heart that not all the labours of thy head could efface it.[12]

21st September 1765 to Hume in France:
[…] I am just returned from a Highland expedition, and was much delighted with the magnificence of nature in her awful simplicity. These mountains, and torrents, and rocks, would almost convince one that it was some being of infinite power that had created them. Plain corn countries look as if men had made them; but I defy all mankind put together to make anything like the Pass of Gilicranky [Killiecrankie].

16th December 1768 to Hume in London, trying to persuade him to return to Edinburgh: she will hire him a house and, if she gets the specifications, procure him a wife:
But no fear, come along; bring you vices we shall find objects for them. As for the Godly, there is not one here. They are all gone to England to Whitefield and Wesley.[13] […] All, all are worshippers of mammon. I am to dine with Baron Mure tomorrow, and shall remember you. The Baron is quite sober, and Mrs Mure drinks hard;[14] everything is changed since you were here – quite topsy-turvy. I am grown a laddier. I hate any man that's above sixteen: your Joseph is one of my greatest Joes. […] Pray be good to poor Rousseau. You are a good Christian after all. It was jealousy alone, and over affection for you, that put him mad.[15][…] Adam [her son] never writes; I am angry at him just now; but I know what he waits for – Lady Balcarres and her lovely lasses in town for the winter.[16] The town is too big, and I am the reverse of you; I am grown too little, and hide myself in my own shell. I am, yours faithfully,   A. COKBURNE [*sic*]

Selection from correspondence with the Reverend Robert Douglas, minister of Galashiels:
28th November 1775 :
As for printing, never fear. I hate print, and though I have been sung at wells to the flowers of the forest, I never was in print that anybody but a street singer could decipher. I have many curious researches to set you on: I wish you to tell me why I should have suffered real martyrdom all last winter by the distress of my son, why I should foresee he was a cripple for life, submitting to that patiently, and willing to devote every hour I lived to attending upon him; yet, now that he writes to me he is in perfect health, walks 10 miles a day, in fine spirits and happy, I do not feel as much joy as I suffered misery? Answer all this […]

17th November, 1784 on her receipt of a birthday letter from Douglas:
A lady, a particular favourite was alone with me when I got it.[…]You are right not to trust me with good letters. You might as well send me an ortolan to eat alone.[17] That she heard me read the letter, that she put it in her pocket, is as certain as that many have read it, though it discovers my antiquity day and date. That it met with applause you will be sure; but (to mortify you and myself) I read it to one lady, no bad critic, and religious too. She stopped me and said it was a shame to treat sacred subjects in so ludicrous a manner! I put my letter halfway read in my pocket, and said I would not cast pearls before swine, and asked her whether she worshipped God or the devil?

October 1793:
'You have lived so long!'
   What? Can I help it? These are the first words of your letter, Douglas. I'm sure I am as weary of it as you can be; and yet it's very impious and ungrateful to say so, as I have every blessing that fourscore can enjoy, and not a gray hair in my head, nor a spoiled tooth in my mouth. Yet I have plenty of hair, and can send you a lock if you won't believe me. I can also send you plenty of teeth to convince you. Like a female, I begin with my remaining beauties! next, free from pain and distress. When my maidens carry me from my bed to my chair or *vice versa*, I sing to them all the way to cheer the weariness of attendance. Both my maids were taken ill – my particular attendant has been ill 5 weeks, the other a sprained leg. Good luck, all my domestics are my friends. A married one sent in a daughter of 10 year old, and I am very well served. Next, I come to my friends – you know they love me. But some go to Heaven and leave me.

Alison Cockburn died in Edinburgh thirteen months after writing this letter.

NOTES
  1. David Hume (1711-76), the celebrated philosopher and historian, was born in Edinburgh. In 1739 he published his *Treatise of Human Nature* and in 1748 his *Enquiry Concerning Human Understanding*. James Burnett, Lord Monboddo (1714-99), Scottish judge and pioneer anthropologist, published in 1773-92 *Of the Origin and Progress of Language* and *Antient Metaphysics* (1779-99).
  2. According to Craig-Brown's note the nobleman was James, 6th Duke of Hamilton, notoriously profligate in money matters and quixotic in love. In Scots law a cautioner provides security or surety.
  3. Much of Scotland did not remember Alison Cockburn's father-in-law with such affection. Adam Cockburn of Ormiston was Lord Justice-clerk of Scotland, thus vice-president of the High Court of Justiciary. Craig-Brown quotes a contemporary, Dr Houston: 'Of all the [Whig] party, Lord Ormiston was the most busy and zealous in suppressing the rebellion [1715] and in oppressing the rebels, so that he became universally hated in Scotland, where they called him the curse of Scotland; and when ladies were at cards playing the nine of diamonds, commonly called the curse of Scotland, they called it the Justice-clerk' (p.26).
  4. Craig-Brown confirms that the date of her marriage in Ormiston Parish Register is 12 March 1731. March 12 was probably the date of calling of the banns (announcing the marriage from the pulpit) and Alison Cockburn seems to have got the year wrong.

5. Craig-Brown's note: 'Seems to point to the family of John Pringle, Lord Haining, and his wife Ann Murray of Philiphaugh, whose son Andrew Pringle, Lord Alemoor, was much troubled with gout.'

6. These details are supported by a letter from Anne, Countess of Balcarres, to her daughter, Lady Anne Lindsay Barnard, in the collection of manuscripts in the Crawford Family Papers in the National Library of Scotland (27/1/105). The Countess remarks that it was 'a sad piece of work to poor Mrs Cockburn'.

7. Craig-Brown quotes Chambers's *Traditions of Edinburgh*: 'The neat first floor of a house in Crichton Street, with windows looking along the Potterow.'

8. Harrowgate, now usually 'Harrogate', Yorkshire, was at the time the leading spa in the North with nearly 90 springs. Smollett's episolary novel, *Humphry Clinker,* 1771, testifies to its eighteenth century popularity.

9. 'John Pringle of Crichton, who had married Mrs Cockburn's niece, Anne Rutherford, heiress of Fairnilee. Their daughter Anne was the object of Captain Adam Cockburn's love': Craig-Brown's note.

10. 'It is not very clear whether this means that Adam was averse to being bled by a surgeon, or that he was of too pacific a disposition to draw blood himself': Craig-Brown's note. The former seems more likely: the effusions of blood would probably at the time have been taken to indicate that he had too much blood and to refuse to be bled would have been regarded as unwise.

11. John Pringle became bankrupt.

12. Alison Cockburn's chief intellectual quarrel with Hume is, of course, over his religious scepticism.

13. George Whitefield (1714-1770) and John Wesley (1703-91), the Methodist preachers. See also Sinclair (p.192, n.4).

14. William Mure (1718-1776) was from 1761 Baron of the Scots Exchequer and in 1764-65 Lord Rector of Glasgow University. His close friends included John Stuart, the third Earl of Bute, and David Hume. Mrs Mure, if she did indeed 'drink hard', survived her drinking and died in 1820 in her 86th year. She was the daughter of James Graham, Lord Easdale, one of the judges of the Court of Session and according to her grandson, William Mure, was known for her beauty, wit and 'lively eccentricity of character'. See Mure, p.33.

15. Hume brought Rousseau to England in 1766. Rousseau responded with suspicion and unwarranted complaints, including the accusation that Hume was reading his correspondence. Alison Cockburn had a soft spot for Rousseau as a man of feeling, which would probably not have survived a reading of *The Confessions*.

16. Lady Anne Lindsay Barnard (*q.v.*) was the eldest of the 'lovely lasses'.

17. Ortolans are small birds about 16 cm. long with brown plumage, yellow throat and pinkish belly. They are quite plentiful in the south of France and in Spain Italy and Greece. Just before their autumn migration they store large amounts of fat and it is this which has made them a great, although very expensive delicacy. In different times and places elaborate rituals have attached to the eating of ortolans.

Elizabeth Mure of Caldwell (1714–1795)

'Elizabeth Mure probably spent the greater part of her life at Caldwell, the family estate in Renfrewshire and Ayrshire – there she was born in 1714 and there she died in 1795. Her father, William Mure of Caldwell, died in 1722, leaving a young family. For a time the Rev. William Leechman, afterwards Professor of Divinity in and Principal of Glasgow University, was tutor to the eldest son [later Baron Mure], and it is not at all improbable that Elizabeth was also one of his pupils. But very little is known of her life, except that she had charge of the estate during the minority of a nephew, and that, owing to her careful management, it was relieved of the heavy burdens caused by the extensive improvements carried out by the previous owner' (Fyfe, p.61). In a note to the selections from the Caldwell family papers the editor, William Mure, Baron Muir's grandson and Elizabeth Mure's grand-nephew, says that 'her memory is still fondly cherished by the more aged tenantry of the estate' (p.259). In the Introductory Memoir William Mure credits her with an interesting observation about David Hume whom she had known since her youth: 'It is very remarkable that those persons who have distinguished themselves the most for scepticism, or even for atheism, have often a stronger belief in dreams, presages, and omens, than other people. I have frequently been led to this remark by conversing with David Hume. No man more credulous than he, or sees a judgment inflicted sooner than he does. Three others I could mention, all of whom are professed sceptics, yet on many occasions declare their belief in dreams, presages, and omens. How strange a thing it is for a wise man to doubt of every revelation made to the world by God or angels, and yet give credit to his own or other people's dreams!' (p.41). The essay on the manners of her time may have been composed by Elizabeth Mure towards the end of her life; it was, says, William Mure, 'surreptitiously printed in one of the few numbers of the short-lived periodical set on foot in Edinburgh in 1818, under the title of *Constable's Magazine*' (p.258).

Selections from the Family Papers Preserved at Caldwell, ed. William Mure, 1799-
1860, 2 vols in 3; New Club series [Maitland Club] (Paisley: A. Gardner, 1883-85)

Further reading:
DNB (for Baron Mure); Fyfe

From *Selections from the Family Papers*. I have modernised most spelling but left period expressions such as occur in the first paragraph; the different convention for noting dates has been retained.

     Some remarks on the change of manners in my own time. 1700-1790.
Had we a particular account of the manners of our country, and of the changes that has taken place from time to time since the reign of William the III, no history could be more entertaining; but those changes has been so little marked, that what knowledge we have of them we owe it more to the essay writers in Queen Anne's

time than to any of our historians. Addison, Pope, Swift, learns us the manners of the times they wrote in. Since that period the information we have had from our parents, and our own observation, may instruct us. It were to be wished that some good author would make his observations on this subject during his own life, which if carried down would contain both useful, and entertaining knowledge.

Nobody that has lived any time in the world but must have made remarks of this kind, though it's only the men of genius that can make the proper use of them, by representing the good or ill consequences the changes may have on society. Those I have lived myself to see I wish to remember and mark for my own use. I'm sensible that in order to make these remarks properly it's necessary one should have been more in the world than I was during the times I write of, as the manners in the chief towns would be something different from those in the country; but as our fashions are brought from the Metropolis, the people of fashion in the country cannot be far behind.

My observation cannot go much further back than the 30, which period I reckon verged on the age of my Grandfather, who was one of those born betwixt the 60 and 70 in the last century, many of whom remained beyond the time above mentioned. Their manners was still peculiar to themselves as some part of the old feudal system still remained. Every master was revered by his family, honoured by his tenants, and awful to his domestics. His hours of eating, sleeping, and amusement, were carefully attended to by all his family, and by all his guests. Even his hours of devotion was marked, that nothing might interrupt him. He kept his own seat by the fire or at table, with his hat on his head; and often particular dishes served up for himself, that nobody else shared of. Their children approached them with awe, and never spoke with any degree of freedom before them. The consequence of this was that except at meals they were never together; though the reverence they had for their parents taught them obedience, modesty, temperance. Nobody helped themselves at table, nor was it the fashion to eat up what was put on their plate. So that the mistress of the family might give you a full meal or not as she pleased; from whence came in the fashion of pressing the guests to eat so far as to be disagreeable.

The 1727 is as far back as I can remember. At that time there was little bread in Scotland; manufactories brought to no perfection, either in linen or woollen. Every woman made her web of wove linen, and bleached it herself; it never rose higher than 2 shillings the yard, and with this cloth was everybody clothed. The young gentlemen, who at this time were growing more delicate, got their cloth from Holland for shirts; but the old was satisfied with necks and sleeves of the fine, which were put on loose above the country cloth. I remember in the 30 or 31 of a ball where it was agreed that the company should be dressed in nothing but what was manufactured in the country. My sisters were as well dressed as any, and their gowns were striped linen at 2s. and 6d. per yard. Their heads and ruffles were of Paisley muslins, at 4 and sixpence, with four penny edging from Hamilton; all of them the finest that could be had. A few years after this, weavers were brought over from Holland, and manufactories for linen established in the West. The dress of the ladies were nearly as expensive as at present, though not so often renewed. At the time I mention hoops were worn constantly four yards and a half wide, which required much silk to cover them; and gold and silver was much used for trimming, never less than three rows round the petticoat; so that though the silk was slight the price was increased by the trimming. Then the heads were all dressed in laces from Flanders; no blonds nor coarse-edging used;[1] the price of those was high, but two suit would serve for life; they were not renewed but at marriage or some great event. Who could not afford those wore fringes of thread.

Their tables were as full as at present, though very ill dressed and as ill served up. They ate out of pewter, often ill cleaned; but were nicer in their linen than now, which was renewed every day in most gentlemen's families, and always napkins besides the cloth. The servants ate ill; having a set form for the week, of three days broth and salt meat, the rest meagre, with plenty of bread and small beer. Their wages were small till the Vails[2] were abolished; the men from 3 to 4 pounds in the year, the maids from 30 shillings to 40. At those times I mention few of the maids could either sew or dress linen; it was all smoothed in the mangle but the ladies' head-dresses, which were done by their own maids, and the gentlemen's shirts by the housekeeper. They in general employed as many servants as they do at present in the country, but not in the towns; for one man servant was thought sufficient for most families, or two at most, unless they kept a carriage, which was a thing very uncommon in these days, and only used by nobles of great fortune. The prices of provisions were about a third of what they are now; beef from $1^1/_2$ to 2 pence per pound; butter 2 pence $^1/_2$ penny; cheese 3 farthings or 1 penny; eggs 1p. the dozen; veal 5 shillings the whole; a hen 4 pence; geese and turkeys 1 shilling. Neither was the provisions much raised till after the Rebellion in the forty five, when riches increased considerably.

Before the union, and for many years after it, money was very scarce in Scotland. A country without trade, without cultivation, or money to carry on either of them, must improve by very slow degrees. A great part of the gentlemen's rents were paid in kind. This made them live comfortably at home, though they could not anywhere else. This introduced that old hospitality so much boasted of in Britain. No doubt we had our share in it according to our abilities; but this way of life led to manners very different from the present. Nothing could affect them more than the restraint young people were under in presence of their parents. There was little intercourse betwixt the old and young; the parents had their own guests, which consisted for the most part of their own relations and near neighbours. As few people could afford to go to town in the winter, their acquaintance was much confined. The children of this small society were under a necessity of being companions to one another. This produced many strong friendships and strong attachments, and often very improper marriages. By their society being confined their affections were less diffused, and centred all in their own small circle. There was no enlargement of mind here; their manners were the same and their sentiments the same; they were indulgent to the faults of one another, but most severe on those they were not accustomed to; so that censure and detraction seemed to be the vice of the age. From this education proceeded pride of understanding, bigotry of religion, and want of refinement in every useful art. While the Parents were both alive the mother could give little attention to her girls. Domestic affairs and amusing her husband were the business of a good wife.

Those that could afford governesses for their children had them; but all they could learn them was to read English ill, and plain work. The chief thing required was to hear them repeat Psalms and long catechisms, in which they were employed an hour or more every day, and almost the whole day on Sunday. If there was no governess to perform this work, it was done by the chaplain, of which there was one in every family. No attention was given to what we call accomplishments. Reading and writing well or even spelling was never thought of. Music, drawing, or French were seldom taught the girls. They were allowed to run about and amuse themselves in the way they choiced even to the age of women, at which time they were generally sent to Edinburgh for a winter or two, to learn to dress themselves and to dance and to see a little of the world. The world was only to be seen at Church, at marriages, burials and baptisms. These were the only public places where the ladies went in full dress, and as they walked the street they were seen by everybody; but it was the fashion when in undress always to be masked. When in the country their employment was in coloured work, beds, tapestry, and other pieces of furniture; imitations of fruit and flowers, with very little taste. If they read any it was either books of devotion or long romances, and sometimes both. They never ate a full meal at table; this was thought very undelicate, but they took care to have something before dinner, that they might behave with propriety in company. From the account given by old people that lived in this time, we have reason to believe there was as little care taken of the young men as of the women; excepting those that were intended for learned professions, who got a regular education through schools and colleges. But the generality of our country gentlemen, and even our noblemen, were contented with the instructions given by the chaplain to their young men. But that the manners of the times I write of may be shown in a fuller light, I shall give Mr Barclay's[3] relation of the most memorable things that past in his father's house from the beginning of the century till the 13, in which year he [*i.e.*, Sir James Stewart] died.

My brother was married (says he) in the four, at the age of twenty one; few men were unmarried after this time of life. I myself was married by my friends at 18, which was thought a proper age. Sir James Stewart's[4] marriage with President Dalrymple's second daughter brought together a number of people related to both families. At the signing of the eldest Miss Dalrymple's contract the year before, there was an entire hogshead of wine drunk that night,[5] and the number of people at Sir James Stewart's was little less.

The marriage was in the President's[6] house, with as many of the relations as it would hold. The Bride's favours was all sewed on her gown from top to bottom and round the neck and sleeves. The moment the ceremony was performed, the whole company run to her and pulled off the favours: in an instant she was stripped of all of them. The next ceremony was the garter, which the Bridegroom's man attempted to pull from her leg; but she dropped it through her petticoat on the floor. This was a small white and silver ribbon which was cut in small morsels to every one in the company. The Bride's mother came in then with a basket of favours belonging to the Bridegroom: those and the Bride's were the same with the liveries of their families; hers pink and white, his blue and gold colour. All the company dined and supped together, and had a ball in the evening. The same next day in the Advocate's. On Sunday there went from the President's house to Church three and twenty couples, all in high dress: Mr Barclay then a boy led the youngest Miss Dalrymple who was the last of them. They filled the lofts of the kirk from the King's seat to the wing loft. The feasting continued every day till they had gone through all the friends of both families, with a ball every night.

As the baptism was another public place, he goes on to describe it thus:

On the fourth week after the lady's delivery she is set on her bed on a low footstool; the bed covered with some neat piece of sewed work or white satin, with three pillows at her back covered with the same; she in full dress with a lapped head dress and a fan in her hand. Having informed her acquaintance what day she is to see company, they all come and pay their respects to her, standing or walking a little through the room (for there's no chairs). They drink a glass of wine and eat a bit of cake and then give place to others. Towards the end of the week all the friends were asked to what was called the Cummer's feast.[7] This was a supper, where every gentleman brought a pint of wine to be drunk by him and his wife. The supper was a ham at the head and a pyramid of fowl at the bottom. This dish consisted of four or five ducks at bottom, hens above, partridges at top. There was an eating posset in the middle of the table, with dried fruit and sweetmeats at the sides. When they had finished their supper, the meat was removed, and in a moment everybody flies to the sweetmeats to pocket them. Upon which a scramble ensued, chairs overturned and everything on the table; wrassalling[8] and pulling at one another with the utmost noise. When all was quieted, they went to the stoups [flagons] (for there was no bottles) of which the women had a good share. For though it was a disgrace to be seen drunk, yet it was none to be a little intoxicate in good company. A few days after this the same company was asked to the christening, which was always in the Church; all in high dress; a number of them young ladies, who were called maiden Cummers. One of them presented the child to the father. After the ceremony they dined and supped together, and the night often concluded with a ball.

The burials is the only thing now to be taken notice of. It was always on foot.

The magistrates and town Council were invited to every person's of any consideration; 1500 burial letters were wrote (says Mr Barclay) at my Father's death. The Assembly was sitting at the time,[9] and all the clergy were asked; and so great was the crowd, that the magistrates were at the grave in the Greyfriars Church-yard before the corpse was taken out of the house in the foot of the Advocate's Close. A few years before this it had ceased to be the fashion for the ladies to walk behind the corpse, in high dress with coloured clothes; but formerly the Chesting[10] was at the same time; and all the female relations asked who made part of the procession.

At this time acts of devotion employed much of their time; see the same gentleman's account of a Sunday past in his father's house: 'Prayers by the chaplain at nine o'clock; all went regularly to Church at ten, the women in high dress.' He himself was employed by his father to give the collection for the family which was a crown. 'Half after twelve they came home; at one had prayers again by the chaplain; after which they had a bit of cold meat or an egg, and returned to Church at two; was out again by four, when everybody retired to their private devotions, except the children and servants who were convened by the chaplain and examined. This continued till five, when supper was served up, or rather dinner. A few friends generally partook of this meal, and sat till eight; after which singing, reading, and prayers was performed by the old gentleman himself; after which they all retired.'

Whether the genius of a people forms their religious sentiments, or if religion forms in some measure the manners of a people, I shall leave the wise to decide. I shall only observe, that while that reverence and awe remained in the minds of man for masters, fathers and heads of clans, it was then that the awe and dread of Deity was most powerful. This will appear from the superstitious writing of the times. The fear of Hell and deceitful power of the Devil was at the bottom of all their religious sentiments. The established belief in witchcraft (for which many suffered) prevailed much at this time; ghosts too and apparitions of various kinds were credited; few old houses was without a ghost chamber that few people had courage to sleep in. Omens and dreams were much regarded even by people of the best education. These were the manners of the last century, and remained in part for 30 years in this.

The change of manners in the new generation was very remarkable. The Union with England carried many of our nobility and gentry to London. Sixty of the most considerable people being obliged to pass half of the year there would no doubt change their ideas. Besides, many English came to reside at Edinburgh. The Court of Exchequer and the Boards of Customs and Excise were mostly all of that nation; at least all the under officers were. These were people of fashion, and were well received by the first people here. As this intercourse with the English opened our eyes a little, so it gave us a liberty of trade we had not before. From the Union many of our younger sons became merchants and went abroad. It likewise became the fashion for our young men of fortune to study for some years in Holland, after which to make a tour through France. On their return home they brought to Scotland French politeness grafted on the self-importance and dignity of their fathers. May we not suppose it was at this time our nation acquired the character of poverty and pride?

About the 24, a weekly Assembly for dancing was set up at Edinburgh. This with private balls carried on by subscription took place of marriages, baptisms, and burials. Their society now came to be more enlarged, but it required time to have a proper effect. The men's manners, though stiff and evidently put on, yet were better than the women's, who were undelicate in their conversation and vulgar in their manners. As the awe and reverence for parents and elder friends wore off, they brought into company the freedom and romping they had acquired amongst their brothers and near relations. Many of them threw off all restraint. Were I to name the time when the Scotch ladies went farthest wrong, it would be betwixt the 30 and 40. I'm at a loss to account for this, if it was not owing to our young noblemen bringing home French manners; and lest they should be led into marriages, made their addresses to those only that were in that state. No doubt the contrast betwixt the young men educated abroad and ours who were close at home would be very great. Besides, the manners of the ladies might lead the men to more freedom if they were so disposed, as they had not yet learned that restraint so necessary where society is enlarged. Yet this was far from being general.

There was still in the country a taste for good morals, which was improved by a set of teachers established among us, most of whom had their education abroad or had travelled with young gentlemen. As every body at this period went regularly to Church, I may justly mention ministers as teachers: Professor Hamilton and the two Mr Wisharts at Edinburgh; Professor Hutchison; Craig, Clark and Principal Leichman in the west;[11] these taught that whoever would please God must resemble him in goodness and benevolence, and those that had it not must affect it by politeness and good manners. Those lectures and sermons were attended by all the young and gay. They were new and entertaining and matter for conversation and criticism.

In well regulated families there was still kept up a reverence for parents and for elderly friends; and when the young was admitted to their society, there was a degree of attention paid the old, yea even servility, that this age knows nothing of; and whoever was wanting in it was unfit for company. Nobody in those times thought of pleasing themselves. The established rule was to please your company; endeavour to make them think well of themselves and they will think well of you for doing it.

Society was not yet so much enlarged as to weaken the affections of near relations. This may be easily ascertained by every one now alive that is turned of fifty. Not only brothers and sisters, but brothers- and sisters-in-law, mothers-in-law, and even more distant connections, would leave their own families for ten or twelve days, and attend with the utmost care a friend in a fever or dangerous disorder. These were the nursekeepers for the first 30 years of this century, who by every method endeavoured to lessen their distress, nor left them night or day till recovered or buried. The intercourse betwixt relations and friends was kept up in another way, which was by small presents, mostly consisting of meats or drink. Anything rare or good of its kind was in part sent to a friend whatever rank of life they were in. These presents were received with thanks, and returned in kind on proper occasions. Neither was strangers or people of high rank sought after in their entertainments. It was their relations, the friends they loved, that shared their delicacies. Those manners still remain in many places in Scotland. At Glasgow two brothers will vie with one another who will give the most elegant meal. Though this may proceed more from vanity than affection yet I believe it to be introduced by the last.

When this restraint was thrown off every character appeared in a natural light, of which there was great variety. Prudes and coquettes, romps and affected fine ladies, they were at no pains to disguise, as every one had their own admirers. The regular tea-tables which commenced about the 20 was the meeting of all the young and gay every evening. There they pulled to pieces the manners of those that differed from them; everything was matter of conversation; religion, morals, love, friendship, good manners, dress. This tended more to our refinement than anything else. The subjects were all new and all entertaining. The bookseller's shops were not stuffed as they are now with novels and magazines. The women's knowledge was gained only by conversing with the men not by reading themselves, as they had few books to read that they could understand. Whoever had read Pope, Addison and Swift, with some ill wrote history, was then thought a learned lady, which character was by no means agreeable. The men thought justly on this point, that what knowledge the women had out of their own sphere should be given by themselves, and not picked up at their own hand in ill chosen books of amusement, though many of them not without a moral, yet more fitted to reclaim the desolate than to improve a young untainted mind, that might have passed through life with more happiness and purity than they could with the knowledge those books contained. Neither was there any sceptics in these times. Religion was just recovered from the power of the Devil and fear of Hell, taught by our mothers and grandmothers. At this period those terrors began to wear off and religion appeared in a more amiable light. We were bid draw our knowledge of God from his works, the chief of which is the soul of a good man; then judge if we have cause to fear. The Christian religion was taught as the purest rule of morals; the belief of a particular providence and of a future state as a support in every situation. The distresses of individuals were necessary for exercising the good affections of others, and the state of suffering the post of honour.

The intercourse of the men with the women, though less reserved than at present, was full as pure. They would walk together for hours, or travel on horseback or in a chaise, without any imputation of imprudence. The parents had no concern when an admirer was their guide; neither had they cause. The men showed their attachment by correcting their faults, informing them what the world thought of them, and what was most agreeable to the men if they choiced to please them.

About the 40 riches began to increase considerably. Many returned from the East and West Indies with good fortunes who had gone abroad after the Union. These picked up estates through the country, and lived in a higher style than the old gentry. The Rebellion in the 45 still more increased our riches. From this time the country took a new form. Whether the dread of arbitrary power disposed us for more liberty, or if another cause, I shall leave the more knowing to determine, but surely it had powerful effects on the manners. It was then that the slavery of the mind began to be spoken of; freedom was in everybody's mouth. The fathers would use the sons with such freedom that they should be their first friend; and the mothers would allow of no intimacies but with themselves. For their girls the utmost care was taken that fear of no kind should enslave the mind; nurses were turned off who would tell the young of witches and ghosts. The old ministers were ridiculed who preached up hell and damnation; the minds was to be influenced by gentle and generous motives alone. These methods of instruction has been on the increase since the time mentioned above. What may be the effects none knows. May not even the love of liberty become the disease of a state; and men be enslaved in the worst way by their own passions? The word menial becomes of late years to be much used; every degree of denying one's self to please others is menial; and for fear of the imputation of this we are in hazard of tricking ourselves out of the finest feelings of humanity; devotion, love and friendship; as in each of them there's a degree of self denial. Nobody will at present share a family dinner with the friend they love for fear of being menial. Neither will they attend them when in distress for the same cause; but satisfy themselves with daily enquiring after them.

About the same time that tea-tables were established, it was the fashion for the men to meet regularly in Change-house, as it was called, for their different clubs. There they spent the evening in conversation, without much expense; a shilling reckoning was very high; and for people of the first fashion it was more general from four pence to eight pence the piece, paying besides for their tobacco and pipes which was much in use. In some of those clubs they played at Backgammon or Catch honours for a penny the game. All business was transacted in the forenoon and in the Change-houses. The lawyers were there consulted and the bill paid by the employer. The liquor was sherry in mutchken stoups. Every new mutchken was chalked on the head of the stoup. It was incredible the quantity that was drunk sometimes on those occasions. Every body dined at home in private, unless called to some of the entertainments mentioned above; but the tea-tables very soon introduced supping in private houses. When young people found themselves happy with one another they were loath to part, so that supping came to be the universal fashion in Edinburgh; and lest the family they visited might be unprepared, they sent in the morning to know if they were to drink tea at home, as they wished to wait on them. Amongst friends this was always considered as a supper, and any of their men acquaintances asked that they could command to make up the party. The acquaintance made up at public places did not visit in this way; they hired a chair for the afternoon, and run through a number of houses as is the fashion still. Those merry suppers made the young people find a want when they went to the country, and to supply the place of them was introduced collations after supper; when the young people met in some one of their bed chambers, and had either tea or a posset, where they sat and made merry till far in the morning. But this meeting was carefully concealed from the parents, who were all enemies to those collations. Those manners continued till the sixty, or near it, when more of the English fashion took place, one of which was to dine at three, and what company you had should be at dinner. These dinners lasted, the women sat for half an hour after them and retired to tea; but the men took their bottle and often remained till eight at night. The women were all the evening by themselves, which put a stop to that general intercourse so necessary for the improvement of both sexes. This naturally makes a run on the public places; as the women has little amusement at home. Cut off from the company of the men, and no family friends to occupy this void, they must tire of their mothers and elderly society, and flee to the public for relief. They find the men there, though late in the evening when they have left their bottle, and too often unfitted for everything but their bed. In this kind of intercourse there is little chance for forming attachments. The women see the men in the worst light, and what impression they make on the men is forgot by them in the morning. These late dinners has entirely cut off the merry suppers very much regretted by the women, while the men pass the nights in taverns in gaming or other amusement as their temper leads them. Cut off in a great measure from the society of the men, it's necessary the women should have some constant amusement; and as they are likewise denied friendships with one another, the parents provided for this void as much as possible in giving them complete education; and what formerly begun at ten years of age, or often later, now begins at four or five. How long it's to continue the next age must determine; for it's not yet fixed in this. Reading, writing, music, drawing, French, Italian, Geography, History, with all kinds of needle work are now carefully taught the girls, that time may not lie heavy on their hand without proper society. Besides this, shops loaded with novels and books of amusement, to kill the time.

NOTES

1. Blonde-lace was originally made from raw silk.
2. 'Customary fees from the master or his guests, at particular seasons': note in Maitland Club edition. In the seventeenth and eighteenth centuries servants were largely paid by these vails, that is gratuities or tips, and the practice of giving them, particularly when guests left a house, is frequently referred to in the literature of the period. In his *Directions to Servants* Swift advises those who 'expect vails, always to stand rank and file when a stranger is taking his leave'.
3. Her uncle; a younger son of Sir James Stewart, Lord Advocate (1692-1709; 1711-1713), who took the name of Barclay: note from Maitland Club edition.
4. Sir James Stewart, Solicitor-General from 1714 to 1717, eldest son of Sir James Stewart (the Lord Advocate): note by Fyfe.
5. A hogshead is a variable quantity; but a cask called a hogshead would contain between 46 and 63 gallons.
6. Sir Hew Dalrymple, Lord North Berwick, was Lord President of the Court of Session from 1698 to 1737.
7. A corruption of the French *commère*, gossip or companion.
8. More commonly 'wrastling' for 'wrestling'.
9. The General Assembly of the Church of Scotland is the highest court of the Presbyterian Church; it meets in the Assembly Hall in Edinburgh.
10. 'Also called Coffining, of the body': note from Maitland Club edition.
11. Robert Hamilton (1707-1787), minister of Old Greyfriars, Edinburgh, from 1750 till 1754; Professor of Divinity, University of Edinburgh from 1754; Moderator of the General Assembly in 1754 and 1760. William Wishart (1660-1729), minister of the Tron Parish, Edinburgh from 1707 till 1729. Moderator in 1706, 1713, 1718, 1724 and 1728. In 1716 appointed Principal of Edinburgh University. His son, George Wishart (1703-1785), minister of the Tron from 1730 till 1785. Moderator in 1748. His other son, William (1707-1753) became Principal of Edinburgh University in 1737. Francis Hutcheson (1694-1746) was Professor of Moral Philosophy at the University of Glasgow from 1729-46. His system of philosophy, known as the common-sense school, was published by his son in 1755. The Rev. William Leechman (the more common spelling) afterwards became one of the most distinguished divines of the Church of Scotland, and in 1761, partly through the influence of Baron Mure, became Principal of the University of Glasgow. William Craig was a Glasgow minister, distinguished for his preaching; James Clark, minister of the Tron Parish, Glasgow, 1702-1723, preached violently against the Union of the English and Scottish Parliaments in 1707.

Mrs Margaret Stewart Calderwood, (1715–1774)

Margaret Stewart Calderwood was the eldest of four daughters of Sir James Stewart of Coltness, who was Solicitor-General for Scotland from 1714-1717; her mother, the witty and beautiful Anne Dalrymple, was the daughter of Sir Hew Dalrymple, Lord President of the Court of Session, and thus the niece of the Bride of Lammermuir, daughter of the first Viscount Stair and heroine of Scott's novel. Margaret Stewart was born in 1715, and in 1735 married Thomas Calderwood of the Polton estate, six miles south of Edinburgh. During the 'Forty-Five' Rising her brother, Sir James Stewart, was thought to have assisted the Jacobites and was, as a result, forced to flee to the Continent. In 1756 Mrs Calderwood, anxious about his comfort, travelled to the Continent to see him. With her husband, her two sons and two family servants, she journeyed down through England to London; crossed the Channel and proceeded through the Low Countries. This was her first trip outside Scotland and she kept a journal to record her impressions of her new experiences. Mrs Calderwood, it should be remarked, is violently anti-catholic throughout her record.

The Journal, which takes the form of letters home, was eventually published in 1884, but had previously been circulated among relatives and friends and in 1842 privately printed for the Maitland Club and issued to its members among the Coltness Collections. The letters are characterised by sharp and often prejudiced observation of English and Continental manners and customs. Everything is measured against her sense of the importance of her native country: she often feels it pitiable not to be a Scot. Her language is forthright and to the point, whether it copes with description or argument. Her anti-English prejudices are certainly lively and a general unwillingness to be impressed by 'abroad' makes her a more delightful female Smollett. The vigour of her body and mind seems typical of her class of educated eighteenth-century Scotswoman the disappearance of which was so lamented by Scott.

After her travels Mrs Calderwood probably settled for the rest of her life at Polton, remaining closely involved in the management of the family estates. Her rent rolls and account books are still extant. She is said to have studied mathematics under Professor Maclaurin,[1] the friend of Newton, and the way in which she increased the rental of the family estates would suggest that she profited from the study. She also apparently wrote a novel, *The Adventures of Fanny Roberts*, which remains unpublished.

Alexander Fergusson remarks in his Introduction to her letters and journals that 'she is as cogent, and as much to the point, as ever her brilliant nephews were. Her sister, Agnes, married Henry David, tenth Earl of Buchan and her children were Henry Erskine, the Lord Advocate of Scotland, and Thomas Erskine, Lord High Chancellor of Great Britain' (p.x).

Margaret Calderwood died in 1774 eight months after the death of her husband, having had two sons and one daughter. The estate of Polton passed to the daughter's children.

Margaret Calderwood, *Letters and Journals of Mrs Calderwood of Polton from England, Holland and the Low Countries in 1756*, edited by Alexander Fergusson (Edinburgh: Printed for David Douglas, 1884)

Further Reading:
DNB; Fyfe; *HSWW*

From *Letters and Journals from England, Holland and the Low Countries* (spelling is modernised):

Mrs Calderwood began her journey in June 1756, setting out from Polton in the afternoon and sleeping at Pilmure. On 9 June she met at Barnet 'a squinting, smart-like black girl' who spoke to her in what she thought was Irish, and so she said,

'Are you a Highlander?'

'No,' said she, 'I am Welsh, are you not Welsh?'

'No,' said I, 'but I am Scots, and the Scots and Welsh are near relations, and much better born than the English.'

'Oh!' said she, 'the maid said you was Welsh, and sent me to see you.'

She took me by the hand, and looked so kindly that I suppose she thought me her relation, because I was not English; which makes me think the English are a people one may perhaps esteem or admire, but they do not draw the affection of strangers, neither in their own country nor out of it.

Before describing London she gives her impressions of England on the journey south:

I admired the cattle much more than the people, for they seem to have the least of what we call smartness of any folks I ever saw, and totally void of all sort of curiosity, which perhaps some may think a good quality. In our first day's journey in England, I asked the post-boy to whom the lands on each hand belonged?

He said, 'to Sir Carnaby.'[2]

I knew who he meant, and, to try him, asked 'what Sir Carnaby, or what other name he had?'

But he answered, 'Just Sir Carnaby, who lives yonder,' and that he had never enquired the surname of the man in whose ground he was born.

As for the enclosing in England, it is of all the different methods, both good and bad, that can be imagined; and that such insufficient enclosures as some are keeping in the cattle, (which is so hard with us in Scotland) is entirely owing to the levelness of the grounds, so that an English cow does not see another spot than where she feeds, and has as little intelligence as the people; whereas, with us, there are few places which does not hang on the side of a hill, by which means the cattle sees what is above or below them, and so endeavours to get at it. I was convinced of this, by some oxen a butcher was driving to market, very large and fat. They walked along betwixt the hedges very well, but, no sooner were they come to a place where there was only an old ditch and no hedge on the one hand, but they scrambled over it very cleverly into a field of rye.

Once in London she remains tart and sceptical about the English, high and low:
You will think it very odd, that I was a fortnight in London, and saw none of the
royal family, but I got no clothes made till the day before I left it, though I gave them
to the making the day after I came. I cannot say my curiosity was great: I found, as I
approached the Court and the grandees, they sunk miserably in my opinion, and
came so far short of the ideas I had conceived, that I was loath to lose the grand ideas
I had of Kings, Princes, Ministers of State, Senators, etc., which I suppose I had
gathered from romance in my youth.

We used to laugh at the English for being so soon afraid when there was any
danger in state affairs, but now I do excuse them. For we, at a distance, think the
wisdom of our governors will prevent all these things; but those who know and see
our ministers every day see there is no wisdom in them, and that they are a parcel of
old, ignorant, senseless bodies, who mind nothing but eating and drinking, and
rolling about in Hyde Park, and know no more of the country, or the situation of it,
than they never had been in it; or how should they, when London, and twenty miles
round it, is the extent ever they saw of it.

*Margaret Calderwood's impressions of Rotterdam and the Dutch in general are a mixture
of approval and amazed reprobation:*
Their streets are kept as clean as any parlour floor, washed from the door of every
house cross to the canal every day, with a besom made of small twigs. The Dutch
maid-servants do nothing on earth but wash the house and the streets, and the
vessels of the house and kitchen.
[…]
I cannot commend their architecture by no means.

They look upon a stair as a necessary evil, so put it in as little room as possible,
and in as dark an out of the way corner as they can find. If the street runs a-squint
the town, then all the houses run a-squint in the fore wall, and every room is two
foot longer on the one side than the other. The chimney places are very droll like;
they have no jambs nor lintel, as we have, but a flat wall the grate is set to, and then
projects over it a lum [chimney], in the form of the cat-and-clay lums in the country
houses of timber, and commonly a muslin or point ruffled pawn [valance] round it;
above that several other little cornices for setting china upon, which every house
must be decked with.

They have excellent bedding here, fine down and feather beds; most of the
bottoms are timber, and over that a straw mattress, then a large down bed, then a
wool mattress very thick; a Dutch bolster is at least three quarters broad, and not
made round as ours are, but in the pillow shape; the pillows are in proportion, and
made square. The finest bed I lay in in Rotterdam had no blankets, but a soft calico
quilt, very thick with cotton, and very slightly quilted together. I thought I should
not have enough clothes, so took another, but soon found it too warm.
[…]
The thing I think the oddest about the Dutch is their appearance; there [are]
almost none of them have the look of gentlemen or ladies. The men are tolerable;
they have the air of sober men of business, but, for the ladies, they look like
chambermaids, put on them what you please, and they dress very plain. A fine gilt

coach will pass, and in it a chamber-maid in her Sunday clothes, or an old worn-out housekeeper; and, when you see them walking from church, dressed, they are just like a lady from the country, who has not had on a hoop, nor a fan in her hand, for twenty years, looking very prim, with her elbows into her sides, her two hands straight out before her, holding the fan out likeways, as if she was to red [to clear] her way by it, and hageling,[3] as if she thought all her petticoats were coming off.

This kind of detail characterises Mrs Calderwood's perceptions of life in Amsterdam and Utrecht and numerous smaller places. Her sharp eyes and pen carry her through Spa and Liège and at last to Brussels where she admires the town hall in the market square:

The great fair, which was since I came here, holds in it, and in the market-place; there was a terrible crowd, and all this building was employed by the shops, but I saw nothing very curious, nor very cheap, except carved work, looking-glass frames, and small picture frames, crucifixes, etc.: but what I would fain have bought (could I have got them easily sent you) were brackets for candles or flower-pots, very well carved, unpainted, for tenpence-halfpenny the pair. From this great square a street goes off at every corner, and all round it are shops; and, indeed, for shops, this town surpasses any one I have seen: it is a mart for Dutch and English goods, for Germany and the country round about, as it is impossible that the town can find them business.

[…]

It is vastly well supplied with water, and the fountains are some of them, very pretty: the oldest, and what is greatly valued by the town, in one called *Manicky*. This is a little gilded statue about the size of your Jamie; round this is a rail of iron, and a place for one to put in a thing to take the water. When the French took the town, they imagined that *Manicky* was certainly made of gold, and they stole him; upon which the town was in an uproar, and complained to Marshal Saxe,[4] who ordered him to be replaced; and to make up for this outrage, gave him a complete suit of clothes, with a hat and feather, in which he is dressed on St Michael's day, and the day of the Holy Trinity.

Mrs Calderwood is amusingly pleased with her own powers of observation and presentation but she does concede that Europeans do exhibit openness of mind:

All I shall say by way of conclusion is, that travelling may be an advantage to wise men, and a loss to fools, and the weight of anybody's brain is well known, when they are seen out of their own country. The proper use of it is to learn to set a just value upon every country, or the things they possess; and I believe, when accounts are balanced, the favours of Providence are more equally distributed than we rashly imagine: what one country wants another can supply, which links men into one common society; and it is curious to observe the contrivances they fall on to supply those wants [that] either cannot be purchased, or are too expensive for the generality.

The people on the continent have their minds more at large with regard to the rest of the world than those in an island; they have the opportunity of converse with all nations, which takes off prejudice, except when it is political, and even then it does not extend to individuals. Their behaviour is politer, because they are often amongst strangers, and it makes just the same difference betwixt them and us, as it does on the same man when he is in company and at home; he is the same man in head and heart, when he is entertaining a great visitor, as he is when lolling at his own fireside.

After setting a just value upon others, I must next set it on myself. I think I have done wonders, that, in the midst of all my hurry, I have found time to write so many pages, as all this is wrote since I came to Brussels; and I have gone so much through this town that I know it as well as Edinburgh.

NOTES

1. Colin Maclaurin (1698-1746) became Professor of Mathematics at Marischal College, Aberdeen in 1717.
2. 'Sir Carnaby Haggerston of Haggerston, Bart., Country Northumberland. Into his family married, in 1758, the Lady Winifred Maxwell of Nithsdale, the heir of an ancient name and of many romantic memories': note by Fergusson.
3. 'Not translatable by any word in English, nor at all without much circumlocution': note by Fergusson. Clearly it refers to a kind of swaying movement of the hips as if to hold up slipping petticoats.
4. Maurice, Comte de Saxe (1696-1750), Marshal of France, fought heroically in the French army during the War of the Austrian Succession (1740-48).

Lady Anne Lindsay Barnard (1750–1825)

Anne Lindsay was the eldest child of the eight boys and three girls of James Lindsay, 5th Earl of Balcarres, and his wife Anne Dalrymple, daughter of Sir Robert Dalrymple of Castleton, whom he married when he was sixty and she twenty-two. The family fortunes had been much depleted during the Jacobite Rebellion: Lindsay had fought for the Stuart cause in 1715, although he later supported George II, and much of Lindsay's political effort went into restoring them. Lady Anne spent her childhood in Fife under the stern discipline of her mother which she describes in the extracts below. The family often spent the winter in Edinburgh which meant that Lady Anne was admitted from an early stage to a social circle which included David Hume, Henry Mackenzie, Lord Monboddo and other luminaries.[1] Dr Johnson was introduced to her when he visited Edinburgh in 1773. Later she moved to London to live with her much loved sister, Margaret, whose husband Alexander Fordyce had fled to the continent to escape his debts (see Lonsdale). She was courted by but refused Henry Dundas, who became Secretary of State for War in Pitt's first administration, is said to have been in love with William Windham, but in 1793 married Andrew Barnard, the talented but poor son of Thomas, Bishop of Limerick, when he was twenty-eight and she forty-three. Barnard, with Dundas's patronage, was appointed colonial secretary to the Cape of Good Hope under the Governorship of Lord Macartney. Barnard died at the Cape in 1807 and Lady Anne spent the rest of her life in London, at first with her sister until Margaret's second marriage in 1812. Burke, Sheridan, Windham and Dundas were in their circle as well as the Prince of Wales: Lady Anne had made a trip to Paris before the Revolution (1784-85) with Mrs Fitzherbert, the Prince's mistress. She always had what the *DNB* calls the 'dubious honour' of the attachment of the Prince Regent. Lady Anne died on 6 May 1825, in her seventy-fourth year.

Lady Anne became famous primarily because of her ballad 'Auld Robin Gray', the genesis of which is explained in the extracts below. But her letters and journals will surely in the end be her most enduring monument. Her letters to Dundas (published first incidentally, towards the end of the Boer War) are very clearly the letters of a woman writing to a man, and of a private individual, placed in a position of public trust, writing to a great public figure. In them Anne Lindsay characterises herself as 'a poor weak woman', but patently does not believe her own characterisation. And although we cannot be sure how much attention Henry Dundas paid to her advice and political analysis, we can, with hindsight, see how much of her policy was good policy. We can also see how peculiarly gendered her perceptions are: indeed some of her most acute analyses either come out of transactions with her own 'feminine' bitchiness or self-protectiveness, or are generated by the gendered discourse of the house-wife.

Lady Anne's letters to her sisters are rather more social and less politically engaged than her letters to Dundas but they are always characterised by precise and witty observation and with a nice sense of the nuances of social relationships. Since she also left a Journal of her early life in her family, I have chosen extracts not from the letters to Dundas but from the familial letters and journals, from *The Lives of the*

Lindsays, which cover both of the aspects of my grouping 'at home and abroad'.

Lady Anne left, however, a huge quantity of written material much of it still unpublished and she hedged it about with conditions. The present Earl of Crawford and Balcarres, to whom I am indebted for permission to extract from *The Lives of the Lindsays* as well as to include letters from Sophia (Sophy) Johnston to Lady Anne, is organising a systematic programme of editing and publication of these materials.

Lady Anne Lindsay Barnard, *South Africa a Century Ago: Letters written from the Cape of Good Hope (1797-1801)*, ed. with a memoir by W. H. Wilkins (London: Smith, Elder, & Co., 1901); *The Letters of Lady Anne Barnard to Henry Dundas, from the Cape and Elsewhere, 1793-1803, together with her Journal of a Tour into the Interior, and Certain Other Letters* (Cape Town: A. A. Balkema, 1973); *The Cape Journals of Lady Anne Barnard, 1797-1798*, ed. A. M. Lewin Robinson, Margaret Lenta and Dorothy Driver (Cape Town: Van Riebeeck Society, 1994) (Van Riebeeck Society Series, 2nd ser., no. 24)

Alexander Crawford Lindsay, Earl of Crawford, *Lives of the Lindsays, or, A Memoir of the Houses of Crawford and Balcarres*, 3 vols (London: J. Murray, Printed by W. Clowes and Sons, 1849)

Further Reading:
Jose Burman, *In the Footsteps of Lady Anne Barnard* (Cape Town: Human & Rousseau, 1990)
Dorothea Fairbridge, *Lady Anne Barnard at the Cape of Good Hope, 1797-1802* (Oxford: Clarendon Press, 1924)
Madeleine Masson, *Lady Anne Barnard: The Court and Colonial Service under George III and the Regency* (London: Allen & Unwin: 1948)
Gwen M. Mills, *First Ladies of the Cape* (Cape Town: Maskew Miller, 1950)

Anderson; *DNB*; Elwood; Lonsdale; *HSWW*; Todd 1 & 2

From *Lives of the Lindsays* vols II & III:
There had long existed a prophecy that the first child of the last descendant of the House of Balcarres was to restore the family of Stuart to those hereditary rights which the bigotry of James had deprived them of. The Jacobites seemed to have gained new life on the occasion; the wizards and witches of the party had found it in their books; the Devil had mentioned it to one or two of his particular friends; old ladies had read it from the grounds of their coffee, – no wonder if the event was welcomed by the grasp of expiring hope. Songs were made by exulting Tories, masses were offered up by good Catholics, who longed to see the Pope's Bull once more tossing his horns in the country, – every one was glad to hear what the Countess longed for; if devout, she would produce a pious man, – if she set her heart eagerly on anything, it was a sign the young Earl would be ardent and successful in his pursuits, – if she wore white much, it was the child's attachment to the white rose; but the Countess was a woman who longed for nothing, and thereby afforded no key

to unlock the secrets of futurity. She went on prosperously, however, and in due course of time the partisans of the Pretender, the soothsayers, wizards, witches, the bards, fortune-tellers, and old ladies, were all in a group, amazed, disconcerted, and enraged, to learn that Lady Balcarres was brought to bed of a daughter after all, absolutely but a daughter, – while Lord Balcarres, though he too privately would have been flattered with a boy, received the present she had made him with transport, thanked his young wife as if she had conferred a boon on him he had no right to expect from her, and both parents united in that partiality to their eldest child which they ever afterwards so kindly continued to it. That child was the Anne Lindsay who now addresses you, and in the arms of my nurse I promised to be a little heiress, perhaps a heroine worthy of having my name posted on the front of a novel. But twelve succeeding years robbed me of my prospects by enriching me with ten friends whom I would not now exchange for that crown which it was foretold I was to have placed on the brows of the Pretender.[2]

[…]

To my mother Lord Balcarres gave up the entire management of the family and the children; he knew her prudence, and rarely interfered in her jurisdiction, except when he found little misdemeanours punished as crimes, and then I have heard him say, 'Odsfish, Madam! you will break the spirits of my young troops, – I will not have it so!' – But while the tearing of clothes or fracturing of tea-cups might be too rigorously chastised, or while needless privations might be imposed on us to fit us 'for the hardships of life', let us not forget that from Lady Balcarres' conversation and practice we learnt those general rules of equity and honour, of independence of mind and truth, which have through life, I am convinced, governed the mind of many a brother.

Had she but accompanied this sometimes with a little of a mother's fondness, what a foundation of tenderness as well as veneration would have been laid in our hearts! But unfortunately for the contents of our nursery, it was not the system of that century (1700) to treat children with gentleness; everything was done by authority and by correction.

[…]

As we conceived that the tasks of languages, geography, arithmetic, under which we laboured, were harder than those laid on the children of Israel which produced a revolt, Margaret, who had a taste for public speaking, taking the lead, assembled us one day in our favourite temple,[3] and mounting the sacred fane, proposed an insurrection.

She complained of hard laws and little play, and assured us, if we would be ruled by her, that she would carry us to a family where she had once spent a week after the whooping-cough very agreeably indeed. She was certain they would receive us kindly, and, as they had no children of their own, they would make us welcome to live with them, which would be much better than the 'horrious' life we lived at home.

This being the only word in the course of Margaret's life that she was ever known to slip-slop, I am glad to transmit it against her to posterity.

The proposal was agreed to with acclamations of joy, and we instantly set out on the journey, intending by forced marches to reach the neighbour's house that night, as it was but three miles distant and by the side of the sea; but as we could not think of leaving little James behind, who had not yet got into breeches, it considerably retarded us, as we had to carry him by turns. Our flight was discovered by Auld Robin Gray, the shepherd – 'All the young gentlemen and the young ladies, and all the dogs are run away, my lady!' – a messenger being despatched, not to negotiate but to bring us back *nolens volens*, the six criminals were carried before the Countess, who declared that on this occasion whipping was too good for us, and that we should each have a dose of tincture of rhubarb to teach us to stay at home – a punishment classically just in its last degrees, as the eldest, consequently the most guilty, had the last and most offensive glass of the bottle.

Lady Anne goes on to describe the pleasures (often in the open air) as well as the pains of childhood. She remarks that Robert, often chastised or shut up in a closet, shows now that 'thoroughly good minds pardon severity arising from right meanings' and so it is with him and his wife and children at Balcarres that 'our dear old mother […] derives the solaces of her extreme old age, eighty-five'.
My mother said that we saw more company than anybody, and we were convinced of it. The parson – an excellent bust of Homer, and his wife of Seneca – with their daughter, came frequently to see us, – a few neighbours did so too, but seldom; they were honest country gentlemen, living on the produce of grounds they cultivated themselves, but we were told they were as genteel as people ought to be. However, the society at home was so numerous that we did not much feel the want of any other.

This consisted of my father, my mother, my grandmother, Lady Dalrymple – a placid, quiet, pleasing old woman, whose indolence had benevolence in it, and whose sense was replete with indolence, as she was at all times of the party for letting things alone, – of Miss Sophy Johnstone [sometimes 'Johnston'], an original whom I shall mention by and by, – of the Miss Keiths, three maiden cousins of my mother, – of Mrs Cockburn, an intimate friend of Lady Balcarres, who had goodness, genius, Utopianism, and a decided passion for making of matches, for which reason she was the confidante of all lovesick hearts, – of the eleven children, who made no inconsiderable addition to the society, – of my brother's tutor; who occupied a chair,[4] – and of a young woman, or rather a young lady, to whom I dare hardly, even at this moment, give the title governess.[5]
[…]

Miss Sophy Johnstone was, as I have before mentioned, an original in her way not less extraordinary.[6] Her father was what is commonly called 'an odd dog'; her mother that unencroaching sort of existence, so universally termed 'a good sort of woman'. One day after dinner, the squire, having a mind to reason over his bottle, turned the conversation on the 'folly of education'. The wife said, she had always understood it was a good thing for young people to know a little, to keep them out of harm's way. The husband said, education was all nonsense, for that a child who was left to Nature had ten times more sense, and all that sort of thing, when it grew up, than those whose heads were filled full of gimcracks and learning out of books.

Like Mrs Shandy, she gave up the point,[7] and, as he stoutly maintained his argument, they both agreed to make the experiment on the child she was ready to produce, and mutually swore an oath that it never should be taught anything from the hour of its birth, or ever have its spirit broken by contradiction.

This child proved to be Miss Sophy Johnstone, – the dispute and covenant were known in the country, and the neighbours, in jest, calling her 'Hilton's Natural Daughter', in a few years she passed *bona fide* for his illegitimate child.

I scarce think that any system of education could have made this woman one of the fair sex. Nature seemed to have entered into the jest, and hesitated to the last whether to make her a boy or a girl. Her taste led her to hunt with her brothers, to wrestle with the stable-boys, and to saw wood with the carpenter. She worked well in iron, could shoe a horse quicker than the smith, made excellent trunks, played well on the fiddle, sung a man's song in a bass voice, and was by many people suspected of being one. She learnt to write of the butler at her own request, and had a taste for reading which she greatly improved. She was a droll ingenious fellow; her talents for mimicry made her enemies, and the violence of her attachments to those she called her favourites secured her a few warm friends. She came to spend a few months with my mother soon after her marriage, and at the time I am speaking of, had been with her thirteen years, making Balcarres her head-quarters, devoting herself to the youngest child, whichever it was, deserting him when he got into breeches, and regularly constant to no one but me. She had a little forge fitted up in her closet, to which I was very often invited.[8]

One anecdote of Sophy Johnstone is most poignant:
My own good friend Miss Sophy Johnstone, having constantly declared that her attachment to us was such that she would never leave our family, although she was tormented beyond measure to share her time with others, and that she daily expected a letter fron her first cousin, old General Cranville, who had been appointed governor of Gibraltar, inviting her to go there with his wife who was a dull formal woman of whom he was tired, and whom she had never seen, we had constantly been expecting the arrival of this letter; but as it never came Margaret observed that it was a sad pity that Miss Johnstone could not have this letter and the pleasure of sacrificing this invitation to her love of us. The idea lighted the gas of my brains, and the letter was written in a moment with a good pen on a fine sheet of paper, and I returned myself member of parliament on the occasion. A formal unexceptionable invitation was sent to Miss Johnstone by Mrs Cranville to accompany her and the general to Gibraltar, – with an assurance that a little forge should be fitted up for her in the garrison.

We supposed she would send her refusal in a day or two, and meant to take measures to prevent her letter from being sent, as the village was close at hand. We proposed to thank her afterwards, and tell her the truth.

The post arrived, and the letter was carried up to her room. We dined together, – not a word was said, but there seemed to be many cheerful hints passing to and fro amongst the seniors of the family. Margaret and I were leaving the room when the cloth was withdrawn, but Miss Johnstone in an encouraging tone bid us to stay. She said that we had sense and discretion above our years, and that she was not ashamed to call us into the council which she had been holding with her friends here on a letter that she had received from her good friend Mrs Cranville, – putting my own letter into my hand. I trembled from head to foot. 'Well!' said I, when I had read it, 'and you will answer this by saying that you will never leave us?' 'My dear child,' said she, 'I should wish to give that answer; but, to tell you the truth, I ought not. Though I am old, I am now almost fifty, they are older, and very rich – I am poor,' – (poor! Oh, what a poignard was in that word!); – 'I am sensible of the advantages it might be of to me to be with them, and, however, painful to me, I am not only resolved to accept of their invitation, but I have already sent off my letter doing so.'

Confounded by this, and afraid to speak, I laid down the letter, and Margaret and I disappeared, letting it be supposed that we were very sorry to lose her, but really in despair at what we had done. Nothing remained for it but instant confession. She had gone to her own room to settle the particulars of her wardrobe, given all her clothes to be mended, cut out the shape of her travelling trunk, ordered herself a new wig, which she had never before confessed to wearing, – this fact, together with her poverty, we had wrung from this poor woman by our jest!

We threw ourselves on our knees before her, and told her all. Never did I see anybody more cruelly disappointed, but her manly strong mind took it as a hero would the loss of his army. The lecture she read to us, and the internal groan I heard suppressed, were never afterwards erased from my memory. She did not lose in the end, for every attention was doubled, and Margaret and I at a small price purchased the invaluable experience of 'never playing a trick to anybody'.

Of Alison/Alicia Cockburn, who was a good friend of her mother's, Lady Anne writes:
Lady Balcarres looked upon her as a second mother; she was ten years her senior, but her mind was so gay, enthusiastic, and ardent, her visions were for ever decked with such powers of fancy, and such infinite goodness of heart, her manners to young people were so conciliatory, and her tenets so mild, though plentifully Utopian, that she was an invaluable friend between the mother and the daughters.

And of her grandmother:
I now remember, with a smile, the different evolutions that grandmamma's daily fidgets had to perform, though at the time, they plagued me a little. Good woman! she had a right to exercise her own troops as she pleased, but no major of cavalry had a greater variety of manoeuvres to go through than she had every day, – and why? If she chanced to do something on Monday that was new to her, she thought it right to do it on Tuesday, and all the future days of her life.

At ten she came down stairs, always a little out of humour till she had her breakfast. In her left hand were her mitts and her snuff-box, which contained a certain number of pinches; she stopped on the seventeenth spot of the carpet, and coughed three times; she then looked at the weather-glass, approached the tea-table, put her right hand in her pocket for the key of the tea-chest, and, not finding it there, sent me up stairs to look for it in her own room, charging me not to fall on the stairs.

'Look,' said she, 'Annie! upon my little table, – there you will find a pair of gloves, but the key is not there; after you have taken up the gloves, you will see yesterday's newspaper, but you will not find it below that, so you need not touch it; pass on from the newspaper to my black fan – beside it there lie three apples – (don't eat my apples, Annie! mark that!) – take up the letter that is beyond the apples, and there you will find – 'But is not that the key in your left hand over your little finger?' – 'no, Annie, it cannot be so, for I always carry it on my right.' – 'That is, you intend to do so, my dear grandmamma, but you know you always carry it in your left.' – 'Well, well, child! I believe I do, but what then? is the tea made? put in one spoonful for every person, and one over – Annie, do you mark me?'

Thus, every morning, grandmamma smelt three times at her apple, came down stairs testy, coughed on the seventeenth spot, lost her key, had it detected in her left hand, and, the morning's parade being over, till the evening's nap arrived, (when she had a new set of manoeuvres) she was a pleasing, entertaining, talkative, mild old woman. I should love her, for she loved me; I was her god-daughter, and her sworn friend.

In a letter to Sir Walter Scott, 8 July 1823, Lady Anne admits authorship and explains the origin of 'Auld Robin Gray' – she says that she is
[…] transmitting to him, fairly and frankly, the Origin, Birth, Life, Death and Confession, Will and Testament, of 'Auld Robin Gray' with the assurance that the author of *Waverley* is the first person out of my own family who has ever had an explanation from me on the subject.

Robin Gray, so called from it being the name of the old herdsman at Balcarres, was *born* soon after the close of the year 1771. My sister Margaret had married and accompanied her husband to London; I was melancholy, and endeavoured to amuse myself by attempting a few poetical trifles. There was an ancient Scotch melody of which I was passionately fond, – Sophy Johnstone, who lived before your day, used to sing it to us at Balcarres: she did not object to its having improper words, though I did. I longed to sing old Sophy's air to different words, and to give to its plaintive tones some little history of virtuous distress in humble life, such as might suit it. While attempting to effect this in my closet, I called to my little sister, now Lady Hardwicke, who was the only person near me, – 'I have been writing a ballad, my dear, – I am oppressing my heroine with many misfortunes, – I have already sent her Jamie to sea, and broken her father's arm, and given her Auld Robin Gray for a lover, but I wish to load her with a fifth sorrow in the four lines, poor thing! help me to one, I pray.' 'Steal the cow, sister Anne,' said the little Elizabeth. The cow was immediately *lifted* by me, and the song completed.[9] At our fireside, amongst our neighbours, 'Auld Robin Gray' was always called for; I was pleased with the approbation it met with, but such was my dread of being suspected of writing anything, perceiving the shyness it created in those who could write nothing, that I carefully kept my own secret.

The following selections are from Volume 3 of the 'Lives of the Lindsays' which consists of Lady Anne Barnard's 'Extracts from the Journal of a Residence at the Cape of Good Hope, and of a Short Tour into the Interior':
We sailed into Table Bay at the hour of noon on Thursday the 4th of May, 1797. – And now, mine own good souls, *myne lieve moye goede vrowen*, let us *causer* of Caffres [Kaffirs], Hottentots,[10] men, women, unicorns, mountains, cameleopards, ostriches, flowers both wild and tame, bays both False and true – permitting me sometimes to regret, as always I must do, the bad use I have made of my earlier years, which, had they been improved as much as you two have improved your later ones, would have made my journal here more worthy of your reading.

The taking of the oath of allegiance to George III is the occasion for the farmers and settlers from the interior to arrive in the Cape:

The people of the Cape having had it notified to them that during a certain portion of time (which was an ample one) they might come from all quarters and take the oath of allegiance to King George III, the gates of the castle were thrown open every morning, and I was surprised at the number I saw of well-fed, rosy-cheeked men, well-powdered, and dressed in black, walking in pairs and with their hats off – a regulation on entering the castle on public occasions which in former days Dutch pride imposed. They were succeeded by the *boors* from the country – farmers and settlers, – who arrived from a great or greater distance; I thought that many of them seemed but ill affected to the errand they came on, – they shook hands with each other, but they shook their heads too in a manner that said, 'There is no help for it! We must swear, for they are the strongest.'

The size of these sulky youths, all dressed in blue cloth jackets and trousers, and very large flat hats, was enormous; most of them were six feet high and upwards and stout in proportion, – I was told that at five or six hundred miles' distance they often reach seven feet. All came in their waggons, bringing a load of something to market at the same time. The Hottentot servant who crept behind each, carrying his master's umbrella, seemed to owe but little to Nature for beauty, constitution, or worldly gear; a piece of leather round their waist, and a sheep's skin round their shoulders, was all their dress, – sometimes a scarlet handkerchief was tied round the head, sometimes an old hat was ornamented with ostrich feathers, but the head was generally bare, and studded only with black curls of the size of peas, through which no comb can pass. I cannot say that I think the Hottentots so uncommonly ugly or disgusting as they are reported to be; their features are small and not ill-shaped, the expression of their eyes is sweet and inoffensive, their cheek-bones are certainly immense, and one misses the cheek altogether; but they are not uglier than the slaves from Mozambique, who have uncouth features but fine persons. I must try to catch a face of every different caste or nation here; the collection cannot be short of twenty.

A ball is given to mark the arrival of the Governor, Lord Macartney:[11]

When we entered the ball-room we found it lined with two rows of ladies, all tolerably well dressed, and all 'mad in white muslin'.[12] I had expected to find them handsomer; but here was no real beauty to be seen, no countenance, no manner, no graces, no charms, though plenty of good looks and the freshness of health, with a vulgar smartness accompanying it, which spoke the torch of Prometheus which animated them to be made of mutton-tail. They danced without halting a moment, and in a sort of pit-a-pat tingling little step, which they have probably learnt from some beauty on her way to Bengal. Upon the whole, they were much such women as may be found at an assize ball a great way from the capital, – and, saying so, I do not think I disparage their appearance.

What they want most is shoulders and softness of manners, – the term, 'a Dutch doll', was quite explained to me when I saw their make and recollected the dolls; but what is more exceptionable about them is their teeth and the size of their feet. A tradesman in London, hearing they were very large, sent a box of shoes on speculation which almost put the colony in a blaze, so angry were the fair ones –

but day by day a pair were sent for by a slave in the dark, till at last the shoes vanished.

The Barnards acquire a small country house from the conversion of an old farmhouse at a 'pretty little place called Paradise at the back of the Table Mountain, half-way up the hill'. Since it could at first be reached only on foot, the road to the house was improved to enable easy access:

We walked to the house [...] between rows of aromatic bushes which scented the air with an odour potent and pleasant in the extreme.

I was enchanted by the flowers and stopped to pluck up their roots. Barnard laughed at my ardour, saying, 'Stop, stop, you will find plenty of time for this by and by.'

At last we reached a small house where wood is kept for the use of Government, and, shadowed by the silver-trees which clothed the brow of the hill, turned round to admire the wide plain before us, bounded by the Hottentot hills and by a range of numberless mountains rising behind each other, the sea appearing to the right, and after it made the circle of the continent, rolling into the little Bay of Memenburg before it proceeded on to the larger one of Simmons Town.

The world indeed seemed all before us,[13] and mental vision might have painted the distant country fertile, but here there was not a trace of anything but sand and rock, – on turning round, tired of the cheerless prospect, a sequestered low road appeared, over which oaks met in cordial embrace. We pursued the path, which suddenly turning, presented to us an old farm-house, charming in no point of architecture, but charming from the mountain which raised itself three thousand feet perpendicular above its head, with such a variety of spiral and Gothic forms, wooded and picturesque, as to be a complete contrast to the hill we had ascended or the plain over which we had gazed.

Before the house, which was raised a few steps from the court, there was a row of orange-trees loaded with fruit both ripe and green, which shadowed the windows. A garden, well stocked with fruit-trees of every description, was behind the house, through which a hasty stream of water descended from the mountain, and to the left there was a grove of fir-trees, whose long stems, agitated by the slightest breeze of wind, knocked their heads together like angry bullocks in a most ludicrous manner.

The refurbishment of the house and road gave rise to some resentment among the military personnel of the Cape and thence birth to a poem entitled 'Paradise Gained', – 'had it been good I suppose I should have had it from someone, but it was only ill-natured'.

I had long been desirous of ascending to the top of the Table Mountain, and, the expedition being determined on, Barnard, to render the plan still more interesting to me, procured a dozen of slaves to carry up a tent, mattress, blankets, a little table, and camp-stool, together with provisions, that we might sleep on the top of the mountain, and see the sun rise and set, when I could have the opportunity of making what drawings I pleased. It was an expensive party of pleasure, as it cost us five rix-dollars (a Guinea) for each slave, but the occasion was an uncommon one, and in all countries particular jobs must be paid well to be cheerfully performed.

We left the castle at six in the morning on horseback, attended by as many of our servants as chose to be of the party, and by Colonel Lloyd, Mr Barrow, Dr Patterson, and other gentlemen, together with a couple of female slaves.[14] We ascended for the first mile by a winding path through rocks, each side of which was clothed with the waggonbomb,[15] with its bright yellow flowers, the silver-tree,[16] whose leaves have the appearance of white satin, and the sugar-tree, which was covered with beautiful pink flowers with black seeds, – when the flowers are boiled they produce a syrup as rich as honey, and with this all the preserves in the colony are made. The ascent then became so tremendously steep that we were obliged to dismount and send our horses back to the castle, scrambling up amongst rocks where cascades tumbled down and lost themselves in gullies beneath. The air was perfumed with the most delicious fragrance of numberless bushes, which composed a concord of aromatic harmony perfectly wild, and such as no one can imagine to themselves.

Here Barnard was obliged to consign me to the particular care of Mentor, a most intellectual slave, who knew the safest paths to ascend by; I might have reckoned myself his Telemachus if dress had decided the sex, as I had stolen a part of Barnard's wardrobe for precaution, which I found was eminently useful, but which made him, as I bounded up the rocks, laugh and call out, 'Hey-day Anne, what are these?' – 'Yours! *myne lieve vriende*, my dear friend!' said I – 'you must acknowledge it is the first time you were ever conscious of my wearing them.' Mentor, our guide, smiled, as he saw us smiling, and called me a *braave vrow*, a rare wife – so in gratitude you shall have his picture, which I drew when I got home. After crawling up an immense sheet of small stones, almost perpendicular – stones broken into pieces by the force of the torrents which the clouds discharge in volumes during the rainy seasons, we proceeded up though the gully which nearly cuts the mountain in two, and began to rise above the world. The weather was mild and charming; the sun, now fully risen, warmed us with his fervent rays, which the mountain threw back on us with intolerable heat. I was surprised here to find so many pieces of leather as I did; it appeared as if the mountain had quickly made old shoes of new ones; but I suppose other scramblers had done as I did, – I took with me several pairs of the oldest I could muster, which are far pleasanter to climb in than new ones.

While Barrow darted at plants and fossils in hopes of finding something to report favourably of to the Governor, I got out my pencil to draw the rocks and jackalls, but Mentor pressed us to go on, which we did, making a turn in the ascent which at once brought us into the shade, and lowered the thermometer fifteen degrees. We all felt the sudden chill, and hurried to get out of this atmosphere, when, coming to a milder spot, I proposed a glass of port-wine to each, to counteract its bad effects and fortify us before we proceeded. We found here a cave, where slaves who have run away for crimes hide themselves, and where wood-cutters halt as they return with their burthens; the traces of bones and cooking were seen but our party was too numerous to have anything to fear. At last a thousand feet more of rock were surmounted, – I left all the gentlemen behind, envying the 'braave vrow' for the lightness of her heels, the effect perhaps of the lightness of her heart, and reached the top as tired as it was possible to be, but perfectly refreshed before they joined me.

What a wide extended barrenness presented itself all round! Oceans, points of coast, and hills were the only objects the eye had to dwell on. The Lion's Head (a high mountain) appeared a mole-hill beneath – to find oneself three thousand five hundred feet above the level from which we had set out – to behold a considerable town more invisible than the smallest miniature which could be painted of one – to feel the pure air raising one up – it gave me a sort of unembodied feeling such as I conceive the soul to have which mounts, a beatified spirit, leaving its atom of clay behind. The view, the sensation, was full of ether – and I hope of something better. The plan of rendering the grey expanse 'parlant' by my pencil was fixing my eyes to the scene.

'Well!' cried the honest Welshman, Colonel Lloyd, rubbing his hands, 'I don't know how it is with you – but I am very hungry – you said something about cold beef, did you not?'

I confessed I had, but as it was too soon an hour yet to make a regular dinner, I would give him just enough to keep body and soul together in the interim.

When dinner comes it is copious:

While Pawell, Mr Barnard's Brabanter servant, and the slaves pitched our tent on the top of the mountain on a bit of dry ground, I pitched the little camp-table Barnard had procured for me, and with my sketch-book and colours traced the effects of the setting sun before he dropped into the ocean, which encompassed in a zone the peninsula where we were placed. This done, Pawell surprised us very agreeably with a pan in which Revel had cooked forty snipes the day before, ready for warming up, as he knew my ladyship loved a bit of hot supper. Delighted with the snipes, which we put to flight in a manner which the pure air of the atmosphere I hope will apologise for – N.B. I believe we ate a dozen apiece at least – we begged our slaves might have our nice rump of beef, fowls, and ham; but not one of them would *scoff* or eat, – they shook their heads with a look of horror – 'nae, nae,' – and I found that, owing to the ham having been put up in the same basket with the other articles, everything was contaminated to them. But they too had their pan, and their stew, which smelt so savoury and so odd, that I begged leave to taste it. It was composed of wild herbs fried up with coriander and many aromatic seeds, to which was added a little mutton-tail grease, which is more pure than butter, and plenty of the fish called *snook*, which I thought, when salted and dried, was one of the best fish at the Cape. This made a most incomparable mess, though one I never desired to partake of again from its unaccountable singularity.

Supper over, and no fear of wild beasts existing so near the town, the slaves lay down round the fire, and Barnard and I within the tent found a good bed, on which two hearts reposed themselves which were truly grateful for all the blessings conferred on them, but most so for their happiness in each other.

On a visit to the Landrost (viceroy) in Stellenbosch, Lady Anne goes to church, an experience which tends to bring out her anti-Boer bitchiness and her insecurity about being childless:

How very fat we found the people! many of them showing evident tendencies to dropsy, all of the women passing thirty years of age weighing from fourteen to sixteen stone, and so prolific withal, that the Sunday before twelve children had been baptized there, belonging to five mothers only. On asking from whence those useful mothers came, the reply was, 'From over Berg Yarrow', from over the hills, whence everything good, greasy, and in quantity comes, I find.

Since I came to the Cape I have discovered that it is a bit of a reflection to be without a family here. One of the civilised of the Dutchmen, on hearing me say we had no children, exclaimed, 'Oh miserauble, miserauble!' in such a doleful tone, that I believe I must give myself credit for half a dozen boys left at school for the future.

In April the Barnards move to Paradise:

I amuse myself here rather as necessity obliges me than as taste directs, as I have, owing to the illness of my cook and the loss of my maid, who is obliged to go to England from bad health, to attend to many household matters when I would rather be employing my pen or pencil.

At six I rise, and, after I have made breakfast for my *mann*, I reserve a good one for a half-starved pussy that was found in the shrubbery with five poor kittens reared out of her own misery half way on to cat's estate. Next comes the breakfast of a hundred and fifty very very young chickens, at which I act as groom of the chambers, standing by while they eat it, as I have too much reason to think a hundred have been starved to death by the tyranny of force over feebleness, the turkeys, ducks, etc., having made it their practice to frighten the chickens from their breakfast, and of course, though the little ones came well out of their shells, and lived for a few days while attended to, all vanished; and it broke my heart to think what a number of wretched creatures I had called into life, to have a poor specimen of it, and to die before they had had their little bellies full.

One of our dogs expects to be confined directly – a serious beast, who I had no idea was given to such follies; but she is mild and affectionate, so I have made up a bed for her and her heirs of entail at the top of the staircase in a hole in the roof.

Our two black cooks from town are come to assist me in the absence of Revel to dress dinner, as a dozen of people are to dine here, whom my husband has invited, finding them anxious to see this little place. I cannot convince the cooks that so great a lady as 'my vrow' understands anything of the kitchen, though I give my directions with Mr Fairley, head *cuisinier* to the London Tavern, in my hand, and have lately succeeded so well in a vegetable soup, that I can make no greater present to the persons reading this (if they reside in the country) than by giving them the following

Receipt for a meagre vegetable soup

Take one large head of celery – shred it down, stopping before you reach the green part, which is bitter – take one onion, a handful of spinach, three heads of cabbage, each about the size of your two hands, half a dozen leaves of sorrel, twenty carrots twice as long as your finger, two or three handfuls of green peas, and after you have shelled them, if the peas are young (but not otherwise), you may cut the shells in pieces and throw them in with the rest – all these must be cut into bits about the size of your little finger, and the carrots smaller than sixpences – put all in a large wash-hand basin, which will be sufficient to make a small tureen-full.

Meantime take a quarter of a pound of butter, put it into a frying-pan, and, when melted, dust in a handful of flour, stir it well about in the pan, till it is of the colour of brown tanned leather – then put your vegetables and that into a saucepan, with as much gravy or weak broth as will cover them all over, and stand two inches above them – let it stew gently for two or three hours till all is quite tender – put a large teaspoonful of salt to it, and another of pepper – then, having given it five minutes more, serve it up hot in your tureen. – If the liquid is taken from it, it will be equally good as stewed vegetables.

Our friends arrived, and did it ample justice.

In May 1798 the Barnards make a tour into the interior. Lady Anne points out that May in the Cape is the equivalent of November and the commencement of the rainy season but that they did not wish to pass up their opportunity for fear of not having another. They visit the Fathers, or Herrn-hütters, Moravian missionaries sent to convert the Hottentots, who live at the foot of the Baviaan and Boscheman's Kloof. The three Fathers work at their original professions – miller, smith, carpenter and tailor in one. The Barnards go to Church:

I regretted much that it was Thursday and not Sunday, when I should have found the whole community, about three hundred Hottentots, assembled to divine worship; but I found I should have only seen them more dressed, and such as had acquired any clothes by their industry would have worn them, – I should also have seen a greater number; but that I should still see plenty, as at sunsetting every day, when business was supposed to be over, there were prayers. We retired to our parlour, and, the church-bell now ringing to bring them all together, when the church was full and all was ready, we begged leave to make part of the congregation.

I doubt much whether I should have entered St Peter's at Rome, with the triple crown itself present in all its ancient splendour, with a more awed impression of the deity and his presence that I did this little church, of a few feet square, where the simple disciples of Christianity, dressed in the skins of animals, knew no purple or fine linen, no pride, no hypocrisy. I felt as if I was creeping back seventeen hundred years, to hear from the rude but inspired lips of evangelists the simple sacred words of wisdom and purity.

The service began after the Presbyterian form with a psalm. Then indeed the note that raised itself to heaven was an affecting one; about one hundred and fifty Hottentots joined in the twenty-third psalm in a tone so sweet, so loud, but so just and true that it was impossible to hear it without being surprised. The Fathers, who were the sole music-masters, sang their deep-toned bass along with them, and the harmony was excellent. One fault only I found, – the key on which they took the psalm was too high, by which means the shrill pipes of the women rang upon the ear too sharply, and made one apprehensive of their own voices being injured by it. This over, the miller took a portion of the Scripture, and expounded as he went along, – how I wished to have understood him! but by the chapter he spoke from (Matthew, viii, 11), and a word now and then, I knew the subject he dwelt on, – that the Dutchman who was great and rich, with abundance of slaves and cattle, was not more sure of a place in a better world than the Hottentot who was good, and who would find a seat in heaven kept for him to eternal happiness.

Mild and tender by nature, oppressed by the Dutch and often sinking under it, the poor creatures blessed God as they listened, while the artless tears of gratitude and hope fell down on their sheepskins. The Father's discourse was short, and seemed to be whatever came first without study, the tone of his voice had no puritanism in it, it was even and natural; but when he used as he often did, *Myne lieve vriends*, 'my beloved friends', I thought he felt to them all as his children. Not a Hottentot did I see in this congregation that had a bad passion in the countenance; I watched them closely – all was sweetness and attention.

The Fathers explain that they are in some danger from the farmers because they encourage self respect and self sufficiency among the Hottentots and the farmers as a result lose a source of cheap labour.

The Barnards are shortly afterwards made particularly welcome at the house of Jacob van Rhenin. Lady Anne recounts an embarrassing experience there which sheds light on the relationship of some of the less oppressive Boer farmers with their slaves:
Dunira, a pretty back slave, wife to Adonis [the gamekeeper], came into my room, and in a bashful way pointed to one of the white bead necklaces which lay on the table, and then to her own neck, seeming to beg for a row. This threw me into a sad quandary – to give a slave a necklace the same that I had given to the young ladies of the family! it would have been nearly as much as my life was worth in some houses, and to have displeased my hospitable landlord and landlady after all their civility to me – No, no! – I therefore shook my head, and made Dunira suppose I had no more – 'All done!' – but promised she should have something better. She left me, mortified. I thought that if I could manage the matter, that it was worth the trying, so I bade Mr Barnard tell the story to Van Rhenin before his wife, and at the same time mention my objections to her request, that I had given of them to the young ladies.

They both laughed, and cried aloud, 'Not to think anything of that, – that she had been born in the house, and was a sort of child of the family, and that, if I had the beads, to give her them,' – which I did, making her happier than a young beauty would be with a diamond necklace.

At the end of the tour Lady Anne's reflections are characteristically more sympathetic to the Hottentots than to the Dutch, although, of course, she is still patronising in her feeling for the Hottentots and slaves:
Our tour finished and all well, the 1st of June, Mr Barnard thanked our kind Governor for the pleasure he had afforded us, and we were all glad to have made the journey. Though small the portion of ground we had gone over, it showed me at least the face of seven hundred miles of Africa, and enabled me to judge a little of the peasantry, whom upon the whole we found hospitable and good-humoured, at least to travellers, but without industry or emulation, or capacity, attached to habits and careless of improvement – in their persons and houses slovenly and dirty, a few excepted; but, while improved minds are happy from religious contentment, from philosophy, or from a combination of blessings, these good folks seem to me to be equally so from their want of care, thought, or feeling, from a good deal of self-conceit, and from the charms of power, experienced by every master, mistress, and child, of every house.

The slaves and Hottentots, on the other hand, seem happy too upon the whole, from knowing no other state than that which they are in, – the idea of drawing a comparison between themselves and their masters is one belonging to the first step of civilisation, and they have not reached to it, as far as I could judge. Their pleasures consist in eating what is given them, and in sleeping whenever they can; and all their pains are bounded by the lash of the whip, which is occasionally applied if they are disobedient, or what the master may call insolent. Could we weigh happiness in a scale, I do not believe, on the average, they are less happy than ourselves, though they have much less reason to be so, and meet death with an apathy which one would be apt to imagine proceeded from the dislike to life, were it not that it certainly arises from the want of strong or precise feeling about anything.

Lady Anne concludes this part of her journal with a statement of her unabated love for her sisters.

Letters from Sophy Johnston to Lady Anne Lindsay Barnard:
The letters are from the Crawford Family Papers deposited in the National Library of Scotland:

(Crawford Family Papers 27/2/118)
Dun (?) June 3 [n.d.]
My dearest Pupil's most wellcome epistle comes in a good hour for I was almost persuaded, she was to cherish the heart of her poor old mistress no more, indeed my Dear Lassie I was afraid London and its Environs, had buried in oblivion, all that was left behind, which is often the case with those that are much older than you, but I rejoice to find you are still the same which I think is giving you a higher character than writing a volume in your praise. I am exceedingly oblig'd to you for taking the trouble to tell me what you are about, I hope everything you hear, and see, will continue to give you pleasure, but I wonder you did not mention the masquerades of all the entertainments in, and about London, that is the one wou'd take my fancy most, a kiss of Geordys fatt cheek not excepted;[17] I suppose you have not seen Pugg, as you say nothing about her, by the description you give me of your dress, I think it has been genteel and elegant, and make no doubt but you was pretty bonny, and full of dignity, – O my Dear Lady come dance to my Jigg – seriously my beloved Pupil your kind attention, in writing to me, gives me very great satisfaction; I wrote to one of your friends in the Neighbourhood of Edn. that I had the pleasure of a letter from you, some encomiums I made upon that subject which is needless to repeat but I thought pretty proper, – had your mother been dead, I shoud have seen it in the Newspapers, so I hope she is still in this Valley of Tears, tho' she seems to have got a comfortable draught of the Water of Lethe, and a most desirable potation it is, no help for those things my Burdie. I wish I had anything entertaining to tell you, but from hence you can expect nothing, we live an innocent, Rural Uniform Life, go a Fishing, eat and drink, etc.: if I did not know you despise all pityful pecuniary considerations, I wou'd delay'd writing to you till I coud procure a Frank but I really was impatient to tell you how much I think myself obligd to you for your very kind

remembrance – Moll Baird desir's to return an affectionate Tendre and says she honours you for your attachment to old friends –

Now my Dear Lady I dare say you are more than tir'd of this uninteresting discourse which is not worth reading far less postage, so with wishing the accomplishment of all your desires, believe me to be most affectionately yours ever.
                    S. J.
I wish this may be properly directed as you sent me none.

(27/2/119)
Edn. May 7 1785
Well My ever Dear and best beloved Pupil how are you this long time? Your mother says 'pretty fat' and I'm truly glad to hear it, but what giv's me still greater pleasure is, that you have not forgot your poor old mistress – I'm told you have sent me a propine [gift] for my Palace, and tho' I have not seen it yet, I return you ten thousand thanks my own Dauty, the De'el care what it be; your remembrance is the Tongue of the Trump to me Lassie, so I say again monie thanks t'ye –

O my Lamb what think ye o' Cousine B's kindness? and sick a present as Lady M has sent me? truly I think the world's beginning to cast a smile upon me. I'm pretty light-hearted at present. E' what'll a dae? I hope you will provide yourself with a large assortment of Musick before you come down as I have nothing worth telling you. Shall conclude with wishing you God's blessing.

My Dear Bairn
                    Soph Johnston

(Crawford Family Papers 27/2/120)
On the back of this letter Lady Anne has written: 'This letter from my constant Friend Old Sophy Johnston named in the memoirs of Louisa Price Western was written on my marriage with Mr Barnard in 1793 – she was about 80.' Sophy Johnston's hand-writing is very shaky.
[1793]
To be so kindly and affectionately recognised by my Dearest and Best beloved Pupil gave me more pleasure than I thought myself now capable of feeling and what you tell me of your situation and prospect through Life is most excellent, the description of your Master charming in every respect, may God almighty continue to bless you to the last moment of your life – you desire some account of my self, alas my Dear Pupil I can give but a very dismal one, having outliv'd my facultys, if ever I had any (which indeed I'm very doubtfull of) and a constant gloom hangs over me, in short every comfort is withdrawn, and I am most impatient to be reliev'd, but not without terror – My hand shakes so abominably that it's with the greatest difficulty I have wrote this, which I fear you will not be able to understand, indeed I should not have made the attempt to any mortal but yourself, for I'm totally incapable of everything.

I beg your pardon My Dear Lady Anne for troubling you with this desponding horrid scrawl, but its in obedience to your desire – God for ever bless and make you happy is the sincere wish of your most affectionate

S.J.

Crichton Street

I put no date, as I don't know when I shall get this sent.

NOTES

1. For Hume and Monboddo see Cockburn (p.31, n.1). Henry Mackenzie (1745-1831) became comptroller of the taxes for Scotland, but is best known as the auther of the sentimental novel, *The Man of Feeling*, 1771.

2. Charles Edward Stuart (1720-88) was known as the 'Young Pretender', 'Bonnie Prince Charlie'. After the final defeat at Culloden, the Prince escaped to France and lived the rest of his life there and in Italy. He died 31 January 1788 in Rome.

3. Margaret was the third child and second daughter; her insurrection was proposed in the privy in which the children used to hide to eat such delicacies as they were able to steal from the kitchen or the garden.

4. 'The Rev. Alexander Small, a pious but very absent man, and highly valued by the Balcarres family, by whom he was afterwards presented to the living of Kilconquar': note from *Lives of the Lindsays*.

5. This was a Miss Henrietta C– whom Lady Balcarres had found 'weeping and painting butterflies in the garrett of an Edinburgh house where she lodged for a few days' (*Lives etc.*). By a mixture of innocence, guile and sheer eccentricity Henrietta became accepted as a member of the Balcarres family where she performed some of the duties of a governess as far as it suited her. She took against Lady Anne because of the latter's friendship with Sophy Johnstone.

6. Craig-Brown's notes to Alison Cockburn's *Letters* (see p.22) quote from Sir Walter Scott's letter to Lady Anne in 1823: 'Well do I remember Soph's jockey coat, masculine stride, strong voice, and, occasionally, round oath. I remember also many of her songs […] In short, I saw this extraordinary original both at home and at Mrs Cockburn's, and am like to laugh even now whenever I think of her.' 'Poor Soph,' Craig-Brown continues, 'had a miserable ending. A sceptic without hope, but not without terror, she lived to extreme old age, and latterly in great misery through penuriousness, her first salutation to visitors being always, "What hae ye brocht, what hae ye brocht?" – stretching out her skinny arm to receive the offering.'

   Sophy Johnstone remained devoted to Lady Anne who equally was kind to her until she died. I have included at the end of the entry on Lady Anne letters from Sophy Johnstone to Lady Anne written in Sophy Johnstone's old age.

7. In Sterne's *Tristram Shandy* Mrs Shandy generally gives way to her forceful and argumentative husband. His insistence that she have the man-midwife attend Tristram's birth results in Tristram's nose being crushed by his forceps.

8. 'The result of this strange experiment was, morally, a most unfortunate one. She lived and died an unbeliever.– the family of Hilton, to which she belonged, is now extinct:' note from *Lives of the Lindsays*.

9. 'Auld Robin Gray' tells the story of Jenny whose lover Jamie goes to sea to make enough money for them to marry. While he is away the family falls on hard times, the last straw being the stealing (lifting) of the cow. At last believing Jamie to have perished in a shipwreck, Jenny agrees to marry her aged suitor, Robin Gray: of course, Jamie returns after the wedding.

O sair did we greet, amd mickle did we say,
We took but ae kiss, and we tore ourselves away;
I wish I were dead! but I'm no like to die,
And why do I live to say, wae's me!

I gang like a ghaist, and I carena to spin,
I darena think on Jamie, for that wad be a sin;
But I'll do my best a gudewife to be,
For auld Robin Gray is kind unto me.

The moving dignity and stoical decency of Lady Anne's version of the story has given it a lasting place in Scottish writing. The unsentimental finality of 'but I'm no like to die' locates the poem in the realities of female lives.

10. Kaffirs was the former collective name for the Pondo and Xhosa peoples of the East Cape Province of South Africa; the Hottentots, originally a Bushman-Bantu cross, called themselves Khoi-Khoin, 'men of men'.

11. Earl Macartney (1737-1806) Envoy-Extraordinary to St Petersburg in 1764, Governor of Madras, 1781, Ambassador in China in 1792 and Governor of the Cape of Good Hope 1796-8, when he resigned because of ill health.

12. In Sheridan's *The Critic*, 1781, the conventional presentation of Ophelia's madness in *Hamlet* is parodied by the stage directions: 'Enter Tilburina stark mad in white satin, and her confidante stark mad in white linen' (Act III, scene ii).

13. Picking up the notion of Paradise, Lady Anne quotes Milton, *Paradise Lost*, Book xii, l. 646: 'The world was all before them'.

14. Colonel Lloyd was a fellow-passenger on the journey to the Cape; John Barrow (1764-1848) was a career diplomat; he acted as private secretary to Macartney and was sent by him on a good will mission to reconcile the Boers and the Kaffirs. He was knighted in 1835; 'modest, well-bred' Dr Patterson, his wife and her 'crumb of a sister' were also fellow-passengers.

15. The waggonbomb or wagenboom is so named because its wood was used in making wagon wheels.

16. The silver-tree, of the mainly Australian family of Protaceae, is native to South Africa.

17. Lady Anne was a close friend of the Prince of Wales, later Prince Regent and George IV. She made a visit to Paris in 1784-5 with Mrs Fitzherbert, the Roman Catholic woman with whom George contracted a form of marriage, later declared illegal. Lady Anne's diary of the trip is written in 2 note books, deposited among the Crawford Family Papers in the National Library of Scotland.

Anne Grant (née Macvicar)
Mrs Grant of Laggan (1755–1838)

Anne Grant was born Anne Macvicar in 1755 to Highland parents from Argyllshire who were at that time living in Glasgow. Soon after Anne's birth Duncan Macvicar joined the army and was posted to America where his wife and daughter joined him in 1758. Although the Grants originally landed at Charleston, South Carolina, they had by 1760 settled near Albany, New York, and they continued in this area until in 1768 they returned to Glasgow so that Duncan Grant could recover from an illness. Because of the War of Independence they never returned and Grant lost some property he had acquired there. But the American experience shaped Anne's attitudes to the virtues of 'primitive' societies and she became close to Catalina Schuyler, from a prominent New York family, who was a second mother to her as well as providing much of her cultural education. Anne Grant later celebrated her mentor and Albany society in her *Memoirs of an American Lady*, extracts from which are given below.

Anne Macvicar found her second 'primitive' society in the Scottish Highlands, first in Fort Augustus, where her father had been posted, and then in Laggan where she moved with her minister husband, James Grant, on their marriage in 1779. For the next twenty-three years Anne Grant lived in Laggan and brought up her large family there. She had altogether twelve children of whom three died in infancy and one at fifteen. In her Highland community Anne Grant found all the virtues of simplicity and family values that she felt were increasingly being threatened elsewhere in Britain and Europe. She was unsurprisingly a devoted believer in the authenticity of the poems of Ossian, which is noteworthy given her deep knowledge of Highland culture and of the Gaelic language.[1] When her husband died in 1801, Anne Grant was left with two small pensions and eight children, and when the family moved to Woodend, near Stirling, she began to write with the intention of publishing to provide her with an income. She began with poetry but soon found that the publication of her letters was more remunerative. Her *Letters from the Mountains* appealed to a new class of reader who enjoyed their detailed accounts of ordinary lives in remote places. Grant supplemented her income from writing by taking live-in pupils, at first young boys and then adolescent girls.

By the time Grant moved to Edinburgh in 1808 she was an established writer who was able to take an active part in Edinburgh literary life. She wrote in her posthumously published letters about her many encounters with such luminaries as Scott and Francis Jeffrey[2] and, of course, Elizabeth Hamilton, Eliza Fletcher and, when she visited Edinburgh, Joanna Baillie. And she had breakfast with Southey,[3] when he was passing through Edinburgh. Fletcher and Jeffrey were, interestingly, politically opposite from the extremely Tory Grant who loved them in spite of their politics.

Her successful literary life was not matched by private happiness. Her elder son, Duncan, got into serious trouble during a mutiny at his military academy, causing Grant emotional and financial distress: he was sent to India as a cadet but died there ten years later. Indeed, the steady loss of her children makes harrowing reading in the letters: only one of Grant's children, John Peter, a Writer to the Signet, survived her and was able finally to support her in his home when he married in 1833. She died five years later aged eighty-three, unshaken in her faith, despite the many tragedies of her life.

Her most important work, *Essays on the Superstitions of the Highlanders of Scotland*, is, I think, probably less attractive to the modern reader than her more informal letters and memoirs from which I have, therefore, made my selections.

Anne Macvicar Grant, *Poems on Various Subjects* (Edinburgh and London: Longman and Co., 1803); *Letters from the Mountains; being the Correspondence with her Intimate Friends between the Years 1773 and 1803*, 3 vols (London: Longman and Co., 1806; ed. in 2 vols with notes and additions by J. P. Grant, London: Longman, Brown, Green and Longmans, 1845: text is taken from the 1845 edition); *Memoirs of an American Lady with Sketches of Manners and Scenery in America as They Existed Previous to the Revolution*, 2 vols (London: Longman and Co., 1808; New York: Research Reprints, 1970); *Essays on the Superstitions of the Highlanders of Scotland, with Translations from the Gaelic*, 2 vols (London: Longman and Co., 1811; reprinted Norwood, Pa: Norwood Editions, 1975); *Eighteen Hundred and Thirteen: A Poem* (1814); *Memoir and Correspondence of Mrs Grant of Laggan*, ed. J. P. Grant, 3 vols (London: Longman, Brown, Green and Longmans, 1844)

Further Reading; Agnes Douglas Black, *Mrs. Anne Grant of Laggan: A Highland Journey – 1773* (Oban: Agnes D. Black, 1971)
Peter Womack, *Improvement and Romance: Constructing the Myth of the Highlands* (Basingstoke: Macmillan, 1988)

see also the *Corvey Project*: http://www.shu.ac.uk/corvey/

Chambers; *DNB*; *HSWW*; Irving

From *Letters from the Mountains*, 1806 (text is taken from the 1845 edition, ed. by J. P. Grant):
Although Anne Grant came to know many celebrated people, her letters are generally not written to the great, but rather to private people, and it is this that gives them their special tone of friendly intimacy:

Lochfyne, near Inverary,
April 28, 1773

My dearest Harriet[5]

The beginning of the letter describes her journey up Loch Lomond side:
I have already forgotten the name of the place we breakfasted at [probably Tarbet or Arrochar]; but there our fellow-traveller, or attendant rather, forsook us; and there we picked up an original of quite another kind. The carriage was detained

while one of the horses was shod, and I took that opportunity of gathering some of the freshest primroses I had ever seen, from the roots of a weeping birch, that actually 'wept odorous dews' upon me, as I sheltered under its drooping branches. How I do love these artless bowers, and how much I wish to have you with me here, to tell you things that no other mortal would understand or care for! My walk was stopped by a stream, whose descent into the lake was covered by thick shades of alder and hazel, that reminded me of the creek where Ulysses went on shore in Phaeacia, and then I wished I had my Odyssey out of the chaise. But, alas! no Odyssey was to be had. Then I was called to breakfast, in an upper room, the floor of which was much worse than that at Luss; and indeed pervious to every sound. We had taken possession of the only tolerable room, and a newly-arrived traveller was heard growling for his breakfast below. He did not swear, but was so fretful and querulous; so displeased with everything that was given or said to him, and his manner of growling, too, was so amusing, he showed so much ingenuity in discovering faults in everything, that I burst out a-laughing, and said we were certainly haunted by the ghost of Smelfungus, of whom Sterne gives such an amusing account.[5] By the by, we had the previous day passed, with 'reverence due', the monument of the original Smelfungus, which rises near his native spot, beside his favourite lake, which he delights to describe in Humphry Clinker. Tea was prepared, but still thunder muttered hoarse below.

My father, inquiring about the stranger, and finding he was a gentleman's son of the country, very good-naturedly sent him an invitation to breakfast; for he concluded the house, a very poor one, could not furnish two breakfasts, with their apparatus, of equal elegance, and that this occasioned the ill humour by which we were incommoded. He was a student, travelling home from college: he left all his irritability below, and came up with an air so manly, well-bred, and accommodating, that, had we not received some previous intelligence of his character through the floor, we should have thought highly of him; yet, through the strong lines of a marked and sensible countenance, the scowl of discontent was but too obvious. I, who for my part detest every mode of selfish luxury, could not endure to see a native Highlander make his good humour dependent on a good breakfast, and was moreover disgusted by certain learned strictures on new-laid eggs, which I am sure made no part of his college acquirements.[6] Then his appearance was so manly, that this puppyism was doubly provoking; however, he sweetened by degrees into an agreeable and intelligent fellow-traveller. But, O! not a single spark of enthusiasm. Ossian himself was never blinder than he is to the soul-moving beauties of that bard.

Why, after tiring you and myself with such a detail, should I tell you of the horrors of Glencroe, through which we travelled in a dismal rainy day? In one particular, I dare say, I agreed with the stranger, for I really thought dinner the most interesting event of this day's journey, not merely as a repast, but the manner of it was so novel. There was a little inn, thatched, and humbler than any of the former; we came very cold to it; we found a well-swept clay floor, and an enlivening blaze of peats and brushwood, two windows looking out upon the lake [Loch Fyne] we were to cross, and a primitive old couple, whose fresh complexion made you wonder at their silver hairs. All the apparatus of fishing and hunting were suspended from the roof; I thought myself in Ithaca, though Homer does not speak of peats or trout, and far less of grouse. The people showed an alacrity in welcoming us, and a concern about our being wet and cold, that could not have been assumed. I never took such a sudden liking to people so far out of my own way. I suppose we are charmed with cheerfulness and sensibility in old people, because we do not expect it; and with unservile courtesy in the lower class for the same reason. 'How populous, how vital is the grave!' says your favourite Young;[7] 'How populous, how vital are the glens!' I should be tempted to say here: but after the 'stupendous solitude', through which we had just passed, the blazing hearth and kindly host had peculiar attractions.

Shall I tell you of our dinner? Never before did I blot paper with such a detail; but it is instructive to know how cheaply we may be pleased. On a clean table of two fir deals we had as clean a cloth; trout new from the lake, eggs fresh as our student's heart could wish; *kippered* salmon, fine new-made butter and barley-cakes, which we preferred to the loaf we had brought with us. Smelfungus began to mutter about the cookery of our trouts; I pronounced them very well drest, out of pure spite; for by this time I could not endure him, from the pains he took to mortify the good people, and to show us he had been used to lodge and dine better. I feasted, and was quite entranced, thinking how you would enjoy all that I enjoyed.

To Harriet Reid from Oban, 1 May 1773: Anne Macvicar reflects on her removal from the life of towns:
People in the country may be abundantly silly and selfish, but the passion for despicable and corrupting novelties is not so constantly fed. When the heart is chastened by adversity, or softened by sorrow, the salutary impression is not too often effaced. The mind is in a manner forced on the contemplation of nature; and I do not know how any one can see one's Maker in his greatest works, without being the better and the wiser for it. Yet to those who are truly desirous of improvement, the town offers greater choice of society. That, and that alone, I regret in leaving it.

Again to Harriet Reid from Oban, 3 May 1773 describing Soroba and its inhabitants:
It is a sweet place, sheltered by a small hill; a brook, fringed with willows and alder, runs by it; beautiful meadows lie below, and towering mountains rise opposite. I never saw a place of more pastoral aspect. I love the good old people; there is something so artless, primitive, and benevolent about them. I think I could guess them, by their looks, to be what everyone describes them. Do you know, the Highlanders resemble the French, in being poor, with a better grace than other people. If they want certain luxuries or conveniences, they do not look embarrassed, or disconcerted, nor make you feel awkward by paltry apologies, which you do not know how to answer; they rather dismiss any sentiment of that kind by a sort of playful raillery, for which they seem to have a talent. Our visit, if not a pleasant, was at least a merry one. The moment tea was done, dancing began; excellent dancers they are, and in music of various kinds they certainly excel. The floor is not yet laid but that was no impediment. People, hereabouts, when they have good ancestry, education, and manners, are so supported by the consciousness of those advantages, and the credit allowed for them, that they seem not the least disconcerted at the deficiency of the goods of fortune; and I give them great credit for their spirit and contentment, though it should prove the appellation of poor and proud, which

vulgar minds are so ready to apply to them. Is it not a blessed thing that there yet exists a place where poverty is respectable, and deprived of its sting?

Once settled in Fort Augustus, Anne Grant becomes the interpreter of Highland manners to the southerners, Scottish and English:

Did you ever know so good a creature as Sandy the primitive? See now, he insists on his mother and his sisters coming to live with him, and means to support the whole family in ease and abundance. Is it not like Joseph sending for his brethren – and Joseph too, was factor. [...] It just now occurs to me, why, in a country so near as England, and even in one so assimilated as Ireland, Scotch manners are so little understood. They never write a page on these subjects without making some blunder, which to a Scotchman seems very ludicrous. This comes from confounding the peculiarities, dialect, etc., of the Highlanders with those of the Lowlanders, the two most dissimilar classes of beings existing, in every one particular that marks distinction; the former, indeed, are a people never to be known unless you live among them, and learn their language.[8]

After her marriage to James Grant (who incidentally proves a more passionate and lover-like husband than she expected) Anne Grant moves to Laggan. In a letter, August 27, 1787, she describes a day in Laggan:

I shall, between fancy and memory, sketch out the diary of one July Monday. I mention Monday, being the day that all dwellers in glens come down for the supplies. First of all, at four o'clock, Donald arrives with a horse loaded with butter, cheese and milk. The former I must weigh instantly. He only asks an additional blanket for the children, a covering for himself; two milk tubs, a cog, and another spoon, because little Peter threw one of the set in the burn; two stone of meal, a quart of salt, and two pounds of flax for the spinners; for the grass continues so good that they will stay a week longer. He brings the intelligence of the old sow's being the joyful mother of a dozen pigs, and requests something to feed her with. All this must be ready in an hour; before the conclusion of which comes Ronald, from the high hills, where our sheep and young horses are all summer, and only desires meal, salt, and women with shears, to clip the lambs, and tar to smear them. He informs me that the black mare has a foal, a very fine one; but she is very low, and I must instantly send someone to bring her down to the meadows, before he departs. The tenants who do us service come next; they are going to stay two days in the oak-wood, cutting timber for our new byre, and must have a competent provision of bread, cheese, and ale for the time they stay. Then I have Caro's breakfast to get, Janet's hank to reel and a basket of clews [balls of thread] to dispatch to the weaver; Caroline's lesson to hear, and her sampler to rectify; and all must be over before eleven. Meantime, his Reverence, calm and regardless of all this bustle, wonders what detains me, urging me out to walk, while the soaring larks, the smiling meadows, and opening flowers, second the invitation; and my imagination, if it gets a moment loose from care, kindles at these objects with all the eagerness of youthful enthusiasm. My tottering constitution, my faded form and multiplying cares, are all forgotten, and I enjoy the pause from keen exertion, as others do gaiety and mirth.[9] How happy, in my circumstances, is that versatile and sanguine temper which is hoping for a rainbow in every cloud; nay so prevalent is this disposition, that were a fire to break in the offices, and burn them all down, I dare say the first thing that would occur to me, would be to console myself by considering how much ground would be manured by all these fine ashes.

By 1792 Anne Grant is wholly at home in Laggan and anxious to interpret the wrongs of the Highlanders to her friends: in a letter to Miss Ourry in London she remarks on the importance of northen affairs:

Our tumults in the north appear aggravated and formidable to you in London, which is the region of political panics. […] The only cause of complaint in Scotland is the rage for sheep-farming. The families removed on that account are often as numerous as our own. The poor people have neither language, money, nor education, to push their way anywhere else; though they often possess feelings and principles that might almost rescue human nature from the reproach which false philosophy and false refinement have brought upon it. Though the poor Ross-shire people were driven to desperation by the iron hand of oppression, they even acted under a sense of rectitude, touched no property, and injured no creature. […] The only real grievance Scotland labours under, originates with landholders.[10]

A letter of 1802 is of particular interest since it estimates the 'poetesses' of the period:

It is among the lovers of truth and nature alone that I am to look for my partisans. Who that admires Mrs Robinson or Miss Seward will ever tolerate me? I have read no modern authors, except in extracts that I have chanced upon here and there. But the only female writers of poetry that I can recollect at present, who have kept their garments unspotted, are Carter, Barbauld and Williams.[11] All the rest have sat too long at their toilette, and are so bedizened, – they nod such spangles, and trail such pompous plumes, – that, like every other artificial and superficial thing, they are only calculated for the fashion of the day – to please and dazzle for a moment: but of the two former, particularly one might say:

> The teeth of Time may gnaw Tantallon;
> But they're for ever.[12]

Miss Williams has since disfigured her style with the slang of party: but how elegant were her first productions! I am told the song,

> Where Avon mingles with the Clyde,[13]

is hers. I should have been charmed though I had seen that only. Burns's poems always excepted, I have seen no lyrical production of latter days that has power over my feelings.

Laggan, August 9, 1796 (To Mrs Macintosh whom she had recently journeyed to meet in Dunkeld):

One of my first cares after my return home was to prepare for Sandy Kennedy's wedding, which proved, in his own way, a very splendid one. The day before the marriage we had the bride's friends, with all the servants, dancing all the evening; and on the wedding-day, we had the same party at dinner, in the nursery. You are to understand that the bride served us eight years, and her swain seven, at a former period; so we could not withhold our countenance. The Sheriff is rich, according to Anne's estimate of wealth, and excels in strong sound sense; you know he is our tenant in the glebe which forms an additional tie.[14] He is counted penurious, but shone on this occasion. Four fat sheep, and abundance of game and poultry, were slain for the supper and following breakfast, which was served only in *the Chinese manner* to the inferior class. At this feast above a hundred persons assisted, three score of which consisted of our children and rustics, our tenants and servants, and the teachers of *arts* and sciences from the neighbouring hamlets. At the head of the long table was a cross one, raised higher, a humble imitation, I presume, of the dais, at which the courteous knights and noble dames sat in the days of Queen Guinever. [...] And there were poultry, and plovers, and a roast joint, and grouse in perfection. [...] The music and dancing were very superior to anything you could imagine; do not whisper anything so treasonable, but both were superior to many fashionable performers in each way. Mr Grant took a fancy to be very wise and serious; and reproved the Sheriff for killing so many sheep, and collecting so many people; and wondered at me for being so pleased. I never saw him ungracious before; but he was not well. My versatility stood me in good stead. Everyone was quiet, orderly, and happy in the extreme. I considered it was hard to grudge this one day of *glorious felicity* to those who, though doomed to struggle through a life of hardship and penury, have all the love of society, the taste for conviviality, and even the sentiment that animates and endears social intercourse, which constitutes the enviable part of enjoyment in higher circles. It would be cruel to deprive such of the single opportunity their life affords of being splendidly hospitable, and seeing all those to whom nature and affection has allied them, rejoice together, at a table of their own providing; and by seeing that table graced by such of their superiors, as they have been used to regard with a mixed sentiment of love and veneration. I myself never dance, and on those occasions join very little, outwardly, in the amusement; I rather sit rapt in reverie, or gaze in mute triumph at the collective felicity before me. The wedding was in a large barn. After breakfast, they danced a while on the green, and the scene closed with the young couple going home. The following evening we had to dress all the children for the concluding ball in our itinerant dancing-school; so you must allow for my being fatigued with festivities.

I am sure I have tired you with the history of Anne's wedding. Had it been a fine ball, such as you are used to, I should not say half so much about it; but I thought the scene would be new to you. It is such, indeed, as cannot take place but in these regions: here only you may condescend without degradation, for here only is the bond between the superior and inferior classes a kindly one. I cannot exactly say where the fault lies; but cold disdain, on the one side, and a gloomy and rancorous envy on the other, fix an icy barrier between the upper and lower classes with you. Your low people are so gross, so sordid; but if you treated them as we do ours, they would not be so coarse and hard; they are now, however, past recovery. It grieves me to think that the iron age of calculation approaches fast towards the sacred retreats of nature and of sentiment.

From *Memoirs of an American Lady*, 1808:

Anne Grant points out that it is 40 years since she lived through the experiences she describes but is confident that the 'simple manners' and 'primitive notions' of an 'infant society' will give an interest 'for reflecting minds'. In her account of the Five Nations, or Mohawk Indians, and the visit of four of their Sachems or chiefs to London with Colonel Philip Schuyler to the court of Queen Anne, Grant is very insistent that the Mohawks were not savages:

The high spirited rulers of the boundless wild, who, alike heedless of the power and splendour of distant monarchs, were accustomed to say with Fingal, 'Sufficient for me is the desert, with all deer and woods'¹⁵ [but] in the present depressed and diminished state of these once powerful tribes, so few traces of their wonted energy remain, that it could scarce be credited, were I able to relate with what bold and flowing eloquence they clothed their conceptions.

Then Grant turns her narrative focus, however, on the white, originally Dutch, settler society of Albany and its environs. The women, she explains, had charge of the training of children and plants. The issue of slavery remains an embarrassment to be apologised for. The Albanians provided 'neat cottages for their slaves':

These cottages were in summer occupied by some of the negroes who cultivate the grounds about them, and served as a place of joyful liberty to the children of the family on holidays, and a nursery for the young negroes whom it was the custom to rear very tenderly, and instruct very carefully. [...] Let me not be detested as an advocate for slavery when I say that I think I have never seen people so happy in servitude as the domestics of the Albanians.

Slaves, Grant continues, were initially brought up with the family, sharing food, clothing, religious instruction and sometimes even the same cradle as the children of the house, and at the age of three the slave was given to a household child of the same sex: thus extremely close bonds were formed. Slaves who failed out of 'drunkenness or levity' were sold to Jamaica and often had to be stopped from commiting suicide:

But they never considered that they held the slaves except by right. [...] They sought their code of morality in the Bible, and there they imagined they found this hapless race condemned to perpetual slavery; and thought nothing remained for them but to lighten the pains of their fellow Christians, after having made them such.

They regarded miscegenation with horror as productive of
an ambiguous race which the law does not acknowledge; and who (if they have any moral sense, must be as much ashamed of their parents as these last are of them) are certainly a dangerous, because degraded part of the community.

A relation of Colonel Schuyler's 'of weak capacity' had fathered a child by a negro woman and the resultant son was carefully educated and married to a destitute white woman from one of the older colonies. The couple were given a well-stocked and fertile farm in the depth of the wood. Anne Macvicar visited the Chalks, as they were called:

I have been in Chalk's house myself, and a most comfortable abode it was; but considered him as a mysterious and anomalous being.

Grant describes the education and early habits of the Albanian community. The children were divided into companies from the age of five or six until they were marriagable. All their education and amusements centred round the company and it was considered 'a sort of apostasy to marry out of one's company'. Because of these early habits:
Inconstancy or even indifference among married couples was unheard of, even when there happened to be a considerable disparity in point of intellect. […] Marriage in this colony was always early, very often happy, and very seldom indeed interested. […] Nor must it be thought that these were mean or uninformed persons. Patriots, magistrates, generals, those who were afterwards wealthy, powerful and distinguished, all […] set out in the same manner and later delighted to recount the humble toils and destiny obscure of their early years!

When a boy, as all males were called until marriage, wished to marry:
He demanded of his father forty or at most fifty dollars, a negro boy and a canoe; all of a sudden he assumed the brow for care and solicitude, and began to smoke, a precaution absolutely necessary to repel aguish damps and troublesome insects. He arrayed himself in a habit very little differing from that of the Aborigines, into whose bounds he was about to penetrate, and in short commenced Indian trader. That strange amphibious animal, who uniting the acute senses, strong instincts, and unconquerable patience and fortitude of the savage, with the art, policy, and inventions of the European, encountered in the pursuit of gain dangers and difficulties equal to those described in the romantic legends of chivalry.

Grant digresses to remark on the beauties of the natural world with which, despite its dangers, these young men became intimate and to remark too that the Indians were noble people until seduced from their former probity by the bad examples and liquor of the Europeans: 'while faith was kept with these people, they never became aggressors'. On their return from their trading ventures, the traders themselves were more like Indians:
Lofty, sedate, and collected, they seem masters of themselves, and independent of others. […] One must have seen these people (the Indians, I mean) to have any idea what a noble animal man is, while unsophisticated. […] Of [this] class of social beings (for such indeed they were) of whom I speak, let us judge from the traders who know their language and customs, and from the adopted prisoners who have spent years among them. How unequivocal, how consistent is the testimony they bear to their humanity, friendship, fortitude, fidelity and generosity.

Much of Grant's narrative is concerned with the history and politics of the area, with the relationships of the Dutch and English speaking settlers with the French and of the various military engagements of the time. Given her consistent didactic intent, Grant always uses her ethnographic observations to criticise what she feels to be the short-comings of her contemporary society. Although the overt aim of the 'Memoirs' is to pay tribute to Catalina Schuyler and her family, the more general detail about community and about travel is probably most interesting for the modern reader. 'Madame' or 'Aunt Schuyler' is, however,

the constant theme of the 'Memoirs' and it is clear that she was important not merely as
Anne Grant's mentor but as a source of hospitality, stability and political and social
acumen in the early community of Albany: Anne Grant's 'Memoirs' remain an important
source for her biography. I conclude the entry, however, with Grant's account of her
journey from Albany to Lake Ontario. When Grant's father, who has seen very little of his
family, is required to journey to Fort Oswego on the lake's south-eastern shore, it is agreed
that Anne Grant and her mother are to accompany him:

In the month of October he set out on this journey, or voyage rather, in which
it was settled that my mother and I should accompany him. We were, I believe, the
first females, above the very lowest ranks, who had ever penetrated so far into this
remote wilderness. Certainly never was joy greater that that which lulled my
childish mind on setting out on this journey. I had before seen little of my father,
and the most I knew of him was from the solicitude I had heard expressed on his
account, and the fear of his death after every battle. I was, indeed, a little ashamed
of having a military father, brought up as I had mostly been, in a Dutch family, and
speaking that language as fluently as my own; yet, on the other hand, I had felt so
awkward at seeing all my companions have fathers to talk and complain to, while I
had none; that I thought upon the whole it was a very good thing to have a father
of any kind. The scarlet coat, which I had been taught to consider as the symbol of
wickedness, disgusted me in some degree; but then, to my great comfort, I found
my father did not swear; and again to my unspeakable delight, that he prayed. A
soldier pray! was it possible? and should I really see my father in heaven! How
transporting! by a sudden revolution of opinion I now thought my father the most
charming of all beings; and the overflowings of my good will reached to the whole
company, because they wore the same colour, and seemed to respect and obey him.
I dearly loved idleness too, and the more, because my mother, who delighted in
needle-work, confined me too much to it. What joys were mine! to be idle for a
fortnight, seeing new woods, rivers, and animals, every day; even then the love of
nature was, in my young bosom, a passion productive of incessant delight. I had,
too, a primer, two hymns, and a ballad; and these I read over and over with great
diligence. At intervals my attention was agreeably engaged by the details the soldiers
gave my father of their manner of living and fighting in the woods; and with these
the praises of Madame were often mingled.[16] I thought of her continually; every
great thing I heard about her, even her size had its impression. She became the
heroine of my childish imagination, and I thought of her as something both awful
and admirable. We had the surgeon of the regiment, and another officer with us;
they talked too of Madame, of Indians, of battles, and of ancient history. Sitting
from morning to night musing in the boat, contemplating my father, who appeared
to me a hero and a saint, and thinking of Aunt Schuyler, who filled up my whole
mind with the grandeur with which my fancy had invested her; and then having my
imagination continually amused with the variety of noble wild scenes which the
beautiful banks of the Mohawk afforded, I am convinced I thought more in that
fortnight, that is to say, acquired more ideas, and took more lasting impressions,
than ever I did, in the same space of time, in my life. This, however foreign it may
appear to my subject, I mention, as so far connecting with it, that it accounts, in
some measure, for that development of thought which led me to take such ready

and strong impressions from Aunt's conversation when afterwards I knew her.

Never, certainly, was a journey so replete with felicity. I luxuriated in idleness and novelty; knowledge was my delight, and it was now pouring in on my mind from all sides. What a change from sitting pinned down to my sampler by my mother till the hour of play; and then running wild with children as young and still simpler than myself. Much attended to by all my fellow travellers, I was absolutely intoxicated with the charms of novelty, and the sense of my new found importance. The first day we came to Schenactady, a little town, situated in a rich and beautiful spot, and partly supported by the Indian trade. The next day we embarked, proceeded up the river with six batteaux, and came early in the evening to one of the most charming scenes imaginable, where Fort Hendrick was built; so called, in compliment to the principal Sachem, or King of the Mohawks. The castle of this primitive monarch stood at a little distance, on a rising ground, surrounded by palisades. He resided, at the time, in a house which the public workmen, who had lately built this fort, had been ordered to erect for him in the vicinity. We did not fail to wait upon His Majesty; who, not choosing to depart too much from the customs of his ancestors, had not permitted divisions of apartments or modern furniture to profane his new dwelling. It had the appearance of a good barn, and was divided across by a mat hung in the middle. King Hendrick, who had indeed a very princely figure, and a countenance that would not have dishonoured royalty, was sitting on the floor beside a large heap of wheat, surrounded with baskets of dried berries of different kinds; beside him, his son, a very pretty boy, somewhat older than myself, was caressing a foal, which was unceremoniously introduced into the royal residence. A laced hat, a fine saddle and pistols, gifts of his good brother the great king, were hung round on the cross beams. He was splendidly arrayed in a coat of pale blue, trimmed with silver; all the rest of his dress was of the fashion of his own nation, and highly embellished with beads and other ornaments. All this suited my taste exceedingly, and was level to my comprehension. I was prepared to admire King Hendrick by hearing him described as a generous warrior, terrible to his enemies and kind to his friends: the character of all others, calculated to make the deepest impression on ignorant innocence, in a country where infants learned the horrors of war from its vicinity. Add to all this, that the monarch smiled, clapped my head, and ordered me a little basket, very pretty, and filled by the officious kindness of his son with dried berries. Never did princely gifts, or the smile of royalty, produce more ardent admiration and profound gratitude. I went out of the royal presence overawed and delighted, and am not sure but what I have liked kings all my life the better for this happy specimen, to which I was so early introduced. Had I seen royalty, properly such, invested with all the pomp of European magnificence, I would possibly have been confused and over-dazzled. But this was quite enough, and not too much for me; and I went away, lost in a reverie, and thought of nothing but kings, battles, and generals for days after. The journey, charming my romantic imagination by its very delays and difficulties, was such a source of interest and novelty to me, that above all things I dreaded its conclusion, which I well knew would be succeeded by long talks and close confinement. Happily for me we soon entered upon Wood-creek, the most desirable of all places for the traveller who loves to linger, if such another traveller there be. This is a small river, which winds irregularly through a deep and narrow valley of the most lavish fertility. The depth and richness of the soil here was evinced by the loftiness and the nature of the trees, which were, hiccory, butter-nut, chestnut, and sycamores of vast circumference as well as height. These became so top heavy, and their roots were so often undermined by this insidious stream, that in every tempestuous night, some giants of the grove fell prostrate, and very frequently across the stream, where they lay in all their pomp of foliage, like leafy bridges, unwithered, and formed an obstacle almost invincible to all navigation. The Indian lifted his slight canoe, and carried it past the tree; but our deep loaded batteaux could not be so managed. Here my orthodoxy was shocked, and my anti-military prejudices revived by the swearing of the soldiers: but then again veneration for my father was if possible increased, by his lectures against swearing provoked by their transgression. Nothing remained for our heroes but to attack these sylvan giants axe in hand, and make way through their divided bodies. The assault upon fallen greatness was unanimous and unmerciful, but the resistance was tough, and the process tedious; so much so, that we were three days proceeding fourteen miles, having at every two hours' end at least, a new tree to cut through.

It was here, as far as I recollect the history of my own heart, that the first idea of artifice ever entered my mind. It was like most female artifices, the offspring of vanity. These delays were a new source of pleasure to me. It was October: the trees we had to cut through were often loaded with nuts, and while I ran lightly along the branches, to fill my royal basket with their spoils, which I had great pleasure in distributing, I met with multitudes of fellow plunderers in the squirrels of various sizes, who were numberless. This made my excursions amusing: but when I found my disappearance excited alarm, they assumed more interest. It was so fine to sit quietly among the branches, and hear concern and solicitude expressed about the child.

I will spare the reader the fatigue of accompanying our little fleet through

Antres vast and desarts wild[17]

only observing, that the munificent solitude through which we travelled was much relieved by the sight of Johnson hall, beautifully situated in a plain by the river; while Johnson castle, a few miles further up, made a most respectable appearance on a commanding eminence at some distance.

We travelled from one fort to another; but in three or four instances, to my great joy, they were so remote from each other, that we found it necessary to encamp at night on the bank of the river. This, in a land of profound solitude, where wolves, foxes and bears abounded, and were very much inclined to consider and treat us as intruders, might seem dismal to wiser folks. But I was so gratified by the bustle and agitation produced by our methods of defence, and actuated by the love which all children have for mischief that is not fatal, that I enjoyed our night's encampment exceedingly. We stopped early wherever we saw the largest and most combustible kind of trees. Cedars were great favourites, and the first work was to fell and pile upon each other an incredible number, stretched lengthways, while everyone who could was busied in gathering withered branches of pine, etc. to fill up the interstices of the pile, and make the green wood burn the faster. Then a train of gun-powder was laid along to give fire to the whole fabric at once, which blazed and crackled magnificently. Then the tents were erected close in a row before this grand conflagration. This was not merely meant to keep us warm, though the nights did begin to grow cold, but to frighten wild beasts and wandering Indians. In case any such Indians, belonging to hostile tribes, should see this prodigious blaze, the size of it was meant to give them an idea of a greater force than we possessed.

In one place, where we were surrounded by hills, with swamps lying between them, there seemed to be a general congress of wolves, who answered each other from opposite hills, in sounds the most terrific. Probably the terror which all savage animals have at fire was exalted into fury, by seeing so many enemies, whom they durst not attack. The bull frogs, the harmless, the hideous inhabitants of the swamps, seemed determined not to be out-done, and roared a tremendous bass to this bravura accompaniment. This was almost too much for my love of the terrible sublime:[18] some women, who were our fellow-travellers, shrieked with terror: and finally, the horrors of that night were ever after held in awful remembrance by all who shared them.

The last night of this eventful pilgrimage, of which I fear to tire my readers by a farther recital, was spent at Fort Bruerton, then commanded by Captain Mungo Campbell,[19] whose warm and generous heart, whose enlightened and comprehensive mind, whose social qualities and public virtues I should delight to commemorate did my limits permit; suffice it, that he is endeared to my recollection by being the first person who ever supposed me to have a mind capable of culture, and I was ever after distinguished by his partial notice. Here we were detained two days by a premature fall of snow. Very much disposed to be happy anywhere, I was here particularly so. Our last day's journey, which brought us to Lake Ontario and Fort Oswego, our destined abode, was a very hard one; we had people going before, breaking the ice with paddles, all the way.

All that I had foreboded of long talks, confinement, etc., fell short of the reality. The very deep snow confined us all; and at any rate the rampart or the parade would have been no favourable scene of improvement for me. One great force of entertainment I discovered here, was no other than the Old Testament, which during my confinement I learned to read, till then having done so very imperfectly. It was an unspeakable treasure as a storybook, before I learnt to make any better use of it, and became, by frequent perusal, imprinted on my memory.

Grant concludes this section of her 'Memoirs' with a tribute to the Commanding Officer, Major (afterwards Colonel) Duncan of Lundie, who treats the men like sons, firmly and kindly, and who, therefore, enables them to pass the long winter months profitably.

From *Memoir and Correspondence of Mrs Grant of Laggan*, 1844:

It seems appropriate to conclude with Anne Grant's tribute to Joanna Baillie:
Mrs Baillie (for so her elder sister chooses to be distinguished) people like in their hearts better than Mrs Joanna, though they would not for the world say so, thinking that it would argue great want of taste not to prefer Melpomene [the muse of tragedy]. I, for my part, would greatly prefer the Muse to walk in a wood or sit in a bower with; but in that wearisome farce, a large party, Agnes acts her part much

better. The seriousness, simplicity, and thoughtfulness of Joanna's manners overawe you from talking commonplace to her; and as for pretension or talking fine, you would as soon think of giving yourself airs before an Apostle. She is mild and placid, but makes no effort either to please or to shine; she will neither dazzle nor be dazzled, yet, like others of the higher class of mind, is very indulgent in her opinions: what passes before her seems rather food for thought than mere amusement. In short she is not merely a woman of talent, but of genius, which is a very different thing; which is the reason I have taken so much pains to describe her. Joanna's conversation is rather below her abilities, justifying Lord Gardenstone's maxim, that true genius is ever modest and careless.[20] Agnes unconsciously talks above herself, merely from a wish to please, and a habit of living among her intellectual superiors. I should certainly have liked and respected Joanna, as a person singularly natural and genuine, though she had never written a tragedy. I am not at all sure that this is the case with most others.

NOTES

1. James Macpherson (1736-96) claimed to have discovered remains of the poetry of the legendary poet, Ossian or Oisin, in the Highlands and published his 'translations' between 1760 and 1763. Controversy over whether the poems are better described as 'forgeries' than translations has raged more or less ever since: see *The Poems of Ossian and Related Works*, ed. Howard Gaskill with an Introduction by Fiona Stafford (Edinburgh: Edinburgh U.P., 1996).

2. Francis, Lord Jeffrey (1773-1850) was educated at Edinburgh and Glasgow Universities and became a judge and an MP. His political sympathies were Whig and with Sydney Smith and Henry Brougham he founded the *Edinburgh Review* in 1802, being editor until 1829. As a critic Jeffrey approved of Byron, Scott and Keats but is known as the scourge of Wordsworth and the 'Lake Poets' – his review of Wordsworth's *The Excursion* famously begins 'This will never do'. He was also severe, although less so, on Joanna Baillie (see headnote, p.91).

3. Robert Southey (1774-1843) was appointed poet laureate in 1813: he subsequently regretted accepting the position which seemed to some of his contemporaries the final betrayal of the radical principles of his youth. His longer narrative poems were admired by a number of his contemporaries, although he was lampooned particularly by Byron in *Don Juan*. Southey was a friend of Coleridge and married Elizabeth Fricker, sister of Coleridge's wife, Sarah; he showed his generosity in his kindness to Coleridge's more or less abandoned family. Southey made his regular income largely from his association with the *Quarterly Review* – the copy of Anne Grant's *Memoirs of an American Lady* which Dorothy Wordsworth read was probably given to her by Southey.

4. 'Miss Henrietta [presumably called Harriet by her friends] Reid was a very amiable and deserving young lady, connected by marriage with Miss Ewing; and by the more endeared intimacy both with her and the author': note by J. P. Grant. Isabella Ewing, later Mrs Smith of Jordanhill, Glasgow, was one of Anne Grant's earliest friends and correspondents. Harriet Reid also lived in Glasgow.

5. Smelfungus is the hyper-critical tourist of Laurence Sterne's *A Sentimental Journey*, 1768. He is based on Tobias Smollett whose travels are full of complaint about France, etc. At Renton, near Balloch and Smollett's family home at Dalquharn, there is a monument to Smollett with a Latin inscription by Dr Johnson; in Smollett's novel *Humphry Clinker*, 1771, he celebrates the beauty of Loch Lomond: 'I have seen the Lago di Garda, Albano, De Vico, Bolsena, and Geneva, and upon, my honour, I prefer Lough Lomond to them all'.

6. 'Among the peculiarities of Highland manners, is an avowed contempt for the luxuries of the table. A Highland hunter will eat with a keen appetite and sufficient discrimination; but were he to stop in any pursuit, because it was meal time, to growl over a bad dinner, or visibly exult over a good one, the manly dignity of his character would be considered as fallen for ever': note by J. P. Grant.

7. Edward Young, *Night Thoughts*, 1742, I, l.116.

8. Anne Grant learned, and had her children learn, Gaelic.

9. It is perhaps worth reminding the reader that Anne Grant lived more than 50 years beyond this point.

10. The Highland Clearances have still not settled into history. It is argued that the Highlands became more prosperous after the forced and 'unforced' departures from the land; it has equally been argued that no subsequent prosperity could compensate for the sufferings of the dispossessed of the time.

11. Mary Robinson (1758-1800), novelist, poet, dramatist, essayist, etc., is perhaps better remembered for her success as an actress and her affair with the Prince of Wales, later George IV, than for her writings. Anna Seward (1742-1809) was known as the 'Swan of Lichfield'; her poetry might be felt to violate canons of truth and nature by its gushing sentimentality. Elizabeth Carter (1717-1806) was probably the most erudite of the eighteenth-century Bluestockings, or intellectual society hostesses. Her linguistic ability was remarkable: she learned Latin, Greek and Hebrew from her clerical father and taught herself at least five other languages including Arabic. Mrs Barbauld (1743-1825), poet: for more detail see Fletcher (p.115, n.2) and Joanna Baillie (p.90). Helen Maria Williams (1762?-1827) memoirist, poet and novelist, spent much of her life on the Continent. Although she deplored the Terror, she never retreated from the libertarian principles of the French Revolution and Grant's approval is a little surprising.

12. Robert Burns, 'Poem on Pastoral Poetry': 'The Tooth o' Time may gnaw Tantallan/But thou's for ever', referring to Allan Ramsay: see p.8, n.1.

13. Helen Maria Williams, from 'Slow spreads the gloom my soul desires': 'All, all my hopes of bliss reside/Where Evan mingles with the Clyde.' Janet Hamilton uses the phrase again in 'Reminiscences of the "Auld Hie Toon of Hamilton", sixty years ago'. Note too that Joanna Baillie played during her childhood where the Avon joins the Clyde (see p.106).

14. 'Alexander Kennedy, a favourite servant of Mr Grant's, was called the Sheriff in the parish from the deference which the neighbours had for his decisions on all occasions': note by J. P. Grant. Anne was his bride. The 'glebe' is the land attached to a parish church.

15. 'Fingal', book VI: 'The desart is enough to me with all its deer and woods', *The Poems of Ossian*, ed. Gaskill, p.101.

16. Catalina Schuyler is generally referred to as Madame.

17. Shakespeare, *Othello*, I, iii, 140.

18. By the Romantic period the sublime had crystallised into a virtually technical term in the description and depiction of both landscapes and feelings. To use it was to invoke notions of a lofty wildness which chastened humans by reminding them of their smallness within God's creation, yet simultaneously the sublime was inspirational. The poems of Ossian fed a taste for the sublime. Here the addition of 'terrible', also a favourite term of the poets of the period, reinforces Anne Grant's self-irony. For eighteenth-century uses of the term, see Andrew Ashfield and Peter de Bolla, eds, *The Sublime: A Reader in British Eighteenth-century Aesthetic Theory* (Cambridge: Cambridge University Press, 1996).

19. 'Colonel Mungo Campbell was killed leading the attack of Fort St Anne, at the Battle of White Plains, 1777': note from original edition.

20. Frances Garden, Lord Gardenstone (1721-1793), was an advocate, Lord of Session from 1764. He built a model village at Laurencekirk, Kincardineshire. He was eccentrically and inordinately fond of pigs!

Elizabeth Hamilton (1758–1816)

Elizabeth Hamilton was born, the youngest of three children, in Belfast. Her mother, Katherine MacKay, was Irish but her father, Charles Hamilton, was Scottish; her father died shortly after she was born and her mother when she was only nine. She went to live with her father's sister, Mrs Marshall, in Stirlingshire when she was six and after the death of her parents she continued to live there. She thus learned early to identify herself closely with Scotland and Scottish affairs and manners. Throughout her writing life she showed an unusual interest in Scots which she used in her poems and, although only for lower class characters, in her last satirical and didactic novel, *The Cottagers of Glenburnie*, 1808.

She was educated in a mixed school between the ages of nine and thirteen, but she was not classically educated. Although she was not brought up with him, she later became exceptionally close to her soldier brother Charles (1753-92): she corresponded with him while he was in India and visited him in London after he returned in 1788 from a fourteen year tour of duty. Charles was a scholar as well as a soldier and worked after his return on a translation of the *Hedaya*, one of the principal commentaries on Muslim law. Elizabeth lived with her brother in London from 1790 until his premature death in 1792. This meant that she shared his intellectual acquaintance and this fed an existing thirst for knowledge. After Charles's death she lived with her married sister Katherine Black in various places in England before the two sisters settled in Edinburgh. By the time she returned to Edinburgh in 1804, Hamilton had already written two satirical, philosophical novels, *Letters of a Hindoo Rajah* (1796) and *Memoirs of Modern Philosophers* (1800), which features a pretentious blue-stocking, Miss Bridgetina Botherim, who is supposed to be based on the feminist, Mary Hays. Other works included the didactic (and rather dully humourless) *Letters on Education* and and a biography of Agrippina.

Back in Edinburgh her interest in Scotland and Scottish affairs and language was rekindled: she wrote a number of Scotch songs and her most enduring work, *The Cottagers of Glenburnie* which transcends its 'soup and sanitation' didacticism by its wit. Hamilton's invented the now famous Mrs MacClarty whose *canna-be-fashed* (can't be bothered) philosophy tends to win supporters when it was, of course, intended to excite disapproval. Mrs Mason, the builder of the social fabric, overcomes the dirt and laziness of her cousin but it is hard to imagine a *novel* without the McClarty dirt.

Elizabeth Hamilton never married, although she was in her later life given the courtesy title 'Mrs'. It was certainly the life of ordinary women that she was most anxious to improve, but modern readers will probably find Elizabeth Hamilton patronising and perhaps unselfcritical. In many ways, however, her message was radical and her publishing programme aggressive. Unlike Mary Wollstonecraft she lived a blameless and pious life and so her concern for female education seemed benign instead of threatening. Hamilton was particularly friendly with Joanna Baillie and Maria Edgeworth, who wrote an appreciation of her in *The Gentleman's Magazine* in 1816. When *Sense and Sensibility* was attributed to Hamilton, Jane Austen was pleased that 'such a respectable writer' had been named.

In her final years Elizabeth Hamilton suffered from bad eyesight and gout but she appears to have remained pleased with the company of both young and old. She moved to London shortly before her death in Harrogate, where she had gone because of an eye problem, in 1816.

Elizabeth Hamilton, *Translations of the Letters of a Hindoo Rajah; Written Previous to, and During the Period of his Residence in England. To Which is prefixed a Preliminary Dissertation on the History, Religion and Manners of the Hindoos* (London: G. G. and J. Robertson, 1796); *Memoirs of Modern Philosophers: A Novel* (Bath: R. Crutwell, 1800; reprinted 1992 with an introduction by Peter Garside); *Letters on the Elementary Principles of Education* (Dublin: H. Colbert, 1802); *Memoirs of the Life of Agrippina, the Wife of Germanicus* (London: G. G. and J. Robertson, 1804); *Letters Addressed to the Daughter of a Nobleman on the Formation of Religious and Moral Principle* (T. Cadell and W. Davies, 1806); *The Cottagers of Glenburnie: A Tale for the Farmer's Ingle-nook* (Edinburgh: Manners & Miller, 1808; reprinted New York: Garland, 1974); *Exercises in Religious Knowledge* (Edinburgh: Manners & Miller, 1809); *A Series of Popular Essays Illustrative of Principles Essentially Connected with the Improvement of the Understanding, the Imagination, and the Heart* (Edinburgh: Manners & Miller, 1813); *Examples of Questions Calculated to Excite and Exercise the Infant Mind* (Edinburgh: Walker & Greig, 1815); *Hints Addressed to the Patrons of Schools: Principally Intended to Shew that the Benefits Derived from the New Modes of Teaching May be Increased by a Partial Adoption of the Plan of Pestalozzi. To Which are Subjoined Examples of Questions Calculated to Excite and Exercise the Infant Mind* (London: Longman, Hurst, Rees, Orme & Brown, 1815); *Memoirs of the Late Mrs Elizabeth Hamilton with a Selection from Her Correspondence and Other Unpublished Writings*, 2 vols, ed. Elizabeth Benger (London: Longman, Hurst, Rees, Orme, Brown and Green, 1818)

Further Reading:

Virginia Blain, 'Letitia Elizabeth Landon, Eliza Mary Hamilton, and the Genealogy of the Victorian Poetess', *Victorian Poetry* , vol.33 no.1 (Spring 1995), 31-52

Margaret Doody, 'English Women Novelists and the French Revolution', *Actes du colloque tenu à Paris, les 24 et 25 octobre 1975* : 'La Femme en Angleterre et dans les Colonies américaines aux XVIIe et XVIIIe siècles' (Lille: Pub. de l'Univ. de Lille III, 1976), 176-198

[Maria Edgeworth], 'Character and Writings of Mrs Elizabeth Hamilton', *Gentleman's Magazine* Supplement 86, 2 (1816)

Gary Kelly, *English Fiction of the Romantic Period 1789-1930* (London: Longman 1989)

Emma Letley, *From Galt to Douglas Brown: Nineteenth Century Fiction and Scots Language* (Edinburgh: Scottish Academic Press, 1988)

Janice Farrar Thaddeus, 'Elizabeth Hamilton's Domestic Politics', *Studies in Eighteenth-Century Culture*, vol.23 (1994), 265-84

Eleanor Ty, 'Female Philosophy Refunctioned: Elizabeth Hamilton's Parodic Novel', *ARIEL: A Review of International English Literature*, vol.22, no.4 (October 1991), 111-29

DNB; *DLB* 116, 158; *HSWW*; Irving; Todd 1 and 2

From Elizabeth Benger, *Memoirs of the Late Mrs Hamilton*, 1818:
'Biographical Fragment' by Mrs Elizabeth Hamilton

Having often thought, that there is no person, however insignificant, who might not by a fair and impartial statement of the circumstances of his early life, render an essential service to the investigator of the human mind, I sit down to recall and to record every event which I can imagine to have been in any way conducive to the formation of my character and sentiments. Should what I now write never be seen by human eye, the retrospect may at least to myself be useful; as where it gives rise to reflections that mortify, the mortification may be salutary; where it produces a more lively view of the divine goodness, that view must be attended with corresponding sentiments of pious gratitude.

I have laughed at the philosophers for assigning to remote causes a mighty influence over human character; but it is only since domestic education has been in a great measure exploded, that the peculiar traits of family character cease to be distinguished. While children were, from generation to generation, brought up in the bosom of their own family, we may believe that they must, in many instances, have succeeded to prejudices as to an inheritance. Of all these prejudices, the pride of birth was in Scotland the most predominant. Its effects seem to have been injurious, or otherwise, according as the leading members of the family had distinguished themselves by their abilities, or been contented with the consciousness of superiority which they derived from the number of their vassals, and the extent of their estates. In the latter case, I have ever observed family pride to be the bane and ruin of the individuals who composed the inferior branches. In them it gave rise to such absurd ideas of their own importance, as precluded all active exertion, and seldom failed to engender a spirit of malevolence against those who, without the same pretensions, had risen to superior consequence in the eyes of the community. Where, on the contrary, the chiefs of an ancient family have been distinguished by valour or talents, the pride of birth having been associated with an honourable exertion of the faculties, will be found to produce a superior degree of vigour throughout all the younger branches. It is thus that the actions of a remote ancestor may continue to operate in forming the character of those who scarcely preserve the remembrance of his name.

As the Hamiltons of Woodhall, not only boast of being *one* of the first of the Saxon *family* established in Scotland, but of being the stock whence all the branches that have been ennobled in these kingdoms, in France, and in Germany, have sprung; it is probable that some such sentiment as that I have been describing gave an impulse to the energies of the race, which it never could have received from the extent of its possessions. Nor is this mere conjecture: the estate of Woodhall (now the seat of Mr Campbell of Shawfield) was granted by a charter from Pope Honorius to one of my ancestors, 'for good deeds done in the Holy Land', in the first crusade.[1] Nor does it appear that the spirit which led this ancient chief to combat the enemies of the faith, was soon extinguished in the family.

In the reign of the Charles's it accommodated itself to the fashion of the times, and blazed out in zeal for the Covenant, and hatred of episcopacy.[2] My great grandfather, unable to endure with patience the establishment of the liturgy, left Scotland in discontent, and going over to Ireland with his family and a few chosen friends, took up his residence in a remote part of Ulster, where he hoped to enjoy what was then called liberty of conscience. Though only a younger son, he took with him sufficient property to enable him to purchase a track of land, in the county of Monaghan, of such extent as, had his family been possessed of wordly *wisdom*, would have raised them to influence and distinction. But to perpetuate in his family a zeal for the Covenant, was, in his eyes, an object of greater importance than to be the founder of a race. Of his numerous children, four sons only remained with him in Ireland, and to these he at his death bequeathed his fortune in nearly equal lots. A great part of the lands thus divided were, however, afterwards united by his grandson Sir James [Hamilton] who, following the example of his grandfather, has again divided them among his children. To my grandfather Charles no part of this property was assigned. He, at the age of fifteen, entered the army, and went over to Scotland to join a regiment of cavalry, in which, through the interest of his friends, he expected quick promotion. To finish his education, he at the same time entered at the University of Edinburgh, where he acquired such a disrelish for a military life, as made him gladly relinquish the service for a civil appointment; soon after which he married a lady of distinguished beauty, and who possessed what was at that time deemed a very considerable fortune.

My grandmother, who, in manners and accomplishments, as well as in a taste for show and gaiety, seems to have anticipated the fashions of a succeeeding age, resolved not to discredit her husband in the eyes of the world by an appearance inferior, in point of expense, to any of his great connections. She consequently vied with the people of rank among whom she lived; and, being much too fine a lady to be a good manager, did not, as is often done, make up by secret deprivation for ostentatious display. In vain did her too indulgent husband remonstrate; in vain did he change his place of residence to different parts of the kingdom, in order to find a society with whom he might live on equal terms without exceeding his income. My poor grandmother did not understand reasoning; she piqued herself on being one of the best of wives, and most affectionate of mothers, and, in all the pride of virtue, ruined her family, and destroyed the peace of her husband.

Notwithstanding this proof of weakness, my grandfather was universally esteemed as a man of *worth* and sense. The greatest proof he, however, gave of his under-standing was in the assiduous care with which he cultivated the minds of his children in early life. His wife determined that her daughters should be accomplished – he wisely endeavoured to make them rational; and so successfully were his efforts directed, that even the third generation have had reason to bless his memory.

My grandmother's fortune, which, at least, ought to have been secured as a provision to her family, had been gradually dissipated in paying the debts contracted by her habits of expense. Nothing now remained but the emoluments of office; and, unfortunately, my grandfather's employment gave such a command of money, as prevented the immediate feeling of embarrassment. The hour of conviction and of misery at length arrived.

My grandfather saw with horror the impossibility of answering the demands of government; and felt so deeply the stain that he had thus thrown on his honour, as to be unable to support the shock. In the agony of his soul, he went to his friend Mr Basil Hamilton, to unburden his sorrows, and to beseech him to break the distressing intelligence to his wife. With that goodness which was worthy the son of Lord Basil Hamilton,[3] and which has descended as an inheritance to his offspring, Mr [Hamilton] endeavoured to console his unhappy guest. He sat with him, after he had retired to his chamber, till after midnight, and went again to his apartments in the morning, to consult farther on the steps he was to take. On drawing the curtains of his bed, he imagined him to be still asleep, with so little struggle had the perturbed spirit taken its everlasting flight! No death was ever more certainly occasioned by an excess of mental sensibility: but it was the goodness of God that thus removed him from a change of fortune he wanted fortitude to support. The eldest of his daughters thankfully accepted of an invitation from a rich aunt in Ireland, where she soon found herself looked on with an evil eye by the numerous relations who were competitors with her for the old lady's fortune. The fate of the younger was to me more peculiarly interesting. She had her mother's beauty, and her father's understanding, without any of her father's weakness. In her sixteenth year she had made a conquest of the eldest son of Sir A. W.; nor did the baronet make any objection to the match, which, had my grandfather lived, would have taken place in a few months. His death made as great an alteration in the sentiments of the old gentleman, as in the circumstances of his family; and the lover, with true filial obedience, gave up his mistress, as soon as he was desired to seek a richer wife.

With talents of a superior order, and with an education such as few Scotch ladies could at that time boast of, my aunt ought not to have experienced any difficulty in the attainment of independence. But for talents and accomplishments there was for that period no resource, – nothing upon which they could be employed to advantage; she was therefore glad to obtain protection in the house of a distant relation, and to repay this protection by those exertions for which she was eminently fitted by a superior education. Her situation was not, however, void of advantages. Lady G– was a woman of great piety and extensive information: she had at Bath formed acquaintance with some distinguished characters, with whom she kept up correspondence; and as she employed my aunt to write all her letters, gave her thus an opportunity of improving in sentiment and expression. Nor was the opportunity thrown away; for I have never met with the writer who could express so many ideas in so few words, with an equal degree of simplicity and elegance.

On the death of Lady G–, my aunt went with her daughter, Mrs M–, into Stirlingshire. This lady, though not equal to her mother in intellectual accomplishments, was nevertheless extremely amiable, possessing a compassionate temper and charitable disposition. When in her sixteenth year, she had from her own choice married Mr M–, then in the sixtieth year of his age: nor was this considered as a sacrifice, either by herself or others, for the Laird of P– had an estate which had been for many centuries in the family, a circumstance which was then considered as the chief object of glory; and such is the power of general sentiment, that there were probably few young ladies in Scotland who could then have dared to be so singular, or so romantic, as to have condemned her choice. That family pride which my aunt had hitherto considered as a generous and dignified sentiment, and which she had from her cradle been taught to cherish as a virtue, she now saw in a very different light, for she had now an opportunity of contemplating its effects, in giving self-importance to vulgarity and ignorance.

As the necessity of taking the oaths to government shut the door of all the liberal professions against the zealous adherents of the house of Stewart, the younger sons of old Jacobite families were often destined to employments that little corresponded with the high pretensions of their birth. All, however, considered themselves as still superior to the common race of mortals. Weavers, shoe-makers, tailors, all were cousins of the lairds; and, as such, presumed not a little on the high idea of their own importance. The letters written by my aunt to my father, about this period, show how deeply she was affected by the mortifications to which she was now exposed; – mortifications which only ceased to wound when she had obtained that perfect resignation to the divine will, which enabled her to read the dispensations of Infinite Goodness and Wisdom in all the events of her life. When the pride of the heart has been expelled by true Christian humility, half the evils of life are annihilated; – a truth, of which my good aunt was an eminent example.

It was not, however, without a severe struggle, that she obtained this conquest over herself, and over all the prejudices of her education. Not till these were entirely subdued, could she bring herself to listen to the addresses of a man, born as Mr Marshall was, in a very inferior station. Time, however, as it displayed the extraordinary virtues of this best of men, reconciled her by degrees to the thoughts of an alliance, which though little gratifying to her pride, would, as she believed, secure her peace. Nor was she disappointed in this expectation: nor in the two-and-thirty years that she afterwards lived with him did her heart ever experience even a momentary pang of vexation, sorrow, or regret. To Mr Marshall might well be applied what the poet Burns has said of an Ayrshire friend, that 'he held his patent of nobility direct from Almighty God.'[4] But, though the son of a peasant, he had received the advantage of an education superior to his birth; and as the seed that was thus sown fell into a grateful soil, the sentiments it inspired would have done honour to the most exalted station. Whatever repugnance my father might have felt at the idea of such a connection, he had too sound an understanding to take offence at his sister for consulting her own happiness. He had himself experienced the benefit of an early acquaintance with adversity; and though the vigour of his mind enabled him to assert the spirit of independence, he made every allowance for the different circumstances under which his sister was placed, and generously offered to her and her husband all the assistance in his power, towards placing them in a situation equal to their wishes. Obliged, on my grandfather's death, to relinquish the pursuits most agreeable to his taste, my father had, immediately on that event, quitted the University, and gone to London with an intention of seizing the first opportunity of entering business. Through the friendship of the elder Mr A–, this opportunity soon offered. He was taken into the mercantile house of Messrs A– and J–, with the prospect of soon having his name added to the firm, and had reason to encourage the sanguine hope of speedily attaining such a fortune, as would enable him once more to enjoy that place in society, which, from his manners and accomplishments, he seemed destined to adorn. Had the air of London agreed with his constitution, these prospects would soon have been realised; but, unfortunately, it proved so adverse to his health, as to render a continued residence there impossible. He, therefore, with a relation of Lord Macartney's, who was his particular friend, went over to Ireland, where, soon afterwards, he engaged in business.[5] When in Dublin, on his way to Belfast, he went to visit a lady whom he had had the pleasure of seeing in London, and whom he had ever spoken of with enthusiasm, as the most sensible, and best informed of her sex. On going to her house, and enquiring if Miss Mackay was at home, he was answered in the affirmative, and conducted to the drawing-room; where he saw, not the Miss Mackay he was in search of, but a sister many years younger, who to all the understanding of the lady whose intellectual endowments had appeared to him so extraordinary, added all the attractions of beauty, and all the charms of grace. His heart was instantly captivated; and as he was received by this lovely woman with the attention due to the friend of a sister, he entered into conversation with the ease of an old acquaintance, and soon discovered that the talents which nature had so liberally bestowed, had been as liberally cultivated by education. It may be easily imagined, that mutual esteem and admiration soon warmed into mutual love. The want of fortune seemed, for some time, to present an invincible obstacle to their union; but love brought hope, and confidence of future affluence, to support his cause, against the arguments of rigid prudence. They married; and if ever perfect happiness was enjoyed by married pair, that happiness was theirs.

Mutual esteem, and mutual respect, – a perfect congeniality of taste, and temper, and sentiment, and principle, – cemented the bond of mutual tenderness.

The mercantile speculations into which my father had entered wore such a promising aspect as to leave him no fears of being able to provide for his rising family, whose infant smiles repaid him for all the exertions he had made, and for all the anxieties he had ever suffered; and as his health had, from the time of his leaving London, been uninterrupted, no cloud threatened to obscure the future propspect. Alas! no warning cloud prepared my unhappy mother for the fate that awaited her.[6]

[*The end of the fragment*]

Elizabeth Hamilton wrote a number of affectionate letters to Joanna Baillie. She writes from George Street, Edinburgh, November 18, 1808, offering a comic discourse on fame, arising out of domestic observation:

I hope I may congratulate you on the happy effects of your performance on the sofa covers; but really think you ought to have sent for a notary public, and had a regular entry made in some national register at every patch. Who knows what fortune you might thus have secured to the future possesser! What would a stocking darned by the hands of Shakepeare now bring to the lucky owner? – and if the value of a thing be as much money as 'twill bring, how precious, a hundred years hence, will be all the articles on which you have bestowed your time and ingenuity! and yet, I dare say, not one word of this ever came into your simple head. See what a fine thing it is to have such a genius as mine to instruct you!

[…]

Your sincerely affectionate

ELIZA HAMILTON

Again in one of many letters to Joanna Baillie, 9 July, 1814, Elizabeth Hamilton writes of the natural advantages of Wales and the problems of the Scottish Inn-keepers.

I hope you stayed long enough at Capel Cerig to give you an opportunity of exploring the beauties of its glens; and that you have found at Caernarvon such accommodation as you like, or at least find tolerable. But if you have not there found what is agreeable, I should recommend it to you to remove without loss of time to Aber, near Conway, where there is a small country inn, part of which is fitted up for lodgings. The situation is beautiful and retired; and (as a lady who had spent the summer there told us) the lodgings very cheap, very quiet, and very comfortable. She provided her own breakfast, tea, and supper; but got her dinner from the inn, which saved her trouble, and cost a mere trifle. Had we not stopped at Hagley, we should have gone to Aber, on the faith of her description, and intended staying for a month. The same lady had tried Caernarvon, but could not there find accommodation out of the town, and the town she did not like; the recollection of which circumstance has induced me to give you this detail.

I am not afraid of Wales falling short of your expectation; and if the weather is favourable, am sure its scenery will not disappoint you: but I fear this summer will not be so propitious to rural enjoyment as the last. It is here cold and gloomy. After more than two months of bitter east-wind, and continuous drought, we have now got cold rains: but the rain has come too late to save the green crops, which in this neighbourhood are completely destroyed, as is also the small fruit, to the utter ruin of the poor people, who depend on their great strawberry gardens for support. I am told, that some who pay hundreds of rent will not sell ten pints of berries this season. The poor inn-keepers in Scotland are likely to be equal sufferers, though not entirely from the weather, but from the ill-wind (to them) that blows everyone to France. The genius of the Lakes now sits solitary on the deserted Trossachs; nor do Ben Lomond's echoes return the sound of an English voice.

The Journal entry for her last Birthday, July 25 1815, Bridge of Earn:
Again permitted to see a return of the day of my birth, let me offer to the Most High the sacrifice of praise and thanksgiving, and renew the vows I have so often made – of devoting the remainder of my life to his service. Bless the Lord, O my soul, and forget not any of the mighty benefits which he has through life bestowed on thee. But how shall I number up blessings that are innumerable, – mercies that are beyond my comprehension great! From the first hour of my existence, how wonderfully have I been preserved! how mercifully provided for in things spiritual and temporal! In all events that have befallen me, from infancy to the present day, I perceive the wisdom and goodness of an over-ruling Providence, distributing sickness and health, joy and sorrow, as were to me most needful for correction or comfort; and in every instance alike salutary and beneficial. By the glorious light of the gospel, the path to life eternal was early displayed to my view: to walk in it had been the serious purpose of my life. But alas! how often have I been in danger of straying from it, turned aside by the passions and desires of my own corrupt heart! How often in such instances have I been recalled, as if by the voice of my Lord and Master, in gentle accents, warning of my danger! Though dark clouds have sometimes passed over me, never have they been permitted to obscure effectually

the sun of truth. In the darkest hour I have still been enabled to say, 'Lord, I believe; help thou mine unbelief.' Not by my own strength have I been preserved, nor by the exertion of my own intellect enlightened. It is by the grace of God that I have been saved from destruction; and to it alone that I look for aid in working out my salvation by faith and holiness of life. But in taking a view of the goodness and mercy that have conspicuously followed me through the whole course of my past life, I am inspired with confidence, and with the full assurance of hope, in regard to what remains. He of whose love I have experienced such convincing proofs, will not forsake me when my strength fails. On him, then, let me rest my cares; and, firmly confiding in his wisdom and goodness, let me follow wherever his providence may lead; praying that he may so rule and govern the events before me, that if I change my place of residence, the change may be propitious to my eternal interests, – enabling me better to discharge the duties of declining life, and more fully to devote to God the sabbath of my days. One year more, and the period of six tens of years will be completed. One ten years more is the date of human life: so near, so very near do I now approach to that awful and eternal change, to which the few years spent on earth are but the prelude. But glory be to him, who hath divested the grave of its terrors; and in and through whom I have the hope of everlasting life, the promise of eternal joy!

NOTES

1. The first crusade lasted from 1095 to 1099.
2. The National Covenant of 1638 was signed by thousands of Scottish Presbyterians who opposed Charles I's attempt to introduce the English Prayer Book: the subsequent struggles were known as the Bishops' Wars.
3. 'Father to the late Earl of Selkirk': note by Benger.
4. Loosely quoted from the complimentary description of the poem's subject at the head of the 'Elegy on Captain Matthew Henderson', 1793: 'A Gentleman Who Held the Patent for His Honours Immediately from Almighty God'. I am indebted to the celebrated and kind Burns scholar, Thomas Crawford, for this source.
5. Lord Macartney was the Governor of Cape Province where Lady Anne Lindsay Barnard's husband was Secretary (see p.65, n.11).
6. Elizabeth Hamilton's father died of typhus fever in 1759.

Joanna Baillie (1762–1851)

Joanna Baillie, dramatist and poet, was one of the three children of Dorothea Hunter and James Baillie, minister of Bothwell, Lanarkshire and later Professor of Divinity at the University of Glasgow. She had been a twin but the other baby did not live. She and her elder sister Agnes were educated at a boarding school in Glasgow: her experiences there form part of her 'Recollections' below. Her mother's brothers were the celebrated surgeons, anatomists and collectors, William and John Hunter. William Hunter's collection now forms the Hunterian Museum of the University of Glasgow and John's collections are housed in the Royal College of Surgeons in London. In 1783 Matthew, who had been educated at Glasgow and Balliol College under the tutelage of his uncle, William, inherited William's School of Anatomy in Great Windmill Street in London. His mother and sisters who had been living on William's estate at Long Calderwood since the death of James Baillie in 1778, moved to London to keep house for Matthew. When Matthew married in 1791 the three women moved out, living in various locations near London, including Colchester, and eventually settling in Hampstead. After Dorothea's death in 1806 Joanna and Agnes continued to live in Hampstead for the rest of their lives.

In London Joanna and her sister moved in the literary and intellectual circles that surrounded Matthew and his uncle. John Hunter's wife, Anne (1742–1821), wrote and published poetry – 'My mother bids me bind my hair' is perhaps her best known piece – and was close to Joanna throughout her life. And it is perhaps not very surprising that in spite of her retiring nature Joanna Baillie became a writer.

Joanna Baillie became without question the pre-eminent female dramatist of her day, and although her plays had very limited stage success, it was significantly greater than that enjoyed by any of the now more celebrated male romantic poets. She began, however, with poetry: in 1790 she published a volume, first identified by Roger Lonsdale as *Poems; Wherein It Is Attempted to Describe Certain Views of Nature and of Rustic Manners*, which attracted little notice, although it is now generally felt to contain prototype lyrical ballads. The first volume of her *Series of Plays: In Which It Is Attempted to Delineate the Stronger Passions of the Mind* appeared in the crucial year 1798, the year of the *Lyrical Ballads* by Wordsworth and Coleridge: it contained a comedy and a tragedy on love and a tragedy on hatred. Two subsequent volumes were published as well as a number of other plays, one of which, *The Family Legend*, enjoyed some success in Edinburgh and was the only one of Baillie's plays to be published *after* performance.[1] Joanna Baillie collected her early verses and some later productions as *Fugitive Verses* in 1840.

De Monfort, which was performed in 1800, remains the most celebrated of her plays and Wordsworth echoes a speech from it in 'There was a Boy'. Baillie initially published anonymously but after *De Monfort*'s success she acknowledged her authorship. Joanna Baillie was a close friend of Mrs Barbauld and had a wide literary and intellectual acquaintance but her most important friendship was with Walter Scott: they visited each other and corresponded throughout Scott's life. Germaine Greer believes that Scott could not have meant his praise of Baillie as the best dramatist since Shakespeare (Germaine Greer, *Slip-shod Sybils*, 1995) but there is no reason whatsoever to doubt his sincerity. Joanna Baillie theorised her dramatic writing in the Preface to her *Series of Plays*. Francis Jeffrey in a number of articles in *The Edinburgh Review* from 1803 criticises her structuring of her plays round a dominant passion as unlikely to produce great drama but it is a mistake to imagine that Jeffrey did not treat her work seriously, and although Joanna Baillie herself felt sufficiently put out to refuse to meet Jeffrey in Edinburgh, the two became friends at a later stage.[2] Joanna Baillie had a long publishing life, seeing the first edition of her collected works through the press before she died in 1851 aged 88. Her elder sister Agnes lived for ten more years, dying in 1861 at the age of 100.

Joanna Baillie, *Poems; Wherein It Is Attempted to Describe Certain Views of Nature and of Rustic Manners* (London: Joseph Johnson, 1790); *A Series of Plays: In Which It Is Attempted to Delineate the Stronger Passions of the Mind, Each Passion Being the Subject of a Tragedy and a Comedy*, 3 vols (London: T. Cadell & W. Davies, 1798-1812); 'Epilogue to the theatrical representation at Strawberry-Hill, written by Joanna Baillie, spoken by the Hon. Anne S. Damer', November 1800, London, 1804; *Miscellaneous Plays* (London: Longman & Co., 1804); *De Monfort: A Tragedy* (London: Longman, Hurst, Rees and Orm, 1807); *The Family Legend: A Tragedy* (London: J. Ballantyne & Co., 1810); *Metrical Legends of Exalted Characters* (London: Longman & Co., 1821); *The Martyr: A Drama in Three Acts* (London: Longman & Co., 1821); ed., *A Collection of Poems Chiefly Manuscript and from Living Authors*, Longman & Co., 1823; *The Bride: A Drama in Three Acts* (London: Henry Colburn, 1828); *Fugitive Verses*, London: Edward Moxon, 1840); *Ahalya Baee: A Poem* (London: Spottiswoode & Shaw, 1849); *The Dramatical and Poetical Works of Joanna Baillie* (London: Longman, Brown, Green and Longmans, 1851)

The Collected Letters of Joanna Baillie, ed. Judith Bailey Slagle, vol.1 – (University of Delaware Press, 1999)
Joanna Baillie : A Selection of Poems and Plays, ed. Keith Hanley and Amanda Gilroy (Brookfield, Vt.: Pickering & Chatto, 1999)

Further Reading

Catherine Burroughs, *Closet Stages: Joanna Baillie and the Theater Theory of British Romantic Women Writers* (Philadelphia: University of Pennsylvania Press, 1997)
Margaret S. Carhart, *The Life and Work of Joanna Baillie* (New Haven, 1923)
Germain Greer, *Slipshod Sybils* (London: Viking, 1995)
Coral Ann Howells, *Joanna Baillie and her circle, 1790-1850: An Introduction*. (London: Camden History Society, 1973)
Dorothy McMillan, 'Dr Baillie', in Richard Cronin, ed., *1798: The Year of The 'Lyrical Ballads'* (Basingstoke: Macmillan, 1998)
Marjean D. Purinton, *Romantic Ideology Unmasked: The Mentally Constructed Tyrannies in Dramas of William Wordsworth, Lord Byron, Percy Shelley, and Joanna Baillie* (Newark; London: University of Delaware Press, 1994)
Daniel P. Watkins, *A Materialist Critique of English Romantic Drama* (Gainesville,

Florida: University of Florida Press, 1993)
Duncan Wu, ed., *A Companion to Romanticism* (Oxford: Blackwell, 1998)

DNB; *DLB* 93; *HSWW* ; Lonsdale; Todd 2

From the Hunter-Baillie Papers in the Royal College of Surgeons, HB II [59 (55)] 56C. I have generally reproduced spelling and punctuation, etc., of the original Manuscript, except where there are obvious changes of mind or crossings out, which I have not reproduced. The retention of a few obviously wrong spellings may seem pedantic but I do it mainly because of Joanna Baillie's insistence that she is a bad speller: in these mistakes we may a little see the woman. My intention is to retain something of the informality of these memoirs.

Recollections written at the request of Miss Berry[3]
Recollections of Joanna Baillie's daily life by herself 1831

The farthest back thing I can remember is sitting with my sister on the steps of the stair in Bothwell manse, repeating after her as loud as I could roar the letters of the Alphabet while she held in her hand a paper on which was marked in large letters the ABC. I was then about three years old and this was, I suppose, the very beginning of my education. Of the other lessons which followed I have no recollection, and that they were not very successful may be inferred from my not being able to read except in a very imperfect manner at the age of eight or nine. My Mother took pains to teach me and I was sent to a day school at Hamilton where my father was then settled as Clergyman, but even the sight of a book was hateful to me and all this teaching produced little effect. As I was an active stirring child, quick in apprehending or learning anything else, My Parents were the more provoked at my uncommon dulness in learning this most useful of all acquirements. However I ought not to say <u>provoked</u> for they had more patience with me than I deserved. About the beginning of my tenth year (as far as I can remember) they informed me that I was to be sent to a Boarding School in Glasgow, and then I began to consider that it would be a shameful thing for me to be amongst strangers – <u>Young Ladies</u>, without being able to read decently. The detail of any extraordinary pains taken with this prospect in view, I have entirely forgotten, but when I did at length find myself settled in this formidable place amongst the Young Ladies, I was as good a reader as any of them. Indeed several months before I went to Glasgow and I was then just eleven years old, I must have read with some facility; and a little taste for reading was begun in me by my sister to whose kind anxiety in this respect, being herself a natural lover of books, I owe much. Having in some of my out-of-door gambols cut my ancle with bottle glass so severely that I was obliged to lie upon a sofa the whole day for a week on end, she came to me with Ocean's poems in her hand and coaxed me in a very persuasive soothing manner to open the book and read some of the stories to myself: I did so and was delighted with them (as far as I can recollect) the first book which I read willingly and with pleasure.[4]

When the craft of reading was acquired so tardily that of writing could scarcely expect to fare better, and as to spelling I have always been very deficient. If I merely read a name or word, though I may do it many times, when I have occasion to write the same, I don't know how to spell it, and I think I have told you that many a time in writing letters, I have used not such words as I wished and as best expressed my meaning but such as I know how to spell. This defect has made me all my life an uneasy writter[*sic and smudged*] of letters. In short had there been no such arts as reading and writing in the world, I should rather have passed for a clever person, showing more than a common talent for music, some little turn for drawing and above all for needlework, so that I was early consulted and employed as a <u>Contriver</u> of patterns for dresden-work⁵ and embroidery by my companions and also by more experienced workwomen. Perhaps I may also say as a contriver of tales, for having no store from books, when the Girls about me (as they frequently did) told tales round, I was obliged when it came to my turn to invent one upon the spot, and the pleasure they expressed in hearing my tales even after they discovered them to be inventions was a gratification to me.

A great defect and I suppose a natural defect in me has been a want of the power of close attention, so that my memory, bad as it was, had not fair play given to it, and therefore gained but a very superficial knowledge of the books which I read. A story or a book of argument I could follow, but history and moral writings made little impression, and I have often been very melancholy and ready to weep when any very flagrant proof of this defect has been forced upon my notice. – With such defects how I ever came to think of writing either verse or prose is curious. I fear that it first arose from nothing better than a little whimsical, presumptuous self conceit, fostered by a few concurring circumstances. My father had a man servant who was very vain and particular about his dress though at the same time very uncouth and lubberly and laughed at by every body who came about the house. My first verses were composed in ridicule of him and sung by myself and others to a ballad tune to his great mortification and annoyance. In his distress he came privately to me, beseeching me not to sing it, and promising in return to give me a ride behind him every time he took my Father's horse to be watered. I consented: he kept his promise; and this was the first reward I received for what might be termed literary labours. But he had no occasion to take this method of checking my impertinence; for when my Mother knew of it she forbade everything of the kind peremptorily. I might then be about 7 or 8 years old. After that I remember, when my Brother came one day from the Grammar School, somewhat disturbed by the Master's having enjoined him and some of the boys of his class to compose a few couplets on the seasons, – My Father saying to him, 'tut man! Jack (the name I then went by) could do that.' I was set to it forthwith and composed a few common-place lines upon the subject, the copy of which has happily been long since lost. As my Father and Brother were incapable of his schoolmaster['s task]⁶ this precious composition served no other purpose than to make me vain. However my Mother very sensibly knocked that on the head, by saying to me when I had completed my tenth year, 'Remember you are no longer a child and must give up making verses. People would only laugh at you now were you to pretend to do it, though they might commend it and be amused by it from a child.' I followed her advice and thought no more at that time and long after, of writing verses. —

During the heedless period of my teens a few things of no value were written by me and carefully concealed. But during those years, though I had never seen above three or four Plays a love for the Drama took hold of me, and I began to borrow Playbooks and to read them with great avidity, though I must confess that the pictures of Mrs Yates and Mrs Cibber with their wide hoops and high feathered heads, at the beginning of each piece, had more than their due share of admiration.[7] This was during the early part of my teens. The only Dramatic books which my father's library afforded – a copy of Shakespeare with no pictures in – it was sadly overlooked and neglected. Many years after that when my Mother came with my Sister and myself to live with my Brother in London in seeing our incomparable Mrs Siddons and other good actors in theatres not too large for natural expression and effect,[8] my love for the Drama was greatly increased, and one day, seeing a quantity of white paper lying on the floor which from a circumstance needless to mention had been left there and which I knew would be entirely thrown away, it came into my head that one might write something upon it, and then followed a thought, natural enough, that the <u>something</u> might be a play. The play was written or rather composed while my fingers were employed in sprigging muslin for an apron and afterwards transferred to the paper, and though my Brother did <u>not</u> [*arrowed in above the line*] much like such a bent given to my mind, he bestowed upon it so much hearty and manly praise, that my favorite propensity was fixed for ever. I was just two and twenty when we first came to London and this took place I believe the following summer about 9 months afterwards.

When I might be (as well as I can remember) about seven and twenty, my mind for a time became very differently occupied, arising from a casual circumstance but leading to no material result, and only deserving to be mentioned as a curious fact combined with those which I have already detailed. I heard a friend of ours, a Mathematician, talking one day about squaring the Circle as a discovery which had often been attempted but never found out, and naturally supposing that it must be the discovering a Circle and a Square, exactly the same size, I very simply set my wits to work to find it out. 'What composes a circle?' I said to myself. – 'As many imaginary lines as can lie between a point – the centre of the circle, and its circumference, each line being equally distant in all its parts from the Centre, – this must make a Circle; and if one were to cut those lines across from the Centre to the circumference and lay them horizontally, they would form a triangle, having for its base the whole of the circumference and for its altitude the half of the diameter of the circle.' I knew not if this way of proving it would be according to rule, but of the fact I was certain. I had then no difficulty in converting this triangle into an oblong square – for the word <u>parallelogram</u> was yet unknown to me, but I could by no means turn that long square into a direct square which I supposed must be required to make the discovery complete. 'But surely' thought I 'it will be found in Euclid,' so I borrowed from my friend Miss Fordyce, now Lady Bentham, an old copy of Euclid. It would have amused a learned person not a little had he been present when I borrowed the book. After telling her for what purpose I borrowed it and producing my paper with the figures, he would have seen her put my discovery to the simplest of all proofs, had it been a practicable one, while I stood breathless with the fear of its failure. She cut out from the paper my oblong square with her scissors and mincing it into very small pieces covered the circle with them as well as she could and then looking in my face very gravely said, 'indeed I believe you are right.' From various circumstances, very imperfectly remembered by me, a considerable time elapsed before I began my search into Euclid, but I went through it by myself as well as I could, though in no very plodding way, being only intent on this one purpose. My general time for study (we were then inhabitants of a Country Town) was after I was dressed for an evening party till the time of going to it arrived. I thus went through all the books in my own way, having great pleasure when I could work out a problem that at first had appeared difficult, and passing over those which after a reasonable endeavour I could not understand. What I was in search of – how to turn a long into a direct square, I soon found, but the pleasure I took in the study, carried on in this slight superficial way, tempted me, as I have said, to go through the whole. But my disappointment and mortification may easily be guessed, when on arriving at the Apendix [*sic*] to the book, in a small collection of particular discoveries by Archimedes and Matthew[?] Tackenet[?] (I think that was the name) I found my own discovery, though proved in a different manner.[9] 'So I have mistaken what was meant by squaring the circle' said I very bitterly to myself, and thus ended my mathematical pursuits. I had by this time written Basil and De Monfort and very soon consoled myself for such a Wildgoose Chace. In that part of the science which regards the properties of space I had some pleasure as far as I could understand it for that which regards numbers I had none and never could take in any degree to arithmetic, though I always kept my own accounts and those of the family very regularly. Indeed excepting a few simple lessons from my Brother when we were both very young I never had any instruction. Many long years afterwards when I saw my Niece – a mere child multiplying on her slate by so many figures deep I felt ashamed of my own ignorance and thinking that I would not be too proud but even submit to the tuition of a child, I asked little Lizzy to set me a sum. She did so but I could not comprehend the rule and method which seemed so easy to her; so I gave up while she looked up with an innocent amazement in my face and called out 'O Aunty!' —

What little taste I acquired for classical reading (and it was but little) came to me of its own accord as circumstances offered themselves. When I was fifteen, having heard a great deal about Milton I thought I must read Paradise Lost, but after going through the first books, I could not proceed; it was beyond the level of my mind at that time. But when I was about 3 years older I fortunately met with Comus, and read it with so much delight that I took courage and began again to try Paradise; then indeed I did perceive the grandeur, sublimity and beauty of the Poem, and read through it with great admiration and interest, though the many learned allusions of the theology did often make it heavy, and I could not help wishing that the great Poet had been a less learned man. Could I have retained anything of what most delighted me in poetry so as to have repeated it to myself and others, I should have been induced to read more and to have read fine passages repeatedly, so as to have become acquainted with them; but I could not; nothing remained with me but a general impression of having been pleased or delighted and this has always proved a great discouragement to me. When at boarding school after having been all the Sunday evening employed in getting two or three verses of a psalm by heart, and diligent in my endeavours, I never could say them on Monday morning (the time for examination) with any degree of correctness. This defect has continued with me through life: the many verses and songs etc. which I have written myself I cannot repeat, though there are some of them I should be very well pleased to retain – I once set about trying to overcome this when I was still very young and wrote an abridgment from memory of my daily readings in Rollin's history of Alexander's successors,[10] a tangled web which I was then engaged in, and after that an abridgment of the life of Mahomet, as prefixed to Sale's Koran,[11] but the occupation was irksome to me and had not all the effect I had hoped from it. That of Alexander's Successors was taken up from an accident, being the work I was reading when the idea came into my head, that of Mahomet from taking a particular interest in the subject – Traits of human nature whether in Books or in real life have always had most power in arresting my attention and keeping place in my recollection. This has often made me a watcher of children at play or under any excitement, and a frequenter in early life of the habitations of labouring and country people which happily for me I had many opportunities of doing. I might forget the dialogue in which it was displayed and could not therefore make a truthful anecdote of it, but the trait itself remained perhaps for ever. – Ghost stories had a good deal to do in arousing my imagination, which my Sister and I delighted in and received from servants, from some of our young companions and above all from the Sexton of Hamilton parish, who came often to the house upon parish business and was an old man who was very kind to us and with whom we were very familiar; for we were not kept up in a schoolroom or nursery as the decorum of the present time requires. We paid dearly, however, for this fearful delight; for we could not be left in the dark alone without dread, nor even go upstairs alone in the twilight; and there was a garret room in the house, where tradition said a man once hung himself, which we durst not enter alone even at mid-day. My Father and Mother were never aware of the state of our minds in this respect, for we durst not acknowledge it lest we be obliged to be alone in the dark to get the better of our timidity.

From the Hunterian Society Deposit, MS. 5613/68 in the Wellcome Institute for the History of Medicine Library:

Memoirs written to please my Nephew, William Baillie.[12]

My first faint recollections are of Bothwell where I was born and passed the first four years of my life. They are chiefly out of door recollections – running in the garden and looking at the flowers and seeing pigeons flying in the air or gathered on the round roof of a pigeon house that belonged to the Manse and above all an occasional walk to the Clyde with my sister, when our nursemaid put us both into the waters to be drouket [soaked] and dance and splash about as we pleased. It is curious enough that remembering these little circumstances pretty vividly, almost every thing that passed within doors are almost entirely lost: and that the important change of going to a new residence – Hamilton is in my mind a blanc [sic] altogether. My being sent to the reading-school I dont remember, but well do I remember sitting there on a weary bench day after day looking on letters and stories which I did not understand and had no desire to know – the worst or one of the worst scholars in the school. My only bright time was when playing out of doors with other children – playing at make-believe grown people or Gentlemen and Ladies, generally in some open cart or waggon that served us for a house. It is such a common pastime with children that it would scarcely be worth while to mention it only that I was so particularly fond of it and my sister who could read and amused herself with books never entered into it at all. But there was one occupation which we both joined in with equal avidity – listening to Ghost Stories told us by the sexton of [the] parish who frequently came to the house of a Winter evening and sat by the Kitchen fire. We always, I don't know how, contrived to escape from the parlor when we heard that <u>John Leiper</u>, so he was called, was in the house. His stories excited us much, and as the house we lived in was said to be haunted by the ghost of a man who had in former years hanged himself in the Garret, we became so frightened that we durst not go up stairs alone even in broad day light. There was a very small Farmer, little above the degree of a labourer, who lived in a cottage very near us, and in his house my mind got some little insight into human natures homily [*sic*] habits, for his wife was a shrewd eccentric woman and his only daughter was my play-fellow, and my Mother frequently allowed me on a Winterday to go there for an hour or two. There I was, by a make-believe compact, the engaged servant of the good Wife, who was sometimes good natured enough to let me sweep the earthern floor with a little besom or help to teaze the wool that was in preparation for her web of winter clothing. When a jobbing Taylor who with his apprentice came occasionally to the house to make the family garments, then it was a delightful thing; for he knew all the stories of the Parish and told them with an off-hand humour that never failed to produce laughter and amusement. – When visitors from a distance came to my Fathers house and asked, as was frequently the case, that my sister & I might be allowed to accompany them to see the pictures in the Palace and afterwards to see the two famous flower gardens in the neighbourhood of the Town, it was also a delightful thing. We did not learn to be conoiseurs [*sic*] by looking at the pictures, but it opened to our imagination the appearances of great and remarkable people of other days; and in the gardens of Chatlerault & Barn Clugh wandering among a blazing profusion of beautiful flowers in fanciful well-trimd [well-trimmed] parters [*parterres*] and the gay regions of fairy-land opened before us.[13] These visits with a gay excursion at times into what remained of the old Forest, called the wood, did my fanciful untaught mind much good. By the Burn & wilder places in the immediate environs of the Town, near our own doors, we rambled much, but into the town itself I never liked to go except in a Fair-day when the streets were crowded with country people & Lords & Ladies, dressed in their holiday gear, were mingled in the crowd & seen looking out of ale house windows, where the sound of fiddles and dancing gave notice of the merry-making within, to say nothing of the booths with all their tempting treasure and the people & children looking wistfully at them or haggling with the Chapman for a bargain. Yet the fair itself was almost eclipsed by the amusement received by standing at the entry of our house to see the Fair-folk, as we called them, returning home in the evening, jesting & laughing & roaring & glorious as Tam o' Shanter.[14] Every different humour was then to be traced among the motley groups of grave Farmers, whose wool or cheeses or cow had gone off, or had <u>not</u> gone off to their satisfaction. The gay Damsels somewhat tired of foot with gallant sweethearts to escort them, and Damsels younger still perhaps with only a Father or sour-faced Aunty by her side. In short all sorts of people, young and old and every face & gait telling its own tale to our whimsical guessing. – After being a dunce for so many years, how I came to read at last, I dont remember, but I well remember being ashamed of not being able to read, and that, I believe, in a short time effected the business. Still, however, although I could read I had no pleasure in books, when fortunately for me I cut my ancle so much one day by stumbling among broken bottles that I was obliged to be <u>doctored</u> for it, and to keep upon the sofa for some weeks. Then Agnes, like a kind sister came to me with books in her hand and coaxed me to try if reading some story or other would amuse me and make the time less weary. At last reluctantly I took the book she recommended, and then as I proceeded began to like it, and in this way Oceans Poems became the first book I ever read of my own good will without being obliged to do it.

This was a considerable step in my intellectual education. I then read of my own accord various poetical works and afterwards prose, though I had not pleasure enough in the occupation to sit at it long at a time. What first induced me to read history was the pleasure of reading by my Brother, sitting at his side and doing as he did, my love for him was beyond all the affection I felt for anybody else. I got up early of a summer morning and when he took his book I took mine though he never desired me to do so, and went through many volumes of Rolins history perseveringly and with a degree of attention that enabled me to retain the leading facts in my mind for many years.

When the summer was ended, he went to College and I was put to a boarding school at Glasgow. This great change of scene and mingling with so many new companions, quickened my mind and opened my ideas and notions in many respects, both salutary to it and otherwise; but there would be little use in entering on the subject with any detail which can easily be imagined. Two things above the rest made deep impresion and had an effect that did not soon pass away. One evening, before bed time, we were, some six or seven of us, put into a dark room together for what reason I don't know, to say our prayers. Accordingly we each kneeled by a chair and said our prayers; but as we rose from our knees to grope our way out of the room, unfortunately one of the girls discovered a bason or Cannister of sugar which had been recently broken for household store, and this was a temptation that notwithstanding our recently finished devotions, could not be resisted. She took some and told the others who readily followed her example and as I was going out at the door one of them brought the cannister to me and desired me to take some 'We have all taken some' I felt it wrong but yielded to the temptation and took two small bits of sugar, with which I went to my bedroom. But when we were undressing the Lady of the House came in great anger into the door of our bedroom showing us the empty cannister, and accusing us of having taken the sugar. We all denied the charge with one voice and it grieves me still to think that my own voice was mixed in the sound. Our Mistress could not discover where the guilt lay, so she very properly decreed that all the girls who were in that dark room should drink their tea without sugar for a week. A sentence we very well deserved, and fully made amends for all the sugar that was stolen. I had committed a theft and lied to conceal it, but though much mortified, I did not feel it strongly till a day or two after, when my especial friend Lilias Graham who had had nothing to do with it, and was incapable of doing anything so bad, told me that Miss Macdonald (our Mistress's name) said to her, she did not know who had taken sugar but she was sure little Baillie had taken none, for she could perfectly believe what she said and could not believe any of the others. The misery of that moment is not to be expressed; and I was bent immediately to go and confess my guilt to Miss M. that she might no longer think so highly of me when I deserved it so little. I was restrained by the strong arm of my friend from executing my purpose forthwith, saying at the same time 'if you accuse yourself she will immediately question you as to who did take the sugar and you will be obliged to betray your companions'. Immediately I felt that our Mistress would not respect my feelings upon this point, and kept the tormenting secret in my own breast, where it gnawed me in secret for a long time. This opened my thoughts to the working of a strong passion, and traces of it will be found in the character of Edward in the tragedy of <u>Ethwald</u>, who could not bear, after his first battle from which he had fled, to have the honour of pre-eminent valour imputed to him, though he was truly the cause of the victory. – The other circumstance was of a very different nature and had nothing but pleasure connected with it namely going to see a play for the first time. I had seen nothing of the kind before but a puppet show in a poor little out-house when I was a mere child. But now I beheld a lighted up Theatre with fine painted scenes and gay dressed Gentlemen & Ladies acting a story on the stage, like busy agitated people in their own dwellings and my attention was riveted with delight. It very naturally touched upon my old passion for make-believe, and took possession of me entirely. The play was a singing Sentimental Comedy not very interesting in itself but the after-piece was one of Foote's Farces in which Lady Pentwheezle, a City Lady from Blowbladder Street, makes a very conspicuous figure, particularly in the scene where she sits for her picture, and I with my young companions went home with our heads full of it; each repeating all the scraps from it she could possibly remember.[15] But we were not satisfied with repeating, we must needs act it also and Miss M. good-naturedly indulged us some days after, when she invited a few friends to tea and to see the show. Dresses were prepared as well as our scanty means would allow and each character as she entered was received with a merry cheer by the Spectators, but when I made my appearance as Lady Pentweezle there rose a roar of laughter among them that shook the whole house. I was dressed in a wide hoop and paper lappets and ruffles of my own cutting out, and my efforts, such as they were, through the whole scene met with unbounded success. After all this, it may be easily imagined that plays and play acting did not go out of my head or fancy for many a day. Many drole whimsical anecdotes of my school life might be added, but as I am not conscious that they had any influence on my mind, connected with the writings of this after life, it would be useless to mention them here. I believe some of them will be found in a little memoir in the possession of Miss Berry who has promised in case she should die before your Mother, as in the course of nature may be expected, to leave it at her disposal.–

When my Father a few years after my leaving school, was elected to the Divinity

Chair in Glasgow and the family settled there in one of the College Houses, I was in a common way awake to all the changes, domestic and otherwise that took place, of course, but I can remember only one circumstance that fairly belongs to my present purpose. A Gentleman of the Town in whose house my friend and Playmate Miss Graham frequently stayed, had a very fine Library and among his choice books Bell's Theatre with engravings of all the Actors and Actresses in their stage-dresses, at the beginning of each Play.[16] She, knowing how much we delighted in plays, kindly procured for us a loan of this work, one volume at a time, with the new binding carefully covered with paper; and there was no errand I went with such good will as to return one of these books and receive a new one in its stead. I was interested in the story of every piece, Tragedy or Comedy, and both laughed & cried with some degree of rationality. I could indeed detect great departures from nature in many of the speeches, but the high-sounding grandeur of them made some amends; and if the frontispiece represented an actress dressed to my taste, as was often the case, the image went with me through the whole course of the play and covered all defects with a kind of bewitchment or glamourie. In my Father's library stood 8 vols of Shakespeare undisturbed, for it was a mean-looking book, and had no pictures in it; and as it belonged to the house and I could have it at any time, it was naturally held in less estimation.

I have no recollection of when I began to read or have any vivid feelings of the genius of Shakepeare. The Ghost of Hamlet I believe first broke me in to a proper feeling of his power & his knowledge of human nature, but that was several years afterwards when my sister & I lived entirely in the Country at Longcalderwood with my Mother, then become a Widow. But I have neglected to say that in the course of this play-reading from Bell's Theatre, I had been taken to see one or two plays at the Glasgow Theatre and that did not fail to encrease my passion for the art. – When we lived at Long Calderwood we were fortunate in having Professor Millar & his family for our near Neighbours during the summer.[17] He was very fond of theatrical amusements, and when Mrs Siddons in the beginning of her glory, came to Glasgow, he left the country with Mrs Millar and all her children who were old enough to enjoy it, and lived in his College residence all the time she acted there, having a box secured for them every night. How I longed to have been of their party need not be said. It was an exceeding & strong desire, but it could not be gratified; and when they returned again to the Country full of admiration of her wonderful powers I was never tired of listening to their descriptions of her: my imagination followed her with delight. I don't know how long it was after this that in the dining room at Long Calderwood with Miss Graham & Anne Millar, then staying in the house, I attempted to act that scene in Measure for Measure where Isabella pleads with Angelo for the life of her Brother. It had been a favourite scene with me before, and I set myself to follow nature through it as closely as I could. Lilly G. was Angelo, dressed most absurdly & I not less so in an old black gown of my Mother's. Our two maid servants were summoned from the kitchen and they with my Mother & Sister made the audience. First when we began, they all laughed without restraint at our strange appearance, but, as I proceeded in my part, they became grave and ended by shedding tears, and this was a great triumph for me. Every one praised me but my Mother who, very wisely did not like to give me any kind of encouragement. At another time too I acted Hamlet in the Ghost scene with great commendation. But all this passed away and other occupations & fancies came in its place, more suitable to quiet country Gentlewomen. – I have mentioned Bell's Theatre and Shakespeare, but nothing in a dramatic form ever charmed me so much as Milton's Comus which I read (I forget exactly when) a year or two before we left Scotland. I had attempted to read Paradise Lost some years before, but tired of it and gave it up. Now, however, being encouraged by Comus, I again took up Paradise Lost and felt its sublimity & beauty. The great transition from a very retired country home in Scotland to a dark narrow street in London did not do much to awaken my imagination, but my curiosity was busy, and to see all the places I had read of & seen in Pictures and shows etc kept up my spirits though almost everything I saw disappointed me. I had pictured to myself a grandeur & magnificence which I did not find. We had at first few acquaintances; one of those with whom we were naturally most intimate had probably a considerable influence on my mind. This was my aunt in law Mrs John Hunter. She had written some beautiful songs which were then very popular among the cultivated circles of Society, and many pleasing & elegant poems, generally short, known in manuscript to her own more intimate friends which had deservedly gained for her the reputation of a woman of genius. As to lyrical compositions she at that time excelled any other writer. She was very kind to me, I was often with her and she used to read to me every new composition as it came from her pen. To write as she did was far beyond any attempt of mine, but it turned my thoughts to poetical composition. However, it was a very different cause that eventually brought me to the act of putting pen to paper on any serious subject akin to poetry. One dark morning of a dull winter day, standing on the hearth in Windmill Street and looking at the mean dirty houses on the opposite side of the street, the contrast of my situation from the winter scenes of my own country came powerfully to my mind; the Barn, the early sound of the flail, and all the occupations and scenes of a Winter day, among the Cottages in the neighbourhood of Long Calderwood, became present to me in a very vivid way, and with little further deliberation I forthwith set myself to write the 'Winter day' in blank verse. Thomson had written in blank verse,[18] but I must confess I would much rather have written in rhime; only rhimes with me in those days were not easily found and I had not industry enough to toil for them. Ballads in rhime followed afterwards, and when I found I could write them with some degree of ease, I began to be proud of myself and to believe that I possessed some genius. From the Museum library I had all the books I wished for, and took this opportunity of reading the Dramatic Works of the four great French Poets Corneille, Racine, Voltaire and Mollier and also read many of Beaumont & Fletcher's Plays with some of our Old English Dramatists.[19] However I did not find much in our old plays to interest me and whatever impression they might make on my mind soon passed away. You will find in a paper now in the possession of Miss Berry that a very homely sordid & whimsical circumstance was my first immediate inducement to write a play. However, as I proceeded in my work, following simply my own notions of real nature, I began to feel as if I had fallen into an occupation that suited me, all my former imaginary scenes & theatrical representation returned upon me and a Tragedy was finished at odd times as I could find leisure which had, I believe, some good passages in it, but only deserves to be mentioned as the first step in a path that has led to some degree of distinction. The plot is an American story entirely of my own invention or rather I should say the scene is laid in America. It has never been published and I hope never will; I have only preserved it as a curiosity. – Rayner, preceded by a first part in the form of a serious comedy I afterwards burnt, puting all that it contained essential to the story in a retrospective passage in the Tragedy.[20] When it was completed I became busy in preparing my miscellaneous verses for the press and afterwards set out to make a visit to my friends in Scotland where I stayed nearly a year, and there they being ignorant of my poetical pretentions, I almost forgot them myself. On my return to London My Brother was married to your Mother, an event which we have all our life long had cause to bless. We went to reside in the country, changing our place of abode two or three times till we settled at length in Colchester. Our previous home to that was dull enough where there was little or no society and dulness & leisure set me again to create a fanciful world of my own, and the idea of writing Dramas on the stronger passions of the heart, took possession of me strongly. Perhaps having read, not long before, Mercier's Plays, a copy of which Professor Millar had kindly brought me from Paris, had something to do with rousing my natural propensity, but I can scarcely venture to say so.[21] The good sense & feeling of his Pieces, free from the exaggerations that had often offended me in other Dramatic works, pleased me very much. I then with some envigorating hopes that it would not be in vain, began that arduous task which has been so much praised & censured during a long course of years. In writing Basil I took great pains with particular passages, composing them often several times over; and when passion was concerned and I could not find expressions that appeared to me truly to speak the feelings of the moment, I have rejected those that presented themselves a dozen of times before I found one to satisfy me; when the <u>one</u> was found, it generally struck me at once as the truth, though many of the rejected that went before it would have appeared to a common reader much finer writing. The comedy on a similar subject was a relaxation to me that had become almost necessary to my mind before I should deal with the sterner subject of hatred. De Monfort was written more rapidly and with more interruption from visitors & the gaeities of a Country Town, while at the time of the annual fair that lasted several weeks, frequent opportunities of seeing a very good company of actors in a small Theatre, brought scenery and stage effect more under my consideration. Hitherto, I had it may be said worked in the dark, no friendly critic to encourage me but my Brother, to whom when occasion allowed it I showed all that I wrote. I knew very well that he would readily detect anything that was false, foolish, bombastic or affected and when I saw the tears springing into his eyes on reading any passage that I had myself thought pathetic, I felt I must surely be right. His having no turn for poetry himself, made him a critic, I am well convinced not the less useful to me. But it would have been foolish to go on always in the dark, so at my request he sent the Tragedy of Basil to his friend Mr Alison, the celebrated writer on taste, who read it in manuscript, not knowing who was the author and not knowing that it was written on any intended plan for delineating a passion. The answer he received from him was full of the most generous praise of the Piece, and such high commendation from a man of his feeling & refined character, did really elevate me in my own estimation and gave me confidence & courage to proceed. I owed much to him from this well-timed cheering. Faint praise mixed with fastidious censure is what I would probably have received from by far the greatest proportion of the learned critics of that time. I now went on with spirit, and the probability of publishing successfully a volume of plays, different in character from any that had yet been offered to the public, seemed to be considerable, to be worth trying at least. Your mother at this time was let into our secret, and was not sparing in her praise & encouragement; but she was very young and her judgement was not to me of the great value I put upon it afterwards. When all this was going on, what might be called my bye play or amusement was reading Euclid to find out some problem by which a square might be turned into a parallelogram that when found would make a certain discovery of my own prove to be the famous squaring of the circle so often attempted in vain. I soon found what I wanted, but I found also, at the end of the book, that my squaring of the circle was an old discovery and not what learnedly goes by this name. My vanity received a check, and I dealt no more with Mathematics.—

The first volume of Plays lay for several months at the Booksellers, who had refused to publish them at his own risk and cared very little about its success, without being called for or noticed, notwithstanding a review of them full of the highest, most liberal praise, published in the first Review for reputation in those days, the writer of it being equally ignorant of the author with Mr Alison and with whom I had not the pleasure of being acquainted till many years afterwards.[22] But this review had no doubt considerable though not immediate effect.

As my name was entirely concealed, I sent no copies of the book to any of my own friends, but to some literary persons, who might perhaps if they liked it, mention it to others. None of those literary persons, as far as I knew, took any notice of it but Miss Berry, who saw much company at her house and spoke in the highest terms of it to everybody.[23] To her zeal in the cause I have always felt myself to be a debtor. Thus, after a time, it got into circulation, became a subject of conversation in the upper circles, and John Kemble through the medium of my book sellers, asked leave to bring out De Monfort at Drury Lane,[24] while a company of amateurs were preparing to act the Comedy at the Priory, the seat of Ld Abercorn.[25] The last mentioned circumstance was for some reason or other prevented and the former did not take place for more than a year after Kemble's proposal. It was perhaps fortunate for me that during this time of the works greatest popularity, I lived away from the Metropolis, and heard but a very few of its distant sounds; enough to encourage me without exciting any unreasonable vanity, the best thing for my mind that could possibly be. Thus envigorated, without being intoxicated, I began to write Ethwald in two parts, according to my plan, and I have always believed that my talents, whatever they are, were then at their best. So passed away the earlier & brightest part of my career, till the feeble success of de Monfort on the stage and the discovery of the hitherto concealed Dramatist being not a man of letters but a private Gentlewoman of no mark or likelihood, turned the tide of public favour, and the influential critics and Reviewers from all quarters North & South, attacked the intention of the work as delineating in each of the Dramas only one passion, and therefore quite unnatural and absurd.[26] That I had in my preface mentioned this as an error into which such a plan was like to lead the writer, and professed to have taken every pains to avoid it was a circumstance beneath their notice, and the writers of such criticisms by implication taught their readers to suppose that the second characters in Basil & de Monfort – Victoria   [27] Rosenberg, Jane de Monfort and Rezenvelt, for instance, were all dull unempassioned characters, unworthy of attention but for the share they take in the plot. I had also said in my preface that the master passion of the principle [*sic*] character could only be discovered by the opposition it met with from the passions of others which created a necessity for making the second characters spirited and marked. But all this was in vain, the inferences drawn from their <u>own</u> remarks was all that they deigned to lay before their Readers. Yet in the face of all this learned and methodical prosing, Ethwald was received with very considerable favour and the author was by many people reported to have produced a volume superior to the first.[28] My popularity now fallen to a very moderate level, remained stationary and just enough to enable me with some spirit to pursue my original design and to write occasional plays as I might feel inclined, unconstrained by any particular plan.

In the great & deserved sensation of admiration excited by the Poems of Walter Scott, a few years later, I had my share and the generous encouragement I always received from him was certainly of great use in keeping me to my work. The fascination of his heroic Ballads made the drama less interesting for a time and then an idea of Metrical Legends of exalted characters, in which there should be no mixture of fiction in the events & circumstances of their story, feeling & descriptions only being imaginary, came into my head. Hitherto all modern poems or romances having real heroic characters for their subjects, were woven with some fictitious love story, that drew away the feelings & attentions of the Young reader from the real dignity and excellence of the Personage. Though many of these were written with great beauty & delicacy, it appeared to me as injurious both to their virtuous & exalted views and to the moral purpose of their subjects. After considering this, as well as I could, I set to work in my own way, beginning with Collumbus [*sic*] whose story had been early impressed upon my mind by Herrera one of the old books in my Father's library. A better poet no doubt might have been able to compete with the fictitious love-portraits of such worthies, but I made but a faint impression on general readers and endeavoured to be contented with the sober approbation of a few, and that my endeavours have not been in vain, my having not long since in my old age composed a metrical legend of   [29] that admirable Indian Begum whose wonderful history is to be found in Sir J. Malcolm's book on Central India, is a pretty strong proof. – All that I have mentioned of circumstances that helped make my fancy more active may seem to you my dear William very small & common matters, scarcely deserving to be noticed, but as a person who had never seen the ocean might imagine the agitations and undulations of its waves in some degree by blowing from his lips on the surface of water in a bason, so may an imaginary mind from very small indications gather much knowledge of great and important facts. You know that I have been in Switzerland and have seen objects there which you would naturally expect me to notice but during the short time I was in that sublime region, my mind was occupied with anxious thoughts, and excepting the grand view from the Juras of Montblanc and all the grand alps, lakes and fertile shores etc and one other sight I carried nothing home with me to add to the indwelling treasures of my heart. That other thing was, as you perhaps remember, for you stood by my side and beheld it, the immense Hall of clouds which appeared as if prepared for the Gods seen as we ascended the lower part of Montblanc. We were upon a narrow shelf of ground a considerable way up the mountain looking over the mer de glass and the vale of Chamonix which was however veiled at the time by dim vapours, while the side of the mountains that surround it was concealed by a varied drapery of clouds. Some lofty peaks were dimly seen through their skirts but we seemed at that moment to have nothing to do with the earth. Vapour was the pavement of our hall and clouds of heaven the walls thereof. I mention this the more readily because of all our travellers in Switzerland whose works I have read, no notice is taken of such sublime appearance. No; I did not carry home with me what I might have done under different circumstances. The clouds seen in my youthful days floating across Benloman [Ben Lomond] & the Campseys [Campsies], as seen from the high lands of Long Calderwood, were my chief store of Mountain-Ideas and continued so through life.

NOTES

1. *The Family Legend* is a Highland story which has a potent mixture of love and honour, feuding and treachery. It was performed in the Theatre Royal, Edinburgh on 29 January 1810 and for 13 consecutive nights. By some at least it was rapturously received. Scott played a large part in the organisation of the production by Henry Siddons who managed the theatre; Siddons's wife took the main female part.

2. For Francis, Lord Jeffrey (1773-1850) see Grant, p.79, n.2. Given Jeffrey's attack on Wordsworth, Joanna Baillie in any case got off fairly lightly.

3. Mary Berry (1763-1852), celebrated for beauty, wit and most of the other reputedly female virtues, lived a single and singularly happy life with her sister Agnes, who was born a year after her, for nearly 88 years. She and her sister had a famous friendship with Horace Walpole, the landscape gardener, poet and, with *The Castle of Otranto*, inventor of Gothic fiction; they lived in a house owned by Walpole, known as Little Strawberry Hill after the parent house owned by Walpole; Walpole bequeathed the house to them. When Miss Berry received Joanna Baillie's first volume of the *Plays on the Passions*, she apparently sat up all night in a ball dress to read it. From the first she believed the plays to have been written by a woman because the female characters were rational before beautiful.

4. The idiosyncratic spelling of Ossian seems peculiar to Joanna Baillie. Since it is used in both sets of reminiscences, however, it seems deliberate.

5. Dresden-work is presumably china-painting, once, like embroidery, a common activity of young ladies.

6. Some words seem to be missing here but the sense, that she could perform the task, while her father and brother could not, is clear.

7. Susannah Cibber (1714-66) was a notable singer and actress: she was the second wife of Theophilus Cibber, son of Colley Cibber (1671-1757) the famous actor, manager, poet and enemy of Pope, and the sister of the composer Thomas Arne.

8. Sarah Siddons (née Kemble) (1755-1831) was the most celebrated actress of her generation. She made her London debut at Drury Lane in 1782. She played the part of Jane de Monfort in Joanna Baillie's *De Monfort*. Her son, the actor-manager, Henry Siddons, was responsible for the Edinburgh production of *The Family Legend* in 1810 at the Theatre Royal, Edinburgh.

9. The MS seems to read Matthew, the other name is difficult to make out, but I think that the reference must be to the 17th-century mathematician, Andreas (Andrew) Tacquet. Tacquet's commentary would have been in Latin but was translated in the 18th-century: *The Elements of Euclid; with select theorems out of Archimedes. By Andrew Tacquet. To which are added practical corollaries, shewing the uses of many of the propositions. The whole abridg'd and publish'd in English. by William Whiston* (London: 1747).

10. Charles Rollin (1661-1741), celebrated French historian the translation of whose *Histoire Ancienne des Égyptiens, des Carthaginouis, des Assyriens, des Babyloniens, des Mèdes, et des Perses, des Macedoniens, des Grècs,* 1730-38, was widely read.

11. *The Koran* to which is prefixed a preliminary discourse by George Sale (London: Frederick Warne & Co., 1734).

12. A pencil note on the MS suggests that the memoirs were 'written probably in the last years of her life: the writing not so neat towards the end'.

13. Hamilton Palace was built between 1693 and 1701 for the 3rd Duke; it was demolished in 1922. The hunting lodge of Chatelherault, containing dog kennels and a banqueting hall, was designed by William Adam between 1732-42; the walled gardens at the little house at Barncluith were stepped down to the Avon and were created in the late seventeenth century. Dorothy Wordsworth was delighted with them: 'Baroncleugh is in a beautiful deep glen through which runs the river Avon, a stream that falls into the Clyde. The house stands very sweetly in complete retirement [...] The whole place is in perfect harmony with the taste of our ancestors' (*Recollections of a Tour Made in Scotland* (A.D. 1803). See Tim Buxbaum, *Scottish Garden Buildings,* 1989.

14. 'Kings may be blest, but Tam was glorious,/O'er a' the ills of life victorious!' (Burns, 'Tam o' Shanter', ll. 57-8).

15. The farce is *Taste,* a two-act comedy acted at Drury Lane in 1752. The part of Lady Pentweezle was acted by the painter, Mr Worsdale.

16. *Bell's British Theatre* was a formidable collection of the 'most esteemed tragedies, comedies and farces'. It ran to many editions and was illustrated as Joanna Baillie describes. It is still a valuable theatre resource.

17. John Millar (1735-1801), Professor of Law, was educated under Adam Smith at the University of Glasgow. He was a notable Whig. His eldest son John inherited his father's sympathy with the French Revolution and his radical politics. John Millar Junior emigrated to Pennsylvania in 1975. His wife returned to Scotland after the death of her husband and became a good friend of Fanny (Frances) Wright and it was to Mrs Millar that Fanny Wright wrote her letters from America, published as *Views of Society and Manners in America,* 1821. Fanny Wright's interest in America was in part fuelled by Mrs Millar with whom Fanny and her sister, Camilla, lived for a short time in Whitburn. Eliza Fletcher was also a friend of Mrs Millar: see pp. 111 and 159.

18. James Thomson (1700-48) wrote his topographical poem *The Seasons,* 1726-30, in blank verse.

19. Pierre Corneille (1606-84), Jean Racine (1639-99), Voltaire, pseudonym of François Marie De Arouet (1694-1778), and Molière, pseudonym of Jean-Baptiste Poquelin (1622-73), were widely read in Britain in the eighteenth century; the dramatic duo Sir Francis Beaumont (1584-1616) and John Fletcher (1579-1625) wrote about 15 plays together, although their best known play, *The Knight of the Burning Pestle,* which Joanna Baillie would certainly have thought written by both of them, is now believed to be by Beaumont alone.

20. *Rayner* was published in *Miscellaneous Plays,* 1804.

21. Louis Sébastien Mercier (1740-1814) was one of the first French writers of *drames bourgeois.* These middle-class tragedies must have had some influence on Joanna Baillie's avowed intention to write plays which focused on characters in the middle station of life.

22. Archibald Alison (1757-1839) was educated at Glasgow and Edinburgh, where he became acquainted with the philospher, Dugald Stewart (1753-1828), who was from 1785 Professor of Moral Philosophy at Edinburgh University. In 1790 Alison published his *Essay on the Nature and Principles of Taste*. He became a minister of the episcopal chapel, Cowgate, Edinburgh, from 1800, believing that he could secure a better education for his family in Scotland. Henry Brougham (see p.115, n.1) told Alison's son that he had at least half of his father's sermons by heart. Alison's monument in St Paul's Chapel has an inscription by Francis Jeffrey.

23. For Mary Berry's reaction to the plays see note 1.

24. John Philip Kemble (1757-1823), actor, elder brother of Charles Kemble and Mrs Siddons, played a number of Shakespearean roles – Romeo, Iago, Prospero, etc. – with huge success. The first performance of *De Monfort* was at Drury Lane, April 29, 1800. It had a total of eight performances in this run. John Kemble played De Monfort and Mrs Siddons played his sister, Jane de Monfort.

25. The villa of Lord Abercorn, the Priory at Stanmore, was Scott's favourite retreat from Saturday to Monday when he was in London. Scott's brother Thomas managed the Abercorn estates in Scotland. Lady Abercorn was a regular correspondent of Scott's.

26. Jeffrey famously made this objection; see headnote. Joanna Baillie obviously still resented what she regarded as a careless reading of her preface and the plays themselves.

27. Joanna Baillie leaves a gap here as if she had perhaps intended to put in another name.

28. *Ethwald* from the second volume of 'Plays on the Passions' is a two part tragedy on Ambition.

29. The poem in question is *Ahalya Baee*. Her story is told by Sir John Malcolm (1769-1833), soldier and administrator, in his *A Memoir of Central India*, 1823. He also wrote part of the life of Clive. Presumably Joanna Baillie left a blank which she intended to fill with the title of the poem: perhaps she intended to check the spelling. The poem is discussed by Amanda Gilroy in *HSWW*, pp.152-4.

Mrs Eliza Fletcher (1770–1858)

Eliza Dawson Fletcher was not Scots by birth but she spent 37 years of married life and part of the remainder of her life in Scotland, and her *Autobiography* is one of the great illuminators of herself, her contemporaries and her period.

She was born Eliza Dawson at Oxton, near Tadcaster in Yorkshire, on 15 January 1770. Her mother died shortly after Eliza's birth, yet in spite of this her childhood and youth, during which she was cared for by her father and his mother, were most happy: indeed lively happiness is a defining phrase for her whole life, although it had, of course, its fair share of sad event.

In 1787 the Dawsons were visited by a school friend of Eliza's and her husband, Mr Meliss. Meliss was on his way from Perth to London to give evidence before the Commons' Committee on Burgh Reform and was accompanied by Archibald Fletcher, an Edinburgh lawyer, known for his liberal opinions and advanced idealism. J. G. Fyfe says that he 'must be reckoned among the great Scottish patriots' (Fyfe, p.307). The Dawsons were Whigs and Eliza's background was, therefore, such as to make her open to Fletcher's ardent expression of his beliefs. Over the next few years Eliza corresponded off and on with Fletcher and he made several visits to Oxton. Despite his sympathy with Fletcher's ideals, Eliza's father was not happy when in 1791 the two expressed the desire to marry, for Fletcher at 45 was 24 years older than Eliza and not well off. Their love prevailed, however, and they married later in the year. Eliza herself scarcely registers the discrepancy in their years and from its inception until Fletcher died in 1828 it was a peculiarly happy marriage.

The early stages of their marriage were full of financial difficulties for Fletcher's legal practice in Edinburgh suffered as a result of his advanced views. He admired the principles of the French Revolution, although he deplored the violence to which it had led; he worked for Burgh Reform as a preliminary to Parliamentary reform and spoke against corruption in Church and State. Yet the couple had six children, two boys, Miles (b.1792) and Angus (b.1799), and four girls, Elizabeth (Bessy) (b.1794), Grace (b.1796), Margaret (b.1798) and Mary (b.1802). Grace died of typhus fever in 1817 and her mother wrote a moving memoir of her. Archibald Fletcher died in 1828 and Eliza spent most of the rest of her life in England but died in Edinburgh in 1858.

Eliza Fletcher knew everyone: 'the giants of the age were her friends – Scott and Allan Cunningham, Jeffrey and Brougham, Henry Mackenzie and Professor Playfair[1] – she took part in the struggle for reform, she saw the birth of the *Edinburgh Review*, she cheered George IV on his memorable visit, she speculated on the authorship of *Waverley*, and in 1832 she viewed the proceedings at the Cross of Edinburgh when the first popular election of members for the city under the Reform Act took place' (Fyfe, 309). Particularly, however, she knew all the literary women of the period: she was on close terms with Mrs Barbauld, to whom she sent her daughter Bessy for a stay of several months, Joanna Baillie, Anne Grant of Laggan, Mary Somerville and Elizabeth Hamilton.[2] She wrote a little herself in addition to her memoirs, and her dramatic sketches were published to the satisfaction of her friends.

I have added to the extracts from Eliza Fletcher's autobiography selections from the concluding remarks of her daughter and editor, Mary, Lady Richardson, along with extracts from the tributes to her mother that Mary Richardson includes in the volume. I have also included part of a letter to her mother from Grace Fletcher while she was visiting Mrs Barbauld in Stoke Newington.

Eliza Fletcher, Elidure and Edward: Two Historical Dramatic Sketches (London: printed by Thomas Davison, 1825); *Autobiography of Mrs. Fletcher with Letters and Other Memorials*, edited by the survivor of her family. [Mary Richardson] The text below is taken from the 2nd edition, Edinburgh: Edmonston and Douglas, 1875.

Further reading:
Mona Wilson, *Jane Austen and Some Contemporaries*, (London: 1938)

DNB; Fyfe

From *Autobiography*:

At eleven Eliza was sent to the Manor House boarding school at York at which her mother had been educated:
It was a place where nothing useful could be learned, but it did me some service, because I had something to unlearn. It taught me that all my reading was not to be compared with the graces that other girls had acquired at the dancing-school, and my rusticity subjected me to many wholesome mortifications. The dull restraints of a school life were extremely irksome to me; everything was artificial, flat, and uninteresting. One great reason of this, no doubt, was that whereas at home I was everything, at school I was nothing – self-love was in a perpetual state of subjection and humiliation. The four years I spent at that school were not without their use, because if their experiences did not convince me that the making a graceful curtsy was the chief end of human existence, and that an awkward gait was worse than a bad action, they did convince me that, if the acquirements I valued myself upon were not to be more admired by the world than they were by my school companions, I had made a very mistaken estimate indeed of the value of my own knowledge and literary attainments. I formed, however, some friendships at school which both at the time and afterwards permanently contributed much to my happiness. Of these were Miss Forster and her sisters, Miss Ann Cleaver, afterwards Mrs Chapman, and Miss Beckwith, afterwards Mrs Craik[3]. But reflecting on my experience of a boarding-school as then conducted, I cannot but wonder how any one could escape the peril of such association as might have been met with there. The Manor School was in the hands of a very well-disposed, conscientious old gentlewoman, but of so limited an understanding that, under her rule, mischief of every kind (short of actual vice) was going on without her ever suspecting it. Lessons were said by rote, without being understood; servants were bribed to bring in dainties clandestinely; in short, every kind of dissimulation was practised to indemnify the subjects of this petty despotism, for the restraints unnecessarily

imposed upon them. During the four years I was at this school, two chapters of the Bible were read every morning by two of the young ladies as a reading lesson. Prayers were regularly drawled out by the husband of our governess, a choleric old man, who thumped our fingers so often for bad writing, with his mahogany ferule, that we listened to his prayers with any feelings but those of love or devotion. I do not remember to have received a single religious impression at this school, though creeds were repeated, and catechisms taught, and all the formalities of religious service regularly performed. Four volumes of the *Spectator* constituted our whole school library. But besides the negative evils of such school life was the misfortune of having as daily associates some girls of thoroughly depraved character. Two of these, the most remarkable for dissimulation and all evil characteristics, who afterwards married, eloped from their husbands.

[…]

In the summer of 1786 my kind father indulged me with an excursion to the Highlands of Scotland. I had my choice to go for six weeks to London or to Scotland; I chose the latter. I was much attached to Miss Stewart, a young lady who had married the year before (from the Manor School) Mr Meliss, a gentleman of Perth, her native place. This and some romantic associations with Scottish Scenery decided my choice. […] After a visit of three weeks to my friend Mrs Meliss at Rosemount, a pretty villa near Perth, where I witnessed much domestic happiness and received much kindly hospitality, we proceeded through Perthshire and Argyllshire by the ordinary tourist route, and, returning by the Westmoreland and Cumberland lakes, we completed our expedition by the 5th of October, on which day we returned to Oxton.

My taste for and enjoyment in picturesque scenery were much increased by this journey. From Bamborough Castle, on the coast of Northumberland, I first saw the sea. It was on a tempestuous day, and the foaming surge and roaring billows of the German Ocean astonished and affected me. I have never looked on the sea since without a recurrence of the same emotion of dread, which philosophers consider the source of the sublime. It would be impossible for me ever to feel familiar with the sea; I have no feeling of happiness connected with it. I was greatly struck with the noble situation of Edinburgh, and interested in the historical associations of the place, but we did not then know any one there. The frankness and urbanity of Scottish manners were very agreeable to me. I was not discriminating enough to be a good judge of character, or refined enough to be fastidious. I had no very high standard of manners, but I returned gratefully impressed with much personal kindness. I had an unaffected wish to please. This feeling was, I think, compounded of benevolence and a great desire of approbation. I never could flatter or say what I did not think; but I was disposed to think well of others. If it had been the estimation of the good and the wise only, it would have been a desire that all rational beings ought to have; but I was more voracious, and less discriminating in my love of approbation.

[…]

It was about this time [the time of the tour] that I read somewhere of a dispute between Mrs Hannah More and Ann Yearsley, the Bristol milkwoman.[4] It appeared that after Mrs Hannah More had introduced her to the public, by a very high and eloquent eulogium on her genius and her virtue (in a letter addressed to the celebrated Mrs Montagu), she quarrelled with Mrs Yearsley for her requesting to have the uncontrolled disposal of the interest only of her money which, chiefly through Mrs Hannah More's influence, had been raised by subscription for her poems. Mrs Yearsley had readily agreed that the principal sum, about £350, should be vested in the funds for the benefit of her family, under the trusteeship of Mrs Hannah More and Mrs Montagu. Mrs Yearsley's 'narrative' made a great impression on me. I thought it showed a case of direct attempt by the strong to oppress the weak. My father and all our little household sympathized in this feeling, and, authorized by my father, I wrote to Mrs Yearsley offering to collect subscriptions for her new volume of poems advertised for publication. Mrs Yearsley, who had been highly irritated by what she conceived to be Mrs Hannah More's injustice, received the offered assistance of a stranger with exaggerated, but I believe sincere expressions of joy and gratitude. I enlisted with all the zeal of partisanship, as well as the feelings of justice and benevolence, in her behalf, and seldom had I felt more delighted than when my father put a £50 bank-note into my hands to give immediate help to the Bristol milkwoman in bringing out her poems. This sum was nearly replaced by the five hundred subscribers I obtained for her. She afterwards addressed some complimentary verses to me in that volume, and, not being then much given to the practice of self-examination, I daresay I was not aware how much of vanity and self-love mixed with better feelings in my patronage of Mrs Yearsley. The correspondence with this remarkable woman afforded me much interest for several years, and I carefully preserved her letters. When, in the spring of 1834, I visited Bristol and Clifton for the first time, I tried in vain to trace any vestige of her or her family.[5]

[...]

In the spring of 1795 our friends Mr and Mrs Millar took their departure for America, banished thither by the strong tide of Tory prejudice which ran so fiercely against Mr Millar. He had joined the Society of 'The Friends of the People'. He lost his professional employment, and though a most able and honourable man, was so disgusted with the state of public affairs in Scotland that he determined to seek peace and freedom in the United States of America. I felt Mrs Millar's departure as a great loss. In two years she returned a widow, and our friendship continued till her death.[6]

[...]

In the summer of 1799, during the vacation of the Courts, Mr Fletcher's health, as well as my own, seeming to require change of air, we repaired with our children to a very inexpensive cottage, in the Morningside district to the south of Edinburgh, called 'Egypt' (so named in memory of a gypsy colony who, as tradition said, had made their head-quarters in its immediate 'whereabouts', by virtue of a grant of land given to them there by one of the Scottish kings). It was the first time that we could afford ourselves the luxury of a country house, and we enjoyed it greatly, seeing how much it promoted the health and happiness of our children. Our friend Mrs Millar had by that time returned from America, a widow, with all her hopes and prospects blighted. She came to visit us at 'Egypt', and interested us much by her animated and graphic descriptions of America, and of men and manners in the United States. She had often seen and conversed with the greatest man of his age, – General Washington, Philadelphia being then the seat of the federal Government.

She described his demeanour as calm, mild, and dignified, and his domestic character as excellent. I should not omit to record that it was in the latter part of this summer, when we were living very quietly at our country house, that my dear friend Miss Fergusson and her very agreeable sister Ann, brought me to read, for the first time, Wordsworth's 'Lyrical Ballads'.[7] Never shall I forget the charm I found in these poems. It was like a new era in my existence. They were in my waking thoughts day and night. They had to me all the vivid effects of the finest pictures, with the enchantment of the sweetest music, and they did much to tranquillize and strengthen my heart and mind, which bodily indisposition had somewhat weakened. My favourites were the 'Lines on Tintern Abbey', the 'Lines left on a Yew Tree at Esthwaite Lake', 'The Brothers', and 'Old Michael' [sic], and I taught my children to recite 'We are Seven', and several others.

[…]

In the winters of 1805 and 1806 I had much agreeable intercourse with Mrs Elizabeth Hamilton, at whose house I met with a greater variety of people than I had yet mixed with. She did much to clear my reputation from the political prejudice which had, during the first ten years of my life in Edinburgh, attached to all who were not of the Pitt and Dundas faction there.[8] She had good success in persuading her friends that Mrs Fletcher was not the ferocious Democrat she had been represented, and that she neither had the model of a guillotine in her possession nor carried a dagger under her cloak.

[…]

It was during this period also [1810-11], when my children were growing up and able to enjoy variety of intercourse, that several English families of intelligence and agreeableness were attracted to Edinburgh, for the sake both of its society and the advantages it afforded as to education for both sons and daughters. […] Among those whose acquaintance in those days ripened into friendship (which was continued without interruption to the close of her life), Lady Williamson, the widow of Sir Hedworth Williamson of Whitburn, should be especially mentioned. She had a house for many years in Queen Street, a few doors from North Castle Street. Her daughters attended classes along with mine, and a strong theatrical friendship was formed among our young people, both sons and daughters, which led to most pleasant meetings for rehearsals at our respective homes. Lady Williamson's house was large, and one of the drawing-rooms was converted into a little permanent theatre during one winter, when the play of *Douglas*, and some of Joanna Baillie's dramas were got up with great effect, and large audiences sometimes gave their applause *con amore*.

In the summer of 1819 Mrs Fletcher went to London with her daughters, Margaret and Mary: they met Mrs Barbauld in Stoke Newington and passed some time with Joanna Baillie in Hampstead where they also met Mrs Opie, Jane Porter, Mary Berry and her sister and many other luminaries:[9]

It was on this visit to London that we had the happiness to pass some hours in Newgate with Mrs Fry.[10] We heard her read and expound to the female prisoners the third chapter of St John's Gospel. Her voice was melody itself, and the earnest sweetness with which she explained the doctrine of regeneration to her attentive hearers found its way directly to their hearts; many of them shed tears, and all were attentive and appeared deeply interested. [...] Robert Owen, the notorious socialist, accompanied us to Newgate.[11] He was then intimate with Mrs Fry, and we had known him for many years. He had always appeared to us a benevolent and zealous reformer, and we bore with the intense though quiet egotism of his conversation from the belief that he had the good of his fellow-creatures at heart. He had not then so openly avowed those opinions, so fatal to moral and religious truth and happiness, which he has since so unfortunately promulgated. It would be unfair perhaps to refuse him credit for wishing to promote the present good of mankind.

In the spring of 1823 Maria Edgeworth and her two younger sisters spent some time in Edinburgh.[42] We met first at my dear friend and pastor's house, the Rev. Mr Alison.[13] It was the first time I had been introduced to the author of *Simple Susan*, though we were not unknown to each other, as she told me her brothers had often mentioned the agreeable society they met at our house when they were students in Edinburgh. Miss Edgeworth's personal appearance was not attractive; but her vivacity, good humour, and cleverness in conversation quite equalled my expectations. I should say she was more sprightly and brilliant than refined. She excelled in the raciness of Irish humour, but the great defect of her manner, as it seemed to me, was an excess of 'blarney'; and in one who had moved in the best circles, both as to manners and mind, it surprised me not a little. She repelled all approach to intimacy on my part by the excess of her complimentary reception of me when we were first introduced to each other at Mr Alison's. I never felt confidence in the reality of what she said afterwards. I do not know whether it was the absence of good taste in her, or that she supposed I was silly and vain enough to be flattered by such verbiage. It was the first time in my life I had met with such over-acted civility; but I was glad of an opportunity of meeting a person whose genius and powers of mind had been exercised in benefiting the world as hers have been. I feel sure from the feeling of those friends who loved her, because they knew her well, that had this been the case with me, I might have been also one of her friends; so that I only give my impression as arising from that of society intercourse of a very superficial kind.

From a letter, September 11, 1823, to her daughters Margaret and Mary who were in Gloucestershire:

I must hasten to tell you how highly and truly I have been gratified by dining in company with Brougham.[14] [...] When the gentlemen came up to the drawing-room, Brougham stationed himself beside me [...] and I never heard a more animated, pleasant, unforced conversation than that which flowed on for more than an hour. One had but to touch the strings, and it always vibrated the very chord one wished. It was not brilliant sayings or pointed *bon-mots*, it was information given with frankness, energy, and good-nature. He said he had met with Clarkson at Penrith,[15] and bade him go and tell Southey it was a shame that Negro Emancipation had never once been advocated in the *Quarterly Review*;[16] that Clarkson told him he had got the promise of fifteen hundred petitions from the principal towns in England in favour of that measure. He said the friends of Emancipation were determined to debate and divide the House upon every petition, so as to force Ministers to adopt some efficient measure in the next session. He said his Education

Bill was rendered abortive by the prejudices of the Dissenters in England, who refused to send their children to schools where the parish minister had a veto on the choice of the schoolmaster; and the ministers of the Establishment hated the Bill, because they were, generally speaking, averse to educate the people at all, and were only driven to do so by fear of the Methodists and other Dissenters. He said it was proposed to bring forward individual cases and instances of oppression and injustice exercised by magistrates and Orangemen in Ireland, rather than argue any longer on general principles of misgovernment in that country; facts would produce an effect upon the House when argument and reasoning were disregarded. Brougham's manner of treating subjects of vital importance is quite different from our Edinburgh Whigs. There is no affected indifference on subjects of vital importance, no contemptuous sneer at rational conversation. He speaks with animation and deep interest on the subjects I have mentioned.

From *At Home and Abroad* by Margaret Fuller Ossoli,[17] **included in the *Autobiography*:**
Ambleside, August 27, 1846
We also met a fine specimen of the noble, intelligent Scotchwoman, such as Walter Scott and Burns knew how to prize. Seventy-six years have passed over her head, only to prove in her the truth of my theory, that we need never grow old. She was 'brought up' in the animated and intellectual circle of Edinburgh, in youth an apt disciple, in her prime a bright ornament, of that society. She had been an only child, a cherished wife, an adored mother, unspoiled by love in any of these relations, because that love was founded on knowledge. In childhood she had warmly sympathized in the spirit that animated the American revolution, and Washington had been her hero: later, the interest of her husband in every struggle for freedom had cherished her own. She had known in the course of her long life many eminent men, and sympathized now in the triumph of the people over the Corn Laws,[18] as she had in the American victories, with as much ardour as when a girl, though with a wiser mind. Her eye was full of light, her manner and gesture of dignity; her voice rich, sonorous, and finely modulated; her tide of talk marked by candour and justice, showing in every sentence her ripe experience and her noble genial nature. Dear to memory will be the sight of her in the beautiful seclusion of her home among the mountains, a picturesque, flower-wreathed dwelling, where affection, tranquillity, and wisdom were the gods of the hearth to whom was offered no vain oblation. Grant to us more such women, Time! Grant to men to reverence, to seek for such!

Grace Fletcher died when she was only twenty of typhus fever. She was a friend of Mrs Millar, the friend also of Fanny Wright; she travelled to London with the novelist, Mary Brunton and her husband and spent some time in lodgings with them there. She also visited Mrs Barbauld in Stoke Newington. What follows is an extract from a letter written to her mother from Stoke Newington in June 1815.
DEAREST OF MINNIES, – I left Hampstead with great regret on Monday, and came to town for one day and night, which I passed at Dr Baillie's. There was a large party in the evening, where I did not know many people, but where Mrs Joanna was very kind in coming to speak to me very often; indeed, I am truly grateful to her

for her constant kindness and attention. The next morning she took me to see a part of the town I had not before been in – Hyde Park and Piccadilly. I was pleased to find such a place as the park, where the poorest inhabitants of this overgrown and dismal metropolis may see the trees and green grass, and have some chance of feeling that a good Spirit formed the universe. After our return, Mrs Baillie kindly pressed me to stay; but as I had fixed to dine at Mrs Barbauld's that day, I declined. She then insisted upon sending me in her carriage, and Mrs Joanna Baillie was so good as to accompany me. Mrs Barbauld received me most kindly, and I have passed with her a week of a most quiet and gratifying kind of enjoyment. The dreadful fear I had of Mrs Joanna Baillie, the hopelessness of pleasing her, gave a feeling of constraint which I hoped I had got over, but which, whenever I saw her composed figure enter the room, returned with painful force; yet I have seldom seen any human being that excites stronger feelings of respect; and there is something so extraordinary in the union of such excellent poetic genius and such simplicity and even plainness of manner, that your attention is constantly alive to every word she utters, hoping you may hear some poetical or elevated sentiment. She is one illustration of Miss Benger's theory about complicated characters; there is so much left to the imagination, you *must* feel great interest.[19] But, to return to Mrs Barbauld: there is in her so much indulgence for the fancies and even follies of youth, that in one week I feel more at ease in her society, and more attached to her, than I could be to Mrs Joanna Baillie in years. Enthusiasm has not departed from the character of Mrs Barbauld, but has left such deep traces, that you find many of her feelings and opinions still tinged with its magic. In Mrs Joanna Baillie that glowing elevating sentiment has dwelt in such impervious depths, and pursued such secret paths, that the passing eye might think her uninfluenced by its spells.

NOTES

1. Walter Scott (1771-1832) knew and, when possible and appropriate, supported the work of many of the women in this anthology. Allan Cunningham (1784-1842) was a native of Dumfries; as a song and ballad collector (and fabricator) he supplied much of the material for Cromek's *Remains of Nithsdale and Galloway Song*; his publications included *Traditional Tales of the English and Scottish Peasantry*, 1822, and *Lives of the Most Eminent British Painters, Sculptors and Architects*, 1829-33. For Francis, Lord Jeffrey (1773-1850) see Grant, p.79, n.2 and Joanna Baillie, p.91, headnote and n.2; Henry Peter Brougham, Baron Brougham and Vaux (1778-1868), was educated at Edinburgh High School and University and finally became Lord Chancellor; he was a celebrated orator and advocate of Queen Caroline. He published widely on social, political and literary matters. In addition to his literary activities, he effected improvements in the Court of Chancery and assisted in the founding of London University, 1828. Henry Mackenzie (1745-1831) comptroller of the taxes for Scotland, but best known as the author of the sentimental novel, *The Man of Feeling*, 1771: see Barnard p.64, n.1. John Playfair (1748-1819) was Professor of Mathematics and Natural Philosophy at Edinburgh University and was also a noted geologist.

2. The poet, writer of prose and scholar, Anna Laetitia Aikin, Mrs Barbauld (1743-1825), with her husband, Rochemont Barbauld, a dissenting clergyman of French descent, ran a school for boys at Palgrave, Sussex. The school closed in 1785 and after travelling on the continent, the Barbaulds settled at first in Hampstead and in 1802 in Stoke Newington. The mental health of Mrs Barbauld's husband, always unstable, deteriorated greatly until be became

violent towards her and had to be put under restraint. He escaped from his keeper and was found drowned in 1808. In 1812 Mrs Barbauld published a poem, *Eighteen Hundred and Eleven* which lamented the decline of moral, political and artistic life in Britain, although exceptions were made for Scott, for example, who did not appreciate the compliment. The poem was reviewed so harshly by J. W. Croker in the *Quarterly Review* in June 1812 that it put an end to her public career as a writer. It is interesting that, although Mrs Barbauld had a classical education herself, she told the scholar Elizabeth Montagu that she saw no point in producing *femmes savantes* rather than good wives or agreeable companions. See *DNB*, Lonsdale, Todd 1 and 2, *DLB*.

3. A private lady, not the novelist, Dinah Maria Mulock Craik (1826-87).

4. A good, balanced account of the dispute between Ann Yearsley and her patron, the moralist and writer, Hannah More, is given by Lonsdale. Ann Yearsley, having been supported by Hannah More, who helped to raise subscriptions for her *Poems on Several Occasions*, 1785, displayed what More, and most of the fashionable world, regarded as amazing ingratitude by demanding control over the subscription money, the investment and disbursement of which More wished to oversee. The subscription money was eventually handed over but not until an irreparable breach had occurred between the two.

5. Ann Yearsley died at Melksham in Wiltshire, a few miles from Trowbridge where her third son, John, was a clothier, on 8 May 1806. She was buried at Clifton.

6. The Millars were good friends of Frances Wright and it was to Mrs (Rabina Craig) Millar that Frances Wright wrote her letters from America published as *Views of Society and Manners in America*, 1821. Fanny Wright's interest in America was in part fuelled by Mrs Millar with whom Fanny and her sister, Camilla, lived for a short time in Whitburn: see also Baillie, p.106, n.17.

7. Published 1798.

8. Henry Dundas, 1st Viscount Melville (1742-1811), was a member of the Younger Pitt's Tory administrations 1784-1801 and 1804-6. See also Lindsay Barnard, p.00.

9. Amelia Opie (1769-1853), novelist and poet, wife of John Opie, the painter. Her novel *Adeline Mowbray*, 1804, was suggested by the story of Mary Wollstonecraft; Jane Porter (1776-1850) was a prolific writer whose most successful novels, *Thaddeus of Warsaw*, 1803, and *The Scottish Chiefs*, 1810 (about Wallace and Bruce), were translated into German and Russian; for Mary Berry see Joanna Baillie, p.105, n.3.

10. Elizabeth Fry (1780-1845) Quaker prison reformer who first visited Newgate in 1813, aiming to improve the conditions under which women prisoners lived.

11. For Robert Owen (1771-1858) founder of New Lanark and his eldest son, Robert Dale Owen, see Wright, p.000, n.0.

12. Maria Edgeworth (1767-1849), novelist, educationist, writer of moral tales for children. She is best known for her novels, *Castle Rackrent*, 1800, and *Belinda*, 1801. Maria Edgeworth knew Scott well and knew and corresponded with Joanna Baillie.

13. Archibald Alison (1757-1839): see Joanna Baillie, p.107, n.22.

14. Brougham: see n.1.

15. Thomas Clarkson (1760-1846) campaigned for the abolition of the slave trade. With William Wilberforce (1759-1833) and Granville Sharp (1735-1813) he formed in 1787 an anti-slavery society and in the same year wrote *A Summary View of the Slave Trade and of the Probable Consequences of its Abolition*. After Britain abolished the slave trade in 1807, Clarkson worked for abolition by other states.

16. From 1808 the poet Robert Southey (1774-1843) became a regular reviewer for *The Quarterly Review*, founded in 1809 as a Tory rival to *The Edinburgh Review*. Scott was promoter of the venture as was his son-in-law, John Gibson Lockhart (1794-1854). Lockhart was editor from 1825 to 1853.

17. Margaret Fuller (1810-50) was an American pioneer of the women's rights movement there. She settled in Italy where she married the Marquis Ossoli in 1847. She and her husband died in a shipwreck between Leghorn (Livorno) and America.

18. The Corn Laws, which were resented by the working classes because they kept the price of bread high, were repealed by Sir Robert Peel's government in 1846.

19. Elizabeth Ogilvy Benger (1778-1827) was the biographer of Elizabeth Hamilton. Benger had an odd life and ought perhaps to have been more famous than she ever was. Born in Wells, Somerset, she was idiosyncratically educated by her navy purser father who sent her to a boys' school when she was 12 to learn Latin. Her father's death left her quite poor and although she wrote poetry, novels and competent biography, she remained badly off for the rest of her life. She was a member of Mrs Barbauld's literary circle and Mrs Barbauld's writer niece, Lucy Aikin, wrote a memoir of her. See Todd 1.

Mary Somerville (1780–1872)

Mary Somerville became the most celebrated woman writer on science and mathematics of her day, and indeed perhaps of any day. Her name is commemorated in Somerville College and in the Mary Somerville scholarship for women in mathematics at Oxford. She was the daughter of Vice-Admiral Sir William George Fairfax and his second wife, Margaret Charters, daughter of Samuel Charters, Solicitor of the Customs for Scotland. She was born, while her father was at sea, in the Jedburgh home of her aunt and later mother-in-law, Martha Somerville. She loved the open air and the natural world from a very early age as she rambled on the sands and in the country round about her childhood home in Burntisland, Fife. She was sent to a fashionable boarding school in Musselburgh where, she felt, she learned nothing. She was self taught in science and mathematics: she worked her way through Euclid and learned Latin to read Newton's *Principia*. She first married in 1804 her cousin Captain Samuel Greig, the son of the Russian admiral, Sir Samuel Greig, and had two sons but was widowed after three years. Her second husband, also a cousin, Dr William Somerville, actively supported his wife's studies when the family moved to London and then, after his appointment to the Army Medical Board, to Edinburgh. Mary Somerville developed an extensive acquaintance throughout Britain in both the arts and the sciences. In 1831 Lord Brougham, on behalf of the Society for the Diffusion of Useful Knowledge, asked her to write a volume interpreting Laplace's *Le Méchanique Céleste*. The publication of *The Mechanism of the Heavens* secured the fame that increased throughout her life, as well as a civil list pension of £200 and then £300 per annum. After 1838 and the illness of Dr Somerville, the Somervilles lived mainly in Italy. The interruptions of travel and her social life (for Mary Somerville was never reclusive) somewhat interrupted her work, but she continued to learn and to write throughout her life. Her husband died in 1860 and her only surviving son Woronzow Greig in 1865 and she threw herself more intensely into her work as a release from her personal suffering: in 1869, in her eighty-ninth year, she published *Molecular and Microscopic Science*, a summary of the most recent discoveries in chemistry and physics. She died in Naples on 29 November 1872 at ninety-two in full possession of her faculties, and was buried in the English cemetery at Naples.

It is, of course, notorious that it was almost as difficult for some middle-class women to get an adequate education as for their working-class sisters. And this was particularly the case in the classics, mathematics and the sciences. It is hard, given all that was stacked against her, to speak too highly of Mary Somerville's achievement. The distinction of Mary Somerville, as the reviewer of her *Recollections* in *Nature* points out, provides ammunition to feminists and anti-feminists alike. If after all 'such powers as hers had been more generally granted to women, why is she the only woman on record amongst us who has exhibited them?'[1] But Mary Somerville also manages gently to give the lie to nineteenth century male fears that education made women unwomanly. Her daughter remarks in the *Recollections* that 'it would be almost incredible were I to describe how much my mother contrived to do in the course of the day': she wrote for the press, taught her own small children, read newspapers and books and freely visited her friends, being very fond of society. Her life and her opinions impeccably support any valorisation of women, indeed into extreme old age she remained tart about any assumption of female inferiority: her own politics were Liberal from an early stage, she advocated female education, supported female suffrage, knew the notable men and women of her age in letters as well as in science. Her *Personal Recollections* are remarkable for their wit and perception.

Mary Somerville, *The Mechanism of the Heavens* (1831); *On the Connection of the Physical Sciences* (London: John Murray, 1834); *Physical Geography*, 2 vols (1848); *On Molecular and Microscopic Science* (London: 1869); *Personal Recollections from Early Life to Old Age, with selections of her correspondence by her daughter, Martha Somerville* (London: John Murray, 1873; reprinted New York: AMS Press, 1975); *An Unpublished Letter of Mary Somerville, with a Comment by F. E. Hutchison, reprinted from the Oxford Magazine* (Oxonian Press, 1929)

Further reading

W. H. Davenport Adams, *Celebrated Englishwomen of the Victorian Era* (London: F. V. White, 1884)

William Chambers, *Stories of Remarkable Persons* (Edinburgh: Chambers, 1880?)

Julian Lowell Coolidge, *Six Female Mathematicians* (New York: Scripta Mathematica, 1951)

Dame Millicent Garrett Fawcett, *Some Eminent Women of Our Times: Short Biographical Sketches* (London: Macmillan, 1889)

Eva Hope, *Famous Women Authors* (London: W. Scott, 1890?)

Alice Jenkins, 'Mary Somerville as Autobiographer', in *Rethinking Victorian Culture* (London: Macmillan, 2000)

Notable Women in Mathematics: A Biographical Dictionary (Westport, Conn.: Greenwood Press, 1998)

Jane McKinlay, *Mary Somerville, 1780-1872* (Edinburgh: University of Edinburgh, 1987)

Lynn M. Osen, *Women in Mathematics* (Cambridge, Mass.: MIT Press, 1974)

Elizabeth Chambers Patterson, *Mary Somerville, 1780-1872* (Oxford: Somerville College, 1979)

Arthur Gay Payne, *Mrs Somerville and Mary Carpenter* (London: Cassell, 1892)

Allie Wilson Richeson, *Mary Somerville* (1941). Reprinted from *Scripta Mathematica*, vol.VIII, no.1 (March 1941)

George Barnett Smith, *Women of Renown: Nineteenth Century Studies* (London: Allen, 1893)

Margaret E. Tabor, *Pioneer Women: Caroline Herschel, Sarah Siddons, Maria Edgeworth, Mary Somerville* (London: The Sheldon Press, 1933)

Lucy Bethia Walford, *Twelve English Authoresses* (London: Longmans, Green, and co., 1892)

Mona Wilson, *Jane Austen and Some Contemporaries* (London: Cresset Press, 1938)

Mary Somerville is also included in a number of other collections of nineteenth century biographies of famous women, mostly dating from the late nineteenth or early twentieth centuries and a number of them intended for children or adolescents.

DNB; *HSWW*; Irving

Selections from *Personal Recollections*:

Mary Somerville describes life in her childhood in Burntisland:
Men and women of the lower classes smoked tobacco in short pipes, and many took snuff – even young ladies must have done so; for I have a very pretty and quaint gold snuff-box which was given to my grandmother as a marriage present. Licensed beggars, called 'gaberlunzie men', were still common. They wore a blue coat, with a tin badge, and wandered about the country, knew all that was going on, and were always welcome at the farm-houses, where the gude wife liked to have a crack (gossip) with the blue coat, and, in return for his news, gave him dinner or supper as might be. Edie Ochiltree is a perfect specimen of this extinct race.[2] There was another species of beggar, of yet higher antiquity. If a man were a cripple, and poor, his relations put him in a hand-barrow, and wheeled him to their next neighbour's door, and left him there. Some one came out, gave him oat-cake or peasemeal bannock, and then wheeled him to the next door; and in this way, going from house to house, he obtained a fair livelihood.

My brother Sam lived with our grandfather in Edinburgh, and attended the High School, which was in the old town, and, like other boys, he was given pennies to buy bread; but the boys preferred oysters, which they bought from the fishwives, the bargain being a dozen oysters for a halfpenny, and a kiss for the thirteenth. These fishwives and their husband were industrious, hard-working people, forming a community of their own in the village of Newhaven, close to the sea, and about two miles from Edinburgh. The men were exposed to cold, and often to danger, in their small boats, not always well-built nor fitted for our stormy Firth. The women helped to land and prepare the fish when the boats came in, carried it to town for sale in the early morning, kept the purse, managed the house, brought up the children, and provided food and clothing for all. Many were rich, lived well and sometimes had dances. Many of the young women were pretty, and all wore – and, I am told, still wear – bright-coloured, picturesque costume. Some young men, amongst others a cousin of my own, who attempted to intrude into one of the balls, got pelted with fish offal by the women. The village smelt strongly of fish, certainly; yet the people were very clean personally. I recollect their keeping tame gulls, which they fed with fish offal.

Although there was no individual enmity between the boys of the old and of the new or aristocratic part of Edinburgh, there were frequent battles, called 'bickers', between them, in which they pelted each other with stones. Sometimes they were joined by bigger lads, and then the fight became so serious that the magistrates sent the city guard – a set of old men with halberds and a quaint uniform – to separate them; but no sooner did the guard appear, than both parties joined against them.

Mary Somerville speaks movingly of her childhood love of birds which stayed with her throughout her life; birds took the place of dolls for her.

My love of birds has continued through life, for only two years ago, in my extreme old age, I lost a pet mountain sparrow, which for eight years was my constant companion: sitting on my shoulder, pecking at my papers, and eating out of my mouth; and I am not ashamed to say I felt its accidental death very much.

Somerville's education was fairly haphazard; when she was eight or nine her father coming home and finding her a 'savage', it was arranged for her to attend Miss Primrose's boarding school at Musselburgh. She stayed there until she was eleven without, according to her, learning even to write and spell securely.

My mother set me in due time to learn the catechism of the Kirk of Scotland, and to attend the public examinations in the kirk. This was a severe trial for me; for, besides being timid and shy, I had a bad memory, and did not understand one word of the catechism. These meetings, which began with prayer, were attended by all the children of the town and neighbourhood, with their mothers, and a great many old women, who came to be edified. They were an acute race, and could quote chapter and verse of Scripture as accurately as the minister himself. I remember he said to one of them – 'Peggie, what lightened the world before the sun was made?' After thinking for a minute, she said – ' Deed, sir, the question is mair curious than edifying.'

[…]

Although Miss Primrose was not unkind she had an habitual frown, which even the elder girls dreaded. My future companions, who were all older than I, came round me like a swarm of bees, and asked if my father had a title, what was the name of our estate, if we kept a carriage, and other such questions, which made me first feel the difference of station. However, the girls were very kind, and often bathed my eyes to prevent our stern mistress from seeing that I was perpetually in tears. A few days after my arrival, although perfectly straight and well-made, I was enclosed in stiff stays with a steel busk in front, while, above my frock, bands drew my shoulders back till the shoulder-blades met. Then a steel rod, with a semi-circle which went under the chin, was clasped to the steel busk in my stays. In this constrained state, I, and most of the younger girls, had to prepare our lessons. The chief thing I had to do was to learn by heart a page of Johnson's dictionary, not only to spell the words, give their parts of speech and meaning but as an exercise of memory to remember the order of succession. Besides I had to learn the first principles of writing, and the rudiments of French and English grammar. The method of teaching was extremely tedious and inefficient. Our religious duties were attended to in a remarkable way. Some of the girls were Presbyterians, others belonged to the Church of England, so Miss Primrose cut the matter short by taking us all to the kirk in the morning and to church in the afternoon.

In our play-hours we amused ourselves with playing at ball, marbles, and especially at 'Scotch and English', a game which represented a raid on the debatable land, or Border between Scotland and England, in which each party tried to rob the other of their playthings. The little ones were always compelled to be English, for the bigger girls thought it too degrading.

Some of Somerville's education was achieved out of boredom: having nothing else to do, she spent four or five hours daily at the piano and taught herself enough Latin to read Caesar's Commentaries in which she was encouraged by her Jedburgh uncle, Dr Somerville. While visiting her uncle William Charteris in Edinburgh, she was sent to a dancing-school:

They sent me to Strange's dancing school. Strange himself was exactly like a figure on the stage; tall and thin, he wore a powdered wig, with cannons at the ears, and a pigtail. Ruffles at the breast and wrists, white waistcoat, black silk or velvet shorts; white silk stockings, large silver buckles, and a pale blue coat completed his costume. He had a little fiddle on which he played, called a kit. My first lesson was how to walk and make a curtsey. 'Young lady, if you visit the queen you must make three curtsies, lower and lower and lower as you approach her. So–o–o,' leading me on and making me curtsey. 'Now, if the queen were to ask you to eat a bit of mutton with her, what would you say?'

Somerville explains how the anti-Liberal sentiments kindled by the French Revolution influenced her for the rest of her life.

There was great political agitation at this time. The corruption and tyranny of the court, nobility, and clergy in France were so great, that when the revolution broke out, a large portion of our population thought the French people were perfectly justified in revolting, and warmly espoused their cause. Later many changed their opinions, shocked, as every one was, at the death of the king and queen, and the atrocious massacres which took place in France. Yet some not only approved of the revolution abroad, but were so disgusted with our maladministration at home, to which they attributed our failure in the war in Holland and elsewhere, that great dissatisfaction and alarm prevailed throughout the country. The violence, on the other hand, of the opposite party was not to be described, – the very name of Liberal was detested.

Great dissensions were caused by difference of opinion in families; and I heard people previously much esteemed accused from this cause of all that was evil. My uncle William and my father were as violent Tories as any.

The Liberals were distinguished by wearing their hair short, and when one day I happened to say how becoming a crop was, and that I wished the men would cut off those ugly pigtails, my father exclaimed, 'By G–, when a man cuts off his queue, the head should go with it.'

The unjust and exaggerated abuse of the Liberal party made me a Liberal. From my earliest years my mind revolted against oppression and tyranny, and I resented the injustice of the world in denying all those privileges of education to my sex which were so lavishly bestowed on men. My liberal opinions, both in religion and politics, have remained unchanged (or, rather, have advanced) throughout my life, but I have never been a republican. I have always considered a highly-educated aristocracy essential, not only for government, but for the refinement of a people. [...]

In an illustrated monthly magazine with coloured plates of fashions as well as charades and puzzles Mary Fairfax finds a puzzle which depends on elementary Algebra and sets out to find out something about this. When she has drawing lessons from Nasmyth she overhears his recommendation of the study of Euclid for perspective but does not feel she can merely ask for the book in a bookshop. At last the tutor of her youngest brother Henry, not himself a mathematician, is, however, persuaded to buy her the necessary textbooks – Euclid and Bonnycastle's 'Algebra'.

I rose early, played on the piano, and painted during the time I could spare in the daylight hours, but I sat up very late reading Euclid. The servants, however, told my mother 'It was no wonder the stock of candles was soon exhausted, for Miss Mary sat up reading till a very late hour;' whereupon an order was given to take away my candle as soon as I was in bed. I had, however, already gone through the first six books of Euclid, and now I was thrown on my memory, which I exercised by beginning the first book, and demonstrating in my mind a certain number of problems every night, till I could nearly go through the whole. My father came home for a short time, and, somehow or other, finding out what I was about, said to my mother, 'Peg, we must put a stop to this, or we shall have Mary in a strait jacket one of these days. There was X, who went raving mad about the longitude!'

In her late teens Mary Fairfax came out in Edinburgh, chaperoned by the Countess of Buchan to whom her family were related, but in any case young women had a considerable degree of freedom at that time:

Girls had perfect liberty at that time in Edinburgh; we walked together in Princes Street, the fashionable promenade, and were joined by our dancing partners. We occasionally gave little supper parties, and presented these young men to our parents as they came in. At these meetings we played at games, danced reels, or had a little music – never cards. After supper there were toasts, sentiments, and songs. There were also always one or two hot dishes, and a variety of sweet things and fruit. Though I was much more at ease in society now, I was always terribly put out when asked for a toast or a sentiment. Like other girls, I did not dislike a little quiet flirtation; but I never could speak across a table, or take a leading part in conversation. This diffidence was probably owing to the secluded life I led in my early youth. At this time I gladly took part in any gaiety that was going on, and spent the day after a ball in idleness and gossiping with my friends; but these were rare occasions, for the balls were not numerous, and I never lost sight of the main object of my life, which was to prosecute my studies. So I painted at Nasmyth's, played the usual number of hours on the piano, worked and conversed with my mother in the evening; and as we kept early hours, I rose at day-break, and after dressing, I wrapped myself in a blanket from my bed on account of the excessive cold – having no fire at that hour – and read algebra or the classics till breakfast time. I had, and still have, determined perseverance, but I soon found that it was in vain to occupy my mind beyond a certain time. I grew tired and did more harm than good; so, if I met with a difficult point, for example, in algebra, instead of poring over it till I was bewildered, I left it, took my work or some amusing book, and resumed it when my mind was fresh. Poetry was my great resource on these occasions, but at a later period I read novels, the *Old English Baron*, the *Mysteries of Udolpho*, the *Romance of the Forest*, etc.[3] […] We returned as usual to Burntisland in spring, and my father, who was at home, took my mother and me a tour in the Highlands. I was a great admirer of Ossian's poems, and viewed the grand and beautiful scenery with awe; and my father, who was of a romantic disposition, smiled at my enthusiastic admiration of the eagles as they soared above the mountains.

The fear and consequent oppression during the wars at the turn of the century greatly distressed Mary Fairfax, torn between desire for British military success and misery about the sufferings of the people at home. Shortly after this period Mary Fairfax married her cousin Samuel Greig, Russian Consul, who secured, however, the home in London without which Mary's family would not have permitted the marriage. Mary Fairfax had two boys by her first marriage but was shortly widowed. Mary still pursued her love of mathematics with consistent devotion until Wallace, Professor of Mathematics in the University of Edinburgh, gave her a list of the requisite books: she was already thirty-three. During this period, too, she met Henry Brougham and Professor Playfair. Before her marriage in 1812 to her cousin, William Somerville, which put an end to scientific pursuits for some time, Mary Fairfax had so far advanced in her mathematical studies that she had gone beyond the teaching of the available mentors. Her studies were not, however, universally well received and when she remarried to her cousin, although his father was delighted others were less so:

My husband had been present at the taking of the Cape of Good Hope, and was sent by the authorities to make a treaty with the savage tribes on the borders of the colony, who had attacked the boors, or Dutch farmers, and carried off their cattle. In this journey he was furnished with a wagon and accompanied by Mr Daniel, a good artist, who made drawings of the scenery, as well as of the animals and people.[4] The savage tribes again became troublesome, and in a second expedition my cousin was only accompanied by a faithful Hottentot as interpreter. They were both mounted, and each led a spare horse with such things as were absolutely necessary, and when they bivouacked where, for fear of the natives, they did not dare light a fire to keep off the wild beasts, one kept watch while the other slept. After many adventures and dangers, my husband reached the Orange River, and was the first white man who had ever been in that part of Africa. He afterwards served in Canada and in Sicily at the head of the medical staff, under his friend General Sir James Craig. On returning to England he generally lived in London, so that he was seldom with his family, with whom he was not a favourite on account of his liberal principles, the very circumstance that was an attraction to me. He had lived in the world, was extremely handsome, had gentlemanly manners, spoke good English, and was emancipated from Scotch prejudices.

I had been living very quietly with my parents and children, so until I was engaged to my cousin I was not aware of the extreme severity with which my conduct was criticised by his family, and I have no doubt by many others; for as soon as our engagement was known I received a most impertinent letter from one of his sisters, who was unmarried, and younger than I, saying, she 'hoped I would give up my foolish manner of life and studies, and make a respectable and useful wife to her brother'. I was extremely indignant. My husband was still more so, and wrote a severe and angry letter to her; none of the family dared to interfere again. I lived in peace with her, but there was a coldness and reserve between us ever after. I forgot to mention that during my widowhood I had several offers of marriage. One of the persons whilst he was paying court to me, sent me a volume of sermons with the page ostentatiously turned down at a sermon on the Duties of a Wife, which were expatiated upon in the most illiberal and narrow-minded language. I thought this as impertinent as it was premature; sent back the book and refused the proposal.

The couple settled in Edinburgh after spending a brief period in London, Mary Somerville's husband having been appointed head of the Army Medical Department in Scotland. Mary Somerville continued her studies in the classics and now also in geology and minerology. At the same time various members of the Somerville family enjoyed intimacy with Scott, particularly supper-parties at Abbotsford:

I shall never forget the charm of this little society, especially the supper-parties at Abbotsford, when Scott was in the highest glee, telling amusing tales, ancient legends, ghost and witch stories. Then Adam Ferguson would sing the 'Laird of Cockpen', and other comic songs, and Willie Clerk amused us with his dry wit.[5] When it was time to go away all rose, and, standing hand-in-hand round the table, Scott taking the lead, we sang in full chorus,

> Weel may we a' be,
> Ill may we never see;
> Health to the king
> And the gude companie.

At that time no one knew who was the author of the Waverley Novels. There was much speculation and curiosity on the subject. While talking about one which had just been published, my son Woronzow said, 'I knew all these stories long ago, for Mr Scott writes on the dinner-table. When he has finished, he puts the green-cloth with the papers in a corner of the dining-room; and when he goes out, Charlie Scott and I read the stories.' My son's tutor was the original of Dominie Sampson in *Guy Mannering*. *The Memorie of the Somervilles* was edited by Walter Scott, from an ancient and very quaint manuscript found in the archives of the family, and from this he takes passages which he could not have found elsewhere. Although the work was printed it was never published, but copies were distributed to the different members of the family. One was of course given to my husband.

The Burning of the Water, so well described by Walter Scott in *Redgauntlet* (actually in *Guy Mannering*, chapter 26), we often witnessed. The illumination of the banks of the river, the activity of the men striking the salmon with the 'leisters', and the shouting of the people when a fish was struck, was an animated, and picturesque, but cruel scene.

Sophia Scott, afterwards married to Lockhart, editor of the *Quarterly Review*, was the only one of Sir Walter's family who had talent.[6] She was not pretty, but remarkably engaging and agreeable, and possessed her father's joyous disposition as well as his memory and fondness for ancient Border legends and poetry. Like him, she was thoroughly alive to peculiarities of character, and laughed at them good-naturedly. She was not a musician, had little voice, but she sang Scotch songs and translations from the Gaelic with, or without, harp accompaniment; the serious songs with so much expression, and the merry ones with so much spirit, that she charmed everybody. The death of her brothers and of her father, to whom she was devotedly attached, cast a shade over the latter part of her life. Mr Lockhart was clever and an able writer, but he was too sarcastic to be quite agreeable; however, we were always on the most friendly terms. He was of a Lanarkshire family and distantly related to Somerville. After the death of his wife and sons, Lockhart fell into bad health and lost much of his asperity.

Scott was ordered to go abroad for relaxation. Somerville and I happened to be at the seaport where he embarked, and we went to take leave of him. He kissed me, and said, 'Farewell, my dear; I am going to die abroad like other British novelists.' Happy would it have been if God had so willed it, for he returned completely broken down; his hopes were blighted, his sons dead, and his only remaining descendant was a grand-daughter, daughter of Mrs Lockhart. She married Mr James Hope, and soon died, leaving an only daughter, the last descendant of Sir Walter Scott. Thus the 'Merry, merry days that I have seen', ended very sadly.

In 1816 Mary Somerville moved to London after her husband was appointed to the Army Medical Board. In London Mary Somerville enjoyed the friendship of many men and women, pre-eminent in the sciences: the Herschels, Henry Brougham, Whewell, Peacock, Babbage, Sedgwick and Brewster. On the continent too she was received as one of themselves by Laplace, La Croix, Biot, Poisson, Arago, Ampère, and many others. Her acquaintance was not, of course, confined to men and women of scientific genius but took in most of the prominent figures of her period:

Among many others, we were intimate with Dr and Mrs Baillie and his sisters.[7] Joanna was my dear and valued friend to the end of her life. When her tragedy of *Montfort* [sic][8] was to be brought on the stage, Somerville and I, with a large party of her relations and friends, went with her to the theatre. The play was admirably acted, for Mrs Siddons and her brother John Kemble performed the principal parts. It was warmly applauded by a full house, but it was never acted again.[9] Some time afterwards *The Family Legend*, founded on a Highland story, had better success in Edinburgh; but Miss Baillie's plays, though highly poetical, are not suited to the stage. Miss Mitford was more successful, for some of her plays were repeatedly acted. She excelled also as a writer. *Our Village* is perfect of its kind; nothing can be more animated than her description of a game of cricket.[10] I met with Miss Austen's novels at this time, and thought them excellent, especially *Pride and Prejudice*. It certainly formed a curious contrast to my old favourites, the Radcliffe novels and the ghost stories; but I had now come to years of discretion.

Mary Somerville records the coronation of George IV and the scandal of Queen Caroline being refused admisssion. More personally she speaks of the grief occasioned by the death of her eldest daughter, Margaret. Mary Somerville undertook the work that began her fame at the request of Lord Brougham. 'Mechanism of the Heavens', her explanatory version of Laplace's 'Méchanique Céleste', was adopted as a text book at Cambridge and she was elected an honorary member of the Royal Astronomical Society at the same time as Caroline Herschel.[11] The Royal Society of London elected to have her bust, by the sculptor Chantrey, in their great hall. After a period of overwork Mary Somerville went to Paris with her family to recuperate. In Paris she moved socially among a large number of people, many but not all of whom were scientific:

At some […] parties I met Madame Charles Dupin, whom I liked much.[12] When I went to return her visit, she received us in her bedroom. She was a fashionable and rather elegant woman, with perfect manners. She invited us to dinner to meet her brother-in-law, the President of the Chamber of Deputies. He was animated and witty, very fat, and more ugly than his brother, but both were clever and agreeable. The President invited me to a very brilliant ball he gave, but as it was on a Sunday I could not accept the invitation. We went one evening with Madame de Rumford. Her first husband, Lavoisier, the chemist, had been guillotined at the Revolution, and she was now a widow, but had lived long separated from her second husband. She was enormously rich, and had a magnificent palace, garden, and conservatory, in which she gave balls and concerts. At all the evening parties in Paris the best bedroom was lighted up for reception like the other rooms. Madame de Rumford was capricious and ill-tempered; however, she received me very well, and invited me to meet a very large party at dinner. Mr Fenimore Cooper, the American novelist, with his wife and daughter, were among the guests. I found him extremely amiable and agreeable, which surprised me, for when I knew him in England he was so touchy that it was difficult to converse with him without giving him offence. He was introduced to Sir Walter Scott by Sir James Mackintosh, who said, in presenting him, 'Mr Cooper, allow me to introduce you to your great forefather in the art of fiction;' 'Sir,' said Cooper, with great asperity, 'I have no forefather.'[13] Now, though his manners were rough, they were quite changed. We saw a great deal of him, and I was frequently in his house, and found him perfectly liberal; so much so, that he told us the faults of his country with the greatest frankness, yet he was the champion of America, and hated England.

Mary Somerville moved largely in the Liberal set but did also meet some moderate and ultra right-wing 'Legitimistes':
All parties criticised the British Administration in Ireland. A lady sitting by me at a party said, 'No wonder so many English prefer France to so odious a country as England, where the people are oppressed, and even cabbages are raised in hot-beds.' I laughed, and said, 'I like England very well, for all that.' An old gentleman, who was standing near us, said, 'Whatever terms two countries may be on, it behoves us individuals to observe good manners;' and when I went away, this gentleman handed me to the carriage, though I had never seen him before.

Much of Mary Somerville's 'Recollections' discuss her social life: here she writes movingly on Mary Berry. Mary Berry and Mary Somerville were both close also to Joanna Baillie:
Mary, the eldest [of the Miss Berrys], was a handsome, accomplished woman, who from her youth had lived in the most distinguished society, both at home and abroad. She published a *Comparative View of Social Life in France and England*, which was well received by the public. She was a Latin scholar, spoke and wrote French fluently, yet with all these advantages, the consciousness that she might have done something better, had female education been less frivolous, gave her a characteristic melancholy which lasted through life. She did not talk much herself, but she had the tact to lead conversation. She and her sister received every evening a select society in their small house in Curzon Street. Besides any distinguished foreigners

who happened to be in London, among their habitual guests were my friend, Lady Charlotte Lindsay, always witty and agreeable, the brilliant and beautiful Sheridans, Lady Theresa Lister, afterwards Lady Theresa Lewis, who edited Miss Berry's 'Memoirs', Lord Landsdowne, and many others.[14] Lady Davy came occasionally, and the Miss Fanshaws, who were highly accomplished, and good artists, besides Miss Catherine Fanshaw wrote clever *vers de société*, such as a charade on the letter H, and, if I am not mistaken, 'The Butterfly's Ball', etc.[15] I visited these ladies, but their manners were so cold and formal that, though I admired their talents, I never became intimate with them. On the contrary, like everyone else, I loved Mary Berry, she was so warm-hearted and kind. When London began to fill, and the season was at its height, the Miss Berrys used to retire to their pretty villa at Twickenham, where they received their friends to luncheon, and strawberries and cream, and very delightful these visits were in fine spring weather.

In her later life in Florence Mary Somerville met Elizabeth Barrett Browning, a woman, she says:
as much distinguished by her high mental qualities and poetical genius as by her modesty and simplicity [...] Mrs Browning at that time resided in Florence, except when the delicacy of her health obliged her to go to Rome. I think there is no other instance of husband and wife both poets, and both distinguished in their different lines. I can imagine no happier or more fascinating life than theirs; two kindred spirits united in the highest and noblest aspirations. Unfortunately her life was a short one; in full bloom of her intellect her frail health gave way, and she died leaving a noble record of genius to future ages, and a sweet memory to those who were her contemporaries. The Florentines, who, like all Italians, greatly appreciate genius, whether native or foreign, have placed a commemorative tablet on Casa Guidi, the house Mrs Browning inhabited.[16]

During the Italian years the family moved about the country, although Mary Somerville was perhaps most fond of Rome. Here, however, she speaks of an adventure on Lake Como:
We [...] went for a month to Bellagio, on the Lake of Como, at that time the most lonely village imaginable. We had neither letters, newspapers, nor any books, except the Bible, yet we liked it exceedingly. I did nothing but paint in the mornings, and Somerville sat by me. My daughters wandered about, and in the evening we went in a boat on the lake. Sometimes we made longer excursions. One day we went early to Menaggio, at the upper end of the lake. The day had been beautiful, but while at dinner we were startled by a loud peal of thunder. The boatmen desired us to embark without delay, as a storm was rising behind the mountains; it soon blew a gale, and the lake was a sheet of foam; we took shelter for a while at some place on the coast and set out again, thinking the storm had blown over, but it was soon worse than ever. We were in no small danger for two hours. The boatmen, terrified, threw themselves on their knees in prayer to the Madonna. Somerville seized the helm and lowered the sail and ordered them to rise, saying, the Madonna would help them if they helped themselves, and at last they returned to their duty. For a long time we remained perfectly silent, when one of our daughters said, 'I have been thinking what a paragraph it will be in the newspapers, "Drowned, during a sudden squall on

the lake of Como, an English family named Somerville, father, mother and two daughters".' The silence thus broken made us laugh, though our situation was serious enough, for when we landed the shore was crowded with people who had fully expected to see the boat go down. Twice after this we were overtaken by these squalls, which are very dangerous. I shall never forget the magnificence of the lightning and the grandeur of the thunder, which was echoed by the mountains during the storms on the Lake of Como.

We saw fishermen spear the fish by torch-light, as they did on the Tweed. The fish were plenty and the water so clear that they were seen at a great depth. There are very large red-fleshed trout in the lake, and a small very delicious fish called *agoni*, caught in multitudes by fine silk nets, to which bells are attached on floats, that keep up a constant tinkling to let the fishermen know where to find their nets when floated away by the wind.

The Somervilles were in Rome during the political troubles of the forties and fifties:
Under Gregory XVI everything was conducted in the most profound secrecy; arrests were made almost at our very door, of which we knew nothing. The new Pope Pious IX at first was welcomed by the liberals: entirely forgetting how incompatible a theocracy or government by priests ever must be with all progress and with liberal institutions. [...] One evening we were sitting on the balcony of the hotel [in Bologna], when we saw a man stab another in the back of the neck, and then run away. The victim staggered along for a minute, and then fell down in a pool of blood. He had been a spy of the police under Gregory XVI, and one of the principal agents of his cruel government. He was so obnoxious to the people that his assassin has never been discovered.

During a cholera epidemic in Florence in the early 1850s the Somervilles saw a death cart as they returned from an evening visit:
As we were driving home late at night, going down the hill, our carriage ran against one of the dead carts which was carrying those who had died that day to the burying-ground at Trespiano. It was horribly ghastly – one could distinguish the forms of the limbs under the canvas thrown over the heap of dead. The burial of the poor and rich in Italy is in singular contrast; the poor are thrown into the grave without a coffin, the rich are placed in coffins, and in full dress, which especially in the case of youth and infancy, leaves a pleasant impression. An intimate friend of ours lost an infant, and asked me to go and see it laid out. The coffin, lined with white silk, was on a table, covered with a white cloth, strewed with flowers, and with a row of wax lights on either side. The baby was clothed in a white satin frock, leaving the neck and arms bare; a rose-bud was in each hand, and a wreath of rose-buds surrounded the head, which rested on a pillow. Nothing could be prettier; it was like a sleeping angel.

Mary Somerville's faith sustained her through the grief of the loss of her husband and her son; in her late eighties she still had the energy to write to John Stuart Mill about female suffrage and to join a petition to the Senate of London University, praying that degrees might be granted to women: it was rejected. She retained full intellectual control until the last; read Darwin's 'Descent of Man'; and continued to write and work till the day of her

death. In her 89th year she writes:
Although I have been tried by many severe afflictions, my life upon the whole has been happy. In my youth I had to contend with prejudice and illiberality; yet I was of a quiet temper, and easy to live with, and I never interfered with or pryed into other people's affairs. However, if irritated by what I considered unjust criticism or interference with myself, or anyone I loved, I could resent it fiercely. I was not good at argument; I was apt to lose my temper; but I never bore ill will to any one, or forgot the manners of a gentlewoman, however angry I may have been at the time. But I must say that no one ever met with such kindness as I have done. I never had an enemy. I have never been of a melancholy disposition; through depressed sometimes by circumstances, I always rallied again; and although I seldom laugh, I can laugh heartily at wit or on fit occasion. The short time I have to live naturally occupies my thoughts. In the blessed hope of meeting again with my beloved children, and those who were and are dear to me on earth, I think of death with composure and perfect confidence in the mercy of God. Yet to me, who am afraid to sleep alone on a stormy night, or even to sleep comfortably any night unless some one is near, it is a fearful thought, that my spirit must enter that new state of existence quite alone. We are told of the infinite glories of that state, and I believe in them, though it is incomprehensible to us; but as I do comprehend, in some degree at least, the exquisite loveliness of the visible world, I confess I shall be sorry to leave it. I shall regret the sky, the sea, with all the changes of their beautiful colouring; the earth, with its verdure and flowers: but far more shall I grieve to leave animals who have followed our steps affectionately for years, without knowing for certainty their ultimate fate, though I firmly believe that the living principle is never extinguished. Since the atoms of matter are indestructible, as far as we know, it is difficult to believe that the spark which gives to their union life, memory, affection, intelligence, and fidelity, is evanescent. Every atom in the human frame, as well as in that of animals, undergoes a periodical change by continual waste and renovation; the abode is changed, not its inhabitant. If animals have no future, the existence of many is most wretched; multitudes are starved, cruelly beaten, and loaded during life; many die under a barbarous vivisection. I cannot believe that any creature was created for uncompensated misery; it would be contrary to the attributes of God's mercy and justice. I am sincerely happy to find that I am not the only believer in the immortality of the lower animals.

Three years after writing this Mary Somerville died in her sleep on the morning of 29 November 1872. Her remains rest in the English Campo Santo of Naples.

NOTES
1. Review of *Personal Recollections* in *Nature: A Weekly Journal of Science*, vol. IX (Nov.1873 to Apr.1874), 417-18.
2. Edie Ochiltree is a licensed travelling beggar in Scott's *The Antiquary*, 1816.
3. All Gothic novels: Clara Reeve, *The Old English Baron*, 1777; Ann Radcliffe, *A Romance of the Forest*, 1791, *The Mysteries of Udolpho*, 1794.
4. William Daniel (1769-1837) was a landscape painter and engraver. His *Voyage round Great Britain, 1814-25* is perhaps now his most famous series.

5. Sir Adam Ferguson (1770-1854) was the son of Professor Adam Ferguson (1723-1816), Professor of Philosophy at the University of Edinburgh; he was one of Scott's closest friends. Having served with distinction in the Peninsular campaign against Napoleon, he was appointed Keeper of the Regalia of Scotland in 1818 and was knighted during the visit of George IV in 1822. William Clerk (1771-1847), a bachelor, was brother of John Clerk, Lord Eldin (1757-1832). It was said by his friends that only William's diffidence prevented him from being as great a success as his brother, the judge.

6. John Gibson Lockhart (1794-1854) was celebrated as a novelist and critic and editor. He is perhaps best remembered, however, for his controversial biography, 1837-8, of his father-in-law, Scott.

7. See Joanna Baillie's 'Recollections' where it is explained that she lived with her elder sister Agnes and was close to her brother Matthew, the celebrated surgeon and physician who attended both George III and the Princess Charlotte.

8. *De Monfort* must be the most frequently mispelled work in English. The intrusive 't' comes presumably from Simon de Montfort. I have even in otherwise respectable places encountered *De Montford* and in one letter Joanna Baillie herself lets in the 't'.

9. For this production of *De Monfort* see Joanna Baillie, p.107, n.24. Mary Somerville is wrong that the play was not acted again. It was staged again in a revised version at Drury Lane in November and December 1821 with the famous tragedian, Edmund Kean (1789-1833) as De Monfort. Kean performed the part again in June 1822 in Bath and in July at the Theatre Royal, Birmingham. In Scotland the play was performed with Mrs Siddons after the celebrated production of Baillie's *The Family Legend* in 1810 but it was not well received, having no local interest. Scott suggested that if the play had had as much tartan as *The Family Legend* it would have gone down better. The play was also staged in America at a number of locations. See Margaret Carhart, *Joanna Baillie*, 1923.

10. Mary Russell Mitford (1787-1855), *Our Village*, sketches of rural life, was begun in *The Lady's Magazine*, 1819, and published separately 1824-32.

11. Caroline Lucretia Herschel (1750-1848), astronomer, sister of Sir William Herschel and aunt of Sir John Herschel. In 1788 the Royal Astronomical Society published her revision of the *Index to Flamsteed's Observations of the Fixed Stars* which included a catalogue of 561 previously omitted stars. See Todd 2.

12. Her husband Charles Dupin (1784-1873) was a mathematician and politician.

13. James Fenimore Cooper (1789-1851) is, of course, best known for *The Last of the Mohicans*, 1826. His *England, with Sketches of Society in the Metropolis*, a highly critical account of English society, appeared in 1837.

14. The Sheridans, known as the 'Three Graces', were the granddaughters of Richard Brinsley Sheridan, the playwright and politician. The eldest, Helen Selina, became Lady Dufferin, afterwards Countess of Gifford: she wrote songs and a play which was performed at the Haymarket Theatre in 1863; the second sister, Caroline, was a writer who wrote for money when she separated from her husband, the Honourable George Norton, who deprived her of her children and tried to attach her earnings: see p.239, n.2 for divorce law at the time. When he died she married Sir William Stirling; the youngest, and by all accounts most beautiful, Jane Georgina, married the 12th Duke of Somerset and was Queen of Beauty at the Eglinton Tournament in 1839.

15. Lady Davy, wife of Sir Humphrey Davy, was a close friend of Joanna Baillie. Catherine Maria Fanshawe (the usual spelling) (1765-1834): her charade/riddle ran ''Twas in heaven pronounced, and 'twas muttered in hell'.

16. Elizabeth Barrett Browning (1806-61) married Robert Browning in 1846. After their marriage the Brownings lived mostly in Italy. Her poem, *Casa Guidi Windows*, 1851, recorded political events in Italy coloured by Elizabeth Barrett Browning's enthusiasm for the cause of Italian liberty.

Christian Isobel Johnstone (1781–1857)

Christian Isobel Johnstone was born in Fifeshire. Early in life she married a man called McLeish from whom she obtained a divorce, but the circumstances surrounding this are not known. In 1812 she married John Johnstone, then a schoolmaster at Dunfermline. In 1815 she published the novel *Clan-Albin: A National Tale*. In 1817 she and her husband were recommended, probably by the publisher William Blackwood, to the projectors of the new *Inverness Courier* as possible editors. The couple were invited and moved to Inverness where the paper was officially edited by John Johnstone but in practice his wife seems to have contributed more to the paper. In 1824 the Johnstones moved to Edinburgh where Christian wrote for Blackwood her third novel, *Elizabeth de Bruce*, 1827. She also joined her husband in editing the *Edinburgh Weekly Chronicle*, the weekly, *The Schoolmaster* and the monthly, *Johnstone's Magazine*. In 1834 she formed with William Tait what turned out to be her most important literary connection. She began to assist in the management of Tait's popular magazine which in opposition to *Blackwood's Magazine* supported radical politics and in the same year *Johnstone's Magazine* was merged with *Tait's*. According to Anderson, 'She now formed a permanent connexion with [*Tait's*], and although not, strictly speaking, the editor, she had entire charge of the literary department, and was a large and regular contributor. She was to *Tait* what Professor Wilson was to *Blackwood*; the ostensible always, and, indeed the real editors, being the respective publishers (Anderson, III, 713)'. At *Tait's* Christian Johnstone had the opportunity of befriending the radical poet, Robert Nicoll, and many other young writers. Some of her contributions to *Tait's* and earlier periodicals, she edited as *The Edinburgh Tales*. Among other writings were *Nights of the Round Table* and the *Cook and Housewife's Manual*, by 'Mrs Margaret (Meg) Dods' which went into 11 editions. This cookery book is described as 'a practical system of modern domestic cookery and family management, containing a compendium of French cookery, and of fashionable confectionery, preparations for invalids and convalescents, a selection of cheap dishes, and numerous useful miscellaneous receipts in the various branches of domestic economy.' It is of interest to note that *The Diversions of Hollycot; or, The Mother's Art of Thinking*, an instructional tale for children which light-heartedly plays upon Horne Tooke's *Diversions of Purley*, has the mother recounting to her children the story of the exemplary heroine, Lady Grisell Baillie. Johnstone almost ceased to write when *Tait's Magazine* was sold but she had been a thoroughly professional writer with a strong sense of the commercial possibilities of the craft . She died aged 76, and was buried in the Grange Cemetery, a few months before her husband. I have chosen her journalism to illustrate her canny feminism and her persistent refusal of sentimentality. Ralph Jessop (*HSWW*, p.224) deals also with her literary reviews in which, for example, she attacks the Irish novelist Maria Edgeworth for failing to be a true national writer: 'Neither her feelings, mind, nor imagination […] are Irish'.

Christian Isobel Johnstone, *The Saxon and the Gael: or, The Northern Metropolis:*

Including a View of the Lowland and Highland Character (London: T. Tegg & T. Dick, 1814) [this novel is presumed to be by Johnstone]; *Clan-Albin: A National Tale*, 4 vols (London: Longman & Co.; Edinburgh: Macredie, Skelly & Muckersy, 1815); *The Wars of the Jews, as Related by Josephus. Adapted to the Capacities of Young Persons* (London: Harris & Son, 1823); *The Cook and Housewife's Manual: Containing the Most Approved Modern Receipes etc.* (under the pseudonym, 'Mrs Margaret Dods, of the Cleikum Inn, St Ronans') (Edinburgh, for the Author, 1826); *Elizabeth De Bruce: A Novel,* 3 vols (Edinburgh: Blackwood, 1827); *The Students; Or, Biography of Grecian Philosophers* (London: John Harris, [1827?]); *Scenes of Industry Displayed in the Bee-hive and the Ant-hill* (London: J. Harris, 1827); *Diversions of Hollycot; or, The Mother's Art of Thinking* (Edinburgh: Oliver & Boyd, 1828); *Nights of the Round Table: Or Stories of Aunt Jane and her Friends*, 2 series (Edinburgh: 1832 & 1849); *True Tales of the Irish Peasantry, as Related by Themselves.* Selected by Mrs Johnstone from the Report of the Poor-law Commissioners (Edinburgh: P. Brown, 1839); *The Edinburgh Tales* (including some work by others) (Edinburgh: W. Tait, 1845-6)

Robert Nicoll, *Poems* with a memoir of the author [by Christian Isobel Johnstone] (Edinburgh: William Tait, 1842)

Further reading:
Ina Ferris, 'Translation from the Borders: Encounter and Recalcitrance in *Waverley* and *Clan-Albin*', *Eighteenth-Century Fiction*, vol.9, no.2 (Jan. 1997) 203-22
A Highland Newspaper: The First Hundred and Fifty Years of 'The Inverness Courier', 1817-1967 (Inverness: Robert Carruthers & Sons, 1969)

Anderson; Irving; *DNB*; *HSWW*

From 'Marriages are Made in Heaven', *Tait's Edinburgh Magazine* (November 1832) 184-9:

It may be so, but we have our doubts upon the matter. Heaven, we think, would have made neater jobs than most of them are. Not that we incline with certain Manicheans, to give the other power the credit of their manufacture. They are a cut above him. That the devil inhabits hell, we know; but we also know that he did not make it.

We have sometimes wondered that Milton did not think it necessary to prefix a 'Doctrine and Discipline of Marriage' to his 'Doctrine and Discipline of Divorce'.[1] When his hand was in he might as well have done it. Whatever evil rumours may be abroad as to his practical fitness for making the married state happy, 'and keeping it so', it is evident from his account of the life Adam led in Paradise, that he had very pretty theoretical notions on the subject. Perhaps, as some old heathen philosophers held the business of life to be preparation for death, Milton esteemed divorce the great object of matrimony, and, like other great men, forgot the means in the end.

There are two main obstacles to the proper choice of a partner. People are, for the most part, in love, as far as their natures will permit, when they marry; and hence a twofold delusion. Firstly, each party sees the other through the glowing medium of passion; secondly, each is for the time in reality a different being from what he or she was before, and is to be again.

It is madness, then, to marry for love but to marry for any other reason may be to take up marriage as a burden from the start:
Marry then for love, in God's name, all who are fools enough to marry! Love is the only apology for such an absurd step. Burning, over-mastering passion, fusing two beings into one; satisfied with nothing short of a perpetual struggle to attain such an intermixture of soul, body, and interests as nature has rendered unattainable; this alone can justify the tying of the knot which may not be unloosed. It is madness, but it is a madness which is in the order of nature, and must be undergone. The only advice that can be given to those unfortunates who stagger hither and thither beneath the load of the tempest, is to keep their reeling wits as sober as possible, – to speak and act as like rational beings as they can, – to remind themselves, perpetually, that they are living in a world of dreams, out of which they must one day awake, in order that the fading of their garish fancies may be as gradual, and their *exit* into the world of reality, accompanied with as slight a shock as may be.
[…]
There is a period of life, when leisure to brood over one's own thoughts is dangerous and unnerving; the period when those throbbings and longings, vague and undefined, but mighty and bewildering, which form the buoyant and surging couch and canopy of love, are awakening into existence. Lack of such employment as leads the mind out of itself, is then all but inevitable destruction. The tone of our literature, the general tendency of daily conversation, increases the danger. The lyres of modern poets 'have one unchanging theme' – 'Tis love, still love.'
[…]
    Sad is but too often the reawakening to the reality of life, after an inconsiderate marriage; when the passions, which in the beloved object had been overflown and hidden by the spring-tide of love, as the low lumps of rock, rough with shapeless shells, and tangled with brown withered sea-weeds are, by a waveless summer sea, again left bare. That good lady there, whose face is like frozen vinegar, and whose life is one perpetual scold, was once, to all outward appearance, a very loveable person. Now, the first thing you hear in the morning is her sharp voice on the stair, rating the maid for leaving the brush and duster there. During breakfast, she keeps up a perpetual maunder. The water is off the boil and smoked, the toast burned, the milk soured, (no wonder, it is near her) some member of the family has come too late, or some one had been in the parlour before her, which is interpreted into impatience. Should your evil genius keep you within doors during the forenoon, she is to be heard incessantly clattering up and down stairs, like a cat shod with walnut shells; fretting from cellar to garret, and from pantry to bed-room; everywhere finding cause for dissatisfaction, and everywhere venting it in shrill, sharp, peevish tones. Should your avocations call you out, you are welcomed back with a scold. Company at dinner may make her bridle her tongue; but then she only 'puts that tongue into her heart and chides with thinking', her looks giving

terrible evidence of the indemnification she promises herself for this restraint. She repeats through her sleep the objurgations of the day. She even scolds the family to church, and employs the time of divine service looking out for faults which she may reprehend on her return home. A party of pleasure is an excuse for finding fault with all the preparations of her family before-hand, and of their conduct while there. She scolds her husband first into habits of drinking, and then into his grave; her sons into occupations for which they are not fitted; and her daughters into ineligible matches, from their eagerness to get out of hearing. And yet she means no harm. She merely needs like all other people, some excitement to keep her alive; and the only excitement of which she is susceptible is irritation. Hers is not that anger which flows from dislike: it is only a sort of moral itch, seeking to scrub itself against every object with which it comes in contact. And yet in the brief season of love this creature was agreeable. That impulse which seeks pleasure in conferring it, made her look lovely for the time; as accidents of the atmosphere can lend a momentary beauty even to the most barren moor.

It is easy to find a male counterpart to this picture. We would say to all ladies, in search of a husband, beware of a sentimental man. He is a selfish voluptuary: he would take without giving. He has lived over in fancy all that gives happiness in reality, and the edge of his feelings has been blunted. Devoted exclusively to such trains of thought, his mind is empty and without resources. Shrinking from the labours and contests of life, his thoughts are devoid of that manliness and vigour which exercise alone can give. Dull, inane, feeble, loveless, he can feel for no one; protect, support, or cherish no one; cheer the dull path of life to no one. In the prime of life, he will be at best but a negative; and in old age he will sit moping and snivelling by the chimney corner,

> Clownish and malcontent,
> Peevish, impertinent,
> Dashing the merriment;[2]

a clog, a log, a nuisance, and an incumbrance.

What then is to be done:
Seeing that 'he who will to Cupar maun to Cupar',[3] the only advice that can be given to aspirants after connubial bliss is not to expect too much. To the man we would moreover hint, that marry whom they may, they ought to eschew silly women. Sentiment it is that attracts man to woman; and where this is not embedded in, interpenetrated with a goodly portion of intellect; it is shallow and evanescent. To the women we would say, avoid idle men. 'Man's love is, of man's life, a thing apart.'[4] Every man has a certain proportion of the commodity, which, if treasured up for idle hours, will suffice; but if beat out over his whole time, will prove lamentably thin and brittle.

Our sermon, we fear, has proved, on the whole, rather dull; but the indulgent reader will remember that
MARRIAGE IS NO JOKE!

From 'Mrs Hugo Reid's Plea for Woman':[5] *Tait's Edinburgh Magazine* (1844) 423-428:

Reid's book argues for female suffrage and became more influential in America than Britain. Christian Isobel Johnstone, however, stresses the need for female education and training to reduce dependence upon marriage for female subsistence. She also indicates here her optimism: although there is much still to do, great advances have been made in recent years.

The Plea which Mrs Reid urges, is far from being novel in England. It has been maintained, chiefly by women, though eminent men also, philosophers and wits, to take antipodes, Jeremy Bentham and the Rev. Sidney Smith, have taken it up.[6] Mrs Macaulay flung her female gauntlet into the arena sixty years since. Mary Wollstonecraft followed as the eloquent and fearless champion of 'The Rights of Women'.[7] In the earlier period of the French Revolution – now half a century ago – she addressed Talleyrand, the ex-bishop of Autun,[8] as the determined and uncompromising advocate of her sex: contending that, in the general emancipation of society from the civil bondage of ages, women should participate; and that the mass of Frenchmen, who then for the first time claimed to be free, and to think and act for themselves, should, in common justice, approve of the same liberty being extended to that half of the rational creation, hitherto held in civil and political thraldom. Miss Martineau[9] has said something similar of the assertors of American Independence, the framers of the original American Constitution; the fundamental principles of which are contained in the famous Declaration of Rights. If it be seriously asked how such monstrous exceptions are practically made as the whole of the women and the people of colour of Free Republican America, a reply would be somewhat difficult to find by a Republican statesman.

Modern female advocates for the rights of the sex, though contending for the principles of Mary Wollstonecraft, are either ignorant that they are hers, or else are afraid to use a name which prejudice has covered with unmerited obloquy. Women dread something they know not what in her writings; whereas, the fact is, that the philosophy of Mary Wollstonecraft, in her apology for her sex and the Rights of Women, is severe and even stoical. No stoic can more sternly repudiate the fleeting empire of personal beauty, or the fickle, short-lived, disturbing passion of youthful love. Her work would seem to have been written after she had bitterly experienced the miseries too often, in the most powerful minds, attendant on that fatal passion; at a time when hope was crushed, or during the collapse of an agonized heart.

'Who,' – to come to the heart of her theory, she demands, – 'who made *man* the exclusive judge, if women partake with him the gift of reason?' Man, however, according to Mrs Reid, still claims, whether rightly or not, to be the exclusive judge on nearly every point of interest to the species; yet, the women – though silently and indirectly – borne quietly on, as it were, with the stream of social improvement, have come to have much more to say on topics of high and vital interest than they ever had before; and the world, we imagine, is none the worse for it. The last twenty years have been remarkable for the mental development, and social progress, of all the 'inferior orders of society': that is, of the slaves of the British colonies, the working classes of manufacturing England; and the women, at least those of middle rank, in France, England and America: – we may add, of the whole North of Europe. The great, if silent change in the attainments and knowledge, and consequently in the social, if not civil, position of women which has already taken place, portends still greater changes; while it indicates the progress already made. […] The women have made no apparent approximation to results which Mrs Reid regards as not more desirable than just. But we think that she labours under an error, when she asserts that women, whether individually or collectively, have not influence, nay, a great and increasing influence, even on public affairs. […] But, admitting the preponderance of influence, this can never, we confess, counterbalance the want of positive rights; and influence, often tainted by the means of its acquisition, must also be tainted in its action. The alleged natural mental inferiority of women, their 'inaptitude' is an argument, or a fallacy, very generally abandoned in these days, so we shall not enter upon it.

[…] A very great point has been gained for the sex, when it is acknowledged that female ignorance is neither virtue nor the safeguard of the feminine virtues, – if virtues have sex, – and never the best soil in which they may take root and flourish. It is something to have it confessed that knowledge of all kinds – knowledge which next to religion and virtue, is man's highest good, and which is essential to religion and virtue – may coexist with the utmost purity and genuine delicacy, and even heighten and refine the womanly graces. But all is gained when it is confessed, that high mental cultivation, the full development of the reason, and of every faculty and affection with which God has gifted the entire human family, is the best foundation of virtue and preparative for happiness.

Like Mrs Oliphant later, Johnstone points out that some social ills are not borne solely by women: 'we have far too many "gentlemen" as well as "gentlewomen" "without a profession"':
Let this be amended. No one can seriously oppose all or a great many more young women being rendered capable of really useful occupation of some sort. A great amelioration in the social state of women takes place when, instead of being bought from their fathers as wives, they are given in marriage with portions. We would have all women, whether single or married, have portions; if not in their pockets, then in their knowledge, usefulness and power of self-reliance, and self sustenance.

NOTES
1. Milton published his *The Doctrine and Discipline of Divorce* in 1643. He argued that a true marriage was of mind as well as body but admitted that those who had had varied experience in youth were less likely than the wholly chaste to find themselves in unsuitable unions.
2. Charles Lamb, 'Hypochondriacus', *Poems*, 1836, ll.13-15. Johnstone inverts l.13 and l.14.
3. A folk saying: people cannot be prevented from doing what they are determined to do.
4. ''Tis woman's whole existence', Byron, *Don Juan*, canto I, cxciv
5. [Marion Reid], *A Plea for Woman* (Edinburgh: Tait, 1843). Reprinted with an Introduction by Susanne Ferguson (Edinburgh: Polygon, 1988).
6. Jeremy Bentham (1748-1832), political and moral philosopher, principally remembered for the theory of 'Utility' which was modified and developed by John Stuart Mill (1806-73); Rev. Sydney Smith (1771-1845) divine, philosopher and wit, in 1802 founded with Brougham and Jeffrey *The Edinburgh Review*.

7. Catherine Macaulay (1731-91) was a celebrated feminist and republican historian. Her *History of England* in 8 vols, 1763-83, was admired in France and, of course, by Mary Wollstonecraft; Mary Wollstonecraft (1759-97) radical feminist educationist. Her views were, as Johnstone indicates, widely enough held but the details of her scandalous life, somewhat naively revealed by her husband, William Godwin, in his tribute to her memory, led to misreading and rejection of her work, even by those who shared her ideas. His revelation of her affair with Gilbert Imlay and her attempted suicides, completely destroyed her credibility with more conservative readers. As Johnstone indicates, however, her *Vindication of the Rights of Woman*, 1792, remained an inspiration to later feminists. She died, in great pain, shortly after the birth of her daughter Mary. Her daughter, Mary Godwin, is better known as Mary Shelley, the wife of the poet, Shelley, and author of *Frankenstein*, 1818.

8. Charles Maurice de Talleyrand-Périgord (1754-1838), French politician and diplomat, was excommunicated for the part he took in the reform of the church during the Revolution. Talleyrand was a survivor and was foreign minister from 1797 until 1807, when he quarelled with Napoleon. He served again under Louis XVIII. For anecdotes about him see Davies p.177.

9. Harriet Martineau (1802-76), feminist intellectual, advocate of social reform, was a prolific writer throughout her life. She was in her youth a devout Unitarian and her first publication was *Devotional Exercises* in 1823, but she moved steadily away from this, indeed from all, faith.

Charlotte Ann Waldie
(Mrs Stephen Eaton) (1788–1859)

Charlotte Waldie was the second daughter of George Waldie of Hendersyde Park, near Kelso, Roxburghshire, and Ann, eldest daughter of Jonathan Ormiston, Newcastle-upon-Tyne. In 1822 she married Stephen Eaton, a banker, from Stamford whose seat was Ketton Hall, Rutland. He died in 1834 and Charlotte Eaton died in London in 1859 leaving two sons and two daughters. In June 1815 she journeyed with her brother John and younger sister Jane to Brussels. She wrote an account of her experiences there which was published in 1817 and from which an extract is given below. A second edition was published in 1853 and a third with an introduction by E. Bell in 1888. The *DNB* says that the narrative 'takes a high place among contemporary accounts by other than military writers' and indeed its detail about the panic and muddle in Brussels during and after the Battle of Waterloo gives a lively sense of the moment and the description of the surrounds of the field some weeks after the battle feels authentically unpleasant.

Her three volume travel book *Rome in the Nineteenth Century* went into six editions, and she subsequently published two novels. All her work was originally published anonymously. Her sister Jane published an account of her travels in Italy.

Charlotte Ann Waldie, *Narrative of a Residence in Belgium during the Campaign of 1815 and of a Visit to the Field of Waterloo*, by an Englishwoman (London: John Murray, 1817); *The Days of Battle; or Quatre Bras and Waterloo*, by an Englishwoman (London: Henry G. Bohn, 1853); *Waterloo Days*, new edition, with an introduction and appendix by E. Bell (London: G. Bell, 1888); *Rome in the Nineteenth Century: containing a complete account of the ruins of the ancient city, the remains of the middle ages, and the monuments of modern times. With remarks on the fine arts, on the state of society, and on the religious ceremonies, manners, and customs of the modern Romans. In a series of letters, written during a residence at Rome in 1817 and 1818*, 3 vols (Edinburgh: 1820); *Continental Adventures; A Novel*, 3 vols (London: Hurst, Robinson & Co., 1826); *At Home and Abroad: A Novel*, 3 vols (London: 1831)

Further reading:
DNB

From *A Narrative of a Residence in Belgium*, 1817:

On Saturday, the 10th of June, 1815, my brother, my sister, and myself sailed from the pier of Ramsgate at three in the afternoon, in company with Sir – –, Major –, extra Aide-de-camp to the Duke of Wellington, a Mr.–, an English merchant;[1] together with an incongruous assemblage of horses, dogs, and barouches; Irish servants, French valets, and steerage passengers, too multifarious to mention, all crowded together into a wretched little packet. On Sunday evening, the 11th of June, we found ourselves, after a passage of thirty-six hours, many miles distant from Ostend, lying at anchor in a dead calm, and without a hope of reaching it till the following morning. To escape remaining another night amidst the discomforts of this packet, without food, for we had eaten up all our provisions; and without sleep, for we had experimentally proved that none was to be got, our three selves, and our three companions in misfortune, the Knight, the Major, and the Merchant, embarked in a crazy little boat, about nine o'clock in a beautiful summer's evening, as the sun was sinking in golden splendour, and trusted ourselves to the mercy of the waves. The tide was running strong against the rowers, and night closed in long before we approached the shore; but though the light of the heavens had faded, the ocean was illuminated with that beautiful phosphoric fire, so well known in warmer latitudes. The most brilliant magic light played upon the surface of the waters, and marked the path of our little vessel through the deep, with the softest, purest radiances; the oars seemed to be moving through liquid fire and every drop, as it dashed from them, sparkled like the blaze of a diamond. […] But the magic spell was dissolved, and the visions of fancy faded away in a moment; for we suddenly struck upon the sands, when we seemed still far from the shore; waves of fire dashed into the boat; and the sturdy sailors, abandoning their oars, seized upon us without the smallest ceremony, and carried us literally through fire and water to the beach.

The party successfully pass the sentries on shore through the offices of the Major, secure accommodation and supper. The following day they travel to Bruges where they sightsee in the rain until evening.

We left Bruges in the same bark which had once conveyed Napoleon Buonaparte to that city, and which is now used as a côche d'eau. It contained 150 people, of every sort and description, from the courtiers of Louis XVIII down to Flemish peasants; all of whom, however, were obliging, talkative, attentive, flattering, and amusing.

They spend Wednesday in Ghent, setting off the next day for Brussels and stopping to dine halfway at Alost. During a walk in Alost they are forced to shelter in a small house, the mistress of which tells them what perhaps she supposes they want to hear:

Short as our stay was beneath her roof it was long enough for her to express with great energy her detestation of Napoleon and of the French; which she said was universal throughout Belgium. We had a good deal of conversation with her upon this subject, and upon the past and the present state of Belgium. […] She lamented over the trade, the manufactories, the commerce they had destroyed; the contributions they had exacted; the fine young men they had seized as conscripts; the convents they had ruined; the priests and 'les bonnes religieuses' they had turned to the door. Wherever we had gone before, and wherever we afterwards went, we heard the same sentiments from every tongue, and we saw the most unequivocal signs of the inveterate hatred of the whole Belgic people towards their former rulers. […]

The streets of Brussels are narrow, but they have that air of bustle, opulence and animation, which characterises a metropolis. To us everything was new and amusing: the people, the dresses, the houses, the shops, the very signs diverted us. Every notice was stuck up in the French language, and quite in the French style. [...] Everything wore a military aspect; and the number of troops, of different nations, descriptons and dresses, which filled the town, made it look very gay. [...] We caught a glimpse of the magnificent spire of the Hôtel de Ville, far exceeding, in architectural beauty, anything I remember to have seen.

In the Place Royale or Grande Place they meet Major Brown, their travelling companion, who tells them that the festive appearance of the city is deceptive and that the French have attacked Blücher.² *Notwithstanding, the Major rushes off to dress for a ball to be held at the Duchess of Richmond's. The Waldies repair to bed but are rudely awakened:*

Scarcely had I laid my weary head upon the pillow, when the bugle's loud and commanding call sounded from the Place Royale. 'Is that the call to arms?' I exclaimed, starting up in the bed. S– laughed at the idea;³ but I heard it again, and we listened with eager and anxious suspense. For a few moments a pause of doubt ensued. Hark! again! it sounded through the silence of the night, and from every quarter of the town it was now repeated, at short and regular intervals. 'It is the call to arms!' I exclaimed. Instantly the drums beat; the Highland pibroch sounded – it was the call to arms! Oh! never, never shall I forget the feelings of that moment! Immediately the utmost tumult and confusion succeeded to the silence in which the city had previously been buried. At half past two we were roused by a loud knocking at our room door, and J–'s [John's] voice calling to us to get up instantly, not to lose a moment – that the troops were under arms – were marching out against the French – and that Major– was waiting to see us before he left Brussels.

They say good-bye to their friend and watch the 'hurry and skurry for the field':

Numbers of the officers had been out, when the first order to be in readiness to march had been issued, and remained in perfect ignorance of the commencement of hostilities, until the alarm sounded, and called them from scenes of festivity and mirth to scenes of war and bloodshed. As the dawn broke, the soldiers were seen assembling from all parts of the town, in marching order, with their knapsacks on their backs, loaded with three days provision. Unconcerned in the midst of the din of war, many a soldier laid himself down on a truss of straw, and soundly slept, with his hands still grasping his firelock; others were sitting contentedly on the pavement, waiting the arrival of their comrades. Numbers were taking leave of their wives and children perhaps for the last time, and many a veteran's rough cheek was wet with the tears of sorrow. One poor fellow, immediately under our windows, turned back again and again to bid his wife farewell, and take his baby once more in his arms; and I saw him hastily brush away a tear with the sleeve of his coat, as he gave her back the child for the last time, wrung her hand, and ran off to join the company, which was drawn up on the other side of the Place Royale. [...] Many of the soldiers' wives marched out with their husbands to the field, and I saw one young English lady mounted on horseback, slowly riding out of town along with an officer, who, no doubt, was her husband. But even at this interesting moment, when thousands were parting with those nearest and dearest to their hearts, my gravity was suddenly overset, and my sorrow turned into mirth, by the unexpected appearance of a long train of market carts, loaded with cabbages, green peas, cauliflowers, early potatoes, old women, and strawberries, peaceably jogging along, one after another to market. These good people, who had never heard of battles, and who were perfectly at a loss to comprehend what could be the meaning of all this uproar, stared with astonishment at the spectacle before them, and actually gaped with wonder, as they slowly made their way in their long carts through the crowds of soldiers which filled the Place Royale. There was something inexpressibly ludicrous in the contrast which the grotesque figures and rustic dresses of these old women presented to this martial hurry and confusion, that really '*not* to laugh surpassed all powers of face',[4] and that I did laugh I must acknowledge, though it was perhaps very ill-timed levity. Soon afterwards the 42nd and 92nd Highland regiments marched through the Place Royale and the Parc, with their bagpipes playing before them, while the bright beams of the rising sun shone full on their polished muskets, and on the dark waving plumes of their tartan bonnets. We admired their fine athletic forms, their firm erect military demeanour and undaunted mien. We felt proud that they were our country-men: in their gallant bearing we recognised the true hardy sons of Caledon, men who would conquer or die; and we could not restrain a tear at the reflexion, how few of that warlike band who now marched out so proudly to battle might ever live to return. Alas! we had little thought that even before the fall of night these brave men, whom we now gazed at with so much interest and admiration, would be laid low!

Rumours about the subsequent engagements with the French are abundant in Brussels but very little real and reliable information is available. But about some aspects of the engagement at Quatre Bras, Charlotte Waldie speaks confidently:

It is a perversion of words to call the troops engaged in the battle of Quatre Bras the English army. During the greater part of the day a few regiments only, a mere handful of men, were opposed to the immense masses the French continually poured down against them: which were in vain attacked by the French cavalry, 'steel clad cuirassiers', and infantry. [...] The 92nd, 42nd, 79th, the 28th, the 95th and the Royal Scots were the first and most hotly engaged. For several hours these brave troops alone maintained the tremendous onset and the shock of the whole French army, and to their determined valour, Belgium owes her independence and England her glory. [...] The 92nd, 42nd and 79th Highland regiments had suffered most severely. [...] With grief and horror not to be described, we thought of these gallant soldiers, whom in the morning we had seen march out so proudly to battle, and who were now lying insensible in death on the plains of Quatre Bras.

The whole situation is, however, most insecure and the Waldies prepare to leave Brussels if it becomes necessary:

J– had engaged, and made an agreement to pay for, horses, upon the condition of their being in readiness to convey us to Antwerp, at a moment's warning, by day or night, if required. We had not, however, the smallest intention of leaving Brussels for some days to come, unless some sudden and unexpected change in public events should render it absolutely necessary. Thinking it, however, prudent to be prepared, we had sent our *valet de place* to *la blanchisseuse*, to desire her to send home every thing belonging to us early in the morning. *La blanchisseuse* sent back a message literally to this effect, – 'Madame,' said the valet addressing himself to me in French, 'the blanchisseuse says, that if the English should beat the French, she will iron and plait your clothes, and finish them for you; but if, *au contraire*, these vile French should get the better, then she will assuredly send you them all back quite wet – *tout mouillé* – early to-morrow morning'. At this speech, which the valet delivered with immoveable gravity, we all, with one accord, burst out laughing, irrestistibly amused to find, that amongst the important consequences of Buonaparte's gaining the victory, would be our clothes remaining unplaited and unironed; and that the British were, in a manner, fighting, in order that the getting up of our fine linen might be properly performed.

Rumour continues to spread stories of French success and of the imminent arrival of the French army in Brussels, but the English are sceptical:

We were now perfectly incredulous as to the whole story of the French having been seen advancing through the woods to take Brussels; but the Belgians still remained convinced of it; and though they differed about how it would be done they all agreed that Brussels would be taken. Some of them thought that the British, and some that the Prussians, had been defeated, and some that both of them had been defeated, and that the French, having broken through their lines, were advancing to take Brussels; others believed that Buonaparte, while he kept the allies employed, had sent round a detachment, under cover of night, by a circuitous route to surprise the town: but it seemed to be the general opinion, that before morning the French would be here. The town was wholly undefended, either by troops or fortifications: it was well known to be Napoleon's great object to get possession of it, and that he would leave no means untried to effect it. […] Great alarm continued to prevail through the whole night, and the baggage waggons stood ready harnessed to set off at a moment's notice. Several persons took their departure, but we quietly went to bed. S–, however, only lay down in her clothes, observing, half in jest and half in earnest, that we might, perhaps, be awakened by the entrance of the French; and overcome with fatigue, we both fell fast asleep.

In the face of the continuing uncertainty, however, the Waldies move out to Antwerp where they find a confusing scene: Charlotte talks at cross purposes with a man she takes to be German who is actually an English officer going from Antwerp to join the army.

The morning, the eventful morning of Sunday the 18th of June rose, darkened by clouds and mists and driving rain.[5] […] The distress of the crowds who now filled Antwerp, it is utterly impossible to conceive. We were, however, soon inexpressibly relieved, by hearing that there had been no engagement of any consequence the preceding day; that the British army had fallen back seven miles in order to take up a position more favourable for the cavalry; that they were now about nine miles from Brussels; and that a general, and, most probably, a decisive action would inevitably take place today.

The day passes in alarm and rumour:

Towards evening a wounded officer arrived, bringing intelligence that the onset had been most terrible, and so immense were the numbers of the enemy, that he 'did not believe it was in the power of man to save the battle'. To record the innumerable false reports we heard spread by the terrified fugitives, who continually poured into the town from Brussels, would be endless. At length, after an interval of the most torturing suspense, a wounded British officer of hussars, scarcely able to sit his horse, and faint from loss of blood, rode up to the door of the hotel, and told us the disastrous tidings, that the battle was lost, and that Brussels, by this time, was in the possession of the enemy. He said that in all the battles he had ever been engaged in, he had never witnessed anything at all equal to the horrors of this. The French had fought with the most desperate valour, but, when he left the field they had been repulsed by the British at every point with immense slaughter: the news of the defeat had, however, overtaken him on the road; all the baggage belonging to the army was taken or destroyed, and the confusion among the French at Vitoria, he said, was nothing to this.[6] Two gentlemen from Brussels corroborated this dreadful account: in an agitation that almost deprived them of the power of utterance, they declared that when they came away, Brussels was the most dreadful scene of tumult, horror, and confusion; that intelligence had been received of the complete defeat of the British, and that the French were every moment expected. The carnage had been most tremendous. The Duke of Wellington, they said, was severely wounded.

At last by the following morning it is possible to be sure that the British and Prussian forces have been victorious and civilians and military wounded are able to rejoice:
    In the mean time the Highlanders, regardless of their wounds, their fatigues, their dangers and their sufferings, kept throwing up their Highland bonnets into the air, and continually vociferating, 'Boney's beat! Boney's beat! hurrah! hurrah! Boney's beat!' Their tumultuous joy attracted round them a number of old Flemish women, who were extremely curious to know the cause of this uproar, and kept gabbling to the soldiers in their own tongue. One of them, more eager than the rest, seized one of the men by his coat, pulling at it, and making the most ludicrous gestures imaginable to induce him to attend to her; while the Highlander, quite forgetting in his transport that the old woman did not understand Scotch, kept vociferating that 'Boney was beat, and rinning away till his ain country as fast as he could gang'. At any other time, the old Flemish woman, holding the soldier fast, shrugging up her shoulders, and making these absurd grimaces, and the Highlander roaring to her in broad Scotch, would have presented a most laughable scene – 'Hout, ye auld gowk,' cried the good-humoured soldier, 'dinna ye ken that Boney's beat – what, are ye deef'? – dare say the wife – I say Boney's beat woman!' […] the valet de place the soldiers and I, all went to the Hospital together. Our progress was slow, for one of them was very lame, another had lost three of the fingers of his right hand, and had a ball lodged in his shoulder. Some of them were from the Highlands, and some from the Lowlands, and when they found that I came from Scotland, and lived upon the Tweed, they were quite delighted. One of them was from the Tweed as well as myself, he said, 'he cam' oot o' Peebleshire'.

The Waldies are horrified by the notion that they might visit the battlefield while the wounded and the dead were still upon it. They feel helpless too in the face of the sufferings of the wounded:
    Numbers of poor wounded Highlanders were patiently sitting in the streets,

shaded from the powerful rays of the sun. We had a good deal of conversation with several of the privates of the 42nd and 92nd regiments, and their account of the battle was most simple and interesting. They seemed not to have the smallest pride in what they had done; but to consider it quite as a matter of course: they uttered not the smallest complaint, but rather made light of their sufferings, and there was nothing in their words or manner that looked as if they were sensible of having done anything in the least praiseworthy: nothing that laid claim to pity, admiration, or glory.

Ordinary life begins to reassert itself:
The day was extremely hot, and on the outside of the cafés, beneath the shade of awnings, and seated beside little tables in the open street, the Belgic gentlemen were eating ices and fruit, and drinking coffee, and reading 'L'Oracle de Bruxelles', and playing at domino and backgammon with the utmost composure, utterly regardless of the crowds of passengers, and apparently as much at their ease as if they were in their own houses, – or indeed more so; for the Belgians, like the French, are more at home at le Café, or in the public streets, or anywhere, than in their own home, which is the last place in which they think of looking for enjoyment.

As things get back to normal the Waldies tour Holland. Charlotte Waldie is patronising about the Dutch:
We found the Dutch a plain, plodding, pains-taking, well-meaning, money-getting, matter-of-fact people; very dull and drowsy, and slow and stupid; little addicted to talking, but very much given to smoking; but withal pious and charitable and just and equitable; with no wit, but some humour; with little fancy, genius, or invention, – but much patience, perseverance, and punctuality. They make excellent merchants, but very bad companions. What Buonaparte once in his ignorance said of the English, is truly applicable to the Dutch, – 'They are a nation of shopkeepers'; and they used to remind me very much of a whole people of Quakers. In dress, in manners, in appearance, and in habits of life, they precisely resemble that worthy sect; and like them, in all these points they are perfectly stationary. It is singular enough that in all matters of taste and fashion, in which other nations are continually varying, the Dutch have stood stock still for at least two centuries; and in political opinions and institutions, which it requires years and even ages, to alter in other countries, the Dutch have veered about without ceasing. They have literally changed their form of government much oftener than the cut of their coats. They have had Stadtholders, and Revolutions, and Republics, and Despotisms, and Tyrants, and limited Monarchies; and new Dynasties and old; and the 'new Code Napoleon', and the newer Code of King William: and they have changed from the side of England to that of France, and from France to that of England, – and from the House of Orange to Buonaparte, and from Buonaparte to the House of Orange, with a rapidity and versatility which even their volatile neighbours, the French, could not equal.

But while their government, their laws, their sovereigns, and their institutions have undergone every possible transformation – the fashion of their caps and bonnets, their hats and shoebuckles, remains unchanged.

Once the road from Brussels to the field of battle is felt to be safe,[7] the Waldies visit Waterloo

On the morning of Saturday the fifteenth of July, we set off to visit the field of the ever-memorable and glorious battle of Waterloo. After passing the ramparts, we descended to the pretty little village of Ixelles, embosomed in woods and situated close to the margin of a still glassy piece of water. From thence we ascended a steep hill, and immediately entered the deep shades of the forest of Soignies, which extends about nine miles from Brussels. The morning was bright and beautiful; the summer sun sported through the branches which met above our heads, and gleamed upon the silver trunks of the lofty beech trees. On either side woodland roads continually struck in various directions through the forest; so seldom trodden, that they were covered with brightest verdure. At intervals, neat white-washed cottages, and little villages by the road side, enlivened the forest scenery. [...] Upon the doors of many of the cottages we passed, were written in white chalk, the names of the officers who had used them for temporary quarters on their way to the battle; or who had been carried there for shelter in returning, when wounded and unable to proceed farther. Many we knew had died in these miserable abodes; but all, excepting one or two of the most severely wounded, had now been removed to Brussels. It was impossible to trace without emotion the very road by which our brave troops had marched out to battle, three weeks before, and by which thousands had been brought back, covered with wounds, in pain and torture.

[...]

The road had been so dreadfully cut up with the heavy rains and the incessant travelling upon it, that notwithstanding three weeks of summer weather had now elapsed since the battle, the chaussée in the centre was worn into ruts upon the hard pavement, and in many places it was still so deep, that the horses could scarcely drag us through; the unpaved way on each side of the chaussée was perfectly impassable. [...] The road, the whole way through the forest of Soignies, was marked with vestiges of the dreadful scenes which had recently taken place upon it. Bones of unburied horses, and pieces of broken carts and harness were scattered about. At every step we met with the remains of some tattered clothes, which had once been a soldier's. Shoes, belts, and scabbards, infantry caps battered to pieces, broken feathers and Highland bonnets covered with mud were strewn along the road-side, or thrown among the trees. These mournful relics had belonged to the wounded who had attempted to crawl from the fatal field.

Thus the road between Waterloo and Brussels was one long uninterrupted charnel-house: the smell, the whole way through the Forest, was extremely offensive, and in some places scarcely bearable. Deep stagnant pools of red putrid water, mingled with mortal remains, betrayed the spot where the bodies of men and horses had mingled together in death. We passed a large cross on the left side of the road, which had been erected in ancient times to mark the place where *one* human being had been murdered. How many had now sunk around it in agony, and breathed, unnoticed and unpitied, their dying groans! It was surrounded by many a fresh-made, melancholy mound, which had served for the soldier's humble grave; but no monument points out to future times the bloody spot where they expired, no cross stands to implore from the passenger the tribute of a tear, or call forth a pious prayer for the repose of the departed spirits who here perished for their country!

The melancholy vestiges of death and destruction became more frequent, the pools of putrid water more deep, and the smell more offensive, as we approached Waterloo, which is situated at the distance of about three leagues, or scarcely nine miles from Brussels.

[...]

On the top of the ridge in front of the British position, on the left of the road, we traced a long line of tremendous graves, or rather pits, into which hundreds of dead had been thrown as they had fallen in their ranks, without yielding an inch of ground. The effluvia which arose from them, even beneath the open canopy of heaven was horrible; and the pure west wind of summer, as it passed us, seemed pestiferous, so deadly was the smell that in many places pervaded the field. The new turned clay which covered those pits betrayed how recent had been their formation. From one of them the scanty clods of earth which had covered it, had in one place fallen, and the skeleton of a human face was visible. I turned from the spot in indescribable horror, and with a sensation of deadly faintness which I could scarce overcome.

[...]

In many places the excavations made by the shells had thrown up the earth all around them; the marks of horses' hoofs that had plunged ankle deep in clay, were hardened in the sun; and the feet of men, deeply stamped into the ground, left traces where many a deadly struggle had been. The ground was ploughed up in several places with the charge of the cavalry, and the whole field was literally covered with soldiers' caps, shoes, gloves, belts, and scabbards, broken feathers battered into the mud, remnants of tattered scarlet cloth, bits of fur and leather, black stocks and haversacks, belonging to the French soldiers, buckles, packs of cards, books, and innumerable papers of every description. I picked up a volume of *Candide*;[8] a few sheets of sentimental love-letters, evidently belonging to some French novel; and many other pages of the same publication were flying over the field in much too muddy a state to be touched. One German Testament, not quite so dirty as many that were lying about, I carried with me nearly the whole day; – printed French military returns, muster rolls, love letters and washing bills; illegible songs, scattered sheets of military music, epistles without number in praise of 'L'Empereur, Le Grand Napoléon', and filled with the most confident anticipations of victory under his command, were strewn over the field which had been the scene of his defeat. The quantities of letters and of blank sheets of dirty writing paper were so great that they literally whitened the surface of the earth.

While I loitered behind the rest of the party, searching among the corn for some relics worthy of preservation, I beheld a human hand, almost reduced to a skeleton, outstretched from the ground, as if it had raised itself from the grave. My blood ran cold with horror, and for some moments I stood rooted to the spot, unable to take my eyes from this dreadful object, or to move away: as soon as I recovered myself, I hastened after my companions, who were far before me, and overtook them just as they entered the wood of Hougoumont. Never shall I forget the dreadful scene of death and destruction which it presented. The broken branches were strewed around, the green beech leaves fallen before their time, and stripped by the storm of war, not by the storm of nature, were scattered over the surface of the ground, emblematical of the fate of the thousands who had fallen on the same spot in the summer of their days. [...] The trunks of the trees had been pierced in every direction with cannon-balls. In some of them, I counted the holes where upwards of thirty had lodged: yet they still lived, they still bore their verdant foliage, and the birds still sang amidst their boughs. Beneath their shade, the hare-bell and the violet were waving their slender heads; and the wild raspberry at their roots was ripening its fruit. I gathered some of it with the bitter reflexion, that amidst the destruction of human life these worthless weeds and flowers had escaped uninjured.

Melancholy were the vestiges of death that continually met our eyes. The carnage here had indeed been dreadful. Amongst the long grass lay remains of broken arms, shreds of gold lace, torn epaulets, and pieces of cartridge-boxes; and upon the tangled branches of the brambles fluttered many a tattered remnant of a soldier's coat. At the outskirts of the wood, and around the ruined walls of the Château, huge piles of human ashes were heaped up, some of which were still smoking. The countrymen told us, that so great were the numbers of the slain, that it was impossible entirely to consume them. Pits had been dug, into which they had been thrown, but they were obliged to be raised far above the surface of the ground. These dreadful heaps were covered with piles of wood, which were set on fire, so that underneath the ashes lay numbers of human bodies unconsumed.

The Waldies inspect the damage to the Château de Hougoumont, contrasting the devastation caused by the shells with the loveliness of the undamaged garden and chapel. In the nearby cottage of 'La Belle Alliance' Charlotte Waldie finds Baptiste la Coste, Buonaparte's guide:

He is a sturdy, honest-looking countryman, and gave an interesting account of Buonaparte's behaviour during the battle. He said he issued his orders with great vehemence, and even impatience. He took snuff incessantly – but in a hurried manner, and without being conscious that he was doing so: he talked a great deal and very rapidly; his manner of speaking was abrupt, quick, and hurried: he was extremely nervous and agitated at times, though his anticipations of victory were most confident. He frequently expressed his astonishment, rather angrily, that the British held out so long – at the same time he could not repress his admiration of their gallantry, and often broke out into exclamations of amazement and approbation of their courage and conduct. He particularly admired the Scotch Greys – 'Voilà ces chevaux gris – ah! ce sont beaux cavaliers – très beaux,' – and then he said that they would all be cut to pieces. He said, – 'These English certainly fight well, but they must soon give way;' and he asked Soult,[9] who was near him, 'if he did not think so?' Soult replied, 'he was afraid not.' 'And why?' said Napoleon, turning round to him quickly. 'Because,' said Soult, 'I believe they will first be cut to pieces.' Soult's opinion of the British army, which was founded on experience, coincided with that of the Duke of Wellington. 'It will take a great many hours to cut them in pieces,' said the Duke, in answer to something that was said to him during the action; 'and I know they will never give way.'

The Waldies return to England, arriving at Margate exactly six weeks after they had landed at Ostend. Waldie concludes her narrative with reflections on the state of Europe, ending with a burst of patriotic fervour:

With these sentiments [about pride of country] deeply impressed upon my mind; with the proud consciousness, that highly as the fame of England had stood in all ages, she had now attained an unparalleled height of greatness and glory; [...] that her name would descend to the latest times as unrivalled in arms, invincible by land and sea, and pre-eminent, not only in valour, but in faith and honour, – in justice, mercy, and magnaminity, – and in public virtue. – I returned to my country, after all the varying and eventful scenes through which it had been my lot to pass, – more proud than when I left it of the name of

AN ENGLISHWOMAN.

NOTES

1. The copy which I used in Glasgow University Library has the names Stewart, Brown and Small pencilled in.

2. Gebhard Leberecht von Blücher, Prince of Wahlstatt (1742-1819), fought in the revolutionary Wars as well as the wars against Napoleon, whom he defeated at Leipzig.

3. S– seems to stand for some version of 'sister'.

4. I have been unable to trace the source of this apparently familiar quotation.

5. The date, of course, of the Battle of Waterloo. In brief, Napoleon caught Wellington a few kilometres south of Waterloo in isolation from the Prussians. The British lines, however, managed to hold the French columns until the Prussians under Blücher arrived, when a concerted charge finally brought victory and Napoleon's second abdication.

6. Wellington defeated the French under Joseph Buonaparte at Vitoria in 1813.

7. Charlotte Waldie explains that the road was believed to be unsafe because of the numbers of predatory deserters from the 'Belgic', Nassau and Brunswick soldiers; she says, however, that she believes the dangers were much exaggerated.

8. Ironically, of course, Voltaire's *conte* is a story of unquenchable optimism in the face of unbelievable disaster.

9. Nicholas Jean de Dieu Soult, Duc de Dalmatie (1769-1851) French general during Revolutionary and Napoleonic wars. Later he became President of the Council under Louis Philippe.

Janet Hamilton (1795–1873)

Janet Hamilton, née Thomson, described in *The Dictionary of Eminent Scotsmen* as a 'Poetess in humble life, and otherwise an ornament to her station', was born on 5 October 1795 at Carshill in the parish of Shotts, Lanarkshire. Her father was a shoemaker who moved to Hamilton when Janet was three and to the weaving village of Langloan in the parish of Old Monkland, Lanarkshire, in 1802. From 1802 to 1804 Thomson and his wife worked as land labourers on the home farm of the Drumpellier estate and Janet worked at home, spinning and working on a tambour frame.[1] In 1804 Thomson resumed his trade as shoemaker, employing a young man, John Hamilton, to assist him. John Hamilton and Janet were married in February 1809 before she had turned 14. The Hamiltons lived in Langloan for sixty years and had ten children. Janet had learned to read as a girl, her early reading taking in not only the expected Bible but the work of Milton and Shakespeare; she also made herself familiar with the work of Allan Ramsay, Robert Fergusson and Burns and was generally well-read in history and biography as she explains in the autobiographical fragment that is printed below. She taught herself to write and as a result her handwriting is very strange and is described by the *DNB* as being 'of oriental aspect'. She displayed an inclination to write poetry when she was in her teens but the religious verses that she wrote then stood alone of her work for many years as she brought up her family. When she was fifty-four, she began once again and published in Cassell's *Working Man's Friend*. Both her poetry and her prose are robust and often witty: her didacticism is never sententious or dull. She wrote several poems of praise to Garibaldi, warning him to watch out, while he is in London, for 'these wild assassin chaps' ('Auld Scotland's Welcome to Garibaldi') and Garibaldi's son visited her in her old age.[2] Towards the end of her life she became blind and her son James wrote for her, while her husband and her daughter Marion read to her.

Janet Hamilton, *Poems and Essays of a Miscellaneous Character on Subjects of General Interest* (Glasgow: Thomas Murray, 1863); *Poems of Purpose and Sketches in Prose of Scottish Life and Character in Auld Langsyne*; with a glossary (Glasgow: Thomas Murray and Son, 1865); *Poems and Ballads* (Glasgow: Thomas Murray, 1868); *Poems Essays and Sketches* (Glasgow: James Maclehose, 1870); *Poems and Essays* (Edinburgh: Akros, 1995) (Akros pocket classics series, no. 26) limited edition of 130

Further Reading:

Florence Boos, 'Cauld Ingle-Cheek: Working-Class Women Poets of Victorian Scotland', *Victorian Poetry*, 33 (1995) 51-71

'"Oor Location": Victorian Women Poets and the Transition from Rural to Urban Scottish Culture', in Debra Mancoff and Dale Trela, eds, *Victorian Urban Landscapes* (New York: Garland, 1996)

Robert Cochrane, *Earnest Lives: Biographies of Remarkable Men and Women* (Edinburgh: Nimmo, Hay & Mitchell, 1894)

William Findlay, 'Reclaiming Local Literature: William Thom and Janet Hamilton',

Douglas Gifford and Cairns Craig, eds, *The History of Scottish Literature, III: Nineteenth Century* (Aberdeen: Aberdeen UP, 1988) 353-376

Janet Hamilton (Coatbridge: Monklands Library Services Department, 1971)

Brian Maidment, *Poorhouse Fugitives: Self-Taught Poets and Poetry in Victorian Britain* (Manchester: Carcanet, 1987)

Julia Swindells, *Victorian Writing and Working Women* (Minneapolis: University of Minnesota Press, 1985)

Martha Vicinus, *The Industrial Muse: A Study of Nineteenth-century British Working Class Literature* (London: Croom Helm, 1974)

David Vincent, *Bread, Knowledge and Freedom: A Study of Nineteenth-Century Working Class Autobiography* (London: Methuen, 1981)

John Young, *Pictures in Prose and Verse; or, Personal Recollections of the Late Janet Hamilton* (Glasgow: George Gallie, 1877)

DNB; *DLB* 199; Irving; Royle

'Preface', *Poems and Essays of a Miscellaneous Character*, 1863:

I have been requested by some who take an interest in what I have written, to state how I came to acquire the power of language and ability for composition, which is necessary in writing a book that would pass muster with the press, and the public. I can only say, that they must have been acquired during a long course of reading the works of good authors, and thus, insensibly acquiring something of their manner and style. I was never taught, never knew, do not know even now, any of the rules of grammar in composition, the names of its parts I know when I meet with them in the course of reading, but cannot methodically use or apply them. It is chiefly by the aid of a correct and musical ear that I can detect or avoid grammatical inaccuracies, which jar on my ear in reading, or hearing like a false note in music.

I do not remember when I became mistress of the alphabet, but I read Bible stories and children's half-penny books with eager delight before I was five years of age. When about eight, I found to my great joy, on the loom of an intellectual weaver, a copy of Milton's *Paradise Lost* and a volume of Allan Ramsay's *Poems*.[3] I carried them off in triumph to the kitchen, returning day after day to devour the contents. I soon became familiar with, and could appreciate the gorgeous sublimity of Milton's imagery, and the grandeur of his ideal conceptions. With Ramsay I was at home at once, for I was beginning to get rich in the Ballad treasures of my country about that time; and a pathetic 'Aul Warl Ballant', would put the sweetie shop to a discount at any time when I was mistress of a bawbee.[4]

About this time my father became a subscriber to the village library, and I had access to much good and solid reading, history, geography, biography, travels, and voyages; but there was no poetry, novels, or light reading of any sort, and I was obliged to slake my unquenchable thirst for reading, with Rollin, *Plutarch's Lives, Ancient Universal History,* Reynal's *Indies,* and Pitscottie's *Scotland;* but the *Spectator* and Johnson's *Rambler* were the tid-bits of my literary banquet. I was quite familiar with Fergusson, Burns, and McNeil; and, as time wore on, by dint of begging, and borrowing from libraries and individuals, I managed to obtain and read the works of many of our best poets and authors.[5]

Some will say this girl must have done nothing else but read – not so – in justice to myself, I must say I had a daily task assigned me, first at the spinning wheel, and afterwards at the tambour frame, which was never omitted.

My mother, who was a very pious woman, did not at all approve of my ballad singing, poetry, and novel reading, and would often threaten to burn my precious store, but a good fit of crying, on my part, always saved them.

Like Timothy, I was taught from a child to know the Holy Scriptures, for as soon as I could read, she made me read a chapter from the Bible every morning, and this practice was never omitted for a single day, till I married and left the house; and during all the years of childhood, every night when I laid my head on the pillow, my mother's mouth was close at my ear, praying for me, and teaching me to pray for myself.

After I had entered the married state, and was engaged in rearing a young family on small means, I was busy enough, and my reading hours were taken from my sleep; and many an hour have I spent in reading, holding the book in one hand, and nursing an infant on my lap with the other. Did space permit, I could give many similar details, but I have said enough to show, that 'where there is a will there is a way' to attain knowledge, even while struggling with deficiencies and difficulties.

I hope I shall be excused for this egotistical sketch, which I would not have thought of giving, had I not been urgently requested to do so.

From 'The Mother's Mission', *Poems and Essays of a Miscellaneous Character*, 1863: Parents in the upper and wealthier classes of society can, with advantage to their children, transfer their parental responsibilities, in a great measure, to others. They can engage the best masters, and by a judicious choice of tutors and governesses, amply endow their children with the requisites of a refined and liberal education. But the poor mother, the wife of the working-man, has no substitute on whom she can shift the onerous duties which devolve upon her; yet she has a deep sense of the important trust committed to her, a mind imbued with right principles, and a heart full of the undying love of a mother; and although she is endowed with only the very commonest elements of education, and though she has daily to undergo domestic toils and privations in her three-fold character of mother, nurse and servant-of-all-work, yet even she is fully qualified, and will always find time and place for imparting to the little dwellers on her hearth those simple but most effective lessons which stamp on the infant mind the first and most valuable impressions, which often in time ripen into principles of religion and virtue.
[…]
We close this article with a brief notice of the atrocious murderer, Gleeson Wilson. That man cruelly butchered in cold blood a mother with her two children, and a female servant. He was immediately apprehended, and committed for trial; yet neither during that period, nor even after sentence of death was passed upon him, did he appear to feel remorse or fear, either for his present or future state, although the most earnest exhortations to confession and repentance were urged upon him, and the most ardent prayers were offered up in his cell by the ministers of religion on his behalf, yet they produced not the slightest visible impression upon

his obdurate mind. Yet this rocky heart, when stricken by the rememberance of the early instructions of a good mother, poured forth in a stream of tearful emotion these pious words: 'Once I had a good and pious mother, but after she died all went wrong with me. Had she lived, I never would have come to this.' This is indeed a most affecting testimony to the power and value of maternal training, and is worth a thousand commonplace comments on the subject.

From 'Address to Working-Women', *Poems and Essays*, 1863:

I have somewhere read an anecdote of Napoleon I, that one day, in conversation with Madame de Staël,[6] he abruptly proposed to her this question: 'Pray, Madam, what do you suppose to be the most effectual agent for the production of good men and good subjects?' 'Good mothers,' was her brief but most emphatic response – a response which my heart echoed with a throb of pride and pleasure, when I found that this gifted lady must have entertained the same idea, felt the same conviction, and held the same opinion, nay, had expressed herself in the same words which I would have chosen to utter my sentiments on this subject; for I believe that all who are truly interested in the welfare of their own country in particular, and of human nature in general – all who are earnestly inquiring after the best methods for compassing the elevation of the working and lower classes of society – will, after a searching and candid investigation, and a patient tracing of effects to their existing causes, feel a strong conviction while witnessing the vast, I had almost said the hopeless, aggregate of juvenile ignorance, depravity, crime, and wretchedness, that a frightful amount of it is consequent on the want of good mothers, and the presence and influence of the ignorant and the vicious, whether in our crowded cities, large manufacturing towns, populous mining districts, or extensive public works.

From 'Reminiscences of the Radical Time in 1819-20', *Poems, Essays, and Sketches*, 1870:

In this Sketch of the 'Radical Time', it is my purpose to bring out a few of its relative incidents, in which I have either had a personal share or an opportunity of observing in connection with others. I intend also to sketch out a few of the characters which came to the surface, in our village and the surrounding district, during the social and political ferment of that period, and which found vent in the seditious utterances and threats against the existing Government, through a portion of the press, at public meetings, and in private circles. These I do not intend to discuss in the Sketch. I shall only premise that the deep distress of the handloom weavers, occasioned by depression of trade, great reduction in prices, and scarcity of employment, and the consequent pressure on other sources of labour, cotton being then in all its stages of preparation the staple of British commerce, partly accounts for the fact, that the cotton manufacturing districts were hot-beds of radicalism, and the cotton-spinners and weavers constituted a great majority of the malcontents.

How well and how painfully do I remember many of the occurrences in these turbulent years, 1819-20, when many amongst the classes indicated, having had their minds already soured by distress and privation, were poisoned and perverted by reading infamous and seditious publications, chief among which was *The Black Dwarf*[7] – a small, mean-looking sheet, overflowing with scurrilous epithets and venomous invectives against the Government, and utterly subversive of all lawful authority and social order, and interlarded with scepticism and blasphemy, clearly indicating that both the writers and readers of this and similar productions were as inimical to the Word and Government of God as they were to the Government of Britain; and the men, thus prepared and still further inflamed by the rabid speeches of their demagogue orators and leaders, now began to come out on the streets in public processions. And a sorry sight it was to see bands of these would-be insurgents, with their lean, pale faces, unwashed, unshaved, and uncombed, thinly clad, and out at knees and elbows, with reckless and defiant looks, come trampling along to the sound of a couple of fifes, these frequently being their only musical accompaniments; and many 'a banner with a strange device'[8] was borne aloft by them in their disorderly marches through our village to their usual place of meeting, a little to the eastward. Of these devices, the cap of liberty on a pole, or a bundle of willow rods bound together, denoting unity and strength, were carried in front. Then followed a number of flags, bearing such mottoes as these – 'Liberty or Death'; 'Bread or Blood, and no Taxes'. There were other devices, of which I do not remember the purport. During the whole of 1819, and part of 1820, these miserable processions passed almost every week through our village, to the great terror and annoyance of the peaceable inhabitants. It was now that I, in common with many well-disposed persons, felt a strong desire to see what we would at other times have deprecated – parties of soldiers amongst us, to protect property and insure social order; both being endangered by the Radicals in the open avowal of their principles and intentions, which were, that when the rising took place, every poor man should help himself as best he could to the possessions of the rich. Houses, lands, money, and goods, were to be divided amongst the people, who had been too long kept from their rights, and must now eat the fat and drink the sweet in equal proportion with their hitherto more opulent neighbours.

But our village radicals were not wholly occupied with marching and speechify-ing; they were busy collecting arms, ammunition, and all kinds of offensive and defensive weapons, such as pikes, pitchforks, and scythe-blades. These implements were generally abstracted from farmers' or gentlemen's barns and outhouses; several pitchforks were taken from the barn of the home-farm of Drumpellier in our neighbourhood; and there was Will Lightbody, the pulicate weaver,[9] and his son, busy every night with a couple of moulds casting bullets, and compounding gunpowder of wood-charcoal, saltpetre, and sulphur, and Jemmy Gardner of that ilk, also labouring in that vocation; and in addition, being an old soldier, acting as drill sergeant to our small corps. And as time wore on, and the year grew old, it was generally understood that a rising would take place in the spring of 1820; and we lived in a state of continual excitement, for the Radicals made no secret of their intentions to take revenge on those who did not join them before the rising now at hand. The first three months of the new year had passed away, when one fine Sunday morning in April, my father, who had been out for an early walk, roused us from bed with the alarming intelligence that that he had just seen, affixed to a tree in the middle of the village, the radical proclamation for a general rising on Wednesday first (I believe that it was the 3rd of April), to carry out their designs by force of arms, as they were now set forth in this their proclamation. My husband got up and went round the village and vicinity, and sure enough he found posted up on every 'coigne of vantage'[9] this precious melange of treason and inflated, braggart absurdity, the very hyperbole of demagogism. My husband and I had an additional cause of terror from the advent of the rising. He had lately purchased of a childless widow a small thatched cottage, in which we at that time resided. She had a brother with a family of grown sons who lived next door to us. Both father and sons had been heard to say, that when the time came they would take forcible possession of what had been their relative's property. These men, we knew, were radicals of the worst type, and had arms of different kinds in their possession, yet we durst not make this known. We had a great dread of these people, and so we committed ourselves and our children to God, and awaited the even. Next day (Monday) Will Lightbody came into the room where my father and husband were at work with a swaggering gait, and an insolent leer on his face, and said – 'Noo's your time, Jamie, to tak' your side; if ye turn oot wi' us ye'll get yer share o' what's gaun, but if ye wunna, ye'll rue't, min' I tell ye.' While he was speaking my husband never lifted his head from his work, but my father turned round, and after surveying Will for a moment with an amused and contemptuous look, he gave vent to a loud and hearty burst of laughter. Will stood petrified with surprise and rage for a moment, and then, with muttered curses and threats, went off. But the most alarming epoch of our reign of terror was yet to come. It came on the following night, when one of the Glasgow carriers drove through our village spreading the alarming intelegence that the radicals were up in Glasgow, and that there had been fighting in the streets, from whence he had seen them carrying off dead bodies,[11] and, further, that the radicals were coming from the west that very night to force out all the able-bodied men in the village, and compel them to join them in an assault upon Airdrie, which, in their plan of operations, was to be the first point of attack, in order to dislodge the military, of whom above one thousand horse and foot had been thrown into the town. This was dreadful news to us, but our first thought was how to preserve our husbands, sons, and brothers, from being driven like sheep to the slaughter; at last being moved by the tears and entreaties of the women, the men resolved, the night being wet and stormy, to wrap themselves up, sally out one by one, and by different routes meet and spend the night in the woods of Drumpellier. A good many of the men, amongst whom was my husband, went stealthily out to the place of meeting, and sheltered themselves as best they could for several hours. But how shall I describe the agony of terror and suspense which I and a neighbour living under the same roof endured during that fearful night. She was a young woman far gone in consumption. She came to me as I sat crying amongst my five young children, and sat beside me with a child in her lap. We barred the doors and windows, and sat in the dark, as we durst not make a light for fear of attracting the attention of some passer-by, and so we sat in silence and darkness, painfully listening to every passing foot-fall, judging it might be the precursor of (shall I say) the enemy, coming in force; but except a quick and solitary footfall, at intervals, and the plashing and dripping sound of incessant rain, nothing was heard till my neighbour's husband and mine tapped at the window, telling us to let them in. They had seen, they said, from their hiding-place some flying but no fighting radicals. They saw Will Lightbody and his sons carrying what they thought must be cans of powder and bags of bullets; and Jamie Gardner with several rolled up flags. They met at the mouth of an old coal pit near Gartsherrie, into which they cast their burdens. They saw another man they did not know carrying a sack containing, as they thought by its appearance, several muskets, which he threw, sack and all, into the pit; and to crown all, they saw that wicked old radical, our dreaded next-door neighbour, and two of his sons, carrying a number of pitchforks. They proceeded to Drumpellier barn, into which they gained admission by some way known to themselves, and deposited them in the place from whence they had been taken, and where they were found next day to the great surprise of the work-people.

These several items of news were hastily told to us while they were taking off their wet clothes and shoes. Although we were greatly relieved by their safe return, yet, it being only three in the morning and still dark, we felt very anxious for their safety, and afraid that a raid of some kind or other might yet be made upon us by the radicals, we persuaded them to get up the hatch and conceal themselves amongst some straw stored on the loft beneath the thatch. They did so, and we sat watching below, where all remained quiet, till people were up and stirring about in the morning. Then my husband came down from his hiding-place, opened the door, and looked out. He was surprised to see several armed soldiers all along the street, going into houses, searching for arms. They were too late; the arms and their owners had both disappeared. Our old radical neighbour (his sons had absconded) was standing before his door, and accosted my husband with a look of innocent surprise on his face, saying, 'Keep us a' John; ken ye what the sodgers are after in the back raw this mornin'? I'm sure they'll fin' naething but what's richt amang quiet bodies like you an' me, John.' This was almost too much for my husband; but he said not a word in reply, and went off to his work as usual. Every house in the village, whose inmates were known or suspected to be radicals, was searched, but nothing was found. They had been warned in time, and had got out of the way. Now came the surprising intelligence that the dreaded rising, which was to have taken place the night before, was a total failure. The rendezvous was supposed to have been a ravine near Airdrie House gate. From this place the insurgents intended to pour into the town of Airdrie and ransack it; but on the knowledge of the overwhelming military force collected there, they acted on the prudent axiom, that 'discretion is the better part of valour', quietly disposed of their military stores, and kept within doors.[12]

The one exception to the general defalcation is a weaver, Will Marshall, who in spite of the refusal of the radical leader in the area to turn out, goes to the rendezvous and stands in the rain for several hours before returning home:
Drenched and disgusted [he was] 'a sadder and a wiser man',[13] for he laid down the radical and took up the shuttle; and many a smart box on the ear was administered by him to the village imps, who would run and shout after him as he passed along the street, 'There's Radical Will'. But Will outlived all this, attained to a good old age, and died a respected member of our little community.

Hamilton's conservatism and law-abiding nature make her anti-radical but she concedes that the would-be insurgents had real grievances against a government whose measures were 'not very wise and good at that period' and that they paid in any case for their radicalism by losing the respect of the village. And many of them were the dupes of demagogues and spies:

I might, but I will not here denounce the principal actors (government spies included) in this miserable drama who moved the wires that made the poor puppets dance. But as I do not intend to discuss any of the relative points of this abortion of rebellion yclept radicalism, I shall conclude these short and desultory reminiscences of a turbulent period, by congratulating my countrymen on the privileges and the legitimate powers they now possess under our present paternal and enlightened government, and the corresponding progress of enlightened philanthropy, large-hearted benevolence, and heaven-born charity, giving largely and working diligently for the best interests of our common humanity in relation not only to this life, but also in that to come. And who shall say that if our misguided brethren of the times we refer to had enjoyed the same privileges, they would ever have, even in their trying circumstances, supplied us with materials for writing Radical Reminiscences.

NOTES

1. A drum-shaped frame generally used for embroidery.
2. The hero of the Italian Unification Movement, Guiseppe Garibaldi (1807-82), was an enormously popular figure in Britain which he visited in April 1864. It was said that the crowds that gathered to welcome him constituted the largest spontaneous gathering of all time in London.
3. Allan Ramsay (1684-1758), wig-maker, bookseller and poet, committed himself to Scotland's literary heritage both in his own poetry and in the resurrection of older material: see Baillie, p.8, n.1.
4. A halfpenny, but generally used to denote a very small sum.
5. For Rollin see Joanna Baillie, p.106, n.10; Plutarch's *Lives* would probably still be read in North's 1579 version; Guillaume Thomas François Raynal, *Histoire philosophique et politique des établissements et du commerce des européens dans les deux Indes*, 1770, translated 1776; Robert Lindsay of Pitscottie, *The History of Scotland from 1436 to 1565*, 1728; Robert Fergusson (1750-74), Ramsay's successor in vernacular poetry, was prevented by his early death from achieving that success which his remaining poems seem to suggest was possible; Hector Macneill, *Poetical Works*, 2 vols, enlarged ed., 1806.
6. Anne Louise Germaine Necker, Madame de Staël (1766-1817), received in her Paris salon, just before the Revolution, the most progressive elements in French society. Her novel *Corinne*, 1807, was particularly influential in Britain.
7. The radical sheet *Black Dwarf* was published weekly in London by T. J. (Thomas Jonathan) Wooler from 1817 to 1824.
8. Henry Wadsworth Longfellow (1807-1882): 'A banner with the strange device,/Excelsior!' ('Excelsior', 1841).
9. Pullicate or pulicate was a material made in imitation of fabric from Pulicat, a town on the Madras coast.
10. 'no jutty, frieze,/Buttress, nor coign of vantage, but this bird/Hath made his pendent bed and procreant cradle' (*Macbeth*, I, vi, 6-8)
11. 'This was a false alarm': Hamilton's note.
12. In the end there were two 'rebellions' in Scotland early in April 1820. In the first, three Parkhead weavers issued a proclamation establishing a Provisional Government of Scotland, but only a few weavers took up arms. The second was more serious when a band of weavers marched from Glasgow Green to Falkirk with the intention of seizing the Carron Iron

Works and were stopped by a cavalry charge at Bonnymuir. Three were executed and 16 transported to Australia (Michael Lynch, *A History of Scotland*, 1991, pp.390-1).

13. Coleridge, *The Ancient Mariner*, part vii.

Frances Wright (D'Arusmont)
(1795–1852)

Frances Wright is still rather better known in America than in Britain: she became for America a powerful icon of radicalism whose name evoked conservative fears that went far beyond those that might have been justified by her actual writing or behaviour; she was by others, including Walt Whitman, greatly loved and admired. She was born, however, in Dundee on September 6, 1795. She lost both father and mother before she was two and a half; her brother was killed when she was still a girl and she did not marry D'Arusmont until she was 35 and already pregnant by him. And so her closest companion, until her death a few months before Fanny Wright's marriage, was her sister, Camilla. Her father was a wealthy merchant, an antiquarian and radical; his money and a subsequent inheritance from her uncle, Major William Campbell, made both Fanny and Camilla modest heiresses. Fanny Wright's radical conscience owed a good deal to her Scottish origins, although her childhood and early adolescence were passed outside the country of her birth.

Fanny was separated after the death of her parents from both Camilla, who went to a foster family in Dundee, and her brother who was brought up among the family of his great-uncle, James Mylne, Professor of Moral Philosophy in the University of Glasgow. Fanny herself was sent off to her maternal grandfather in London and after his death both she and Camilla lived with their aunt, Frances Campbell, in Dawlish. The wealthy and indolent existence of her grandfather and later her aunt presented a contrast with the suffering poor that fuelled Fanny's radicalism. Disgusted by the conspicuous consumption combined with the oppressive intellectual constraint of her life, Fanny quarrelled with her aunt and removed herself and Camilla to the home of James Mylne. Through Mylne the eighteen year old Fanny had access to the College Library where she consolidated an interest in America, sparked off two years previously by her accidental discovery of Botta's history of America's fight for independence (Carlo Giuseppe Gugliemo Botta, *Storia della guerra dell'independenza degli Stati Uniti d'America*, Paris, 1809). Mylne's wife, Agnes, was the daughter of John Millar, friend of both Smith and David Hume, supporter of the American Revolution, repudiator of the slave trade. Millar's daughter-in-law, Rabina Craig Millar, who had lived with her husband in Pennsylvania until his death, became Fanny Wright's close friend and surrogate mother. Mrs Millar was also a close friend of Eliza Fletcher.[1]

Wright spent summers during these Scottish years in the Highlands of Scotland and took the Highlands of Scotland as part of her intellectual and emotional baggage to America. The most telling Highland event of Fanny Wright's young life actually occurred in the Lowlands, when she saw an emigrant ship in the Clyde packed with Highlanders dispossessed during the period of the Clearances. Her sense of their misery and helplessness, she later affirmed, made her pronounce 'to herself a solemn oath, to wear ever in her heart the cause of the poor and the helpless; and to aid in all she could in redressing the grievous wrongs which seemed to prevail in society' (Lane, p.7). This experience obviously fed her desire to see the country for which they were bound, to find out whether it was in truth the land of opportunity and equality.

And so Frances Wright travelled with her faithful sister to America, provided with letters of introduction from Mrs Millar and warnings from Professor Mylne whose male chivalric sense overcame his intellectual daring in his parting advice that Italy would be a far more suitable destination for two young ladies. Mrs Millar was the original recipient of the letters which form Wright's *Views of Society and Manners in America*. Throughout this record of her first travels in America she tended to take the abstract principle as apology for the specific practice, a tendency that she herself later admitted as seeing America under a 'Claude Lorraine tint' (see extract below). The British journals were mostly outraged by her eulogies of American practice which carried with them explicit or implicit condemnation of British policy during and after the Wars of Independence. *Views of Society and Manners in America* was published as 'by an Englishwoman' and *The Quarterly Review* believed, or pretended to believe, that 'Englishwoman' is an unconvincing pseudonym, certainly for a man, probably for a chauvinistic American. Even American journals worried about the fulsomeness of the compliments Wright paid to the new country: the *North American Review* felt that the whole book could better serve 'as the model toward which [the citizen] should strive to bring his country, rather than as a tablet of actual perfections' (xiv, January 1822, 19).

The loss of her childhood, and the love that might have attended it, may explain her tendency to seek such potential father figures as Jeremy Bentham and in Paris, where she lived from 1821 to 1824, the Marquis de Lafayette.[2] At the same time she obviously throughout her life found universal benevolence an easier matter than personal relationships. She pushed relationships to their limit, often trying the patience of those who loved her.

But just as Frances Wright's deprived family life deeply affected her subsequent relationships, so the absence of a sense of community seems to have affected her subsequent political judgments and behaviour. She understood the message of the Highland emigrants only partially: she responded to human suffering finally in an abstract way and consequently imagined that it could be wholly rationally alleviated. She committed herself to America and to the amelioration of the problems of the negro slaves by means of the altruistic and, to herself, costly establishment of 'Nashoba', a free slave community in Tennessee. In the end, however, Nashoba failed mainly because she understood impersonal compassion without really understanding how communities might work as organic entities. Nashoba was a disaster in emotional, social and economic terms and it was eventually broken up and the slaves shipped to Haiti at Wright's expense.

Fanny Wright's subsequent lecture tours in America made her notorious as did her relationship with Lafayette. She crossed the Atlantic several times in the course of her working life; settled for a while in the ideal socialist community, New Harmony, Indiana, where she co-edited *The New Harmony Gazette* with its founder Robert Dale Owen, the son of the celebrated reformer of New Lanark.[3] The paper later moved to New York and changed its name to *The Free Enquirer* (1829-35). Her marriage to Piquepal D'Arusmont whom she had met in New Harmony was not a success: the couple were estranged and squabbled over the custody of their daughter.

Frances Wright D'Arusmont had faded somewhat from public view when a fall caused her to break her hip and hastened her death in December 1852 in Cincinatti at the early age of 57.

There is much that is admirable in Fanny Wright's early letters from America, particularly a felicitous specificity about the world she describes that is lost later in the polemic of the radical orator. But it is more difficult to read her lectures than her letters which have been republished and so I have included here the Preface to her published lectures and addresses which explains their principles and which also recants some of her earlier over-enthusiasm for America. The lectures themselves lose a lot in mere print, for her public appearances were performances in the fullest sense: Fanny Trollope, who went with Fanny Wright to Nashoba, and quickly fled from it as unbearable, nevertheless paid tribute to Fanny Wright's skills on the platform: 'her tall and majestic figure, the deep and almost solemn expression of her eyes, the simple contour of her finely formed head, her garment of plain white muslin, which hung around her in folds that recalled the drapery of a Grecian statue, all contributed to produce an effect unlike anything that I had ever seen before, or ever expect to see again' (*DNB*). As I have suggested, she was both feared and admired, her irreligion indeed made many suspicious that might otherwise have supported her political radicalism. She was not really a feminist, and although she supported, did not prioritise the female franchise; indeed, sometimes something like contempt creeps into her remarks about women but she insists that women should be educated to make them fitter citizens. One of her greatest admirers was Walt Whitman who called her 'the noblest Roman of them all': she was to him 'one of the sweetest of sweet memories: we all loved her: fell down before her: her very appearance seemed to enthrall us'. And Whitman borrowed lines from *A Few Days in Athens* for his poem 'Pictures' (Goodale). Of all the women in this volume, she is most firmly opposed to simple-minded Christianity and yet her rhetoric is oddly akin to that of a revivalist preacher.

Frances Wright D'Arusmont, *Altorf, a Tragedy* (Philadelphia, 1819; London, 1822); *Views of Society and Manners in America* by an Englishwoman (London, 1821); ed. Paul Baker (Cambridge, Mass: The Bellknap Press of Harvard University Press, 1963); *A Few Days in Athens, being the Translation of a Greek Manuscript discovered in Herculaneum* (London: Longman, Hurst, Rees, Orme, and Brown, 1822); *A Course of Popular Lectures with Three Addresses, on Various Public Occasions, and a Reply to the French Reformers of 1789*, delivered by Fanny Wright in New York, Philadelphia, Boston etc. (London: James Watson, 1828?; New York, 1829; 1831, with additional material; vol.2, Philadelphia, 1836); *Fables* (New York, 1830); *Biography, Notes and Political Letters of Frances Wright D'Arusmont* (J. Myles: Dundee, 1844). (This biography was derived from an interview published in the Dundee newspaper, *The Northern Star*, 1844; printed in Boston by J. P. Mendun, 1849. The text was according to the *Northern Star* reporter revised by Frances Wright during a business visit to Dundee concerning an inheritance in 1844); *England the Civiliser* ; various addresses and tracts.

Further Reading:

Paul R. Baker, 'Introduction' to Frances Wright, *Views of Society and Manners in America*; (London: Belknap, 1963)

Celia Morris Eckhardt, *Fanny Wright: Rebel in America* (Cambridge & London: Harvard University Press, 1984)

David Goodale, 'Some of Walt Whitman's Borrowings', *American Literature* (May 1938) 202-13

Margaret Lane, *Frances Wright and the 'Great Experiment'* (Manchester: Manchester University Press, 1972)

A. J. G. Perkins and Theresa Wolfson, *Frances Wright 'Free Enquirer': The Study of a Temperament* (New York: Harper, 1939; 1972 Porcupine Press reprint)

William Randall Waterman, *Frances Wright* (New York: Columbia University Press, 1924)

DNB; HSWW

From *A Course of Popular Lectures:*

The substance of the three first lectures which appear in the present volume, was delivered in Cincinatti, during the course of the last summer [i.e. summer, 1828].

The motives that actuated me to step forward in a manner ill suited to my taste and habits, which are rather those of a quiet observer and reflecting writer, than of a popular performer or public speaker, will appear sufficiently in the discourses themselves. I may observe, however, that from the age of seventeen, when I first accidentally opened the page of America's national history, as portrayed by the Italian Bocca,[4] the only work on a subject so politically heterodox which had found a place in the aristocratical libraries which surrounded my youth – from that moment my attention became rivetted on this country, as on the theatre where man might first awake to the full knowledge and the full exercise of his powers. I immediately collected every work which promised to throw any light on the institutions, character, and condition of the American people: and as, at this period, little satisfactory information on these subjects could be gleaned in Europe, I visited this country in person. The 'Views' then rapidly formed I published on my return to England, with the single object of awakening the attention of European reformers to the great principles laid down in American government. Those principles had indeed so warmed my own feelings, as to have influenced my perceptions. During my first visit to America, I seemed to hear and see her declaration of independence every where. I studied her institutions, and mistook for the energy of enlightened liberty what was, perhaps, rather the restlessness of commercial enterprise. I saw her population active and thriving, and conceived that to be the effect of wise social regulations, which had, perhaps, rather its source in the temporary state of an artificial market. I saw neither princes not bayonets, nor a church married to the state, and conceived, in very truth, that liberty had here quickened the human mind until it was prepared to act under the influence of reason instead of fear. It was true that I saw this country at a favourable moment, when peace had opened to her the ports of the world, and set a second seal on her republican liberties and national independence. Still, however favourable the time might be, my own enthusiasm doubtless conspired to throw a Claude-Lorraine tint over a country which bore the name of republic.[5] It required a second visit, and more minute inspection, to enable me to see things under the sober light of truth, and to estimate both the excellences that are, and those that are yet wanting.

This second visit, while it has exposed to my view evils and abuses differing in degree rather than in nature from those of Europe, has rivetted me in mind and feeling yet more strongly to a country where are enshrined all the liberties and all the hopes of the human race. From a visitor, therefore, I have become a resident and a citizen.

While yet imperfectly acquainted with the state of things in my adopted country – with the breadth of distance between American principles and American practice – between the theory of American government and its actual application – my attention had been attracted towards the political anomaly and moral injustice presented by the condition of the coloured population of the slave-holding states, as well as by the feelings exhibited, and practices legally countenanced, towards that race generally throughout the union. Four years of extensive and minute observation, with deeper reflection, and more varied, as well as more reasoned experience, have convinced me that American negro slavery is but one form of the same evils which pervade the whole frame of human society. And as, in common with all human errors, it has its source in ignorance, so must one common panacea supply its and their remedy. The spread and increase of knowledge alone can enable man to distinguish that the true interests of each point to the equal liberties, equal duties, and equal enjoyments of all; and that then only, will the principles set forth in the first national instrument of American government, the Declaration of Independence, be practically exhibited – when the law of force shall give place to the law of reason, when wealth shall be the reward of industry, and all things shall be estimated in a ratio calculated in the order of their utility.

Satisfied that the melioration of the human condition can be reached only by the just informing of the human mind, I have applied such powers as I possess to the furtherance of this pleasing, though laborious task. In the citadel of human error, as exhibited in this country, it is easy to distinguish two main strongholds, which, if once carried, the fastness would probably surrender at the first summons. These are: first, the neglected state of the female mind, and the consequent dependence of the female condition. This, by placing the most influential half of the nation at the mercy of that worst species of quackery, practised under the name of religion, virtually lays the reins of government, national as well as domestic, in the hands of a priesthood, whose very subsistence depends, of necessity, upon the mental and moral degradation of their fellow creatures.

Second, the inaptness and corruption of the public press, ridden by ascendant influences, until it is abandoned alike by the honest and the wise, and left in the hands of individuals too ignorant to distinguish truth, or too timid to venture its utterance. The former of these evils, as somewhat unusually exhibited last summer in the towns and cities of the western country, first led me to challenge the attention of the American people.

The city of Cincinatti had stood for some time conspicuous for the enterprise and liberal spirit of her citizens, when, last summer, by the sudden combination of the clergy of three orthodox sects, a *revival*, as such scenes of distraction are wont to be styled, was opened in houses, churches, and even on the Ohio river. The victims of this odious experiment on human credulity and nervous weakness, were invariably women. Helpless age was made a public spectacle, innocent youth driven to raving insanity, mother and daughters carried lifeless from the presence of the ghostly expounders of damnation; all ranks shared the contagion, until the despair of Calvin's hell itself seemed to have fallen upon every heart, and discord to have taken possession of every mansion.

A circumstantial account of the distress and disturbance on the public mind in the Ohio metropolis led me to visit the afflicted city; and since all were dumb, to take up the cause of insulted reason and outraged humanity.

The consequences of the course of lectures I then first delivered, on three successive Sundays, in the Cincinnati courthouse, and re-delivered in the theatre, were similar to those which have been witnessed elsewhere; – a kindling of wrath among the clergy, a reaction in favour of common sense on the part of their followers, and explosion of the public sentiment in favour of liberty, liberality, and instrumental reform, and a complete exposure of the nothingness of the press, which, at a time when the popular mind was engrossed by questions of the first magnitude, sullenly evaded their discussion, betraying alike ignorance the most gross, and servility the most shameless. All that I then observed, conspired to fix me in the determination of devoting my time and labour to the investigation and exposure of existing evils and abuses, and to the gradual development of the first principles of all moral and physical truth, everywhere so perplexed and confounded by the sophistry of false learning, the craft of designing knavery, and the blunders of conceited ignorance.

The two means which presented themselves, were those of popular discourses, and a periodical publication, which should follow up the same objects, consistently and fearlessly, and, by instituting enquiry on matters of real interest, aid in drawing off the public attention from the squabbles of party, the verbiage of theory, the gossipings of idleness, and the ravings of zeal without knowledge.

The present volume contains the first, or introductory course, closing at the seventh lecture; in which I have attempted to sketch an outline of the field of truth, and, at the same time, to expose such existing errors as must tend to blind the intellectual sight to its perception.

The second course, which will be found sketched at the close of the fifth lecture, on Morals, will attempt the development and practical application of those simple principles by which the conduct of human beings, one towards the other, may be justly regulated, and the face of human society be harmonized into beauty.

In the seventh discourse, on 'Existing Evils and their Remedy', I was induced by circumstances, and the impatience of the public mind, somewhat to anticipate a subject whose more complete development will form an important item in the second course, as laid out of the close of the fifth lecture, already referred to, and to which I shall apply myself so soon as some duties of a more private nature may permit.

In attempting reform by means of instructional improvement at the present day, the labourer is perplexed by the alternate dullness and vivacity, inertness and restlessness of the human mind. At first, curiosity is slow to awaken; then it runs too fast; anon it slumbers, as if all truth were seized, and its every feature distinguished, when perhaps not a single impression received is in accurate accordance with fact and with reason.

The effects of a pernicious education are in nothing more conspicuous, than in the universal activity of the imagination and the inertness of the judgment. To treat any subject with perspicuity, a certain order and arrangement are indispensable. Let this order be disturbed, and arrangement interrupted, and things the most simple appear confused, and truths the most evident, difficult or doubtful. But to proceed step by step – to trace the outline and consider the details – to substantiate the first principles, and then trace them out in their various applications, demands attention too patient, and reflection too dispassionate, for minds habitually unsettled by the day-dreams of fancy, and accustomed to adopt conclusions without examining premises. The first effort of the reformer is to awaken, but soon he finds it yet more necessary to compose. The spur is hardly applied when the rein is wanting, and the impatience of curiosity is soon a greater hindrance to progress than the apathy of ignorance.

All this, however, a little perseverance, sustained by zeal and tempered by prudence, might speedily vanquish, were it not, most unhappily, the momentary interest of a large and increasing body of men to feed the worst passions of the hour, and to counteract the labours of truth's advocates by every means possible for art to devise or violence to dare. Still, in this country, the progress of the human mind, if impeded, cannot be arrested. And truly, if regard be had to the conflicting interests and sinister influences which now pervade society, we may rather marvel at the success obtained than at the difficulties encountered.

The views which I have felt it my duty to present to the American people – the only people free to choose between truth and error, good and evil – are as yet but faintly sketched. The outline only is presented, and those first principles laid down in whose general and minute application I shall hereafter seek the law of nations and the law of men. While attempting the development of these first principles, I have been often challenged to their premature application to existing laws and usages; not seeing that with these the enquirer after truth has little to do, and that it must be rather for our laws and usages to bend to principles, than for those to shape themselves to our laws and usages. As a lecturer, therefore, I have rather applied myself to develop what is true then to expose what is false; reserving my comments on the passing opinions and practices of the age for the pages of the periodical of which I am a joint editor.

The Free Enquirer, formerly the *New Harmony Gazette*, was the first periodical established in the United States for the purpose of fearless and unbiassed enquiry on all subjects. It was conducted in Indiana, with more or less consistency and ability, for the space of three years, when I assumed its joint proprietorship, and removed it to New York, under a name more expressive of its character. Since that period, it has been conducted, I am sure, with honesty, and, I hope, not without utility. Its editors have had singly in view the discovery of truth and the well being of man. If their zeal has been warm, their spirit has, I trust, been gentle. If they have spared no error on account of its popularity, they have neither sought the exposure of the erring, nor resented the hostility of the violent. They have kept true to the pledge given in their prospectus – they have sought truth 'alone, and for itself'; 'they have devoted their pages without fear, without reserves, without pledge to men, parties, sects or systems, to free, unbiassed and universal enquiry'; and, while taking for their premises the principles developed in the following discourses, they have tested them as they will continue to test, the laws, opinions, and practices of men, by that only standard of truth, supplied by nature herself, and by the powers of the human mind.

FRANCES WRIGHT

New York, 4th October, 1829

From Lecture II 'Free Enquiry':

Wright insists that knowledge should not be withheld from any capable of reason and claims, however, that in the 'home of liberty' it still often is:

Which of us have not seen fathers of families pursuing investigations themselves, which they hide from their sons, and, more especially, from their wives and daughters? As if truth could be of less importance to the young than to the old; or as if the sex which in all ages had ruled the destinies of the world, could be less worth enlightening than that which only follows its lead! [...] However novel it may appear, I shall venture the assertion that, until women assume the place in society which good sense and good feeling alike assign to them, human improvement must advance but feebly. It is in vain that we would circumscribe the power of one half of our race, and that half by far the most important and influential. If they exert it not for good, they will for evil; if they advance not knowledge, they will perpetuate ignorance. Let women stand where they may in the scale of improvement, their position decides that of the race. Are they cultivated? – so is society polished and enlightened. Are they ignorant? – so is it gross and insipid. Are they wise? – so is the human condition prosperous. Are they foolish? – so is it unstable and unpromising. Are they free? – so is the human character elevated. Are they enslaved? – so is the whole race degraded.

From Lecture IV, 'Religion':

Like a number of other female educational reformers of the period, including at an earlier stage, Elizabeth Hamilton, Wright speaks with enthusiasm of the ideas of Pestalozzi.[6] But it was her rejection of the claims of belief that more alarmed her contemporaries; she refuses the customary capital letter to sects and I have followed her practice:

Every day we see sects splitting, creeds new modelling, and men forsaking old opinions only to quarrel about their opposites. I see three Gods in one, says the trinitarian, and excommunicates the socinian, who sees a godhead in unity.[7] 'I see a heaven but no hell,' says the universalist, and disowns fellowship with such as may distinguish less. 'I see a heaven and a hell also, beyond the stars,' said lately the orthodox friend, and expelled his shorter-sighted brethren from the sanctuary. I seek them both in the heart of man, said the more spiritual follower of Penn, and straightway builded him up another temple, in which to quarrel with his neighbour, who perhaps only employs other words to express the same ideas.[8] For myself, pretending to no insight into these mysteries, possessing no means of intercourse with the inhabitants of other worlds, confessing my absolute incapacity to see either as far back as a first cause, or as far forward as a last one, I am content to state to you, my fellow creatures, that all my studies, reading, reflection, and observation, have obtained for me no knowledge beyond the sphere of our planet, our earthly interests and our earthly duties; and that I more than doubt, whether, should you expend all your time and all your treasure in the search, you will be able to acquire any better information respecting unseen worlds, and future events, than myself. Whenever you shall come to the same conclusion, you will probably think the many spacious edifices which rear their heads in your city, are somewhat misapplied, and the time of the individuals who minister therein, somewhat misemployed: you will then doubtless perceive that they who wish to muse, or pray, had better do it after the manner designated by the good Jesus, namely by entering their closet and shutting the door; and further perceive that the true Bible is the book of nature, the wisest teacher he who most plainly expounds it, the best priest our own conscience, and the most orthododox church a hall of science. I look round doubtless upon men of many faiths, upon calvinists, unitarians, methodists, baptists, catholics, and I know not what beside, and yet, my friends, let us call ourselves by what names we will, are we not creatures occupying the same earth, and sharing the same nature? and can we not consider these as members of one family, apart from all our speculations respecting worlds, and existences, and states of being, for which, in ages past, men cut each other's throats, and for which they now murder each other's peace?

From Lecture VI, 'Formation of Opinions:
Wright is unsurprisingly opposed to proselytising missionaries who import new sources of strife as well as intoxicating liquors:
Oh, when ye afflict strange people and other races with the curse which rests upon yourselves – when, despite their expostulations, and presuming upon your power, ye add the feuds of opinions to the hatred of tribes, and send forth retailers of spirituous and spiritual poison to the dusky children of nature – Oh, think well of the liberty ye outrage, the rights of nations that ye violate, the awful responsibility that ye assume!

Could ye send to your red brethren peaceful instructors in the useful arts of life, enlightened observers of nature, respecters of human feeling, who, without questioning their reverence for the benign spirit whose presence they acknowledge in the heart, would travel with them in peace the paths of life, and exchange with them all the offices of human love; could ye send to the feeble remnant of that race, whose decay has been the price of your greatness, such instructors as these, ye might cancel the remembrance of injury, and preserve in your bosom a happy relic of a people, interesting from your own history, their character, and their wrongs. But, until such ye can send, (and, alas, such how rare!) oh, my friends, *send not at all.*[9]

From Lecture VII, 'Existing Evils':
Time is it in this land to commence [...] reform. Time is it to check the ambition of an organized clergy, the demoralizing effects of a false system of law; to heal the strife fomented by sectarian religion and legal disputes; to bring down the pride of ideal wealth, and to raise honest industry to honour.

Time is it to search out the misery in the land, and to heal it at the source. Time is it to remember the poor and the afflicted, ay! and the vicious and the depraved.

Time is it to perceive that every sorrow which corrodes the human heart, every vice which diseases the body and the mind, every crime which startles the ear and sends back the blood affrighted to the heart – is the product of one evil, the foul growth from one root, the distorted progeny of one corrupt parent – IGNORANCE.

Time is it to perceive this truth; to proclaim it on the housetop, in the market place, in city and forest, throughout the land; to acknowledge it in the depths of our hearts, and to apply all our energies to the adoption of those salutary measures which this salutary truth spontaneously suggests. Time is it, I say, to turn our churches into halls of science, our schools of faith into schools of knowledge, our privileged colleges into state institutions for all the youth of the land. Time is it to arrest our speculations respecting unseen worlds and inconceivable mysteries, and to address our enquiries to the improvement of our human condition, and our efforts to the practical illustration of those beautiful principles of liberty and equality enshrined in the political institutions, and, first and chief, in the national declaration of independence.

And by whom and how, are these changes to be effected? By whom! And do a free people ask the question! By themselves – *the people*.

I am addressing the people of Philadelphia – the people of a city where Jefferson penned the glorious declaration which awoke this nation and the world – the city, where the larum so astounding to tyranny, so fraught with hope, and joy, and exulting triumph to humankind, was first sounded in the ears of Americans. I speak to the descendants of those men who heard from the steps of their old state house the principles of liberty and equality first proclaimed to man.[10] I speak to the inhabitants of a city founded by the most peaceful, the most humane, and the most practical of all Christian sects. I speak to a public whose benevolence has been long harrowed by increasing pauperism, and whose social order and social happiness are threatened by increasing vice. I speak to sectarians who are weary of sectarianism. I speak to honest men who tremble for their honesty. I speak to the *dis*honest whose integrity has fallen before the discouragements waiting upon industry; and who, by slow degrees or in moments of desperation, have forsaken honest labour, because without a chance of success to a thousand chances of ruin. I speak to parents anxious for their offspring – to husbands who, while shortening their existence by excess of labour, foresee, at their death, not sorrow alone, but unrequited industry and hopeless penury, involving shame, and perhaps infamy, for their oppressed widows and unprotected children. I speak to human beings surrounded by human suffering – to fellow citizens pledged to fellow feeling – to republicans pledged to equal rights and, as a consequent, to equal condition and equal enjoyments; and I call them – oh, would that my voice were loud to reach every ear, and persuasive to reach every heart! I call them to UNITE; and to unite for the consideration of the evils around us – for the discovery and application of their remedy.

NOTES

1. For note on Professor Millar see Joanna Baillie (p.106, n.17).
2. Jeremy Bentham (1748-1832), philosopher, pioneer of Utilitarianism, was visited regularly in London by Fanny Wright after the publication of her *Views*; Marie Joseph Gilbert Motier, Marquis de Lafayette (1757-1834), had fought against the English during the War of

American Independence. He became friendly with Fanny Wright during her stay in France and when he later toured America she joined him, despite the probably quite unjustified gossip that this caused.

3. Robert Owen (1771-1858), the socialist founder of the model mill community of New Lanark, also helped to establish New Harmony, Indiana. His eldest son, Robert Dale Owen (1801-1877), joined New Harmony in 1826: by 1827 it had virtually ceased to operate as a community. After his association with Fanny Wright, Dale Owen moved into official politics, being elected to the legislature for the State of Indiana in 1835.

4. Presumably an error for Botta.

5. Claude Lorraine (Claude Gellée) (1600-82), French painter whose idealised, harmonious, sunlit landscapes and seascapes provided a model for 18th-century British painters and travellers, who sometimes carried a 'Claude glass' to compose the landscape pictorially as they looked at it.

6. Johann Heinrich Pestalozzi (1746-1827) was a Swiss pioneer of mass education who made several more or less unsuccessful attempts to establish schools for poor children. Despite his lack of personal success, his ideas had a great deal of subsequent influence, especially his theories on intuitive methods of education. His work is commemorated in the Pestalozzi International Children's Villages, the first of which at Trogen in Switzerland was established in 1946 for orphans of the war.

7. Laelius Socinus (1525-62) was an Italian Protestant reformer who rejected the central Christian doctrine of the Trinity of the Father, Son and Holy Ghost and sought to reconcile Christianity with humanism. His ideas became known as Socinianism and contributed a great deal to the development of Unitarian theology. Joanna Baillie, late in her life, wrote a Socinian treatise on the manhood of Christ which seriously upset Scott.

8. William Penn (1644-1718), English Quaker and founder of Pennsylvania, for which he drew up a constitution which allowed freedom of worship.

9. In her earlier *Views* Fanny Wright had been much more accepting of the treatment of the native Americans.

10. The Declaration of Independence was adopted at Philadelphia's Independence Hall on 4 July 1776; the Liberty Bell is kept there.

Lady Lucy Clementina Davies
(née Drummond) (1795–1879)

Lucy Drummond was born in France at the Château of St Germain on 21 November 1795. Her father, commonly known as Lord Leon Maurice Drummond de Melfort, was fourth son of James, third duke of Melfort in France. He would also have been thirteenth earl of Perth had it not been for the attainder against his ancestor. Her mother was Marie Elizabeth Luce de Longuemarre. In 1848 the House of Lords admitted the claim of her brother, George Drummond, to be heir of the earls of Perth. The attainder was reversed in George Drummond's favour in 1853 and Lucy Drummond was granted a patent of precedence as the daughter of an earl in the same year.

Lucy Drummond lived through 'interesting times' in both Britain and France. She had some education in Scotland with Miss Playfair, sister of Professor Playfair. The various moves with her parents between France and Britain gave her a great deal of experience and material for her *Recollections of Society in France and England*. On 8 September 1823 she married Francis Henry Davies at Marylebone, London. Davies was a registrar of the Court of Chancery, four years older than Lucy Drummond. He died at Coblenz in 1863 and Lady Lucy survived him by sixteen years, dying on 27 April 1879 at the Kensington home of her son-in-law, John Sale Barker. Her two volumes of *Recollections*, published in 1872, are full of fascinating history and anecdote and, since they draw on the memories of her mother and grandmother as well as her own, they cover a lengthy period. Lucy Drummond speaks very little directly of herself, her husband and family: she enters as an interpreter of others rather than as a major player.

The extracts I give cover both the early period of her own family history and the fate of Louis XVI and Marie Antoinette as well as treating of society in Britain and France later in the nineteenth century.

Lady Lucy Clementina Davies, *Recollections of Society in France and England*, 2 vols
(London: Hurst & Blackett, 1872)

Further Reading:
DNB

From *Recollections of Society in France and England*, Vols I & II:
Some account of the family to which I belong will form a fitting introduction to my own more personal reminiscences.

Allied by the twofold tie of blood and gratitude to the Stuarts and through them to the Bourbons, the Chiefs of the Drummonds enjoyed the singular distinction of being proscribed and plundered at both the English Revolution of 1688, and the French Revolution of 1789. My ancestor, John, First Earl of Melfort, was Secretary of State to James II; and, like his elder brother James, Fourth Earl of Perth, Lord

Chancellor of Scotland, he accompanied his royal master in his flight to France. There, as everybody knows, the Château of St Germain was generously assigned by Louis XIV to the exiled King of England and his adherents for a residence. The Earl of Melfort had a splendid suite of apartments beneath those occupied by His Majesty; and during a century afterwards, my immediate progenitors successively, though sometimes only occasionally, occupied those rooms consecrated to them by many historians and personal recollections, up to the time of the French Revolution of 1789, when they were driven from France. But, though domiciled in France, it was only as British subjects that they had resided there. A law was passed by the Parliament of Paris, in 1689, providing that, notwithstanding their enforced residence in France, all the followers of James II were to be considered there, not as French subjects, but to all intents and purposes, and with regard to their legal acts, – such as marriages, etc., – as subjects of His Britannic Majesty. And as my family had immense claims in Scotland, they were most careful in maintaining their rights as British subjects, though resident in France, and the fact of their nationality was always asserted by them on every important occasion: as, for example, when, in the time of Louis XVI and Marie Antoinette, their Majesties stood sponsors for my uncle, born in France, and then, as always, they were described as 'sujets de sa majesté Britannique'.

My father, Lord Maurice Drummond, was the youngest son of James, Third Earl of Melfort. Many were his recollections of Marie Antoinette in that bright time which preceded her unparalleled misfortunes. My father was then scarcely twenty years of age; and, remembering him as I well do, I can quite understand that he should have been considered extremely handsome in those days. Marie Antoinette when at the bijou château of Trianon, not only cultivated flowers, milked cows, and invited her courtiers generally to share her pastoral pleasures, but she there acted in private theatricals, and always the part of a shepherdess or a soubrette.[1] In the former character she illustrated Rousseau's rural scenes in a way which, if he had beheld it, would have mitigated even that philosophic republican's well-known sarcasm on royal performers;[2] and she so far overcame the educational or constitutional shyness of her royal husband in his earlier years as even to induce him to take part on the stage.

There were, however, some inconveniences in Her Majesty's taste for theatricals, for my father has often told me that when she preferred to act her favourite rôle, he felt it most embarrassing to go through his part when it was necessary to *tutoyer* her.[3] Marie Antoinette was happy then. Madame du Barry had shortly before presumed to call the future Louis XVI, 'a lubberly boy';[4] but about the date of his proclamation as king, that monarch had suddenly awakened to a sense of his responsibility as a husband. And so little did Marie Antoinette – *la petite reine de vingt ans* – and her Court anticipate the coming storm of the Revolution that one of their favourite pastimes was a game called 'Le Roi Détroné'. When, at fifteen years of age, Marie Antoinette had arrived in France as Dauphiness, she detected so much absurdity in the *ancien régime* formalities forced on her observation by the Duchesse de Noailles, the Grand Mistress of the Ceremonies, that she then and long afterwards spoke of that august personage by the sobriquet of *Madame Etiquette*. My grandmother belonged to the old Court, and clinging – as did most ladies of her age – to the time-honoured conventionalities of Versailles,[5] she ventured to write to Marie Antoinette after her succession to the throne, on the impropriety, or imprudence, of any divergence on the part of her Majesty from the traditional usages hitherto considered as part and parcel of royal etiquette in France. But the young Queen was intractable upon these points, as may be inferred from the following anecdote, the scene of which was the Bois de Boulogne.

My grandmother and my aunt, Lady Emilia Drummond, were one day there in attendance upon Her Majesty, being, like the rest of the more demure members of the Court, in open carriages. But the Queen was riding on a donkey, as indeed were various of her younger favourites. Suddenly, however, the whole cavalcade was stopped, for Marie Antoinette's donkey, having felt a sudden inclination to roll on the green turf, had thrown its royal rider, and she being quite unhurt, remained seated on the ground, laughing immoderately. As soon, however, as she could command her countenance, she assumed a mock gravity, and, without attempting to rise from her lowly position, commanded that the Grand Mistress of the ceremonies should at once be brought to her side. Nobody could imagine what Her Majesty was about either to say or do; but when the lady thus suddenly summoned to her presence, stood, in no good temper and with dignified aspect before her, she looked up and said – 'Madame, I have sent for you that you may inform me as to the etiquette to be observed when a Queen of France and a donkey have fallen – which one of them is to get up first?' This odd question elicited smiles enough from the younger part of the Court in attendance; but – as was the case with many circumstances not dissimilar in their nature – its tendency was to make enemies for Marie Antoinette among not a few who, standing near the throne of France, were jealous for the maintenance of its dignity, and who – in their circumscribed view of human nature generally – were too apt to mistake the tokens of an innocent young heart, then free from care, for those of indecorous, not to say guilty levity.

Even in trifles, this 'last Queen of France', as she has been pathetically called, could not conceal either her preferences or her distastes; in proof of which I may mention that one day when the Duke of Hamilton, who was dark, and my father, who was fair, were both in her presence, she asked some lady in attendance upon her – 'To which of my Scotchmen do you yield the palm?' And then, without waiting for an answer to this unceremonious inquiry, she added – 'For my own part, I prefer blue eyes.'

It was an unprecedented circumstance to hear a Queen of France express herself thus freely, and it was still more strange to mark the desire for change, the love of adventure, which at that time took possession of the younger part of the noblesse at Versailles. This was most signally instanced in the voluntary flight of the young Marquis de Lafayette (a near connection by marriage of the Duchesse de Noailles, the Grand Mistress of the Ceremonies above named), to fight for the cause of Independence in North America.[6]

In 1800 the family returned to Britain. After a period in London where Lucy Drummond's sister died and her brother, later, at the point of writing her memoir, Earl of Perth, was born, the family moved to Edinburgh:
A short time after our arrival there I was taken to a school kept by Miss Playfair, sister

to the professor of that name.[7] When under her care, I well remember often seeing Sir Humphrey Davy, nor can I forget an occasion on which Sir Humphrey was seated on a sort of throne, when a laurel crown was placed on his head by Mrs Apreece, to whom he was subsequently married, one of the celebrated literary ladies then resident in the 'Modern Athens'.[8]

My father, however, was still so much depressed on account of the recent death of my sister, that he resolved to remove me from my school, so that he might have more of my company, as at that time my mother was absorbed by her attention to my little brother, and I, at a very early age, began to go into society with my father.

The following anecdotes relate to the period when Lucy Drummond was about fifteen years old:

My mother did not enjoy general society equally with my father, but at home formed a *côterie* of her own, which resolved itself chiefly into daily, or rather evening, whist parties. Conspicuous at these were Lady Campbell (who lived at Holyrood House), the old Duchesse de Grammont, a Portuguese lady who had married General Macdonald of Logary, and an old maid, Miss Grace Baillie. The latter, who still dressed quite youthfully, and was really popular in her way, was willing enough to play a rubber at whist as long as it did not cause her to miss a ball. And young people of both sexes in Edinburgh at that time were anxious for her presence at every festive gathering; for, unlike old maids generally, she was anxious to promote their enjoyment in every way, and her house was daily a pleasant afternoon rendezvous from two to five o'clock.

I do not know whether Miss Grace Baillie voted either for or against my going to the 'Queen's Assembly',[9] but, despite the fact of my mother and Lady Buchan both protesting against my *entrée* there and their united predictions that if I were introduced so early in life I should in a few years, and much to my own regret, be considered much older than my actual age, I did go. Lord Buchan assumed a sovereign will upon this point, and my father was delighted to introduce me at that my first grand ball, to some of the Scottish beauties he had met a quarter of a century before at Drummond castle. He had often spoken to me of these northern belles, but I, with the impertinence of extreme youth, had imagined that they long ago must have passed into the 'sere and yellow leaf';[10] what, therefore, was my surprise when he presented me to two of them, and I found them both still beautiful! One of these ladies was Lady Charlotte Campbell (afterwards Lady Charlotte Bury), and the other was Miss Robertson, who lived to a great age, but died unmarried. The ball itself was brilliant. A famous musician of that day, named Niel Gow, was Strauss-like in his influence over the orchestra;[11] but the beauty of the two ladies – my father's old friends – was the one thing chiefly remembered by me, and for years after that, my first evening at the 'Queen's Assembly', they still remained celebrated for their personal charms.

In Edinburgh I often met Sir Walter Scott, and he taught me to play at chess. Never can I forget his kind but somewhat heavy-featured countenance, nor the sound of his friendly voice with its broad Scotch accent. He was frequently at the house of Miss Grace Baillie, and not only seemed pleased with the society of the many young persons he met there, but was always ready to enter into the spirit of any innocent jest that was going on amongst them. For example:– One day poor Miss Baillie having had one of her smart and too juvenile bead-embroidered dresses torn by some practical joke on the part of the mischievous merry Sir William Cumming Gordon, the latter promised her that he would import a lady's costume from France, which should surpass all dresses then in Edinburgh; on condition that, when it did arrive, it should be successively tried on by all the young ladies in the habit of frequenting Miss Grace Baillie's house. Sir William Cumming Gordon kept his promise, and in due course of time a packing-case arrived at Miss Baillie's. At its opening all her fair favourites were invited to be present, and not only these, but some gentlemen also, Sir Walter Scott among the number. The packing-case was opened, and many were the smiles of eager faces as from out of it was first lifted a blue cloth petticoat, all embroidered with gold; then a red jacket, also very grand; afterwards a costly lace neckerchief; then a wonderful Normandy cap, elaborately trimmed with lace to match the neckerchief, and last, not least, a pair of long earrings and large brooch, together with a magnificent cross to be worn round the neck. It was a fancy-dress, but quite correct in all points of Normandy costume.

Eagerly were the cap, the earrings, and the cross tried on by all the prettiest girls then in Edinburgh; but when at last it came to the turn of Miss Mary Stuart to test their effect upon herself, she looked so extremely beautiful in them that Sir William Cumming Gordon fell down on his knees before her, and Sir Walter Scott, looking towards her at the same moment with amused admiration, repeated Pope's well-known lines –

On her white breast a sparkling cross she bore,
That Jews might kiss and infidels adore.[12]

Sir William Cumming Gordon, however, declared that though Jews might kiss the cross, he, as a Christian, would kiss the beautiful wearer of it. Here, however, propriety intervened, and he found himself suddenly prevented from fulfilling his Christian intentions.

Miss Baillie, who was at least fifty years old, and very tall and fat, had the good sense to know that this fancy dress was quite unsuited to her self, and she had also the good nature to form a raffle for it amongst her young friends about a week after its arrival from Paris.

She was certainly unwearied in her endeavours to promote amusement, and as the raffle was to take place at her own house, she made it the excuse for a fantastic fête, at which twelve little girls, dressed as shepherdesses, helped to conduct the numerous guests severally to their seats, before joining in the various Arcadian amusements provided for them. In a leafy bower sat a wizard fortune-teller, so disguised by his growth of venerable beard and imposing costume, that he was unrecognisable, although from his answers to those who came to hear their destinies from his lips, it was evident that he had had many social opportunities of studying the various characters of the company generally. Afterwards there was a ball, at which the lovely Miss Mary Stuart, who had drawn the prize at the raffle, wore the Normandy costume which so admirably became her.

At the Restoration of the French monarchy under Louis XVIII the Drummond family travelled to London preparatory to a return to France:
[…] in the capital […] everybody was eager to gain a glimpse of the King of France, and still more of his companion and niece, his *Antigone*, as he called her – the Duchesse d'Angoulême, daughter of the martyrs Louis XVI and Marie Antoinette, and the sharer in her youth of their captivity, generally known to Europe as the 'Orphan of the Temple'.[13]

Congratulatory addresses were on every side offered to Louis XVIII, whose advent in France was heralded under the *sobriquet* of 'The Father of his People'. The elder of the two surviving brothers of 'Louis the Martyr' was not a hero in appearance, and, therefore, legitimists in France, where tradition still clung to the warlike deeds of Bourbons in bygone times, felt it expedient to prepare the minds of the people for the sight of a King whose infirm legs were cased in red velvet gaiters, whose body, no longer slender, was buttoned up in a blue surtout, and who wore on his head a round English hat. So Louis XVIII was proclaimed beforehand as the father of his people and as 'the Magistrate King', who was coming to give France peace, now that the sanguinary despotism of Napoleon was over, and to grant her a Constitution instead of the fancied glory which had cost her so much blood and treasure.

The attractions of London detain the family:
In London, in 1814, Mrs Drummond Burrell (afterwards Lady Willoughby d'Ereby) was occasionally my chaperon. She was one of the Lady Patronesses of Almack's.[14]

At Almack's, in 1814, Scotch reels and the country-dances of Old England were still in fashion, though the quadrille and valse were then recently introduced. The conventions decreed by the Ladies Patronesses were so strictly adhered to, that one night when the Duke of Wellington arrived a few minutes after twelve, the hour after which it had been decided that no visitor should be admitted, he was refused admission to the ball-room. […] I first met Lord Byron at that time in London and his appearance made a melancholy impression on me. He was extremely handsome, and was much courted by everybody; but his manner, when in general society, was so shy and retiring that he would hardly ever move from the side of the room where he had happened to take a position on his first entrance into it. This peculiarity was, I believe, attributable to his lameness, a defect of which he was ever painfully conscious, and the sense of which no doubt enhanced the air of sadness that generally pervaded his look and manner.

He was an object of general attention among ladies, even before the time when Lady Caroline Lamb is said to have poisoned herself, stabbed herself, and drowned herself – unsuccessfully for his sake. Beautiful women of rank vied with each other in a manifest wish to attract the notice of the poet.[15] They learned his verses by heart, but it is strange that but few, if any, of them had intelligence or individuality enough to attire herself according to a poet's fancy; for anything rather than ideal was the mode of English ladies' dress in those day, especially when it was surmounted, as usual then on grand occasions at Court, by three large white feathers – a 'Prince of Wales's plume' – which rose above the head of the fair wearer to the height of at least half a yard. No wonder that George III, beholding these plumes waving before him when he opened Parliament just at the time when his reason began to totter, addressed himself to 'My Lords and peacocks!'

[...]

Balls and parties rapidly succeeded each other during our short stay in London, for all the embassies vied with each other in the splendour of their several fêtes to celebrate the Restoration; but by many foreigners of distinction at that time in England the Caledonian Ball was considered the most remarkable. The Highland costume worn upon this occasion by all Scotch gentlemen present, was strange to continental eyes. Each chieftain wore his own tartan, and the combination of colours was dazzling. More amazing still to the uninitiated were the Scottish country dances, and particularly the reel, with its rapid steps, its Highland fling, and the wild yell of triumph, like that of the red Indian shouted forth by its dancers.

At that ball all Scotch ladies likewise wore their national costume according to clan; and my cousin, Mrs Drummond Burrell, wore the Drummond tartan dress, trimmed with gold fringe; while I, who accompanied her, felt by no means displeased at myself, arrayed as I was in white, trimmed with Drummond tartan, shoes to match, and a scarf of the same plaid fastened with a large brooch on the left shoulder.

The family shortly moved to Paris which Lucy Drummond found then 'like a fairyland'. She was presented to Louis XVIII and the Duchesse d'Angoulême. In Paris after the Restoration she always stayed with her relatives Mr and Mrs Drummond in a magnificent house which had formally belonged to Madame Tallien:

Count d'Orsay, Moore, and many other celebrities then in Paris, felt at home in Mrs Drummond's house and enjoyed the delightful gardens which belonged to it;[16] gardens where choice flowers bloomed, and on the spacious lawns of which peacocks strutted, in a way to make visitors forget the vicinity of the city [...] Small literary côteries used sometimes to form themselves in Paris in those days, in a way to make one think that, under the pedantic King Louis XVIII, the time of 'Les Précieuses' was not altogether past.[17]

[...]

In the month of March, 1815, the star of Napoleon was once more in the ascendant. The Emperor had escaped from Elba.

Lucy Drummond's father had always found the Emperor 'willing to oblige him' and when Napoleon reoccupied the Tuileries he took his daughter with him for an audience with the great man. She is ushered in by Hortense, the daughter of Napoleon and Josephine and ex-Queen of Holland:

I followed the Queen, and I was in the presence of the Emperor. With his usual impetuosity he advanced towards me, and without making the least salutation to me, he took me by the hand and conducted me to an armchair.

'Sit down,' said he to me.

Then instead of seating himself also, he walked away with rapid strides to the end of the salon. When he came back, he said –

'It is a long time since I have seen you, Madame. You are as pretty as ever.'

'But, Sire,' said the Queen, 'Madame is of my age.'

This interruption was singular, for the Queen was five or six years older than myself; but I replied only by congratulating the Emperor on the excellent health he appeared to enjoy.

'And have you no congratulations to offer me on my return?' asked he.

This repartee, and, above all, the look which accompanied it, confounded me. Bonaparte perceived this and continued, –

'Well, Madame, was Louis XVIII very gallant?'

I gathered up all my courage, and replied, –

'I know nothing on that point, Sire; but I can assure your majesty that he never abused the superior privilege of his rank to torment a woman admitted to his presence.'

'Ah! I have vexed you,' he exclaimed, laughing. 'So much the better; that will avenge me a little for what you have done against me.'

'Neither have I ever uttered a complaint of your Majesty.'

'No; but you have intrigued, caballed, plotted, conspired with people of every colour, – emigrants, ideologists, republicans. See the fine service you have rendered to France! for at last, in spite of you, here I come back, and for a long time, I hope.'

Napoleon's return was, of course, the celebrated 'Hundred Days' before he was defeated at Waterloo and exiled to St Helena. After the second Restoration Lucy Drummond recollects the antagonism of Talleyrand and Louis XVIII:

Prince Talleyrand stands out in my memory [...] because, under a quiet exterior, he was incomparably the most brilliant conversationalist present.[18] Every sentence he uttered was epigrammatic, and often pungent with satire; yet all the time that he gave vent to such utterances his smile was most pleasing; and I must add that, although then and long since quoted by the world as a mere dexterous diplomatist or heartless man of wit, that smile of his emanated from a goodness of heart for which few people but those who knew him well gave him credit. I have seen Prince Talleyrand weep as well as smile; it was upon a day at a later date than that to which this period of my narrative refers, when he told me how in his youth he had loved my aunt Emilia, and how Fate, which in the early years of his life had been too often antagonistic to him, had prevented his marriage with her.

Louis XVIII did not like Talleyrand, and none the more so because he felt that his own somewhat pedantic conversation was overpowered by the Prince's brilliant intelligence. Sometimes a sharp though short encounter of words would take place between His Majesty and the great diplomatist; and one of these encounters I remember to have occurred on a Court day at the Tuileries when I was present. The King and the Duchesse d'Angoulême were both receiving that day; the rooms were almost full, and His Majesty appeared in the most excellent spirits. Presently Prince Talleyrand came in, and it was soon rumoured that he had asked for leave of absence from the King. Now everybody in Paris at that time knew that Talleyrand, though separated from his wife, was often threatened by her with the assurance that she would insist on taking up her abode with him, if he did not at once send her whatever sums of money she happened to require. So the King, being in a merry mood, said quite aloud, to the Prince, as the latter approached His Majesty, 'Why, Prince, I hear that as Madame de Talleyrand has just arrived in Paris you wish to leave;' and as Louis XVIII said this he laughed, his laugh being, of course, echoed instantly by the numerous courtiers present who had heard his words.

But Talleyrand only bowed, and in a clear, sonorous voice replied, 'Yes, your Majesty, it is my 20th of March.'

It was then the King's turn to attempt to get up a laugh at his own expense, but he merely coloured and looked annoyed, for few things galled him more than an allusion to his flight on the date just named – a flight caricatured at the time in Paris by a flock of geese waddling out from the Tuileries, while eagles were flying in.

At the beginning of the second volume of her memoirs, Lucy Drummond contrasts the gloomy Versailles of the first half of the 18th century with its pre-revolutionary days and offers her grandmother's version of Voltaire's return to Paris in 1778, four years after the accession of Louis XVI to the throne, and more than twenty years after the date of his own exile from the Court and capital of France:

[My grandmother] remembered what a strange spectacle Voltaire presented to a generation which had grown up and learned to know him from his writings alone, but which never, until his return to Paris, beheld 'the philosopher of Ferney', who nevertheless had to so large an extent guided the progress of public opinion by his pen.[19] He was banished in the time of his benefactress, Madame de Pompadour, because Louis XV would not accord to him certain political and ministerial favours which his ambition led him to desire; and his exile was afterwards confirmed on account of his collusion with Frederick of Prussia in his designs against France and Austria. At last, after a long proscription, he came back to the capital of his country at the beginning of the reign of the most virtuous of all the Kings of France, who, from the moment of his accession to the throne, in possession of his race for nearly a thousand years, to that of his martyrdom on the scaffold, was doomed to suffer for the sins of his ancestors.

It was carnival time when the aged Voltaire returned to Paris after his long absence; and profane *gamins*, not knowing who he was, hooted at or cheered him when he made his appearance, thinking, in consequence of the strange garments which he wore, that he was in masquerade for their amusement. And, indeed, they were not apparently without good grounds for forming such a supposition, for his out-door dress was a vast pélisse, trimmed with fur, which completely enveloped his frail body. A huge Louis Quatorze wig of wool shaded his thin cheeks, and the wig was surmounted by a red cap trimmed with fur. In form and face he was, as he himself said, a mere skeleton; but his eyes still gleamed with such marvellous brilliancy that their magnetic power was felt by all upon whom they shone. [...]

The French priesthood dreaded Voltaire's presence in Paris; but, notwithstanding the various ecclesiastical designs to check his popularity, it increased daily. The cry of 'Vive Voltaire!' was constantly resounding [...] 'I am stifled,' said he, 'but it is beneath roses'. And the roses were sweet to him, for he loved all this adulation, though the excitement of it was killing him. [...] Among his innumerable guests came the friend of his long-past youth, Madame du Deffand. They were both very old, and she was blind. They were both philosophers, yet she passed her whole life in flying from serious reflection; while he was still feverishly anxious in the attempt to win fresh laurels for himself with a production of his new tragedy, *Irène*.

Madame du Deffand, as every one knows, was the intimate friend and constant correspondent of Horace Walpole,[20] who declared her to be, despite her age and infirmities, one of the most charming of women.

She could not see Voltaire, but she could hear him speak. The sound of his voice, weak with age, was not pleasant to her. He could see Madame du Deffand, but the sight was not agreeable to him; for old age does not like to behold its own shadow, nor to hear its own echo.

The day at last came for the representation of *Irène*. All Paris was mad with excitement, and my grandmother, the Duchess of Melfort, went with Madame du Deffand to the theatre. Men, women, and even children, of all ranks and conditions were there, each full of excitement and eager to catch a glimpse of one whose name was in every mouth.

Louis XVI from his youth had had a horror of Voltaire's writings, and he had imposed such restrictions as he considered necessary to prevent the Court at Versailles from joining in any demonstration in honour of the philosopher. Voltaire had been, and still was, excluded from Versailles; unlike his friend Benjamin Franklin, he was not allowed to appear there; but, nevertheless, on that occasion when *Irène* was produced at the *Comédie Française*, the Comte d'Artois was there *incognito*, and my grandmother used to say that the Queen herself was likewise present, though in disguise.[21] […] In fact all the world was present. The multitude overflowed the enclosure, and the benches, the boxes, the corridors, were filled to suffocation. Even the curtain which still hung before the stage seemed to quiver with excitement while the audience awaited the arrival of Voltaire. He came at last, and as he alighted from his carriage at the entrance there was a general rush forward. Everybody was eager to touch him, to look at him closely, and some even tried to pluck some hair from the fur of his pélisse, that they might keep it as a relic.

When he appeared in his box a simultaneous shout of 'Vive Voltaire!' was raised; and then the actor Brizard approached and placed a laurel crown upon his head. Voltaire shed tears. 'Ah!' he exclaimed, 'do you wish me to die of joy?' The people called out aloud to him to retain the crown, while the various titles of all his most popular works were repeated and echoed from every part of the theatre.

The curtain before the stage now drew up, and the first scene of *Irène* appeared. The play began, but the actors and spectators were so occupied with its author that they scarcely attended to his work, so that 'never was a play so badly played, so much applauded, and so little listened to.'

Presently when the piece was concluded, the sound of trumpets and drums announced that a grand ceremony was about to be performed. The bust of Voltaire was placed upon a pedestal before the drop-scene, and all the actors in the tragedy, who still wore the costumes in which they had played their parts, formed a semi-circle round it, palms and garlands in their hands. A crown of laurel was placed upon the head of the bust by an actor dressed in the garb of a monk, and a favourite actress of the time then stepped forward and recited some verses, the concluding lines of which were –

> Voltaire, reçois la couronne,
> Que l'on vient de te présenter;
> Il est beau de la mériter
> Quand c'est la France qui la donne.[22]

After this, each actor laid the wreath he held round the bust; and after one of the actresses had kissed it, all the other actors and actresses followed her example. The acclamations, which were incessant, were renewed with fresh fervour when Dr Franklin, the 'Liberator of the New World', as he was called, appeared by the side of Voltaire, and embraced him in the sight of the audience.

When Voltaire at last left the theatre, garlands were thrown around him; and it was necessary for guards to clear the path, because of the dense mass of enthusiastic admirers who crowded it. When he was re-seated in his sky-blue carriage studded with stars, to return home from the theatre, the horses were unharnessed, while young poets and literary aspirants disputed among themselves the honour of drawing him to his hotel.

This wonderful reception was, however, too much for the old man's nerves. And after a careless overdose of an opiate that had been sent to him with careful instructions for division of the dose he lapsed into unconsciousness and died before the priests could be sure of securing a last confession from him. The family returned to England after the death of the grandmother who told these stories and arrived in time for the trial and later funeral of Queen Caroline:

She died; but not before she herself had dictated the inscription for her own coffin-lid:–

CAROLINE OF BRUNSWICK,
THE MURDERED QUEEN OF ENGLAND

I saw her funeral as it passed through London. It was followed by a multitude of people. The wishes – or it may be the fears – of the King were known to the Ministers, and not only were the troops called out upon this occasion, but the funeral was turned aside when it reached Hyde Park, now the famous gathering-place for mobs. […] Canning, though much favoured by George IV, always proved himself to the last chivalrously loyal towards the unfortunate Queen, though Ministers, as a rule, seemed to persecute her. Byron said (writing to Moore, from Ravenna), 'I won't talk politics, it is low'; and as I cannot here half describe the differences of opinion which existed concerning 'the Queen, and her bath, and her bottle,' and her '*courser*', as some English journalists called her *courrier*, I turn from the subject.[23]

[…]

I very often met Sir Robert Peel at different dinners, and I was always charmed when he happened to sit near me. One reason why I liked his conversation so much was, not only that he was very clever and agreeable, but also that he spoke French so extremely well.

Byron declared that at Harrow there were always great hopes of Peel, 'the orator and statesman (that was, or is, or is to be)'; and he likewise said that Peel 'never got into scrapes', as he himself did. I cannot say whether this was always the case, but certain it is that in after-life, when Peel was Prime Minister, a connexion of mine was destined to be his scapegoat in a most unfortunate manner.

Mr Edward Drummond was secretary to Sir Robert Peel, and one day, when there was a Cabinet council in Downing Street, he went with him thither. Suddenly, however, Sir Robert Peel found that he had forgotten to bring some papers with him that were immediately wanted; and he requested his secretary to get back into the carriage and go back for them at once.

Mr Edward Drummond hastened to comply: but just as he had stepped into the carriage, and was telling the coachman where to drive, he was shot fatally by an assassin, Macnaughten by name, who wanted to kill Sir Robert Peel, and had mistaken my relative for him.[24]

Lucy Drummond mentions her marriage in 1823, her mother's illness and death shortly after; followed by the death of her father and shipwreck of her brother off the coast of Barbados from which he was, however, mysteriously rescued. When her narrative comes to the time of Victoria's Coronation, she decides, she says, to mention merely a few striking details:
At the moment when the Queen, kneeling, had the crown placed on her brow, a ray of sunshine fell upon her face and head. The day had been quite dull and grey until then; but with the sudden sunshine upon the diamonds in the crown making a sort of glory around the head of the fair young Queen, the effect was very striking. And I remember that when Her Majesty was conducted to King Edward's chair – the throne (to which the Peers came to swear their allegiance) – the Duke of Wellington, having, like the rest, to back down the steps of the throne, threw his robe over his arm, and his great military boots were visible under it up to his knees; but still he succeeded in making a safe and not ungraceful descent.

When, however, among the other peers, it came to Lord Rolle's turn to walk back-wards, he lost his footing, and *rolled* down. Many were the easy jokes made upon this *pas perdu*, but never have I heard any mention made of what I myself particularly noticed at the moment, and this was that when poor Lord Rolle was stumbling backwards from the Throne, the Queen started forward as though to save him.

Subsequent reminiscences take us through the lives of the great and notorious and include the visit of the Emperor Napoleon and the Empress Eugénie to Britain; at last comes the visit of Queen Victoria to France:
Although the Paris season was over at the date fixed for that visit of Her Majesty, Parisians still lingered in their capital, because everybody who had a chance of doing so was eager to catch sight of Queen Victoria.
[…]
Upon the day of Her Majesty's arrival in Paris, the streets were crowded from an early hour with provincials, who had flocked from far and near to behold her, and who had taken up their stand upon the pavements, behind rows of boys – *gamins de Paris* – who, like their London confraternity, have their own peculiar characteristics. The provincials had provided themselves with huge baskets of provisions; the gamins cracked their jokes; and, as the day wore on, the Boulevards grew gay with the various hues of ladies' dresses; all the houses, from their tall roofs downwards, seemed teeming with life, and eager faces peeped forth from every window. The allied colours of France and England were floating in various directions, and especially in that of the International Palace of Industry, while thousands of workmen were ready to present their several petitions, and stood prepared to avail

themselves of the permission, previously accorded, to fall behind the Royal and Imperial cortège when it should appear in sight.

[…]

She came at last; trumpets heralded her approach and further progress through Paris towards the château of St Cloud; cheers long and loud rent the air, and although the day had declined so as perhaps to prevent her Majesty's full appreciation of all the public preparations that were intended to greet her, the people of Paris all expressed themselves enthusiastically pleased with her peculiarly gracious mode of bowing to them in response to their acclamations.

[…]

It was at the Palace of Versailles that the last evening of that royal visit was spent, and thither upon that occasion I had the honour to be invited, for at the time we were staying in the neighbourhood with an old friend of ours, the Comtesse de Boursonne. In the Salle de Miroirs Queen Victoria and the Empress Eugénie were seated. The Prince of Wales, in Highland dress, was also there. The Queen and the Empress occupied raised seats, but amid their brilliant *entourage* of illustrious celebrities, the Princess Royal was especially remarkable. How little at that moment could she imagine that not very many years afterwards, when she herself would be one of the Royal Family of Prussia by marriage, the head-quarters of the Prussians at war with France, would be in the very palace amid the gay scenes of which she herself at that time shone conspicuously![25]

I need hardly remind the reader that the Palace of Versailles was so sacked during the Revolution which closed the eighteenth century, that no monarch since seated on the throne of France has undertaken to restore it, though grand fêtes have from time to time been given there, by one of the most memorable of which the *Musée National* was inaugurated in the reign of Louis Philippe.

Indeed the very name of Versailles, like the portraits and pictures hanging upon the walls of its lofty saloons and vast galleries, evokes a panorama of memory from early times until now.

The innumerable and fantastic fireworks outside, displayed in honour of the Queen's visit, presented a brilliant attraction; and when an illuminated transparency of Windsor castle appeared, greeted by the enthusiastic cheers of the people crowding the grounds of Versailles, and accompanied by the national anthem of England, the delight of the spectators was unbounded.

But, of course, this high point of celebration for both countries was not to last:

How unforeseen at that moment was the destination (in 1870)[26] of the palaces of St Cloud, St Germain, and Versailles! Who could have foretold that the splendid and gilded picture-galleries of Versailles, – galleries that night so illuminated that they looked like fairyland, – would ever become, as they afterwards were, the wards of an immense hospital echoing but the groans of the sick and wounded. And St Germain, that half-ruined but still stately abode of the exiled Stuart monarchs of England in the time of the 'Grand Monarque'[27] – who could have predicted that that château also would be turned into a hospital for the victims of one of the most bitter wars ever known since the date of Christianity – the synonym of a higher civilisation!

When the National Anthem of England echoed through the woods of Versailles, and when the illuminations in honour of the great Peace Alliance between France and England were reflected in the sparkling fountains, none there could have believed that, ere many years were past, the neighbouring woods of St Cloud would be pierced by cannon-balls, that the trees would whistle with the murderous bullets of soldiers lying in ambush beneath them, that the boudoir of the Empress Eugénie, and the flower-gardens where the now exiled Prince Impérial was wont to amuse himself, would be occupied by soldiers exposed at any moment to be launched into eternity by shot hurled from the other side of the Seine, and that the château of St Cloud itself would be burnt down to the ground, – its stately walls being now a heap of ruins.

NOTES

1. The Petit Trianon was built at Versailles in 1762-8 for Louis XV. In comedy and comic opera the soubrette is a pert, coquettish maid-servant.

2. Jean Jacques Rousseau (1712-78) believed that man was naturally good and made corrupt by society. It is doubtful that he would have mitigated his strictures on the frivolity of royal performers, even given this flattery. See also Cockburn (p.32, n.15).

3. *Tutoyer*: to use the familiar form of 'you'. Offstage it would be quite wrong for an inferior to use this form to address the sovereign.

4. Marie Jeanne Bécu, Comtesse du Barry (?1743-93), was the last mistress of Louis XV. She was guillotined during the French Revolution.

5. The Palace of Versailles was built for Louis XIV between 1676 and 1708 by J. H. Mansart (1646-1708); it was the residence of the French kings from 1678 to 1769

6. For Lafayette see Wright (p.168, n.2).

7. For Playfair see Fletcher (p.115, n.1).

8. Sir Humphrey Davy (1778-1829), chemist and inventor of the miner's safety lamp which came to be known as the Davy lamp. He began his career by discovering the usefulness of nitrous oxide as an anaesthetic. He subsequently discovered a number of new metallic compounds and, importantly, encouraged Michael Faraday (1791-1867) (who discovered the connection between electricity and magnetism) by employing him as an assistant. The Davys moved in literary as well as scientific circles and Joanna Baillie corresponded a good deal with Lady Davy.

9. An entertainment and ball celebrated on 18 January. Lady Clementina explains that Lady Buchan was then the representative of Her Majesty for this Assembly and that no one could be present at it without a voucher, a sort of equivalent for a Lord Chamberlain's ticket at the Court balls in London.

10. '[…] my way of life/is fall'n into the sere, the yellow leaf' (*Macbeth*, V, iii, ll.22-3).

11. Niel Gow (1727-1807) was a celebrated violinist and composer, patronised by the Scottish nobility. Raeburn's portrait of him is famous and the original was painted for the painter's own collection.

12. Pope, *The Rape of the Lock*, canto II, ll. 7-8.

13. The King and Queen and their family were imprisoned before their execution in the Temple. The Temple, originally a fortified monastery of the Templars, later became a royal prison. On August 10 the mob forced the removal of the royal family to the *petite tour* of the old Temple and later to the main tower where they remained prisoners of the Paris Commune.

14. One of the fashionable London social and gambling clubs.

15. Lady Caroline Lamb (1785-1828) married William Lamb, afterwards second Viscount Melbourne. She became madly infatuated with Byron, and did at least slash her arm with

scissors when he tried to break with her. After this she included a satirical portrait of him as Lord Glenarvon in her novel, *Glenarvon*, 1816.

16. The Irish poet, Thomas Moore, had been appointed Admiralty Registrar in Bermuda in 1803; he left a deputy in charge and returned to London. When his deputy decamped with the official funds, Moore was declared bankrupt and lived in Europe until his debts were discharged in 1822.

17. Molière's play, *Les Précieuses ridicules*, 1659, makes fun of the circle of the Marquise de Rambouillet (1588-1665). She presided over a salon where the celebrated writers of the day met and conversed, pretentiously and pedantically as Molière would have it.

18. For further detail on Talleyrand see Christian Isabel Johnstone, p.138, n.8.

19. Voltaire (François-Marie Arouet, 1694-1778), the great and controversial French writer and 'philosophe', had gone to live in exile in Ferney on the border of Switzerland in 1753. Voltaire had corresponded from 1754 with Frederick the Great of Prussia (1712-86). Madame de Pompadour (1721-64), the mistress of Louis XV, was a notable patron of the arts.

20. Horace Walpole, 1717-97, the English novelist and prose writer. His novel *The Castle of Otranto* is usually described as the first Gothic novel. He never married but had a number of close friendships with women, including the Miss Berrys: see also Baillie (p.105, n.3).

21. Benjamin Franklin, 1706-90, US diplomat, scientist and author. He helped to frame the Declaration of Independence, 1776. He was particularly famous in France where he was a diplomat from 1776 to 1785.

22. 'Voltaire, receive the crown that we present to you; it is a fine thing to deserve it when it is France that gives it.'

23. Caroline of Brunswick (1768-1821) was unquestionably abominably treated by her husband, the Prince of Wales, later George IV, both before and after their separation in 1796. After their separation he prevented her from seeing their child, Charlotte. Popular support made it impossible for him to divorce her, but she was also her own worst enemy and did little for herself in the scenes associated with her exclusion from the Coronation. She was reputed to drink heavily. George Canning (1770-1827) was Foreign Secretary and, briefly in 1827, Tory Prime Minister.

24. Edward Drummond (1792-1843) was Sir Robert Peel's secretary and was shot by a madman, Macnaghten, who believed he had a grievance against Peel. The assassin was acquitted on a plea of insanity. Drummond's wounds were said at the time to have been inattentively treated.

25. William I of Prussia was victorious in the Franco-Prussian War which ended the reign of the Emperor Napoleon III, nephew of Napoleon I, and the Empress Eugénie. Victoria (1840-1901), the eldest daughter of Queen Victoria (1819-1901) (Queen from 1837) briefly in 1888 became Empress of Germany as the wife of Frederick III.

26. The palaces were used as hospitals during the Franco-Prussian War (1870-71). France capitulated after the siege of Paris and was forced to cede Alsace and Lorraine to the newly established German Empire. France itself was left economically and politically weakened.

27. 'Grand Monarque': Louis XIV.

Catherine Sinclair (1800–1864)

Catherine Sinclair was the fourth daughter of Sir John Sinclair of Ulbster, a man of many talents: statesman, agriculturalist, philanthropist and writer, and his second wife, the only daughter of Alexander, first Lord Macdonald. Sir John was also the organiser of the scheme for a Statistical Account of Scotland, the first volume of the twenty volumes of which he published in 1791. Catherine acted as her father's secretary from the age of fourteen until he died in 1835. She too pursued philanthropic work, taking an interest in all schemes of social improvement: as a member of the Edinburgh Society she assisted in the setting up of cooking depots in old and new Edinburgh, and in the maintenance of a mission station at the Water of Leith. She was partly instrumental in securing seats for crowded throughfares in Edinburgh and she helped to institute drinking fountains in Edinburgh, one of which was called after her. Most of her independent writing comes from the period after her father's death. She is perhaps best known today as the author of *Holiday House*, a once very popular children's novel. As well as a number of other novels she wrote travel books from one of which, *Shetland and the Shetlanders, or the Northern Circuit* (1840), the extract below is taken: this kind of travel writing is, of course, part of that project of coming to understand one's own country which can be dated back to the sixteenth century but which became increasingly important towards the end of the eighteenth century. She also published a study of female education, *Modern Accomplishments, or the March of the Intellect*. Catherine Sinclair enjoyed some popularity as a writer in America. She died in Kensington where her brother John was vicar but was buried at St John's Episcopal Church, Edinburgh.

Catherine Sinclair, *Modern Accomplishments* (Edinburgh & London: 1836); *Hill and Valley* (Edinburgh: W. Whyte & Co., 1838); *Holiday House* (Edinburgh: W. Whyte & Co., 1839); *Shetland and the Shetlanders or, the Northern Circuit* with a map of the route (Edinburgh: William Whyte & Co., 1840); *Scotland and the Scotch* (Edinburgh: Simpkin & Marshall, 1841); *Modern Flirtations; or, A Month at Harrowgate* (Edinburgh: W. Whyte & Co., 1841); *Scotch Courtiers and the Court* (Edinburgh: W. Whyte & Co., 1842); *Charlie Seymour* (Edinburgh: 1844); *Jane Bouverie: Or, Prosperity and Adversity* (Edinburgh: 1846); *The Journey of Life* (London: 1847); *Sir Edward Graham* (London: 1849); *Lord and Lady Harcourt* (London: 1850); *Beatrice; or, The Unknown Relatives,* (London: Ward, Lock & Tyler, 1852); *Popish Legends and Bible Truths* (London: Longman, Brown, Green & Longmans, 1852); *London Homes* (London: 1853); *Lady Mary Pierrepoint* (London: 1853); *Frank Vansittart; or, the Model Schoolboys* (London: 1853); *The Priest and the Curate* (London: 1853); *The Mysterious Marriage* (London: 1854); *Cross Purposes: A Novel* (London: 1855); *The Cabman's Holiday* (Ipswich, London: 1855); *Torchester Abbey* (1857); *Anecdotes of the Caesars* (Ipswich, London: 1858); and others

Further Reading:
Anderson; *DNB*; *DLB*, 163; Irving; Royle

From *Shetland and the Shetlanders or, the Northern Circuit* with a map of the route, 1840:

Dedicated to the Highland Society, with the epigraph:

> O Scotland! nurse of bravest men,
> But nurse of bad men too.
> For thee the good attempt in vain,
> What villains still undo!
>
> (Robertson of Struan)[1]

My dear Cousin, – Every new country is interesting to visit once, though the real compliment is, as you say, to go a second time. I like to ascertain with my own eyes, what is, or is not worth seeing in it, – whether it be better or worse than my own, how people set about being happy there, and how they succeed. At one time I expected quite as much to visit the moon as the Shetland islands, but I have lately indulged a sort of hopeless wish to venture on a voyage of discovery towards the extreme verge of her Majesty's dominions, that I might pass the longest day of my life in that country where two days are turned into one, by having no intervening night.

Islands are troublesome articles to deal with, especially as I have not the courage of a butterfly by steam, therefore it was a considerable exertion the first time I invited myself to go, but after talking it over with myself during some weeks, it became a matter of course, that wind and weather permitting, or even not permitting, the experiment should be tried, consequently one cold stormy morning, to my own great astonishment, we found ourselves on board the Sovereign, a fine large well-grown steam-boat, which touches at Wick once a week, in full boil, on its route from Leith to Lerwick, and picks up all those courageous passengers who may have summoned up resolution and enterprise enough to venture almost within sight of the north pole.

Nearly every gentleman before whom I have happened to mention Shetland during the last year or two, has long intended to take a glimpse of those stormy isles, but while swarms and clouds of travellers are migrating to the most unattainable foreign districts, our own northern Archipelago remains unknown and unnoticed, wasting its sweets, if it has any, on the desert air, and scarcely upon visiting terms with a single individual. Pray, bring your telescope here some day, and try, as we are doing, to get a distant peep of Iceland.

Travellers are not seen to much advantage in steam-boat costume, and it is certainly odd that, wherever a crowd is assembled in a morning, they all look vulgar; therefore we glanced round at the mob of miscellaneous beings assembled on deck, all shivering, in cloaks of every shape, size and colour, little hoping to meet with the very agreeable society which we soon afterwards discovered on board, or indeed with anything that could be called society at all.

The General Assembly of Scotland having recently dispersed, we found a ship-load of divines returning to their congregations in the north, some apparently clever and eccentric, some extra-eccentric, and others pious, learned, and communicative, who added all that was in their power, and that was a great deal, to the pleasure of our voyage, and almost every one of whom gave us most cordial invitations to their fire-sides and manses in Shetland. Mr Hamilton, the very talented and agreeable incumbent of Bressay, near Lerwick, became a perfect encyclopedia of information and entertainment as long as we continued in the ultra-north, and Mr Watson of North Yell afforded us many curious details respecting his parish and people. He officiates in two churches, divided by a broad and dangerous ferry, where frequently on Sunday six rowers have endeavoured in vain to carry him across, but after pulling incessantly for three or four hours, and coming in sight of his church and the assembled congregation, he has been obliged to relinquish all hope of landing, while it was about equally difficult to reach the opposite shore. One of Mr Watson's elders, who had to travel eight hundred Shetland miles, a very vague measurement, besides crossing a wide ferry before getting to church, was so exceedingly zealous that never during many years did he once miss a divine service! This venerable Christian was unfortunately drowned lately while trying to save the crew of another boat lost near his own house. Mr Watson says the people of Shetland, in general, testify an extreme value for public ordinances, and though his parish consists of only eight hundred persons, he generally averages at the sacrament about three hundred and fifty communicants. They are all so indigent that the collection at church seldom exceeds threepence!

The chief or only wealth of Shetland arises from the fisheries, and from the manufacture of wool, which is of so very superior a quality that stockings are knitted by thousands and tens of thousands in these islands, at all prices and are sometimes fine enough to be sold for two guineas a pair! I find it registered in the Rev. Mr Sand's account of his own parish Tingwall, near Lerwick, that 'formerly the stockings of Shetland were sent to Holland, but the difference of their value, since they found their way to other markets, particularly the English, is said to be nearly equal to the landrent of the country, and this difference must be ascribed to the patriotic and benevolent exertions of Sir John Sinclair.'[2] During the eighty years of my father's life, he published one hundred and six volumes, and three hundred and sixty-seven pamphlets, written with the one all-prevailing desire to benefit his native country, and while he has been called from his labours to that rest which remaineth for the people of God, it is pleasing in every part of Scotland to trace the success of so enterprising and persevering a patriot. The universal diffusion of English sheep over our native hills, was an era in our national history, and has nearly doubled the value of many Highland properties, where, owing to ignorance and mismanagement, the Scottish wool had become so exceedingly deteriorated and scarce, that, on average, four million of pounds had to be annually imported from Spain. In consequence of some advantageous discoveries respecting wool, communicated by my father to the Highland Society, a board of enquiry was instantly formed, of which he became chairman, sparing neither time nor expense to render it efficient, and presenting to the committee a hundred sheep, which he had collected from the royal flocks of France, from Spain, Shetland, and England, to the latter of which he gave that name, now so universally known, of 'Cheviot sheep'. He travelled in person to every country where the growth of wool was peculiarly successful, and at an inn twelve miles from Edinburgh, he gave the first sheep-shearing festival which had ever taken place in Great Britain, where a multitude of persons from all countries sat down to a collation, each adorned with pastoral badges and emblems, and where one of the amusements consisted in seeing wool which had been shorn in the morning, spun, dyed, wove, and formed into a coat during a single day.

Sinclair moves from these general observations to specific detail about the towns she visits:

The very ancient and interesting cathedral of Kirkwall, dedicated to St Magnus, was begun seven centuries ago, by Ronald, Earl of Orkney. It is the most perfectly preserved in Scotland, and looks almost as large as the whole city put together. You would fancy it an arrival from Brobdingnag among the Lilliputian buildings around, and the whole structure would do honour to any Episcopal diocese in England, being in truth a sort of country-cousin to Worcester Cathedral, as they are in a similar style of architecture, though the masonry of Kirkwall is coarser, and the plan scarcely so dignified. It is wonderful that the poor inhabitants could produce so magnificent a pile for Divine worship! The roof is quite entire, but the lofty steeple was most unfortunately struck down by lightning several years ago, which causes a sad blank in the *coup d'oeil* at first, though much architectural beauty still remains. The long and solemn ranges of pillars and cloisters inside have at length become so perfectly green with damp, that they appear like some wonderful cave, over which the sea had broken for ages. Indeed the celebrated cave at Flamboroughhead is not very unlike it, and certainly neither more mouldy, nor more weather-stained.

We entered this hoary pile with feelings of profound reverence and admiration, preparing our minds for a solemn remembrance of the great men and the eloquent divines who once frequented those sacred walls, generation after generation, many of whom lie side by side in the last long sleep of death. The first tomb-stone which caught my attention was exceedingly handsome, exhibiting a coat-of-arms on one side, and bearing a long panegyrical inscription on the other. While gazing at this impressive memento with all that profound respect due to the illustrious dead, our guide gravely informed us that this tablet was raised in honour of the late dancing-master at Kirkwall!

Not far off, lie the venerated remains of our illustrious Scottish historian, Laing,[3] whose memory is deserving of the utmost reverence and admiration from all his countrymen; and a few steps distant we were shown a curious tomb placed under a low heavy stone arch, like an ancient fire-place, which was built in this peculiar form by special desire of the person underneath, because an enemy had once threatened to dance on his grave.

[...]

We approached Fair Isle, a bright green spot, like an emerald on the wide ocean. This place is quite a little world in itself, covered with grass of a most vivid and luxuriant verdure, but distant twenty-four miles from the nearest shore, being exactly half-way between Orkney and Shetland, – and there four hundred of our countrymen live and die without the instructions or consolations of any clergyman. The parish to which they belong lies on a far distant island, whence Mr Thomson, the incumbent, used to visit them once in a season, to perform all the marriages and christenings; but now, being eighty years of age, he is unable to encounter the fatigue of such a voyage; and it was mentioned, that the last time a clergyman arrived there, several of the children requiring to be christened were quite old and uninstructed, while one boy, when the service was performed on himself, swore most violently. The anxiety of these neglected people for ministerial teaching is so extreme, that they will laboriously row their boat any distance to bring a preacher, and only ask their expenses for taking him away, as it is considered ample remuneration for a voyage of fifty miles to hear a single sermon; and Mr Watson of North Yell told us, that once, when detained accidentally beyond Sunday, the whole population crowded round him to hear the gospel, and listened with fervent attention.

Many rich people disapprove loudly of foreign missions, confidently saying, 'let charity begin at home,' and for them here is a noble opportunity. Neighbours and brethren of our own, who have little to enjoy here, and no one to tell them of happiness hereafter, suffer the most urgent want, while a small subscription might supply the moderate wishes of some resident clergyman, who would be welcomed with eager and grateful delight, bringing them the knowledge which they seem all to be thirsting for.

The deputations sent by charitable societies travel sometimes now at a most preposterous expense. A lady assured me that once a barouche and four arrived at her house in the highlands, containing four gentlemen, who requested leave to see her pictures, and mentioned that they were a committee of clergymen collecting funds for some religious object. Next day her old poultry-woman found several tracts scattered along the approach, and this expedition cost several hundred pounds, besides taking more than one clergyman away from his own charge. This is a wide world, in which there certainly is a great deal of good to be done, but as none of us are like the tortoise, who could carry the whole world on his own shoulders, men who would really be useful must measure the utmost extent of their own individual ability, and do the very most which is possible, without attempting more, and too many parish clergymen would wander about like Wesley,[4] who during fifty years never travelled less then 4500 miles annually. It was no bad jest on a certain iterating rector of this kind, who frequently transferred his own work to a substitute, and preached in any parish rather than his own, that he should be nick-named 'England, because he expected every man to do his duty'.

These poor Shetlanders can afford no expensive deputations, but the half of what was paid for that one excursion which I have described, would place them permanently under the blessed influences of gospel light; therefore I beg to move a resolution, which you shall second, that our next foreign mission shall be established at Fair Isle.

[…]

This is the first year that a tolerable inn has been established at Lerwick, which is considered a most remarkable era, and the style is about equal to that on board a second-rate steam-boat, being conducted by a most respectable landlord from East Lothian. If any wealthy traveller, wishing to be remarkably comfortable, had brought his own carriage and horses to Lerwick, he could not have penetrated beyond the pier, and by no possible contrivance could his equipage have been available in driving up to the hotel, which is in so narrow a street that [a tall man] could have easily made a long arm to touch the opposite house. I remember once meeting an English lady going by steam to Staffa, who said it was her intention immediately on landing, to order a post-chaise, and drive all round the island, but neither there nor here would the plan be very feasible, as not a wheel is stirring in the noiseless streets. […] The streets of Lerwick are […] a curious assortment of courts, connected by lanes, and intersected by stairs, one of which divides the High Street quite across, and some of the streets are even arched over at the top.

The only road in Shetland goes six miles towards Scalloway Castle, and we were told that but one gentleman ever had a carriage here, when he used to drive his wife several times up and down the whole distance, to give her an idea what a journey means. […] Walking is, of course, a most necessary accomplishment in this country, where the shoes are made of materials so very substantial that an old gentleman used to say, he wore in the morning three rows of nails on the sole, but for full dress only two rows.

[…]

The introduction of a weekly steamboat to Shetland had begun a new era in this country, Formerly all communication with other places became so tedious and uncertain, that none could be safely depended on. A few years since, one of the principal merchants here, who possessed more than twenty ships of his own, became so anxious for letters, that he sailed off to enquire for them personally at Edinburgh. There the postmaster objected to deliver any, saying, it would be too great an advantage to give him over the other mercantile houses at Lerwick, if he obtained his correspondence so prematurely, and it was not until after the greatest difficulty and legally proving his identity he could obtain the packet.

The lower orders in Shetland seem rather beneath the middle size, especially when compared to the tall Dutch skippers, stalking about in loose tunics, high caps, and heavy wooden clogs, which seem a most uncomfortable article of dress, being excavated in a solid block of wood, as if the foot had supernaturally forced its way in. We used to read in the Richmond play bills, of a hornpipe to be danced on the stage in wooden shoes, but here it could neither be light nor fantastic, as these slippers, liable to be shuffled off at every step, seem made to impede walking. The Dutch sailors exchange shoes with the Shetlanders for stockings, so that their traffic is easily set on foot.

The sheep in these islands look like goats or greyhounds, having long legs and lank bodies, and their colour is of that peculiar brown and blue which the Shetland stockings usually exhibit. Some are speckled of various hues, and go by the name of Jacob's sheep, though not lineal descendants of that flock. All the ladies here employ their long evenings in knitting; and even the hard-working women, when carrying on their backs the enormous heavy 'creels' which are used here instead of carts, yet contrive to have a perpetual stocking on hand. I met one cleanly dressed chatty old gossip, the sort of looking personage who hobbles on the stage at the beginning of a farce, exclaiming, 'How my old bones do ache!' and she assured me with great exultation, that she manufactured a stocking per day; and that every article she wore was entirely of her own spinning. I liked to see her honest pride, and if the gown had been French cambric, she could scarcely have expected me to admire it more.

Before inns were invented at Lerwick, the proprietors and merchants kept open house for all strangers without exception, and must often, I should guess, have found occasion to look over the inventory of their plate, when exercising such boundless hospitality. A party of well-dressed, plausible looking foreigners arrived here once, and having previously ascertained the names and connections of all the chief inhabitants, they passed muster during several weeks, living at the principal house on the island. One Sunday, however, their hospitable host was privately beckoned aside by a friend, who had observed his companions in the pew at church, and recognised them as a party of well-known black-legs from Paris![5] He recommended their being ejected from the house, in the most expeditious manner possible, but their entertainer replied, with characteristic liberality, that, 'though he would now be on his guard against imposition, yet while his guests continued to behave like gentlemen, he would persevere in treating them as such.' Previous to departing, the ungrateful visitors attempted some swindling transactions, which were, of course, counteracted, owing to this timely detection, and they were opprobriously dismissed from Shetland; but, unfortunately, their schemes prospered better in Orkney, where they afterwards cheated some merchants to a large amount; and it was a curious termination of the whole affair, that upon leaving Kirkwall, they very handsomely transmitted to the parish clergyman £5 for the poor! This was an amusing sort of Robin Hood generosity, but some who deem it right to refuse money collected for charitable purposes, unless they approve of the means by which it had been raised, would be rather perplexed how to dispose of such a donation.

Among countless instances of peculiar hospitality, it may be mentioned, that a Mr Bruce received into his house some years ago, forty Russian shipwrecked sailors, maintained them during the whole winter, and sent them back to their native country. He declined receiving any recompense, but the Empress Catherine privately obtained an impression of the family seal, sent it overland to China, and ordered a magnificent dinner service of the finest porcelain to be manufactured for him without delay. By some unfortunate oversight the box containing this precious gift was seized at the custom-house, and sold to a Mr Reid, in whose possession it still remains, though I cannot but grudge him every dinner he eats of it. Mr Bruce, while he lived, lighted a large fire every winter night close to the shore, and had a barrel of meal ready to be cooked into porridge, for distribution among any number of poor sailors visiting those distant shores. They were also allowed clean straw to sleep on at night, when unable otherwise to procure a bed.

The gentry at Lerwick are still so extremely kind to strangers, that our landlord should lock up his guests, as the only chance of keeping any, or he may perhaps be provoked at last to act like the innkeeper at Luss, who, finding himself nearly ruined by the parish clergyman beguiling away all his visitors, at last one night carried his sign to the manse and nailed it over the door.

Catherine Sinclair leaves the islands rather reluctantly, partly because of the hospitality she has been shown, and partly because she fears the voyage back in bad weather. The passage from the Shetlands to Sinclair Bay, Wick, takes nineteen hours, but, Sinclair remarks, 'When did you ever hear of a voyage in which people were not within an inch of their lives?' The remainder of the volume comprises travel sketches of places visited on the way back south, including Castle Grant and Blair-Atholl. At the Highland games near Blair-Atholl a display of Highland dancing is affected by heavy rain:

The wives, sisters, and daughters of the performers were all anxiously looking on from beneath their cotton umbrellas with sensations of interest and excitement.

[...] At one moment, when the rain poured down with peculiar vehemence, a crowd of dripping-wet clansmen, to save their gay tartans, put up a multitude of umbrellas, and cowered so near our carriage for shelter, that we saw nothing of the dancing. My teasing dilemma being observed by one of the judges who happened to pass, he obligingly resolved to befriend me, and called out to the men in a tone of indignant astonishment, 'Put down these umbrellas!! Whoever heard before of a HIGHLANDER WITH AN UMBRELLA!!!'

Down dropped every umbrella on the spot, and the poor men looked like convicted criminals, quite humbled at the very idea of being considered effeminate, while I really sympathised in their mortification, aware that, to a Celt, no accusation could have been more unwelcome.

As a learned philosopher once judiciously observed, 'everything that has a limit must come to an end;' and now having introduced you to the scenery, machinery, and decorations of the Highlands, while the whole *dramatis personae* are collected on the stage in a state of perfect happiness, I must remember that, under such circumstances, it is customary to conclude, after which the manager makes his final speech, filled with humility on account of his own deficiencies, and of gratitude for favours received. According, therefore, to established prescription, I shall finish now, in the appropriate words of Shakespeare:

> Thus on your patience evermore attending,
> New joy wait on you! here our play has ending.[6]

Flourish of trumpets, drums, and bagpipes, – enter a procession of Highlanders. They form a group, and the curtain gradually drops, amidst thunders of applause.
[*Exeunt.*

NOTES

1. Alexander Robertson of Struan, *Poems on Various Subjects and Occasions* (Edinburgh: 1851)
2. Not all Sinclair's contemporaries were as complimentary about him: Scott has a series of contemptuous nicknames for him. In his journal he calls him the *Gran Giag'Asso* [...] an admirable Morion. I do not believe there is in nature such a full-acornd Boar'; and again 'Sir John Jackass' or 'Cavaliero Jackasso' (*The Journal of Sir Walter Scott*, ed. W. E. K. Anderson (Edinburgh: Canongate Classics, 1998), pp.10; 288; 291).
3. Malcolm Laing (1762-1818), Orkney born historian, educated at the University of Edinburgh. His *History of Scotland*, 1802, contained an attack on the authenticity of the Ossian poems: see Grant (p.79, n.1).
4. John Wesley (1703-91), founder of Methodism, although the Wesleyan Methodist Church was organised only after the death of John and his brother Charles (1707-88). John Wesley travelled the country on horseback, preaching thousands of sermons.
5. Gamblers and probably dishonest ones.
6. The last lines of *Pericles*.

Anne Chalmers,
Mrs William Hanna (1813–1891)

Anne Chalmers, *Letters and Journals of Anne Chalmers*, ed. by her daughter [Matilda Grace Blackie] (privately printed, London, 1912)

What follows are the 'Biographical Notes' by Anne Chalmers's daughter from the 'Letters and Journals' which I use to stand in for the usual introductory biography:

Anne Chalmers was born at Kilmenny on May 5th, 1813, and was the eldest of six daughters of the Rev. Dr Thomas Chalmers and his wife *née* Grace Pratt.[1]

Daughters were welcome in that household. On the birth of each, their father said, 'the better article' or 'Another of the best'. Each of the little girls had a fanciful name, given them according to the place of their birth. Anne's name was 'The Fifeshire Fairy' or 'The Fair Maid of the Eden'.[2] The next sister who arrived in Glasgow, was 'The Glasgow Girl' and so on. Fifeshire was Anne's home for a very short time. Dr Chalmers got a call to Glasgow,[3] and after some years of hard work there, changed his pulpit for the chair of Moral Philosophy in the University of St Andrews, where he remained for ten years. These six years between the ages of nine and fifteen were always looked back upon with pleasure by my mother. She loved the old historical interest of the place, and to the end of her life would say she enjoyed climbing on the rocks and ruins, and believed she still could do so were she there.

The lifelong friendship with Anne Parker (afterwards Lady Caldwell) began at a very early age, and my mother's letters to her girl friend were evidently valued by her, and preserved and all returned after her death. I feel sure that Lady Caldwell's surviving relatives (she left no descendants) will not object to our using them as we have done. These were the days of long and interesting letters, postage being so dear. The art of letter-writing was a characteristic of my mother's all her life. When in Edinburgh, Mr Gladstone used to frank her letters when he breakfasted in her father's house. At that time, though already an M.P., he was still a student at the Edinburgh University. Long years afterwards, near the end of her life, my mother wrote to Mr Gladstone, pointing out what she thought to be an error on his part, and received one of his usual postcards in reply.[4]

In 1828 the family left St Andrews and went to Edinburgh, where Dr Chalmers became Professor of Divinity in the University. These were very busy days for the eldest daughter, who then met many notable people and helped to entertain them. I think she used to be rather bored by the students when they came to breakfast or evening parties; she found some of them dull and loutish. All the same, she married one of them, William Hanna, son of the Rev. Dr Hanna, of Belfast. One supposes she found him different from the others she criticised! She married in 1836 at the age of twenty-two, and, for some years after, her life was spent in the country at East Kilbride, and then at the small, pretty village of Skirling. During these years, private and public events occurred. Several sons were born, for she did not carry on the family tradition of 'the better article'. Of these, only the eldest survived. The deaths of these babies deeply affected her, and helped her to enter into the feelings of other mothers when they too were grieving over a young life snatched away too soon. At the same time my mother was not a universal adorer of all infants. A cousin of hers once told me that when her mother had a young baby, and was showing it with pride to mine, after duly admiring the little person, my mother said, 'Now let us send away the baby and get the cat'. She wasn't very practical in her upbringing of children. I remember at a very young age enjoying macaroon cheese-cakes and sips of negus in bed.[5] She continued to have vague ideas about food for us. When my own eldest child was about a year old, and we were having crab pie for lunch, a message came from her to say, 'Be careful when you give the crab pie to baby; there may be bones in it.'

The Disruption took place while my father was minister at Skirling, and although both her father and her husband 'came out', my mother's heart was never in the Free Church, and many of her intimate friends remained in the old Church.[6] She often quoted her father, saying 'That he left with pain a vitiated Establishment, and would return with joy to a purified one'. My mother was a member of the Church of Scotland at her death, and for many years before. She was rather fond of ritual, and when abroad liked to visit Roman Catholic churches, where she took holy water and made the sign of the cross with it. I objected to this (it was our only subject of disagreement), and she used to say, 'Oh, you Low Church child!'

She was very fond of music, and played the piano with a clear touch and expression. I can remember her taking music lessons when she must have been fifty years of age.

Languages were among my mother's interests, and her house was much frequented by all kinds of foreigners, except Germans. She always disliked them, and was ardently on the side of the French in the Franco-Prussian war. I remember her annoyance with Thomas Carlyle, next whom she sat at a dinner party at that time. He said, 'The Germans are a moral and a religious people, and the French are immoral and irreligious'. My mother entirely disagreed, and subsequent events have, I think, proved her to have been in the right.

Her health was somewhat feeble – she had a severe bronchial cough – but her spirit never failed, and I fancy I can see her now, sitting up in bed surrounded by her letters and papers related to public as well as private affairs, and interested in all.

She dressed very badly, caring nothing for her personal appearance. One day a cousin met her in Princes Street, dressed in a green dress and a bonnet made entirely of crêpe. 'Anne, why are you dressed like that?' she asked. 'Because I am in mourning for Mr J –. He was only a cousin's husband and no relation, so as I had the bonnet I am just wearing it.' She carried out her ideas in the dressing of her only daughter. When I was a baby, she got me a bright orange-coloured pelisse, quite unlike other children, so that she might easily identify me in the street.

Youth is always ashamed of any eccentricity on the part of its relations, and I remember feeling rather uncomfortable when we were making calls, and my mother, feeling tired, sat down on the steps until the door was opened! She would not, however, have adopted the present-day fashion of easy familiarity and indiscriminate use of Christian names. To the end of her life she called my father 'Mr Hanna', and when he remonstrated with her for coldness of address, said she didn't know him well enough to call him by his Christian name!

A sad change took place when my father died in 1882; he was such a kind genial man. I never heard him say a cross word. My mother's sense of loss was extreme. For the rest of her life she remained with her sister Eliza, widow of the Rev. John Mackenzie, at 64 Great King Street, Edinburgh. These two old ladies passed their last years together. They were very congenial in temperament. They were both interested in what went on around them, though themselves confined to the house. My mother's mind was as clear at seventy-seven as at seventeen, when she passed away on the 27th March, 1891. On the day of her death she discussed many public events. She also repeated the Twenty-seventh Psalm, having just learned it by heart. Like many others, she dreaded death. 'I know even the tables and chairs here, but what will it be like there?' she used to say. When death came, she simply fell asleep. I have always felt that no one else ever had so interesting a mother as I had, and I believe that many of her descendants feel as I do: that her memory is always green, and that the 'Great Divide' has not entirely separated us from one another.

M.G.B.

Her daughter's biographical note is followed by a note by her grand-daughter, Mrs T. Bennet Clark, which explains the preservation of her letters to her friend Anne Parker from 1826-86. Anne Parker married Edward Cardwell, later Viscount Cardwell, and apparently became a rather stiff and correct old lady, but in her youth she was in love with Byron. Mrs Clark's picture of her grandmother is also worth presenting:

So long as I can remember, my grandmother never got up for breakfast. It was always something of an adventure for us to go as little children to her room in the mornings, where she slept with her windows tight shut, the shutters closed, and the curtains, not only of the windows but of the fourpost bed, drawn and pinned together. I have a distinct recollection of getting up on the sofa at the foot of the bed, unpinning the curtains and looking in on my grandmother in bed. She was wearing a white nightcap and a sealskin jacket, in which attire she had passed the night. (I believe she also had on an eiderdown petticoat, but that was not visible.) In this warm, if stuffy garb, she had her breakfast, read and wrote her letters, and received a stream of visitors, more often male than female. The grandparents of the present day, who play tennis and golf with their grandchildren, seem separated from mine by a great gulf.

My grandmother had a whimsical mind. The last, or nearly the last, time she was out of doors, she took me with her in a cab to visit 'the cemetery'. It was a cold raw day in November, just the sort of day when Edinburgh looks its worst. I believe I started under the impression that we were going to visit my grandfather's grave, and did not like to ask questions, so I was surprised when we went to another of the old city cemeteries, and still more surprised when I was told we were going to visit the grave of an old friend of her own, recently dead, and that her old friend had in his youth, twenty years or more previously, embezzled a large sum of money, and had fled from justice, living the remainder of his life as an outlaw. Indeed, I do not think he had ever returned to his old home until he was brought there dead. My grandmother said she had always felt sorry for him, and knew no one was likely to visit his tomb or to sorrow over his grave. This was explained while we walked down various pathways, and it was some time before we found what we were looking for, as there were only two letters, initials of his name, marked on the stone. I have never been back there, and I wonder if any one now knows or thinks about that nameless grave.

It seems a long way between the old lady I knew and the bright young girl of the letters and the journal, the one beginning and the other ending life. It was both long and short, for the experiences of life had set a deep gulf between the two ages, yet the same personality remains true to itself throughout. Anne Chalmers had all through the same power of attracting love and devotion. Few women can have had more; not only her friend, Anne Parker, but her sister Eliza and her daughter, all loved her with an absolute singleness of devotion that is very, very rare, and by all her descendants her name is held in honour and esteem. It is as a memorial of a great friendship as well as for their own sake that these letters and journals are now printed.

A.C.B.C.

Extracts from letters to Anne Parker (I have retained some of the more informal characteristics of the letters such as the use of ampersands):

14th May 1827 from St Andrews

I shall like very much to show you all the places about St Andrews and all the walks. I am in school from eleven until 12 and from 1/2 past 1 till 1/2 past three except on Mondays and Thursdays when I go at ten in the morning and leave at 1/2 past 1. Besides I have to practice 2 hours at home and to learn my lessons. We are obliged the first Monday of every month to go to school for fancy work. If you are here on that day I hope you will come with us and make something. I have a pincushion from the Edinburgh bazaar in the shape of a lyre, and one I got from a young lady in Cupar in the shape of a doll. I hope you got the novel finished in time. I am sure you will have much pleasure in seeing Edinburgh.

St Andrews Monday [1827]

I intend to write a little every day this week. I am going to school just now. I shall resume my letter when I come back.

Tuesday. I had not time to write any more yesterday for when I came from school Susan and Fanny[7] and I went to the Maiden rock from which Susan took a sketch of St Andrews. I should have said began to take, for a mist arising from the Tay spread over the city before she had completed it […] I am netting a red claret-coloured purse for Uncle. I must be very diligent. I am going on with Italian. There are some slight differences between the Grammars. Ours says that the article *lo* is used before words beginning with *s* followed by *any* other consonant as *lo studio*. I think yours says it is only words beginning with *sp*. Fanny has left us tonight!!!!!!! She has distinguished herself by numerous petty ill-natured acts. Nobody dares touch her that is not well acquainted with her. Several people were at dinner here last week & a lady, although Fanny growled and Eliza told her not to touch it, brought her hand into too close contact with Fanny's mouth. The consequence was her glove was torn through & her hand a little lacerated. Fanny is certainly cross but she is very fond of us & that makes us like her. She is to be boarded with an old servant of Grand Mamma's about a mile from us so that we can walk to see her often. If we want her in for two or three days we may go for her. I have been reading over tonight all the letters you have written since we left Fairlie. They revive many recollections of our Fairlie amusements & conversations. I hope you will write often for the pleasure of reading your letters is somewhat similar to that of reading *Corinne*.[8]

Wednesday afternoon. They have all gone out to dinner & we are left to amuse ourselves as we can. I have been playing Duncan Grey and John Anderson my joe. I believe they are favourites of yours & of mine also. I must now relate to you a little adventure Eliza & I had today. We could not support Fanny's absence so we walked to see her. There were two roads which branched off & all we knew of the person we were going to see was that she was boarded at a wright. So we enquired of a person we saw which of the roads it was & she told us the one to the right. So we went on until a girl directed us to cross a field. On coming to the house we heard a dog's bark & saw a black dog approach us whom we supposed to be Fanny. But a moment was sufficient to undeceive us! It was a large, ugly dog that came to frighten us away. I had some pieces of sugar that I had intended for Fanny which I determined to give it if it came too near but however it kept at a good distance. Upon enquiry we discovered we were quite at the wrong place & were shown a way across some stubble fields by which we could get to the right place. There were cows in the field & Eliza had on her tartan mantle but we kept at a distance from them. At last we arrived at the house & Fanny was so glad to see us. I don't think she will like a cottage so well as a large house. I think it was this day nine weeks that a number of people came to tea. I made a boot pincushion that night. [...]

Friday. Has not Eliza sent you some very elegant lines commencing with ''twas Judy Shee You'll all agree?' She has put them in my Album as an accompaniment to 'Paddy was an Irishman'. I finished my purse last night. I have only taken a week to it. It looks very well. [...] What a melancholy day tomorrow will be. It will resemble the sorrowful day of our parting at Fairlie. I hope you will come with Susan to St Andrews in Summer, then you may visit Kinkeld cave and perhaps we may be allowed to go back to Fairlie with you. I daresay when we meet next we shall have become very grave and dignified ladies and shall look with an air of great contempt upon such childish amusements as catching Crabs or sailing little boats. You know I shall then be 15. I like the idea of going to Edinburgh; we shall be so near each other & we can meet in a day's journey, but I fear we shall not have such long visits as formerly.

Friday night. I have been solacing myself with playing 'Isabel' [...] 'Cam ye by Athol' and 'The Castilian Maid'. We are all writing such numbers of letters. Eliza is writing several to you and I am writing. Grace & Margaret are writing to their cousins & I believe they are to write to you & Eliza & I are writing cards of acceptance for tomorrow night to a party at Mrs Cowan's. Somebody had been calling at the house Fanny lives in & been told that she had cried all day after we left her. Poor Fanny! I think we are to call on her tomorrow. [...] I must now end my long letter and leave room for Grace and Margaret. Farewell.

I remain, My dear Ann,

Yours affectly,

ANN CHALMERS

From 'The Journal of 1830':
This is largely a kind of tourist's journal from a visit to London during which Anne Chalmers visited the sights, human and monumental, attended debates in the House, particularly on the slavery question. Here the family visits the invalided Hannah More:[9]

We then proceeded to Clifton to the house of Mrs Hannah More, and were shown into her drawing-room. She was very ill and in bed, but her room communicated with the drawing-room by folding doors. Two maiden ladies who live with her and were quite like English elderly maiden ladies, came to us and said that Mrs More could not see us all at once, but wished Papa and Mamma to go to her. Afterwards I was taken in, when she received me with great kindness. She has a most pleasing countenance and a very kind manner. Afterwards the others were admitted, and Mrs Hannah begged Papa to pray, when we all knelt down and he offered up a short prayer, after which she thanked him, and we took leave of her.

From 'Autobiographical Notes', written in 1880 by Anne Chalmers (Mrs Hanna):
We left Glasgow when I was ten years old. I therefore do not remember seeing any persons of distinction before that, except that at a very early period of my life Sultan Katta Gheri, a Tartar, was in our house. I was sitting on a little stool hemming a handkerchief, which I told the Sultan was for Grandmamma. I thought he said 'Are you hemming a handkerchief for Grandmama *mösel?*[10] and though they said not afterwards, I always fancied he had.

The next person of note I saw was Miss Edgeworth. I was then ten years old, living at Blochairn, where I found a copy of her *Patronage* which I devoured eagerly. My father was invited to meet her at dinner at Mr Graham's. His own account of it to me was that she had been wearying much to meet Mr Clarkson of the Anti-Slavery;[11] that at last they were to be brought together that day at Mr Graham's; that he had requested leave to bring me, that I might see the authoress of so many nice stories. He then explained how the lions in the Tower of London gave rise to the soubriquet of Lions for famous persons. Therefore there would be a Lion and a Lioness. He added, 'Some people even go so far as to call your Papa a Lion.' I said, 'Oh, Papa, that would be great nonsense.' I went to this dinner, but felt very shy, never having been at anything like it before. I kept as close as I could to Papa, and so at dinner was placed between him and Miss Edgeworth. She, misunderstanding my feelings and wishing to sit next Papa, said, 'Now, my dear, we shall change places – in that way you will still be near to me, and I shall be nearer your father.' She was little and plain and elderly. After dinner she had to rest, and I still can see her little form reclining on a sofa in the drawing-room. She had two young sisters who looked pretty, and one of them sang, to my father's delight. I have the song in my desk copied to herself for Papa. It is 'The Lass of Livingston'. I was then rather precocious, and thought these young ladies wanted to play at very childish games with me, who had just read *Patronage*.[12] I must thus have seen Clarkson too, but the only impression that remains is that of Miss Edgeworth and her sisters, which I feel to be something gained after the lapse of half a century.
[...]
No one who was in Edinburgh when George IV visited it, can ever forget that scene.[13] I was eight years old, but I have never forgotten it. The enthusiasm of loyalty was so fresh and true that, young as I was, it thrilled my heart. It was met on the part of the King with a royal grace peculiarly his own. He wore tartan ribbons and had bunches of heather; there were medals too. Somewhere about the east of Princes Street my eyes rested for the only time on Sir W. Scott. He was walking somewhat

lame, between the two rows of soldiers on each side of the street. The band was playing 'Highland Laddie', which I had never heard. I though it a most beautiful tune. I saw George IV, but what a transitory pleasure it is to see a passing King! I knew he was there because of the intense excitement of Papa, who waved his hat and cheered with an enthusiasm no one could be near, without being carried along with it. And after half a century I feel it still, when I think of these days.

[…]

I accompanied [my father] on a visit to Broomhall, where we were received by Lord Elgin, who is known as the collector of the Elgin marbles.[14] We spent a very pleasant week there. I never heard my father converse on general subjects with so much ease as he did there, owing to the congeniality and intelligence of Lord and Lady Elgin. [...] We went into a coal pit with Lord Elgin one day. I was dressed in clothes belonging to one of the women, while Papa and Lord Elgin got men's things over their own. I remember the lurid light down below, and his lordship being drawn in a sort of bath chair through the caverns, conversing kindly and genially with the colliers, who seemed delighted to see him there.

On our return to Edinburgh we set off by the United Kingdom steamer for London, where Papa was to be examined by a Committee of the House on Pauperism. My father, mother, and I were in London six weeks, during which time we saw many interesting people, and were very kindly received by some. Among these were Mr Spencer Percival, son of the murdered Prime Minister[15] – a truly charming person. He often called at our lodging and used to speak of his misgivings about having more wealth than others, and enjoying luxuries that many were deprived of. I heard my father answer these scruples of his, as Political Economy would answer them.

With Wilberforce, whom Anne Chalmers and her father meet at an evening party, they pay a visit to Coleridge, 'then living with Dr Gillman at Highgate':
It appeared to me the most intense half hour I ever spent in my life, owing to the beauty of his tones and language, while he poured forth a monologue on Mr Irving, on the Book of Revelations, which he described as a poem perfect in its metaphors, with one exception.[16] That exception I am not sure of, but I think it was the mighty angel that had one foot on the sea, the other on the earth. The effect of his monologue was on me like that of listening to entrancing music. I burst into tears when it stopped and we found ourselves suddenly in the open air.

The first thing that threw cold water on my enthusiasm was what Miss Wilberforce said when we reached her father's house. She had no admiration for Coleridge – indeed, she had no poetry in her own nature and no toleration for the caprices of genius. She was disgusted with his treatment of his daughter, whom he hardly ever saw, because he said his feeling for her was too intense to permit him to indulge in so great a luxury without harm. One can easily see how ordinary minds do not see it in the same light. He called her his 'lovely daughter'. She does not seem to have felt his neglect, as her own memoirs show a great identity of feeling with her father.

[…]

We left St Andrews in 1828-9. While there, the likeness of a little girl with large black eyes appeared in shop windows playing on the harp. She was called the 'Infant

Lyra', and made a great sensation, being about four years old and playing out of her own head. So I never forgot her, and when I was grown up and visiting in a country house, spoke of her to the young lady of the house. She said, 'Did you like her playing?' I began to explain that I never heard her, being at St Andrews at the time. 'But you have heard her – she is in this house.' Then to my great excitement I found that her cousin, Izy Rudkin, now about seventeen, had been the 'Infant Lyra'. 'So you know about me,' the girl said, quite pleased to be able to talk about the past. She was the daughter of an Irish proprietor, and had an uncle a baronet, who went with her in part of her tour. She had wonderful success; they said the Princess Victoria had walked up and down the room with her, their arms round each others' waists. She got jewels showered on her and had large audiences. But all had melted away, the jewels sold, the money spent. She had still the large black eyes, the charm of the Southern Irish with their careless ways. She had not been instructed in the harp, so her playing was not then remarkable. She married first her cousin George Kingston, a clergy man in Ireland; after him, Mr George Rainy, whom she survived. She is possibly still alive, as I know her to be younger than myself a good deal. I last saw her in London – a stout matron, still untidy and extravagant in giving to Irish relations, but the same fine eyes.[17]

NOTES

1. Thomas Chalmers (1780-1847) was born in Anstruther and educated at the University of St Andrews. He was minister in both Kilmenny and Glasgow before becoming Professor of Moral Philosophy at St Andrews and subsequently Professor of Divinity at Glasgow. After the Disruption in the Church of Scotland (see below) Chalmers became the first Moderator of the General Assembly of the Free Church of Scotland. He was an internationally known philanthropist and worker for the poor, and knew many of the most famous men and women of his time. A memoir of his life was written, 1845-52, by William Hanna, Anne Chalmers's husband.

2. From the Fifeshire river Eden.

3. When a Presbyterian minister is appointed to a Church he is said to have been called by the congregation.

4. W(illiam) E(wart) Gladstone (1809-98), although initially a Tory, joined the Whigs (shortly to be called Liberals) in support of the repeal of the Corn Laws in 1846. He was Liberal prime minister from 1868-74; 1880-85; 1886; 1892-94. With his Conservative opponent Disraeli, Gladstone dominated British politics in the second half on the nineteenth century.

5. Negus is a drink of wine and hot water, sweetened with lemon juice and spices.

6. The Disruption was the name given to the secession of 451 ministers, from a total of 1203, from the Church of Scotland. These ministers, headed by Dr Thomas Chalmers, left their livings largely over the question of patronage and formed the Free Church.

7. The pet dog.

8. *Corinne*, 1807, the celebrated semi-autobiographical novel of Mme de Staël (1766-1817).

9. Hannah More (1745-1833) was educated at her sisters' boarding-school at Bristol where she learned Italian, Spanish and Latin. She went to London in 1774 and became a member of various intellectual circles, joining Elizabeth Montagu as one of the 'Blue Stocking' circle. Her didactic writing covered several genres, from plays to tracts, and she was a brilliant letter writer.

10. 'Evidently "Mademoiselle"': note by M.G.B.

11. Thomas Clarkson (1760-1846) British campaigner for the abolition of slavery. With William Wilberforce (1759-1833) and Granville Sharp (1735-1813) he founded an antislavery society in 1787 and wrote in the same year *A Summary View of the Slave Trade and of the Probable Consequences of its Abolition*. When abolition of the British slave trade was

achieved in 1807, a month after Wilberforce's death, Clarkson turned his attention to abolition by other states.

12. Maria Edgeworth, *Patronage*, 1814.

13. George IV visited Edinburgh in 1822, the first visit to Scotland by a ruling monarch since the 1630s; Sir Walter Scott had a good deal to do with the arrangements for the visit.

14. The Elgin marbles, sculptures and architectural fragments from Athenian buildings, chiefly the Parthenon, were collected by the Earl of Elgin (1766-1841) when he was envoy to the Porte (the Turkish Court) (1799-1803) and brought to England where they were sold to the British Government. They were placed in the British Museum in 1816.

15. Spencer Perceval (1762-1812) was Prime Minister from 1809 until his assassination in 1812. His son Dudley Montagu was a friend of Sir Walter Scott.

16. Edward Irving (1792-1834), the son of a tanner from Annan, was a minister of the Church of Scotland until his excommunication in 1833. Margaret Oliphant wrote his biography in 1862.

17. A later note explains that she died in London in 1888.

Felicia Mary Frances Skene (1821–1899)

Felicia Skene was the daughter of James Skene of Rubislaw, a close friend of Sir Walter Scott, and the sister of the historian, William Forbes Skene. She was born on 23 May 1821 at Aix-en-Provence and much of her early life was spent abroad, particularly in and around Athens between 1838 and 1845. Having returned to Britain she lived in Oxford, concerned herself with prison reform and was one of the first prison visitors appointed by the government. During the Crimean War she corresponded with Florence Nightingale. She wrote for *Blackwood's Magazine* about her travel experiences and about nursing and prison reform. As well as her travel sketches, *Wayfaring Sketches*, 1847, she wrote poetry and novels, of which *Hidden Depths*, 1866, is of interest because of its depictions of the poor and the criminal underworld of Victorian Britain. She died on 6 October 1899 in Oxford.

Felicia Skene's travel writing is probably not greatly to modern taste, being characterised by liberal use of exclamation marks and determined efforts at poetry and piety. Yet she offers experiences and anecdotes which are sufficiently different to deserve survival and she is generally tolerant and observant, even if (as is usual) a little too inclined to patronise the natives.

Felicia Skene, *The Isles of Greece* (London: 1843); *Wayfaring Sketches among the Greeks and Turks and on the Shores of the Danube* by a Seven Years' Resident in Greece (London: Chapman and Hall, 1847); *Use and Abuse: A Tale* (London: F & J Rivington, 1849); *The Tutor's Ward: A Novel* (London: Colburn, 1851); *St Alban's; or, The Prisoners of Hope* (London: 1853); *Hidden Depths* (Edinburgh: Edmonston & Douglas, 1866); *Awakened* (London: The Christian World Annual, 1874); *A Memoir of Alexander Bishop of Brechin* (London: J. Masters, 1876); *The Shadow of the Holy Week* (London: Masters & Co, 1883); *Dew Drops* (Oxford: A.R.Mowbray & Co., 1888)

Further reading
Sophie Raffalovich O'Brien, *Unseen Friends* (London: Longmans, Green and co., 1912)
Edith C. Rickards, *Felicia Skene of Oxford: A Memoir* (London: J. Murray, 1902)

DNB; Royle

Fom *Wayfaring Sketches*, 1847; **I have confined the extracts to the Introduction which gives a sense of Skene's life and, in its choice of anecdote, sentiments:**

In her Introduction Skene describes aspects of summer life in Greece when those who could afford to do so left Athens and moved into the mountain villages:
Those mountain refuges, how cool and fresh, and yet how sunny and how bright they are! Those little nests embosomed in the green luxuriant hills, with their gardens of myrtle and pomegranate, and their sombre olive groves, which the singing birds so

haunt! Where, through the unchanging glory of the long Grecian summer, we may dwell sheltered and at rest; half forgetting, as our eyes grow accustomed to the eternal cloudlessness of that sky, where the serene smile is fixed as on the face of the dead who have departed in peace, that there are climes less favoured, where tempests and mists disfigure the fair face of heaven, and dark clouds blot out the sunshine with tears, as though they wept for a fallen world!

[…]

All of human nature that surrounds us is the scanty population of the village peasantry, whose profound and unaffected ignorance and honest superstition are an unspeakable relief, after having been continually brought in contact with the spirit of small and pitiful intrigue, which poisons everything in the capital. […] The good peasants, too, remind us often that the seasons do not languish, for they never fail to bring us the first produce of their labours – the fresh almonds, and green figs, the cool water-melons, and finally the grapes. Of these there is soon such a profusion, that the very dogs, who in this country are singularly partial to the fruit of the vine, may go and riot in the vineyards till even they are satisfied.

Felica Skene has mulberry trees in her garden and village girls are employed to make silk; one of them, Katinko, has a sad destiny:

This young Greek girl, when she first came to us, was about fifteen years of age, and nowhere, certainly, either in Greece or in any other part of the world, have I seen anything to be compared to the perfect loveliness of her face. The high idea we are apt to form of Grecian beauty is liable to great disappointment on visiting the country. It is only among the very young girls that it is to be found at all, for their bloom is scarce less evanescent than that of a spring flower; and it is undoubtedly replaced by a greater degree of ugliness than usually falls to the lot of old women anywhere.

Even during our long residence there, I cannot recall more than one or two instances of that symmetrical perfection of feature, which is thought to belong especially to this country.

None, however, could stand a comparison with Katinko, the little silk-winder. She came, along with her mother, to be hired, and we soon perceived that there was something very peculiar in the manners and appearance of both. There were many traces of former magnificence in the dress of the old woman, who had a truly remarkable countenance. A white veil, of the most delicate silk gauze, was wrapped round her head, and half covered her dusky, sun-burnt face, which was lit up by the blackest and fiercest pair of eyes I ever beheld. These she was continually turning to and fro, with a startled, cunning look; and she used to sit watching her child, when she was at work, with the air of a tigress glaring on her prey. We soon learnt her history, which easily explained these singularities.

She had been one of the slaves of Muhktar, the son of Ali Pasha, Satrap of Jannina,[1] and had consequently passed the greater part of her life in that luxurious palace, overhanging the beautiful lake there, within whose stately walls more deeds of horror and bloodshed have been committed, than ever before perhaps defiled a human habitation. Her days were spent, of course, in the harem, with the other women; and she could tell us little of the incidents of the aged Pasha, of the grey-haired Ali's most sanguinary and eventful life. The women knew nothing of what occurred beyond the limit of their own apartments. It may be that they often heard the echoes of shrieks dying into ominous silence, or confused sounds which instinct told them was the voice of human suffering; and at dead of night, doubtless they could distinguish, through their gay dreams, the dull, heavy plash of some unresisting weight sinking into the lake, whose still waters rippled up against the wall beneath their very windows; but with the true Turkish philosophy, in which they were unconscious adepts, they gave little heed to such things, and occupied themselves in the hourly decoration of their persons, and in quarrelling with one another.

The little Katinko was but a few months old, when her wretched mother discovered, to her utter consternation, that a rival slave had accused her to Muhktar of having entered into a conspiracy to poison him.

However unjust the accusation, the unhappy woman knew that her doom was sealed! No one ever lived four-and-twenty hours under suspicion in the palace of Ali Pasha. The lake and the sack were at hand, and death ever ready to come at the tyrant's beck. She gave herself up for lost. But fortunately one of her brothers was engaged as a soldier in Muhktar's service. He heard of the circumstances just in time, and was determined to save her. Having conveyed to her his intentions, he managed to come directly under her window. It was raised to some height above the water; but one who leaves certain death behind, does not shrink from any peril in attempting to escape. She made a rope of the cashmere shawls which served to gird her waist, and having fastened it securely, she first lowered down her little infant in a basket, and then followed herself, and was received into her brother's arms in perfect safety. In another moment they were skimming the waters with great rapidity, aided by the fresh night breeze. A sleepy sentinel fired a few shots at them, but they succeeded in reaching the opposite shore without injury.

They instantly fled the country, and took refuge in Alexandria, thinking they never could be far enough from their powerful enemies. Since then, the death of Ali, and both his sons, had rendered their poor slave abundantly free; and she returned to Greece, in order to gain a livelihood in her own country, and ultimately to find a husband for her beautiful daughter.

Katinko was more like the most exquisite statue than a human being – the repose of her matchless features, and the marble paleness of her complexion, were quite unequalled. We soon found, however, that she shared in a deficiency common to all inanimate pieces of sculpture, and more general among living beings than we are disposed to admit. The mind, the intellect, that should have illuminated that perfect countenance, existed not, and she was a very child in capacity and in tastes. Still we took a great interest in her; and our distress was extreme when we discovered, after she had been with us two years, that she had consented to enter on a new line of life very different from that we could have desired for her.

Just at this time, some young men, returning from their colleges in Europe, full of enthusiasm for their country and its departed glory, determined to revive several of the ancient tragedies, and have them performed at the little theatre at Athens.

A *prima donna* was, of course, indispensably requisite, and some one had, most unfortunately, caught a glimpse of Katinko, wandering among the vine walks of our garden, when the evening breeze had lifted from her beautiful face the long folds of the floating veil, which completed her native costume.

She was not proof against the golden offers which were instantly made to induce her to go on the stage, and she left us almost secretly for Athens, where she was to be instructed in her new calling. It was in vain we remonstrated; nothing we could offer could compensate to her ambitious old mother for the delight of seeing her child figuring as a princess or queen, were it but for an hour.

Katinko shed many tears at parting; but nevertheless, she went; and it was the last we saw of her, with her simple, childlike manners, and her picturesque Albanian garments.

About a year after, I was accosted in the street by a young woman in the European dress, whose appearance was decidedly remarkable, from the outrageous violation of all good taste which characterized her attire. Not only was she loaded with feathers and ribbons, but her face was positively masked in paint, applied seemingly without any attempt at concealment! It was actually not until she turned towards me the exquisite profile, which nothing could change, that I recognised our once beautiful Katinko!

I believe we should have regretted her far less, had she shared the fate of one of her young companions, who, less singularly lovely, was almost equally celebrated for the extraordinary length and profusion of her beautiful hair.

This poor girl had been compelled one day to go out during the burning heat of noon upon some very urgent errand, for nothing but the most imperative necessity could induce any one to commit such an imprudence during the summer in Greece. Insanity or death may equally be the consequence, and, in this instance, four-and-twenty hours did not elapse before she was stretched on her bier!

I shall not easily forget the funeral of the fair young Greek, on that still and lovely summer evening, as she was borne away with the sound of music and the incense of perfumed flowers around her, to her grave, near the banks of the murmuring Illyssus.

NOTE

1. The rule of Ali Pasha (1741-1822) known as the Lion of Jannina, was based in the city of Jannina in Epirus or North Western Greece. He, and a number of other chieftains, took advantage of the Napoleonic Wars to live like kings. His rule was notorious for bribery, denunciation and murder. Ali and his sons were finally deposed by the Sultan, although it took 20,000 troops to do the job. His head and the heads of four of his sons were sent to Constantinople. Byron visited Jannina and wrote in *Childe Harold*: 'Since the days of our prophet the Crescent ne'er saw/A chief ever glorious like Ali Pashaw' (Canto II, ll.683-4).

Henrietta Keddie ['Sarah Tytler'] (1827–1914)

Henrietta Keddie, who also published as 'Sarah Tytler', a pen name which she explains in her memoirs, *Three Generations*, was given to her by an early publisher, Strahan, was born in Cupar, Fife, on 4 March 1827, where her father, Philip Keddie, was a notary. Her maternal grandfather was a tenant farmer. Henrietta was educated largely at home by her elder sister.

Later her father became a coalmaster at Grange, near Elie, Fifeshire. When her father fell on hard times financially, she and her sisters opened a school in Cupar in 1848, eventually, after some success, developing their original day school into a boarding establishment. In 1870, having already published several novels, she went to London with her sister, Margaret, and subsequently lived by her writing. A few years after the death of Margaret, in 1884, Henrietta Keddie moved to Oxford to be near friends and settled there for the next twenty years. She finally returned to London in 1904 shortly after receiving a civil list pension for services to literature. Of the six Keddie children who reached adulthood, five girls and a boy, all died unmarried, although the children of Keddie's aunt Margaret Gibb had 'numerous descendants scattered over the four quarters of the globe' (*Three Generations*).

Henrietta Keddie's novels are less well known now than the work she and her friend Jean Watson did for Scottish women's poetry in *Songstresses of Scotland*. And in truth with the exception perhaps of *St Mungo's City* and *Logie Town* her novels do not have a great deal to offer a modern reader. But the best qualities of the novels, wit, generosity and precise observation, are to be found in her autobiographical writing which deserves to be better known.

as **Sarah Tytler**, *Jane Austen and Her Works* (London: Cassell, 1880)
as **Henrietta Keddie**, *Phemie Millar*, 1854; *The Nut Brown Maids*, 1859; *My Heart is in the Highlands*, 1861; *Heroines in Obscurity*, 1871; *A Douce Lass*, 1877; *Kincaid's Widow*, 1895; *Three Generations: The Story of a Middle-Class Scottish Family* (London: John Murray, 1911); and others
as **Sarah Tytler**, *Citoyenne Jacqueline*,1865; *Songstresses of Scotland*, with J. C. Watson (London: Strahan, London, 1871); *St Mungo's City* (London: Chatto & Windus, 1884); *Logie Town* (London: Ward & Downey, 1887); *Miss Nanse*, 1899; and over 100 others

Further Reading:
HSWW

From *Three Generations: The Story of a Middle-class Scottish Family*, 1911:

'Three Generations' is dedicated to 'J. M. Barrie, who has touched homely things and made them divine. For this great service a heavy debt of gratitude is owing to him from

his generation'.

I have chosen to give most of the first chapter because of its fascinating detail on the way of life of Keddie's grandfather's time, followed by some of her observations on the education of women and a few of her encounters with some of the literary figures of her time.

In the peaceful lovable country kirkyard of Dairsie, in Fife, Scotland, stands an old headstone bearing the dates of 1682-1745, together with an inscription, more graphic than polite, that here lies 'the cauld corp of Dauvit Gib', who in his lifetime had been the tenant of the neighbouring farm of Blebo. He was my great-great-grandfather, and his wife, whose maiden name is not recorded, was my great-great-grandmother. She must have been the covenanting ancestress of whom a characteristic tradition survives. She was addicted to attending field conventicles, then forbidden by law, and liable to be dispersed by soldiers like Claverse's Dragoons.[1] Nevertheless, the good-wife of Blebo went to these meetings dauntlessly, and as she sat, one of the open-air congregation, consisting chiefly of hinds, shepherds and their families, gathered on the bleak hillside in the wintry weather, she was so absorbed by the words of the preacher that in the course of the service, which lasted long, the snell wind that caught her grey duffle coat froze it to the ground.

The son of that heroine and her husband, Dauvit Gibb, was Andrew Gibb of Balass, a man well-to-do in his circumstances, who married Marget Barclay of Dairsie Mill, a woman of some position and substance in her middle-class rank. Their son, Harry Gibb of Balass, in the room of his father, was my grandfather. I distinctly remember him as he was in my childhood.

The farm and farmhouse of Balass were in the near neighbourhood of Cupar, the county town of Fife, and the seat of the Law Courts, which lent it a certain intellectual dignity.

Scotch farmers of the past often held their tenancies for several generations. Within my own day, Sir Ralph Anstruther, the Laird of Balcaskie – by no means a parvenu – made the statement in connection with one of his tenants in a public assembly that he believed there had been Coopers in Stenton before there had been Anstruthers at Balcaskie.

[...]

During the Peninsular War, when high prices for grain prevailed, it so happened that, however severely the rest of the nation suffered, the stackyards of the farmers were not infrequently synonymous with moderate fortunes. There were counterbalancing influences which led to the reverse in my grandfather's case, but my great-grandfather's affairs were so flourishing that his much-prized only son was accustomed to keep company with the young Laird and the Laird's fellows on something like equal terms. These bucks attended, by way of relaxation, all the 'maidens', or harvest-homes, as well as all the markets, ploughing-matches, and horse-races, within their reach, in order to be the privileged partners of the bonniest lasses who had previously proved their skill and industry in reaping the corn.

My grandfather did not arouse the wrath of humbler swains, nor did he fall a victim to any one of the rustic heroines. His Laird was more susceptible. He was one of the parties in an irregular but perfectly legal Scotch marriage, which he did not find courage to confess to his mother, who presided over his primitive mansion-house, till he was seized with a dangerous illness, and was believed to be at the point of death.

The old lady, a well-connected woman of high spirit and a somewhat high hand, at once sent for the humbly-born wife, and, meeting the scared, distressed young creature on the doorstep, hastened to reassure her with the magnanimous declaration, 'I don't blame you, my dear; it was my son who was in fault.'

Nevertheless, till the day of her death the proud mother kept her place as the qualified mistress of her son's household, sitting at the head of his table, while the wife on sufferance submitted meekly to sit at the side.

My grandfather sometimes dined with his old friend the Laird and the two ladies, not without an uneasy sense of what he and everyone else knew, that there had been days, not so very far away, when he had stooped to the young lady sitting so demurely opposite to him and patronized her on a free-and-easy footing. He had lived long enough to understand why she had always refused to grant him the customary kiss at the end of the dance when the young Laird was by. She was not yet the mistress of the mansion in possession, but she would be in due season. She was no longer dressed in short petticoats, a buff or blue short gown, her head protected with a child's sunbonnet, or at a 'maiden' with her brown clustering curls intertwined with a real snood. She wore now trailing silks and laces, with glittering chains and brooches, every day. She had her hair every afternoon powdered and drawn up over a cushion. It was not so winsome as the soft-cropped curls had been, but no doubt it was far grander and more imposing, and she had learned pretty table manners, and was learning pretty behaviour of every kind.

Not for the world would Harry have put the young lady out, or drawn down on her a frown from the old madam, the real lady, by venturing on delicate ground or being guilty of dangerous allusions.

It was only when the frank, friendly Laird, sure of himself and his position, would not be deterred, by the presence of his mother, from a joking reference to past scenes that my grandfather would take heart of grace and respond, 'Aye, it was you, Mistress Alan, who was wondrous saucy to all your poor partners at the ploys. Aiblins [perhaps] I would not say that there might not be an exception in favour of a gentleman who, as he is in the present company, it is not needful to name him.'

My grandfather's bachelor days were soon ended. He was a bridegroom at nineteen to a bride of sixteen, and I have not found that there was any objection made either to the youthfulness of the pair or to the prematureness of the union. My grandmother, Helen Burn, was not a yeoman's daughter. (I am using the term 'yeoman' in the broad sense in which it was employed in my mother's day, when it was applied freely to the tenants no less than the owners of all the larger farms.) Neither was she a daughter of Fife. She came from one of the three Lothians; and different counties were then farther removed than different countries are today. She belonged to a family of architects to whom various public buildings in Scotland are owing. The young girl had arrived in Fife on a visit to an elder sister, the second wife of the master of the Grammar School in the county town. When one considers the comparative difficulty and rarity of such visits at the period, one may conclude this visit was probably meant to last for several months, perhaps years. But fate and the ardour of a handsome, well-endowed lad brought the story to speedy conclusion. The first encounter of the couple was when Helen Burn was returning from bathing in the clear water of the pleasant little River Eden, which flowed past both Eden Bank and Balass, and reflected the queen of the meadow, the marsh marigolds and kingcups, which grew on its banks. The girl's fresh youthful beauty did its work on the spot. It was a suitable and desirable marriage – on that the relations on both sides were agreed. My great-grandfather – the father of the bridegroom – was particularly pleased with the match. One result of his satisfaction was that he immediately bought the small farm and farmhouse of Eden Bank, and retired to it with his wife and daughter, Elizabeth, transferring the tenancy of Balass to his son. So strong was the impression of his family that he intended Eden Bank not only for his own residence, together with his wife and daughter, but that he regarded it as a future dower-house for his daughter-in-law should she survive her husband, that this belief was chronicled in the family, and remained an article of faith with the next generation. Eden Bank was well suited for the purpose he intended it to serve. There it stood, with its garden, its pasture for a cow and a pony, and its fields, so that if Harry Gibb died and the lease of Balass passed into other hands, his widow might have close at hand, ready prepared for her, a comfortable home and means of support to which she could retire. The only stipulation in the will, by which he devised the farm to his son Harry in the first place, was that there should always be a room in the house set aside for Harry's unmarried sister Elizabeth. Two quaint items added to this arrangement were that, as an exception to the rest of the furniture of the room, the eightday clock was to belong to Harry, and that the said Harry was to do a near kinsman's duty in regularly carting the coals necessary for Elizabeth's fire from the nearest coal-hill.

It seems odd, in the circumstances, to proceed with an account of the pair's elopement. But the readers of Fanny Burney's 'Diary'[2] may have noticed that the frequent elopements of the day did not uniformly signify revolt on the part of young blood against constituted authorities. It was sometimes merely a sign of reaction against the inordinate display and publicity with which marriages had come to be celebrated. It was positively more modest and decorous for the young people to steal away by themselves, and be quietly married in the nearest town or manse, than consent to play the principals' part in the noisy parade and jovial uproar with which more formal marriages were usually accomplished.

Scotch marriages were easily compassed. English marriages were not such simple affairs. But one may read in Fanny Burney how some fastidious gentlefolks managed to conduct them. There might be a slight, small family dinner, at which a clergyman was present. At the close of the feast the ladies of the family retired to the drawing-room and occupied themselves as usual with their needlework and tatting. When the gentlemen joined the ladies the clergyman – aware that one of the gentlemen carried a special licence and a wedding-ring in his pocket – responded to a slight signal by taking his place behind a small table furnished with the necessary Prayer-Book. At the same moment a self-conscious pair disengaged themselves from the surrounding company, advanced and stood side by side before the table, a second gentleman following and remaining a little behind, in order to represent the necessary authority who gave away the woman, when the knot was tied without more ado.

In my grandmother's case the proceedings were even more simple, and the couple still more left to themselves 'to gang their ain gate',[3] and that with the full consent of all concerned. One can imagine them stealing forth in the early summer morning, before the rest of the world was astir, to keep their last lovers' tryst, at which Harry's horse, provided with a pillion, was a dignified, significant figure. A tradition has survived to this day among the descendants of the eloping couple, who seem in the far distance so young and childlike, that their combined ages, together with that of the horse which bore them, did not amount to forty years. So they set out on their happy yet tranquil flight, undisturbed by fears of pursuit, accompanied by bitter reproaches and a humiliating capture.

I conclude, from other crumbs of evidence which have drifted down to me, that the innocent culprits after their privileged escapade and the fulfilment of their marriage, had the grace to take a further journey by repairing straightway to Helen Burn's home in the Lothians, in order that she might introduce her husband to her parents and relations. The two seem to have been cordially received, without a shade of blame, except in one small particular. The wedding-ring plays no part in the original simple Scotch marriage-service. However, convention demands the ring, and all Scotch married women wear wedding-rings, put on in private on the wedding-day, or shortly afterwards by the bride herself, by the bridegroom if the couple are shyly sentimental, or by some favoured friend.

Now, Harry, in his blundering eagerness, had forgotten to get a wedding-ring, and the bride arrived at her father's house without the sign on her hand that she had entered the honourable state of matrimony.

Mrs Burn, whose maiden name was Helen Hogg, was jealous for the proprieties. That a married daughter of hers should appear without a token of her promotion was not to to be thought of. The Christian names of mother and daughter were the same, and the initials of the matron corresponded to what had been those of the maiden. Mrs Burn slipped off her own wedding-ring, with its H. B., and put it on her daughter's finger. The mother's ring would not be missed, and could be easily replaced the next time she was in Haddington or Edinburgh. The young wife's hand should not remain another day without the distinctive mark. Thus it happened that Harry Gibb's wife's wedding-ring had first been her mother's, and that its initials were those of her girlhood, and not of her wifehood.

The bride of sixteen lived to be an elderly woman of over sixty, but I do not find any trace of her having once more crossed the Forth and traversed the once familiar roads. My mother stood midway in her father and mother's family, but she could never have been under her maternal grandmother's roof. With a single exception, she had little personal acquaintance with the uncles and aunts on the mother's side, though she knew their names and the principal events in their lives, as doubtless communications passed between the families on such important occasions as those of births, marriages, and deaths, while the members of either family were not otherwise given to letter-writing.

One of the most difficult things for us to realize is how familiar distances, which we are accustomed to regard as trifles, loomed large in the eyes of our middle-class grandfathers and grandmothers in the days when a voyage to India occupied half a year, and the coach journey between Edinburgh and London meant days and nights on the road. We must count what sounds as grievous waste of time, marked by unknown fatigues and dangers, in order to understand how limited was the environment of our predecessors, how circumscribed were the lives they led, how deep and unchecked their partialities and prejudices.

That early, unceremoniously enacted marriage was a notably happy one. The couple faced many troubles and sorrows together, with a cloud of adversity drawing nearer and nearer and gradually closing down on them. But where their mutual relations were concerned there, at least, was 'no defeat'. Whatever illusions my grandfather had to renounce, whatever disappointments he had to suffer, the image of his wise and gentle 'Nellie' as the flower of womankind was never eclipsed in his estimation. And to her he remained the beau-ideal of manliness and kindness. His generosity might be taken advantage of, his trust abused, but these were his neighbours' shortcomings, and in no way impaired his merits. After a faithful union of many years, death took her from him, but during the time he survived her the memory of her lasted with him, the sweetest thing he possessed. When he was an old man, crippled by rheumatism and paralyzed, a prisoner in his wheeled chair among grandchildren playing round him, the little girls who bore the Christian name of the wife of his youth were always recognized as having a special attraction for him.

The homely old farmhouse, situated in the centre of its barns and byres, and encompassed, not only by the dwellers in the stalls, but by the inhabitants of the bothy and the cot-houses, might not be an elegant nor, in the judgment of modern critics, an altogether sanitary habitation; but no one could deny its cheerful sociability. It was a little colony and kingdom in itself, well expressed in the old term 'Farm-town', which described its character.

In those days of frugal habits and simple living a farmhouse was a byword for a bountiful establishment, not only because of its sheltering rows of stacks, but on account of its general abundance, signified by its dairy and poultry yard, its pigs, sheep and oxen, with its 'mart' (ox) killed at Martinmas, its pork and mutton hams, its puddings, black and white, made all the year round. Tea was drunk in the farm-houses by the good-wife and good-man even when it cost fifteen shillings a pound.

The working class had little variety in their food, but it was sufficient, so far as farm-labourers were concerned; their diet was wholesome and enough for their support. At stated intervals their sacks of oatmeal and potatoes were weighed out and delivered to them, and morning and evening their measures of fresh, sweet milk were supplied. If a man chose to make 'brose' (that is, hot water poured into a portion of salted oatmeal in a wooden 'cap', or bowl, and taken with new milk) instead of betaking himself to the troublesome preparation of porridge, that was his own business. The wooden 'cap' and the horn spoon with which he had been started in his herding days might still constitute his sole table equipage, but he wanted no more. Without doubt his ruddy cheeks and stalwart arms were maintained in full force in what was apt to strike a stranger as meagre fare.

When the young ploughman grew older and took to himself a wife he was promoted to porridge instead of brose and 'kail', the little garden of his cottage furnishing the necessary 'greens'. By the time he attained the rank of a full-blown foreman he had his own pig and pigsty at the end of his garden; he might even, if a valuable servant, rise to the possession of a cow's grass in the pasture and a cow's stall in one of the byres. The foreman's cow and pig have before now been pointed out with a grim smile, by the farmer himself, as being the best-fed and best-cared-for stock on the farm. Such conditions represented a certain amount of plenty and prosperity in the widespread suffering and starvation of war-times. Take note, also, that in the period between herdboy and foreman, master and servant lived on too close a footing for the servant by any misadventure to suffer unaided. In old age, when the ploughman's strength was gone, he was frequently kept about the place as 'hagman', or cattlefeeder.

These old dying relics of a gone-by feudal system stood in the way of individual independence and enterprise, and the world's progress was to sweep them away; but while they lasted they served a purpose, and that not an unkindly one.

The old farmhouse abounded in homely comfort, though foreign – even native – luxuries were carefully limited or shunned. Self-indulgence or idleness were held at arm's-length. Wheaten or loaf-bread was not in common use in Scotland, where ovens for baking bread were not to be found in the houses of the middle class; but there was an abundance and an agreeable variety of 'bannocks' and 'scones' and oat-cakes, which took the place of, strictly speaking, 'bakers' bread'.

Candle-light, the only artificial light, was counted expensive, though the candles were sometimes made in the farmhouses from the mutton-fat of sheep killed for the use of the household. In these later days, one is struck by the Scotch economy, which gratified itself by not only providing the dinner-table with food, but also supplying the light for the hospitable from the same source. The women-servants were either limited to 'cruizies' (rude simple oil-lamps with the wick made of the plaited pith of rushes), or, in order to enable the women to spin the hanks of yarn, a certain quantity of which they were bound to produce by the terms of their engagement, the open kitchen grate was fed with blazing 'parret' coal, round which the spinners sat in a circle, with their wheels and reels, just as in summer they sat round the open kitchen door till the glory of sunset, and the gloaming, merged into 'black mirk'.

The carpets in the ordinary living-rooms were, as a rule, of drugget; the tables and chairs were of homegrown wood – pine or birch: oak was not plentiful in Scotland. If something superior was wanted, cherry-wood was chosen. The ornaments were chiefly trophies of sport – foxes' brushes, stuffed birds – owls, partridges, long-tailed pheasants – behind panes of glass in small wooden boxes fixed on the walls, sometimes on the side-table, and chimney-pieces, keeping in countenance foreign coral and shells, a silver cup or two, prizes gained at agricultural shows and curling matches, interspersed with the remembrances of beast and bird. On the walls were a few engravings of Biblical subjects. The farmer's womenkind were not yet so cultivated as to furnish pencil drawings to mingle with the prints, as in the case of the daughters of the Vicar of Wakefield; but if any youthful member of the family was sufficiently skilled in needlework she might be commemorated by a laboriously executed sampler, in which were recorded, in addition to the name of the sampler-worker, the names of her father and mother, brothers and sisters, in their proper order, so that it has happened a child's worked sampler has been received in a law court as a proof of some candidate or client's birth and descent.

The family Bible was in a place of honour, but other books were commonly conspicuous by their absence. I never heard that my grandfather and grandmother were given to reading, save the newspapers, which, to be sure, in those stirring times told many a thrilling tale of battle and siege in which our soldiers were engaged.

Over such a home, a human hive, a girl good-wife – a title still freely employed – came to preside at Balass, to be cherished and petted; and when the elder generation passed away from the neighbouring farm of Eden Bank, which occurred before long, to reign as a queen with unquestioned supremacy over her rustic kingdom. The men-folk, from the chubby herd-boy to the white-haired hagman, paid her whole-hearted honour. The women – 'cot-wives' and house-servants – were more critical; but it was only till they had satisfied themselves that she was a woman of sense far beyond her years, just and kind in all her dealings; then they awarded her loyal regard and faithful service. But her subjects were not confined to human beings; every animal in the stalls, every horse and its foal, every cow and cackling hen, were the joint property of herself and her husband, to be cared for by her, no less than by him. There was no excuse for her being idle, no lack of interest to fill her days, no temptation for her to sink into the disgraceful habits of those sorely left to themselves – good-wives spoken of by their neighbours with bated breath as gaping fine ladies, sitting with their feet on the fender, *nouvelles* in their hands, and pampered lap-dogs on their knees.

Neither was Mrs Gibb of Balass a stranger in a strange land. She might never again see the Lothians, the home of her childhood, her father and mother, or those of her near kindred who were not adventurous enough to cross the Firth and seek her out, the central figure in her Fife 'Farm-town'; while according to us, in our new ideas, they they were little further off than next door to her. But she had her own elder sister near at hand to consult when she wanted advice. She had her husband's two sisters, Marget and Helen, married to two brothers, Arthur and David Edie, whose farms of Nydie and Dron were at no great distance. Nearer still were her husband's father and mother, and their unmarried daughter Elizabeth, occupying the farmhouse of Eden Bank. She was in a circle of congenial friends and neighbours, among whom young Harry Gibb, frank and guileless, who kept an open heart and an open hand, as well as a hot head and a pretty stock of dogged prejudices, was a high favourite. There was one drawback to this idyllic experience, which Mistress Helen shared along with most of the women of her set a hundred years ago, in the convivial habits of the men with whom the women had to do. It was only at a very little earlier date that it could be recorded Duncan Forbes of Culloden, one of the best men and most perfect gentlemen of his generation, when he visited his Highland kin, was not in a condition to pull off his boots, or have them pulled off by a servant, for a fortnight on end. Take note, however, that such excesses in respectable members of the community were largely for exceptional occasions, such as markets, sales, visiting hospitable friends, celebrating victories of the British arms, housewarmings, marriages, 'dergies',[4] and the like. If the excesses were periodical they were on a smaller scale; they were anticipated, came to be regarded as a matter of course, and were judged and condoned accordingly. Harry Gibb's perennial outbreaks were on the afternoons and evenings of the weekly corn-markets in Cupar, when he and his fellows visited the town to compare and sell their grain and stock.

By an ill-fated custom, my grandfather dined regularly on those market-days with his cousin, an astute business man, the agent or manager for the County Bank. But this by no means diminished the conviviality which was the established rule on such occasions. It would have been an unheard-of, wellnigh an unsatisfactory thing for the hearty sociable yeoman to have returned sober from the market. His wife used to tell her daughters in after-years how in her early married days she used to sit late by an open window in her quilted petticoat, her feet drawn under her, a kerchief tied over her matron's cap for warmth, listening wistfully for the approaching beat of a horse's hoofs, unable to restrain a shiver at the consciousness that their father's safety depended more on the horse's sure-footedness than on the rider's clear sight and steady hand. Her relief came when she heard by a peculiar wooden 'thud' that the pair were in the act of crossing a bridge over a burn not far off, and that the worst of the road was passed.

With regard to the triumphant celebration of the good news from the seat of war, it was not always of a public character. That stalwart, friendly Harry Gibb, of more than a third generation back in Fife, was, as might have been expected, one of the most patriotic of men, in a style which became a leading citizen soldier in the county's troop of yeomanry cavalry. With his abounding bonhomie, he was under the necessity of calling together his swarm of retainers to rejoice with him at the receipt of the last glorious tidings in the local newspaper. Was not the humblest ploughman a Briton? Was not he entitled, with his wife and children, to hear the news of the conquering heroes abroad, to share in the country's exultation? Accordingly, the servants, indoor and out, were summoned to meet and listen to the reading aloud of the welcome announcement of the army's success.

Probably, in his zeal, Harry anticipated the unyoking of his horses and the leaving of his crops and flocks to their fate, and brought in their keepers to play their part in listening to the more important concerns of the nation.

The largest room in the house, and the most suitable for the gathering, was the stone-flagged kitchen, with its cross-beamed roof, from which hung suspended a goodly wealth of flitches of bacon, hams, smoked fish, nets of onions, bundles of dried herbs, etc. The whitewashed walls glittered and shone in the red glow from the open fireplace with pewter plates and mugs, a copper warming-pan, a brass preserving pan, brass candlesticks, the shelves laden with an ample array of blue-and-white stoneware. It may sound strange, but Harry himself was not the proud reader to the gaping audience. He had received a fairly good education in the neighbouring town, but he did not reckon himself a scholar. He could hold forth on ordinary topics, municipal and political, on market prices, and so forth, with the best; but in his partial estimation his elocution was not equal to that of his Nellie. He tackled with difficulty the strange names which abounded in these foreign despatches, but with his unbounded faith in Nellie's powers he had no doubt that she would grapple with the most 'fichly' (difficult) word in the language or the most outlandish term in the dictionary or geography book.

So Nellie was installed in the principal chair, not without reluctance, for she was a specially modest retiring young woman, considerably tried by the charges addressed to her by her husband, bidding her 'speak up' and let everybody hear. At the same time, she was spurred on to raise her soft voice to its utmost pitch, in order not to fail or disappoint Harry, whose love for and pride in her made him exacting where her gifts were in question.

Where the war news contained any reference to the gallant deeds of a well-known Scotch officer like Sir Thomas Graham [...] the interest and excitement were redoubled.⁵ Then Harry would call on his mistress to halt for a minute while he proclaimed enthusiastically that the company should drink the hero's health and that of the Commander-in-Chief.

If the season was not in or close upon harvest-time, and the great barrel of harvest beer could not be resorted to, there would be a serious attack on the 'greybeard' (the big brown jug), containing the whisky in ordinary use for the master's tumbler of toddy and the supply of drams regarded as the perquisite of messengers travelling a distance of miles with communication from friends. If the messengers were men, the refreshment of a glass of whisky was considered their due; if the messengers were women, in plaid shawls worn all the year round, and, in lieu of bonnets, broad-bordered mutches, or the quainter, more becoming high sow-back caps, with their broad black ribbon bands, the refreshment was modified, as it was to the women on the present occasion. They had a glass of the mistress's sweet cowslip or elder-flower wine, or of her cinnamon waters.

By the time the couple who resided at Balass had reached the age of full manhood and womanhood, but while their children were still young, a bombshell fell on the quiet, peaceful farmhouse. It came from across the seas by one of those curious links which bind the great and renowned ones of the earth to their simple and obscure brethren. It was by an action of the arch adventurer and conspirator, the all-conquering Corsican soldier Buonaparte, that the safety of Balass was threatened. The French Emperor's troops were encamped ready to sail from the French seaport, and neither friends nor foes questioned that the next colossal move of the man who had laid the pride of Continental Europe in the dust would be to invade Great Britain. Britain thrilled, but did not quake at the prospect; rather she regarded with stern congratulation the opportunity of coming at last to close grips with a foeman worthy of her steel. For twenty years or so he had been ruining her trade, and reducing many a household, including thousands of her population, to starving misery. Her brave sons had shed their blood like water, holding in check the encroachments of the enemy, while Britain struggled with his great marshals and captains; now she was to come face to face with the mighty Corsican in a tug of war in which one of the two must perish. English, Scotch, and Irish were to fight under the most sacred obligation of all, when men should stand up to do battle to their last breath for their country and their hearths, for 'the ashes of their fathers and the temples of their Gods'.⁶

Harry Gibb's troop of yeomanry cavalry was called out to lie in camp on Kelly law, a low green hill on the coast of Fife, as a lively expectation was entertained that Buonaparte would seek to enter the adjoining Firth of Forth and land on its shores.

Dearly as my grandfather loved his wife, his children, and his home, his warlike ardour sustained him. But alas, for his poor Nellie and for his chicks!

It afforded a desirable diversion, as the dread moment of parting drew near, when a neighbour yeoman, who was likewise bound to the supposed seat of war, arrived at Balass with the ostensible purpose of bearing its master company to the rendezvous of the troop.

To the sympathizing neighbour the wife and mother appealed. In the middle of her awful apprehension that her warrior was departing never to return, she was troubled and fretted by a minor fear. It might be a blessing in disguise to save her stricken heart from breaking. There would be time enough in which to grieve and tremble when the travellers were gone. In the meantime there must be something to think of and do for her dear man. Harry's credit and comfort must occupy her to the last. Harry had never been able to tie his neckcloth properly, never since she had known him. He had always been forced to come to her for assistance. She did not know what he had done in the inconceivably far-off days before they two were acquainted, before his wardrobe came under her care – whether he relied on the assistance of his mother and sisters, or appeared in public in a state of dishevelment. Anyhow, times were changed; she was responsible for him now. If the worst came to pass, and he was called upon to meet the King of Terrors, she could not endure to foresee her 'braw lad' in the last grim moment a spectacle to men and angels, with his dress in slovenly disorder. Would his friend and hers come to their aid, and see that Harry's neckcloth was rightly tied?

My grandmother was of the mind of the consumptive English girl who, when her end came, called to her circle of relatives: 'Bring me a clean nightcap, for I am going to die.'

Everybody knows that the expected invasion did not come to pass. Even Buonaparte withdrew the challenge he had himself thrown down. Harry Gibb, like many another citizen soldier, returned safe and sound to his home at Balass, to be received with a jubilant welcome.

The life of Keddie's grandparents did not continue to be prosperous and happy, financial loss and loss of life dimmed the happiness of their later days. Keddie's parents too had their share of emotional and financial problems. Keddie celebrates her father's love of adventure and his 'admiration of learning and love of culture in women'. Her mother was interested in current literature and contemporary topics like the stories of Lord and Lady Byron, Princess Charlotte and the Empress Josephine. Six of the Keddies' children, five girls and a boy – Margaret, Mary, Helen, Robert, Jessie and Henrietta – survived infancy. With this family to provide for Keddie's father ventured into coal mining with little success. Partly as a result of the failing family finances the girls decided to open a school:

My elder sisters had already been governesses for several years. Eventually, we young women combined forces, and began a school for girls in the little town of our birth [Cupar] which we knew so well. [...] The system of modern education for women is still on its trial, still very much of a novelty. It will grow mellow with time. The hard, aggressive edges will be rubbed off. As it is, one can see its capacity for the development of sundry excellent qualities in which critics have pronounced women deficient – to wit, sterling truthfulness, justice, enterprise, and independence.

As a last word for the schools of a former generation, it is well to remember that Hannah More and her clever bright sisters had a notable school for girls in Bristol, and that later Mary Carpenter, with her mother and sister, had, in the same favoured locality, another girls' school far before its time in the nature of the studies it offered and the attainments it achieved.[7] With regard to the deterrent or destructive influence of the atmosphere on the peculiar gifts of the pupils, Jane Austen, whose genius was that of the highest common sense, finished her education in one of those ladies' schools, which have been satirized as hot-beds of pretence and folly. Mary Russell Mitford, whose love of the English country life was so genuine and thorough, spent years of the most impressionable period of her life as a pupil-boarder in a fashionable London ladies' school. In neither instance was the ruling passion, the dominant faculty, crushed. It was rather stimulated and matured by what was reasonable and natural in the change of air and scene in its environment.

So we were to be school ma'ams, beginning in 1848, that year of national and political convulsions, when more than one throne suffered overthrow.[8] We were not so badly qualified as hasty readers may imagine, while the requisitions of 1848 differed considerably from those of 1911. We were almost all studiously inclined. More than one of my sisters had some experience in teaching, all of us had been taught music from childhood, and those of us who were musically endowed had received special lessons in that direction. The degree of importance which the study of music (generally in the form of piano-playing) held then in the education of middle-class girls was so great as to be positively ludicrous. Not only was the fee for music lessons much the highest – because each girl had to be taken separately, and a considerable portion of the time given to her alone – the scrupulous attention which was paid to music until nothing was allowed to interfere with a girl's hour's or two hours' practice was in broad contrast to the careless negligence which was suffered to attend on her other studies.

The well-taught proficiency of members of all classes in part-singing in musical Germany was a different attainment, with a different origin and end, from the English mode of exhibiting love of music.

There would have been some warrant for the marked preference if it had been confined to musically endowed children. But no; whether tuneful or the reverse, whether the child loved or hated the study, she was sentenced to the long grind, often wasting many hours which might have been more profitably spent in other departments of higher value in the work of life. This was a crying grievance to me, who was not musical, though I had been perforce taught music; I resented the slight to other branches of education in the extravagant favour shown to one branch. The only argument for the injustice which seemed to me to hold water was that which compared the effect on the small girls of being forced to learn the technique of music to a similar effect produced on the small boys who were obliged to master the Latin grammar, which was the great burden of their lives. It might lead to one or two of them becoming learned scholars. Who could tell? Anyhow, it was excellent discipline, bracing to their mental powers in teaching them application, and forcing them betimes to take pains. Even so, application to music in the abstract, with its signs and calculations, its bars and crochets, quavers and semi-quavers, could not be accomplished without beneficial toil and trouble on the part of the small girls in their brave attempt to comprehend what was otherwise incomprehensible by reducing to memory hard words and strange definitions, though the process was apt to be watered by oceans of tears.

The demand for the higher education of women, with the foundation of women's colleges, has done much to remedy the lack of balance in their former studies.

Keddie explains that she read well in French and German which she had been taught by a Hungarian officer in exile after the Hungarian Revolution, although she did not speak either with any fluency. Her brother, who had some talent for drawing and proficiency in geography, supported the efforts of his sisters.

We were four in number teaching in the school, and our ages ranged from twenty-two to thirty-one.

In the early days of the school my father and mother could drive over to see us. We had the great pleasure of welcoming them to our very own house, and they had the relief and joy of seeing that we could maintain a comfortable home for ourselves. I mention something which may encourage those similarly situated, for a school means much drudgery, not a little wearing responsibility, and the relinquishment in a large measure of the happy equal companionships and light-hearted joys dear to young hearts. But the result of the school was worth it, for my father told my mother after bidding us good-bye the first time they visited us that it was the happiest day of his life, since he had seen that their daughters could provide for themselves, and so were safe in the unknown future.

We were in our native town, among our own and our father's and mother's friends. Our pupils, taking them as a whole, were innocent young girls, with good principles, well trained, and well guarded from evil. Individual girls were occasionally rebellious, but no difficulty in managing classes was found. The members were as a rule, of fair average intelligence.

[…]

We started school-keeping in an unpretentious little flat above a druggist's shop, taking only day-pupils. Then we had two better flats in adjoining houses, with a door broken open between the flats to enable my sister Mary, already very much of an invalid, to escape the fatigue of the stairs, and the necessity of facing the open air of the street. When our position was fairly established, and we began to have boarders, we settled in an old house which had been the town-house of Lord Balmerino. He was, with Lord Kilmarnock and Lord Lovat, among the last sufferers who were beheaded on Tower Hill in the Jacobite Rebellion of '45. It was he who, on driving back after he had received his sentence, begged that the coach might be stopped in order that he might buy a pennyworth of 'honey-blobs'[sweets], perhaps in remembrance of his gooseberries in the garden of his great house by the Tay, or in that Cupar house-garden we knew so well. His was an interesting house, in spite of a large modern addition. Among its relics of the past was one fine corridor and a dainty little drawing-room with panels painted white. There was a large pleasant garden extending to the small River Eden, and opening on the 'Water Ends', an ancient promenade of the townspeople, bounded on one side by the 'Cart Haugh', the town's spacious washing-green, with its one venerable tree of local renown.

As is often the case in women writers' memoirs Keddie spends more time discussing other people than her own work but she tells an amusing story about her second novel:

Though the [first] novel was well enough reviewed for the firm to take a second from the same source, both fell flat. Certainly they were not calculated to set the Thames on fire, and I received no remuneration. That was conditional on a certain sale, which was not attained. I remember with regard to the second novel that after I had said all I wanted to say and disposed of the manuscript, I got a sudden alarming request to supply another chapter, as the material was not sufficient to fill the regulation three volumes. I saved the situation by the simple device of inflicting some of the principal characters with a sharp, but not fatal, attack of fever. I recollect also that the publication was a little delayed in order that there might be space found for notices of the book in the newspapers, which were crammed for the moment with the accounts of the funeral of the Duke of Wellington.[9]

The final section of Keddie's memoirs is called 'Men and Women Met by the Way' and it is from this section that the final extracts are taken. I have chosen passages which deal with women met elsewhere in this volume. Keddie reports that Isabella Bird was 'one of the three ladies, the two others being Miss Gordon Cumming and Miss Marianne North, who elected to class themselves as the three women "globe-trotters" who at least once met together and compared notes'. Isabella Bird was known to two of Henrietta Keddie's friends and they took her to be introduced on 'one of the comparatively few occasions when she was to be found in her Scotch home':

She was a slight, fragile-looking woman, having suffered in her youth from an internal disease, and been subjected to a serious and then rarely performed operation.

She bore a resemblance to the pictures of Elizabeth Barrett Browning in the very prominent mouth, which in both women approached to a physical defect. When I saw Miss Bird she was lying on a sofa, her frequent attitude when at home, free from ceremony. It was difficult to imagine how, under the inspiration of travel and novelty, she could ride whole days, man's fashion, and undertake solitary expeditions in the wilds, depending for refreshment on the way on the raisins in her saddle-bag and the springs by the road, while she sighted grizzly bears with philosophic coolness, or lived for days and nights with a party of – what shall I call them? bravos, bandits, half-breeds, to whom the most worthless cowboy would have been a model of virtue and civilisation, keeping house for them, washing their clothes, etc., and in the end treated by them with the utmost respect, according to the cue given them by their leader, the greatest bully and most dreaded bandit among them.

Keddie writes at length on Mrs Oliphant and her work: 'she wrote many books, not all of equal merit, though most of them attained a high standard of excellence; while her public, misled by the number of her stories, lost its head in an "embarras de richesses", and failed to recognize their "rare value"':

[Mrs Oliphant's Scotch] was the cultured Scotch which had belonged in its day to Courts and colleges. It had been spoken by gentlemen and gentlewomen in the past, while it was full of pith, humour, and pathos.

It was Burns's Scotch, and was as free from the illiteracy as from the radical coarseness and vulgarity which is to be found in the degenerate and debased Scotch, uniformly given by those practically unacquainted with the language in its purity. This is the Scotch unfortunately too often heard and read, misquoted, mispronounced, and misspelt by our neighbours across the border, who imagine they are using, when they are simply abusing, a fine old language.

[...]

I was introduced to her in St Andrews, while her sons were still alive, by one of her friends, a member of the Tulloch family.[10] Probably she came first to the little University town by the sea in connection with the occupation by her publishers, the Blackwoods, of the country house of Strathtyrum, in the near neighbourhood. But she grew in the end a familiar figure among the quaint old houses, on the links and the sands, because of her close intimacy – possibly the closest and dearest she ever formed beyond her own family – with the Principal of the University, his wife, and their large household.

[...]

In person and on slight acquaintance Mrs Oliphant was neither striking nor very attractive. She was not tall, and she had a tendency to the stoutness which she was apt to describe in her mature women characters under the style of 'matronly bountifulness'. Her complexion was good, she had brown eyes, but the face must have been rather marred in its bloom by the slightly projecting teeth. She was reserved and reticent to a degree, rather repellent from her abstraction and apparent indifference to the company in which she found herself. People might view her as a woman to be respected, but not one to be readily liked and trusted. It was as if her energies were all monopolised by the work which was so much with her that she had no interest to spare for her surroundings unless in so far as they were connected with that work. And what she did not feel she did not assume. Yet her work was absolutely unobtrusive, and at one time done late at night, in hours carried into the early morning, that her days might be free from it. I should suppose the plan was in force on the few occasions when she went with any regularity into society. [...] Still, it is a pleasure to me that she invited me to her house at Windsor. It was not in my power to accept that invitation, but I like to remember that merely in the light of conventionality she would not have troubled to give the invitation.

[...]

Margaret Oliphant was a gifted woman, courageous and devoted, and it will not be to the credit of English literature and English readers if her sound and varied work is slighted and forgotten.

Keddie knew or at least encountered most of the celebrated literary figures of the age – Isa Craig, Mrs Ward, Jean Ingelow and many more – she speaks, however with particular affection of Mrs Craik who had all the openness that Mrs Oliphant lacked:[11]

In looks Mrs Craik was very fair, with light eyebrows and eyelashes, otherwise her kind face was handsome and attractive on a rather large scale, for she was a big woman, while her tall figure set off her size. She showed something of the 'willowy grace' attributed to one of her heroines. In her later years she acquired more of Mrs Oliphant's dignified 'matronly bountifulness', which decidedly became her, and caused her to look her best.

I knew her well, and liked her much. Our intercourse stretched over more than a dozen years. [...] Mrs Craik had no children of her own – she adopted a baby girl left in the snow on a road in the neighbourhood. To her she was a devoted mother – no mother and child could have been more warmly attached to each other. It was a peculiar token to me how significantly and characteristically one of Mrs Craik's motherly instincts for her daughter could express itself. She was fond of making the child's frocks, capes, and bonnets, with her own hands, even more than of fabricating her own dress, for which she had a similar taste. She was essentially a domestic woman, desiring to entertain and fulfil domestic duties and occupations – not for economy, never for mere entertainment, but loving to take them upon herself as belonging to the woman's kingdom. It was in perfect sincerity that she had carved on her dining-room chimney-piece the homely proverb:

Seek east, seek west,
Hame's best.

NOTES

1. John Graham of Claverhouse, 1st Viscount Dundee (1648-89), Royalist soldier, served in the French and Dutch armies and when he returned to Scotland in 1677 was charged by the Privy Council of Scotland with putting down the militant Covenanters in south-west Scotland. From then until 1685 he was generally employed in the suppression of conventicles, or open air religious meetings. He came to be called 'Bloody Clavers' but is now generally felt not to have been the sadistic killer that this implies. He suffered the fate of many others in this politically up-and-down time: he supported James II against the Glorious Revolution and was killed in the Battle of Killiekrankie on 27 July 1689.

2. The *Early Diary (1768-78)* of the novelist Fanny Burney was not published until 1889; her later *Diary and Letters (1778-1840)* had, however, been published in 1842-6.

3. 'To go their own way.'

4. Dergies or more often 'dirgies' were funeral feasts usually involving drink either at a wake or after the burial. Under her pseudonym, 'Sarah Tytler', Henrietta Keddie writes in *Mrs Carmichael's Goddesses*, 1898: 'The heads of the dead were still propped on big Family Bibles and there was still a lamentable amount of solemn hard-drinking at their "dergies".'

5. Thomas Graham, Baron Lynedoch (1748-1843), general, was aide-de-camp to Sir John Moore in Corunna, and fought at Cuidad Rodrigo and Badajos. He was knighted in 1814.

6. Macaulay's *Lays of Ancient Rome*, 1842, Horatius speaks before he 'keeps the bridge' against the forces of Lars Porsena:
   And how can man die better
      Than facing fearful odds,
   For the ashes of his fathers,
      And the temples of his Gods? (*Horatius*, i, xxvii)

7. For Hannah More (1745-1833) see Chalmers (p.200, n.9). Hannah More acquired Italian, Spanish and Latin at her sister's boarding school in Bristol in 1757. Mary Carpenter (1807-77) was the daughter of the celebrated Unitarian divine and educationist, Dr Lant Carpenter (see *DNB*), in whose school in Bristol she taught when she was only fifteen. With her mother she started a school for girls in Bristol in 1829. In 1846, however, she made educational history by opening the first of the so-called 'ragged' schools in one of the worst parts of Bristol. Her work with, and advocacy for, poor and delinquent children helped to shape the Industrial Schools Act of 1857. She wrote widely on educational and criminal reform, and travelled and lectured on these subjects as well as the female suffrage, in India, Germany, the United States and Canada.

8. The first revolution of 1848 broke out in France where the 'July monarchy' of Louis Philippe was overthrown; subsequent feuds between left and right factions led to the election of Louis Napoleon, the nephew of the Emperor, as president. Louis Napoleon later became Emperor as Napoleon III. In Italy the revolutionary movements had constitutional aims which had some success in Piedmont but the movement also worked to remove the Austrian presence in Italy. In Austria riots in Vienna forced the resignation of Metternich who had dominated post-1815 reaction; trouble in Budapest and Prague was suppressed but in Prussia Frederick William IV was forced to convene a constituent assembly. Although the revolutions were quelled in one way or another, 1848 is generally felt to be the date at which the old Europe ended.

9. Arthur Wellesley, 1st Duke of Wellington, died in 1852. He was buried on 18 November in St Paul's with unexampled magnificence: his funeral procession was watched, it was estimated, by crowds of one and a half million.

10. Dr Tulloch (1823-86) was Principal of St Mary's College, St Andrews, and Professor of Theology.

11. Isa Craig Knox (1831-1903), poet, won the prize for a Burns centenary poem at Crystal Palace. Mrs Ward (11851-1920) was the granddaughter of Thomas Arnold of Rugby. Her most famous novel was *Robert Elsmere*, 1888. Her most significant contribution to thought was her insistence that Christianity should emphasise its social over its evangelical mission. The poet Jean Ingelow (1820-97) was best known for her three series of *Poems*, 1871, 1876 and 1885. She also wrote stories for children. Dinah Mullock Craik (1826-87) was best known for her novel *John Halifax, Gentleman*, 1857, which seeks to define the true nature of gentility as moral rather than inherited.

Margaret Oliphant (1828–1897)

Margaret Oliphant is probably the best known writer to appear in this volume: she wrote more than one hundred best-selling novels, including the well-known series of Carlingford Chronicles. Her *Autobiography* is also now fairly well-known and the recent full edition by Elizabeth Jay opens up the harrowing and courageous experience of her private life in which, after the early death of her husband, she wore a hole in her finger writing to support her children and the extended family for whom she inherited responsibility because of her brother's alcoholism. All her children predeceased her: her *Autobiography* famously and tragically ends, 'And now here I am all alone. I cannot write any more'. She was a personal friend of the publisher, Blackwood, who supported her through some of her worst patches; she also wrote a history of Blackwood's publishing house. Her journalistic activities were so extensive that it was said jokingly that she wrote whole issues of *Blackwood's Magazine* single-handed. Margaret Oliphant's literary reviews are always lively, often trenchant and influential (Annie S. Swan never forgot Oliphant's strictures on her first major novel, *Aldersyde*). In her political writing Mrs Oliphant was on the face of it High Tory in keeping with the political position of *Blackwood's Magazine* but both Merryn Williams (see below) and Ralph Jessop (*HSWW*) suggest that this is too simple a characterisation of her stance. Certainly on the woman question she is often inconsistent in both theory and practice. It is not possible to show the whole range of her responses to the franchise, work and so on and so I have perhaps a little unfairly chosen to give her in her most reactionary mode, arguing against alteration in the custody provisions in separation and divorce. I do this partly to show how much in this kind of issue opinion is conditioned by personal experience. Margaret Oliphant brought up her family single-handed but clearly cannot imagine a situation in which anyone would have tried to prevent her doing so. Caroline Norton, on the other hand, was deprived of her children, and so pamphleteered, and even petitioned Queen Victoria for an alteration in the marriage laws.[1]

Margaret Oliphant, however, was pre-eminently a novelist and there she may be found to be a trenchant critic of steroypical portrayals of women (Thackeray is condemned for creating 'tender pretty fools' instead of 'rational creatures'); and she recognises the narrative practices of *Jane Eyre* as representing the 'true revolution. France is but one of the Western Powers; woman is half of the world'.

Margaret Oliphant, *Margaret Maitland* (London: Colburn, 1849); *Caleb Field* (London: Colburn, 1851); *Merkland: A Story of Scottish Life* (Colburn: London, 1851); *Adam Graeme of Mossgray* (London: Hurst & Blackett, 1852); *Katie Stewart* (Edinburgh & London: Blackwood, 1853); *Harry Muir* (London: Hurst & Blackett, 1853); *The Quiet Heart* (Edinburgh: Blackwood, 1854); *Magdalen* (London: Hepburn, Hurst & Blackett, 1854); *Zaidée* (Edinburgh: Blackwood, 1856); *The Days of My Life* (London: Hurst & Blackett, 1857); *The Laird of Nordlaw* (London: Hurst & Blackett,1858); *Sundays* (London: Nisbet, 1858); *Lilliesleaf* (London: Hurst & Blackett, 1859); *Lucy Crofton* (London: Hurst & Blackett, 1860); *The House on the Moor* (London: Hurst & Blackett, 1861); *The*

House of Edward Irving (London: Hurst & Blackett, 1862); *The Doctor's Family, and Other Stories* (London: Blackwood, 1863; ed. Merryn Williams, World's Classics, 1986); *Salem Chapel* (Edinburgh & London: Blackwood, 1863); *The Perpetual Curate* (Edinburgh & London: Blackwood, 1864); *Agnes* (1865); *Miss Marjoribanks* (Edinburgh & London: Blackwood, 1866; ed. Penelope Fitzgerald, London: Virago, 1987); *A Son of the Soil* (London: Macmillan, 1866); *Francis of Assisi* (London: Macmillan, 1868); *The Minister's Wife* (London: Hurst & Blackett, 1869); *John: A Love Story* (Edinburgh: Blackwood, 1870); *Squire Arden* (London: Hurst & Blackett, 1871); *Ombra* (London: Chapman & Hall, 1872); *Innocent: A Tale of Modern Life* (London: Sampson Low, 1873); *A Rose in June* (London: Hurst & Blackett, 1874); *Whiteladies* (London: Chatto, 1875); *The Curate in Charge* (Beccles, 1876; ed. Merryn Williams, London: Alan Sutton, 1987); *Phoebe Junior: A Last Chronicle of Carlingford* (London: Hurst & Blackett, 1876); *Mrs Arthur* (London: Hurst & Blackett, 1877); *A Beleagured City* (London: Macmillan, 1880); *The Ladies Lindores* (Edinburgh: Blackwood, 1880); *A Little Pilgrim in the Unseen* (London: Macmillan, 1882); *Hester* (London: Macmillan, 1883; ed. Jennifer Uglow, London: Virago, 1984); *Sir Tom* (London: Macmillan, 1884); *A Country Gentleman and His Family* (London: Macmillan, 1886); *A House Divided Against Itself* (Edinburgh: Blackwood, 1886); *The Land of Darkness* (London: Macmillan, 1888); *Lady Car* (London: Longmans, 1889); *Kirsteen* (London: Macmillan, 1890; ed. Merryn Williams, Everyman Classics, 1984); *The Railway Man and his Children* (London: Macmillan, 1891); *The Cuckoo in the Nest* (London: Hutchinson, 1892); *A Beleaguered City, and Other Stories* (London: Macmillan, 1892; ed. Merryn Williams, World's Classics, 1986); *The Marriage of Elinor* (1892); *Lady William* (London: Macmillan, 1893); *Who Was Lost and is Found* (Edinburgh: Blackwood, 1894); *Sir Robert's Fortune* (London: Methuen, 1895); *Jeanne d'Arc* (Putnam, 1896); *The Sisters Brontë* (London: Hurst & Blackett, 1897); *A Widow's Tale and Other Stories* (London: Macmillan, 1898); and others

The Autobiography of Margaret Oliphant, ed. Mrs Harry Coghill (Edinburgh: Blackwood, 1899; ed. Elizabeth Jay, Oxford: Oxford University Press, 1990)

Further Reading:

British Women Fiction Writers of the 19th Century (Women Writers and their Work) (Philadelphia : Chelsea House Publishers, 199)

Carolyn A. Barros, *Autobiography: Narrative of Transformation* (Ann Arbor: University of Michigan Press)

John Stock Clarke, *Margaret Oliphant, 1828-1897: Non-fictional Writings: A Bibliography* ([St. Lucia] Australia: Department of English, University of Queensland, 1997)

Vineta Colby, *The Equivocal Virtue: Mrs Oliphant and the Victorian Literary Market Place* (Hamden, Conn.: Archon Books, 1966; 1984)

Susan Hamilton, ed., *Criminals, Idiots, Women and Minors: Victorian Writing by Women on Women* (Peterborough, Ont.: Broadview Press, 1995)

Elisabeth Jay, *Mrs Oliphant, 'A Fiction to Herself': A Literary Life* (Oxford: Clarendon, 1995)

Margaret Oliphant: Critical Essays on a Gentle Subversive (London: Associated University Presses, 1995)

Patricia A. Morelli, *Frances Trollope, Margaret Oliphant and Caroline North: Disavowed Spheres and Disappointing Spouses in Victorian Marriages* (West Hartford, Connecticut: Saint Joseph College, 1992)

A Question of Identity: Women, Science, and Literature (New Brunswick, N.J.: Rutgers University Press, 1993)

Margarete Rubik, *The Novels of Mrs. Oliphant: A Subversive View of Traditional Themes* (New York: P. Lang, 1994) (Writing about Women, Vol.8)

Merryn Williams, *Margaret Oliphant: A Critical Biography* (Basingstoke, Hampshire: Macmillan, 1986)

DNB; *DLB* 18; *HSWW*; Royle; Todd 2

From 'The Laws Concerning Women', *Blackwood's Magazine* vol. 79, no. 496 (April, 1856) 379-387:

This is a notice of 'A Brief Summary, in Plain Language, of the most Important Laws concerning Wives, together with a Few Observations thereon' (London: Chapman, 1856)[2]
The injuries of women have long been a standing subject of complaint and animadversion. Woman's rights will never grow into a popular agitation, yet woman's wrongs are always picturesque and attractive. They are, indeed, so good to make novels and poems about, so telling as illustrations of patience and gentleness, that we fear any real redress of grievances would do more harm in the literary world than it would do good to the feminine. We speak with a very serious and well-meaning pamphlet on the subject before us – no impassioned statement of personal wrongs, but a quiet summary of real laws and positive (apparent) injustices. We have no desire, for our own part, to throw ridicule upon any temperate and well-considered movement of real social amelioration; but words and terms are unchancy things to deal with, and half the quarrels in the world come from different interpretations put by different people on the same phraseology. These laws which concern women do not seem at the first glance either just or complimentary. At the first glance, it is reasonable to suppose that the masculine lawmaker has made use of his advantages for the enslavement of his feebler companion. Mrs Browning's: 'Women sobbing out of sight/Because men made the laws,'[3] appears, in fact, a real condition, when we glance at the surface and outside of the question; and we are disposed, in immediate indignation, to break a lance upon the grand abstract tyrant, Man, who keeps this princess in a perpetual dungeon. Yet let us pause a moment. The law may be unnecessarily particular; but are its opponents upon just ground?

We have small faith, for our own part, in what is called class legislation which could make the man an intentional and voluntary oppressor of the woman. This idea, that the two portions of humankind are natural antagonists to each other, is, to our thinking, at the very outset, a monstrous and unnatural idea. The very man who made the laws which send 'Women sobbing out of sight', had not only a wife, whom we may charitably suppose he was glad of a legal argument for tyrannising over, but doubtless such things as sisters and daughters, whom he could have no desire to subject to the tyranny of other men. There is no man in existence so utterly separated from one-half of his fellow creatures as to be able to legislate against them in the interests of his own sex. No official character whatever can make so absurd and artificial a distinction. Let us vindicate, in the first instance, the law and the law-maker. It is possible that the poor may legislate against the rich, or the rich against the poor, but to make such an antagonism between men and women is against all reason and all nature.

It is impossible, Oliphant continues, to imagine that men might entertain motives of petty jealousy towards the 'abstract Woman'. As far as married couples are concerned 'it is no fallacy of the law to say that these two are one person; it is a mere truism of nature'.

For all the laws complained of as affecting women concern themselves with women *married*; woman unmarried are under no humiliations of legal bondage. It is the *wife* and not the woman, whose separate existence the law denies. This is a fiction in one sense, but not in another; in one point of view, a visible piece of nonsense; in another, an infallible truth. It is hard to enter upon this subject without falling into the authoritative hardness of legal phraseology, or the sweet jargon of poetic nonsense, on one side or the other. 'The wife loses her rights as a single woman, and her existence is entirely absorbed in that of her husband,' says this *Brief Summary in Plain Language* of the formal law. 'His house she enters,' says the poet,

> A guardian angel o'er his life presiding,
> Doubling his pleasures, and his cares dividing.[4]

The one utterance is somewhat humiliating, the other unquestionably pretty; and both fail of the truth. Lawyer and Poet alike survey the surface and external aspect of the question – common experience pronounces a fuller verdict. This question, of all others, is a question which cannot be decided by individual cases – and we are all perfectly aware that, as a general principle, the wife *is* the husband as much as the husband *is* the wife. In truth and in nature – with the reality of sober fact and without romancing – these two people set their hands to it, that they are no longer two people, but one person. And let us not suppose that, in considering any social question, we have to consider principally a succession of sensitive and high-spirited individual temperaments or states of exalted feeling. No law can suffice to baulk of their natural portion of misery those susceptible personages who are alive to every touch of possible offence. The broad general principle crushes over them, regardless of their outcries. Common law and rule take no cognisance of feelings excited and heroical. We grant it is sometimes unjust to judge the chance Edwin and Angelina,[5] as it is right to judge the Johns and Marys of ordinary existence; but how much more unjust to fit our regulations to the chance case instead of to the ordinary! We can come to no true and safe conclusion upon a matter so delicate and personal as this, without carefully discrimating between the common and the uncommon. No law of human origin can reach every possible development of human temper and organisation; injured wives and unhappy husbands are accidents uncurable by law;

and it would be almost as wise to legislate for the race on the supposition that every member of it had a broken leg, as on the more injurious hypothesis that tyranny, oppression, and injustice, rankled within the heart of every home.

Let us not enter upon the tender question of mental inferiority. Every individual woman, we presume, is perfectly easy on her own account that she at least is not remarkably behind her masculine companions; and so long as this is the case, we need fear no grand duel between the two halves of creation. But every man and every woman knows, with the most absolute certainty, that a household divided against itself cannot stand. It is the very first principle of domestic existence.

Oliphant argues that 'one interest and one fortune' is an 'indispensable necessity' and that it is not in 'reality' the case that 'the woman loses her existence and is absorbed in her husband'. Once men and women have entered, as they voluntarily do, the state of matrimony, it may be the case that it is impossible for the law to deal justly with their separation since this means treating again as two, those who agreed to make themselves one.[6] This is particularly the case with respect to custody of the children of broken marriages:

For it is not the question of the wife's earnings or the wife's property which lies nearest the heart of the controversy: there are the children – living witnesses of the undividableness of the parents. You give their custody to the husband. It is a grievous and sore injustice to the mother who bore them. But let us alter the case. Let the wife have the little ones, and how does the question stand? The ground is changed, but the principle is the same.

There is no just way of arranging the custody of children in the event of separation or divorce.

These children – this child – which is the father's share, and which the mother's? Who can divide them? For our own part we can perceive no equitable arrangement, no possibility of justice; and until this delicate point is settled, there is little effectual ground for legislation, so far as we can perceive, in the laws which concern women.

Of course, the children could become children of the State:

For the law has no bowels of compassion, and no capacity for considering the heartbreak of individual agony. Let the man and the woman part as they met, solitary and single persons; let the unhappy children, fatherless and motherless, become the children of the State. This is *justice*; otherwise, on either side there can be nothing but wrong.

As far as the control of income is concerned the problems are less acute but even here the law is unlikely to be able to secure the earnings of a wife to her, if her husband is persuasive or tyrannical:

'It is cruel,' we quote the *Observations*, 'when the support of the family depends on the joint earnings of husband and wife, that the earnings of both should be in the hands of one, and not even in the hands of that one who has naturally the strongest desire to promote the welfare of the children. All who are familiar with the working classes know how much suffering and privation is caused by the exercise of this *right* by drunken and bad men.' Are we deceived, or is this the mere folly we suppose it to be? What is the *right* which brings the earnings of the wife into the hands of a 'drunken and bad man'? Is it the law, or is it the strong hand? – legal authority, or persuasion by force or by kindness? Do we need to give a serious answer to such a question? Labouring people are not so learned in the law; and certain are we that no charwoman of our acquaintance however induced to give her hard-won shillings to her drunken husband, has the remotest idea that he has any *right* to them. She gives them because he would take them – or she gives them for peace – or with the forlorn hope of redeeming him by kindness; but did she suspect for a moment that he had a *right* to such monies, we have too much confidence in her native feminine spirit and pugnacity, to suppose one single coin would be, without a battle, surrendered to his hands. No. The rascal may punch his wife's head, or carry off her small incomings, but he does not believe the one to be a whit more lawful than the other. A drunken and bad man will swallow up anybody's or everybody's earnings, if he can get them; but our experience of the respectable working classes, and of all the grades above the lower strata of the middle class, established quite different principles. It is the wife there who is the Chancellor of the Exchequer. The husband, honest man, has his little sum of pocket money; the income comes direct into the careful keeping of the household manager. This state of things is universal, and 'all who are familiar with the working classes' must acknowledge that it is so. To speak of 'compensating women for the loss of their moral right to their own property and earnings, and for the loss of the mental development and independence of character gained by the possession and thoughtful appropriation of money', is the merest nonsense which ever looked like reason. To whom belongs the 'thoughtful appropriation' of the decent working man's weekly wages? – who is it that, with care and forethought, finds ever so many frocks and pairs of shoes, in the narrow yearly revenue of those social grades which are next above the working man? Everyone knows it is the wife, unless the wife is proved incapable. Everyone is aware how entirely the expenditure and economy of the house lies in her hands. This is no theory of what should be, but the absolute matter of fact which *is* – known to every mind which takes the trouble to note the common things that lie around.

And, indeed, to tell the truth, women are the only born legislators, let them complain of their position as they will. Only a few hundred of us at the best can have a hand, though of the smallest, in affairs of State; but to every of them all, Paul himself, though not much given to compliment, gives the right and injunction – Rule the house. Yes; the merest girl, eighteen years old, who half in love and half in fun, dares to don the fatal orange-blossom – there she is, a child half-an-hour ago, now a lawmaker, supreme and absolute; and yet, most despotic and unconstitutional of monarchs, you hear them weeping over infringed rights and powers denied. Oh, inconsistent humanity! – as if those powers and rights were not seated, innate and indestructible, far away out of the reach of any secondary law!

From 'The Condition of Women', *Blackwood's Magazine* vol. 83, no. 508 (Feb., 1858) 139-154:

Oliphant begins by remarking that Britain has been free from the violent unheavals that have been the lot of the Continent, particularly the French Revolution and the Napoleonic Wars.

But among ourselves, at least, there has been no such catastrophe – the evils of civilisation have counteracted themselves without any violant disturbances of the national life. We have gained our comfort, our security, our luxury, at a less price than that of our national vigour. The wealth of centuries has not bound us in silken chains of imbecility, or left us ready or probable victims to any invasion. On the contrary, though this is not our golden age – though there is no heroic glory in the firmament, no peculiar combinations of good fortune in our position – every circumstance in the history of the time proves that the race never was more vigorous, more irresistible, or less likely to be worsted. We talk of the evils of extreme civilisation and we see them; but those evils, thank Heaven, are not symptoms of that fatal decadence which killed the civilised races of antiquity, and which has again and again left the hopes of the world in the hands of an army of savage and barbarous tribes, possessed of little more than that primitive force of *life* which was necessary for the revival of all the social conditions well-nigh extinguished by living too well. […] We are in no danger of making sumptuary laws, of regulating the burgesses' wardrobe or the nobleman's plate-closet. Burgesses and noblemen alike send out young adventurers, as all the world knows – who would have been Rolands and Bayards in the days of chivalry[7] – to every quarter of this prodigious empire that stand in need of such; and no man in the kingdom grudges to the mothers and sisters – nay, to the aunts, cousins, and sweethearts of these boys – flounces enough to set the island afloat if it please them. Luxury, present or prospective, affrights neither statesman nor philosopher in these realms; and it is not easy to make a British public believe that an American public can mean anything but a jest, when it throws the blame of its bankruptcy upon its womankind. It is possible that the course of years may reverse this picture, that civilisation may sink into effeminacy, and wealth run on to ruin with this kingdom, as with so many others; but at present, so far as human probabilities go, it seems our privilege to hold the balance, and solve to this extent at least every social problem of the world.

Yet certain sections of our society still feel they have legitimate complaints:
Civilisation among us stands at the bar to be judged by domestic juries, for offences against the social economy. In the present case the complainants are women. Let us do their plea full justice: they are not the passionate women, making vehement appeal to public sympathy for personal wrongs too bitter to contain themselves within a private circle, to whose voices the world has not been unaccustomed hitherto. It is not any personal injury, but a general condition which is the object of their statement, and they make their statement with reasonableness and gravity. It is, notwithstanding, somewhat too sweeping and extensive to be received without hesitation – being no less than a charge against civilisation of upsetting the commonest and most universal relation of life, and of leaving a large proportion of

women, in all conditions, outside of the arrangements of the family, to provide for themselves, without at the same time leaving anything for them to do.

This is very hard, if it is true; and that it is true in many special instances, no one will deny. Special instances, however, do not make up a case so universal as we are called upon to believe this to be.

Oliphant suggests that the statistic of one half the female population as unmarried and unmarriagable is probably exaggerated and polemically advanced:

Here is, however, one of the chief accusations brought against our civilisation. Half the women in England are not married, and never will be; consequently a large proportion of Englishwomen have to seek their own maintenance and earn their own bread. But civilisation, while it makes this unnatural and anomalous arrangement, does not unmake the primitive arrangement by which labour out of doors, handicrafts, arts, and manual skills of all kinds, remain in the possession of men. There are consequently crowds of half-starved needlewomen, thousands of poor governesses, and a great many more feminine writers of novels than are supposed to be good for the health of the public; and so the tale is full. A woman who cannot be a governess or a novel-writer must fall back on that poor little needle, the primitive and original handicraft of femininity. If she cannot do that, or even, doing it, if stifled among a crowd of others like herself, who have no other gift, she must starve by inches, and die over the shirt she makes. We are all perfectly acquainted with this picture, and there can be no doubt that, with countless individual aggravations, it is true enough; the only thing doubtful is, whether these unfortunate circumstances are peculiar to women, and whether it is mainly upon them that civilisation imposes this necessity and works this wrong.

Many a sermon has been preached already upon the singular life of Currer Bell. It would be late now to recur to a book which has already had its day of popularity, and waked its own particular circles of curiosity and wonder; yet there is one aspect of it which bears with no small force upon the present subject. In that remarkable but not very prepossessing family, there was one brother equally gifted we are told, and in extreme youth the most hopeful of any of them. Which seems to have had the best chance for life and success? The sisters were governesses all, and hated their disagreeable occupation: the brother was a tutor, and ruined himself disgracefully in his. Wherein stood the peculiar advantages of this young man, putting out of the question the vices by which he made an end of himself? Is a tutor in a private family of moderate rank better than a governess in the same? Is his position more secure, his prospects less discouraging, his pretensions more suitably acknowledged? Everybody knows that it is not so. Most people know also instinctively that the position of the poor gentlewoman who teaches the children of a rich family, is less humiliating than that of the poor gentleman employed in the same office, and that we could admire a hundred petty endurances in a woman which we should despise a man for tolerating. Why? We have no leisure to enter into the psychology of the question; simply, we do so by nature. A woman who endures worthily even the pettiest slights of meanness, has the privilege of suffering no diminution of dignity – whereas for the man in the same circumstances, the best we can wish is that he should throw his Horace at his patron's head, and 'list incontinently, or start for the diggings. He has no such privilege; and his patience must not go too far, under penalty of everybody's disdain.

The presence of the brother in this family of Brontës, which has been the subject of so many dissertations upon the condition of women, seems to us to change the *venue* entirely, and make the subject a much wider one. The women of the house did not like their occupation; what occupation would have contented these restless and self-devouring spirits? But the only one whose end was worse, and lower, and more debased than his beginning, was the brother. Civilisation, if that is the sinner, was far more bitterly in fault towards Branwell than towards Charlotte. It was the man for whose talents there was no outlet, for whose life there seemed no place in the world: it was not the woman, who did her duty, and in her season had her reward; and so far as this example goes, the theory of undue limitation and unjust restraint in respect to women certainly does not hold. The limitation, the restraint, the bondage, the cruel laws and barriers of conventional life, may, notwithstanding, remain as cruel as ever, but their application is certainly not harder upon the daughters of the race than upon its sons.

For who does not know, who knows the world of modern society – and if no such case is near and present to ourselves, let us be thankful – how many young men are to be found throughout England, but especially in London, recently emerged from Oxford or Cambridge, educated after the highest standard of modern education, full of general ability, considerable enough to pass for genius with many of their friends, well-mannered, well-read, and neither idle nor vicious, who, notwithstanding, linger on that eminence of youthful training perhaps for years, feeling themselves able for anything, and doing nothing, till the chances are that, out of pure disgust, the more generous spirits among them throw their culture to the winds, and rush into something for which all their education had tended rather to disqualify than to train them? Perhaps parental intention – poor scapegoat of many a failure – has destined them for the Church; and but for the slight drawback of having no great faith in any particular doctrine, they are, in fact, better qualified to be incumbents of a tolerable living, than for anything else save the position of squire, which would suit them best of all. But the lads bear a conscience, and will not be ordained – not, at least, until the very latest shift. What are they to do? Sometimes, in spite of Mr Thackeray, it happens that a man may be a very clever fellow, without being able even to write a newspaper article. So many as are able to do this feat 'throw themselves into literature', as a matter of course, and something good comes of it in a few instances; but the majority swell the number of those unfortunates who do rueful comic stories, and live upon the humours of London cabmen and street-boys, sometimes advancing for a charmed moment to the beatitude of *Punch*. This is no fiction; we do not say 'one-half' the young *alumni* of our universities are in this position, or represent it as a universal fate; but the class is large, numerous, full of capabilities, able to be of infinite service to its generation, if it but knew or saw what to do; and how in the face of this, we should recognise a special injustice to woman, or groan over a conventional limitation of her powers of working, in presence of the very same restraint acting still more unfortunately upon the more natural and stronger workman, we cannot allow or perceive.

Yes, the rules of civilisation are hard, and conventional life is cruel; but the injury does not limit itself by any arbitrary law of sex, or imaginary line of demarcation between men and women. The burden lies upon all these educated classes, who, without fortune, have yet a position and habits which seem to make it needful that they should earn their bread by the toil of their brain, rather than by the labour of their hands – who must be banished to the antipodes before they can permit themselves to take up the original tools of nature, and who are in a much greater degree slaves of society and of their own social standing, than either the assured rich or the certain poor. In this vast London, which is the centre and focus of our extremity of civilisation, there are crowds of young men, trained to that pitch of bodily perfection and development which English public schools and universities, without doubt, keep up to a higher degree than any other educational institutions in the world[8]– with a high advantage of intelligence, and all the advantages which are to be derived from that system of mental training which this country approves as the most complete – who, nevertheless, are as entirely at sea as to the best method of employing themselves and their faculties, as any woman with a feminine education equivalent to theirs could possibly find herself. Teaching, literature, art, which they have practised as amateurs to the admiration of their own families – or, last alternatives of all, Australia or a curacy, lie before them, which to choose. Even female novels, and the stories in minor magazines about 'proud pale girls' who support themselves by the work of their own hands, are not less profitable or less noble than the stories in other minor magazines about freshmen and town adventures, to which civilisation drives scores who never learnt to dig, and can see no other way than this of helping themselves; and if it is hard to be a governess, let no one suppose it is much lighter or more delightful to be a tutor. The burden, the restraint, the limitation is true, but it is one of no partial or one-sided application; and this bondage of society, of conventional life, and of a false individual pride, bears with a more dismal and discouraging blight upon men, who are the natural labourers and bread-winners, than it can ever do upon women constrained by special circumstances to labour for their own bread.

As for needlewomen, few people who think on the subject will need to be told what a heavy equipoise of this evil all great towns carry within them. Poor penmen, lost far away down the miserable ranks of penny-a-liners – poor, poor, shabby unemployed clerks, as utterly incapable of using any implement of labour, save the sharp iron nibs of the pen, as ever woman was incapable of more than her needle – poor fluctuating vagabonds, who live by directing circulars for tradesmen, and to whom an election is a carnival. There is little comfort in contemplating this widened prospect of misery, nevertheless it is the real state of the case. The pen – not the pen of Savage or of Chatterton,[9] or any other ship-wrecked genius, but the mere mechanical instrument, which makes out cobblers' accounts, and keeps huxters' books, and directs circulars – counts its miserable craftsmen by the thousands, down far below the ken of the criticising world, and sends sighs as pitiful out of cellars and garrets, as any that ever have breathed their melancholy inspiration into the 'Song of the Shirt'.[10]

Let us not attempt to ignore this dark and other side to all the comfort and luxury of our modern life; but at the same time let no special complaint appropriate the greater share of the injury. It is a universal injury, and evil common to the time;

it is not a one sided and newly-discovered aggravation of the wrongs and disabilities of women.

There is, however, in almost all public discussions upon the social position of women, an odd peculiarity which betrays itself here with great distinctness: it is, that writers on the subject invariably treat this half of humankind as a distinct creation rather than a portion of a general race – not as human creatures primarily, and women in the second place, but as women and nothing but women – a distinct sphere of being, a separate globe of existence, to which different rules, different motives, an altogether distinct economy, belong. One would almost suppose, to take modern predilections upon this subject for our guide, that a different and more delicate gospel, a law of finer and more elaborate gradations, must be necessary for this second creation; and that the old morality which slumped the whole race in one, was a barbarous imposition upon the nature, not human, but feminine, which ought to have had more delicate handling. Yet in spite of all the new light which new experience throws, it still remains true that there is only one law and one Gospel, and that God has made provision for one moral nature, and not for two, even in those commandments which are exceeding broad. One fundamental and general ground of humanity is common to men and to women; one faith is propounded to both, without alteration of terms or change of inducements; one hope and one undiscriminated heaven shines on the ending of their days; they are born precisely after the same manner, and by the same event die; – they are, in fact – different, distinct and individual as every detail of their responsible existence may be – one race; and without the slightest inclination to ignore or lessen the essential differences between them, we can see no true philosophy in any view of this subject which does not recognise the ground they hold in common, as well as the peculiar standing which they hold apart.

Let us not be misunderstood: we are not endeavouring to establish the equality of the two. Equality is the mightiest of humbugs – there is no such thing in existence; and the idea of opening the professions and occupations and governments of men to women, seems to us the vainest as well as the vulgarest of chimeras. God has ordained visibly, by all the arrangements of nature and of providence, one sphere and kind of work for a man and another for a woman. He has given them different constitutions, different organisations, a perfectly distinct and unmistakable identity. Yet above and beyond and beneath all their differences, he has made them primarily human creatures, answering, in the unity of an indivisible race, to His own government and laws; rebelling against them with a simultaneous impulse; moved by the same emotions; under all diversities of detail one creation. [...] The two creatures are as different as creatures made for different vocations, and different offices, can well be; yet in all the great fundamental principles of their mind and nature, the two are one. [...]

How then about our unmarried sisters, our unmarried daughters, that alarming independent army which a bold calculator affirms to amount to 'one-half' of the women of these kingdoms? If there is really one-fourth of our population in these astounding circumstances, we fear that the question is one beyond the power of the circulating libraries, and that even the remaining three-fourths, English, Scotch, and Irish, can scarcely solve so big a problem. On the whole, one would suppose that the best expedient for such an emergency was, after all, Australia, where there is no Act of Parliament to compel emigrant ladies to marry within three days of their landing, and where at least there is room and scope for the energy which over-civilisation cramps and keeps in bondage. If it is true that so large a proportion of women stand in circumstances of isolation so entire, and self-responsibility so complete, it is certainly very weak and very foolish of them to sacrifice, for a mere piece of womanly delicacy, that safety-valve which men in the same position avail themselves of so much – especially, we repeat, as it is certain there is no Act of Parliament coercing them to the necessity of marriage as soon as they have touched the wealthy shores of our great young colony; and the benefit of leaving a little room among the crowd might well indemnify an emigrant sisterhood for the momentary joke of going out to be married, which every one among them had it quite in her own hands to prove untrue. If the evil has gone so far, or nearly so far – if the half of British women have to support themselves, and to do that by means of three, or at most four, limited occupations – to wit, teaching, needlework, domestic service, and novel-writing – we humbly submit that a little watchmaking, book-keeping, or jewellery, additional thereto, would be a very inadequate remedy. To upset the ordinary social economy for any clamant grievance of a time, however just, would be the most short-sighted and ruinous policy imaginable. It is, besides, what is still more to the purpose, impossible. These great questions of the common weal are happily impervious to all philosophies, theories, and reasonings. They arrange themselves by laws of their own, which the warmest appeal of eloquence, and the most infallible array of argument, can neither reach nor influence. [...] Inevitable rules of necessity and self-interest sway the whole social economy. [...] Trade, like civilisation, is an irrational and abstract influence, upon which individual hardships make no impression whatever. It has no particular regard for men, none for women, and very small concern for the general interests of the race. When it suits its own purpose to employ women, and even children, though at the cost of all health, loveliness and domestic comfort, it does so without the slightest compunction; and if it had command of an equal amount of female material for other crafts as it has for cotton-mills and had for collieries, would doubtless employ them with the most sublime impartiality. No, let no one suppose it – there is no conspiracy of mankind to keep women excluded from the workshop or the manufactory. On the contrary, the work of women, if it abounded to only half the extent, could always undersell the work of men, and consequently, would always retain a certain degree of unfair advantage. But if civilisation has unduly increased the class of poor gentlewomen – if the advance of education and refinement adds yearly to the number of those who will rather starve genteelly than 'descend in the social scale' – let nobody run away from the real question with a false idea of special or peculiar injustice to women. The real drawback is, that while the rough work of nature always remains in one quarter or another, ready for those who will work at it, delicate labour for delicate hands is not capable of more than a certain degree of extension; and that, under this burden of our social state, women to whose hands Providence has not committed the establishment and support of families, are neither the only nor the primary sufferers.

Mrs Oliphant goes on to deprecate the tendency in women to 'take to philosophy' and discourse on the question of marriage and the relation between the sexes without the experience to support their enquiry:

And it is also true, and a fact worth remembering, that the maiden lady is not an invention of these times. There were unmarried women long ago, before civilisation had made such fatal progress: while all the heroines in all the novels were still married at eighteen – before the life of Charlotte Brontë had even begun, or there was a woman in existence qualified to write it – unmarried ladies existed in this world, where nothing is ever new. Judging by literature, indeed, Scotland herself, our respected mither [*sic*], seems always to have had a very fair average of unmarried daughters; and for the instruction of womankind in general, and novel-writers in particular, we are bound to add that there were three such personages as Miss Austen, Miss Edgeworth, and Miss Ferrier,[11] novelists of the old world, and representatives of the three respective kingdoms, whom none of their successors in the craft have yet been able to displace in the popular liking; so that we might suppose it was rather late in the day to begin *de novo* to teach unmarried women how, in spite of their unfortunate circumstances, it is still possible for them to keep themselves respected and respectable. Many hundred, nay, thousand years ago, there was even a certain characteristic and remarkable person called Miriam, who, wilful and womanlike, and unquestionably unmarried, was still so far from being disrespected or unimportant, that a whole nation waited for her, till she was able to join their journey. Our age, which likes so much to declare itself the origin of changes, is not the inventor of feminine celibacy. There were unmarried women before our time, and there will be unmarried women after it. Nay, not only so – but Paul the apostle, eighteen hundred years ago, gave anything but an inferior place to the unwedded maidens of his time: 'She that is unmarried careth for the things that belong to the Lord, how she may please the Lord,' says the writer of the Epistles;[12] and many an unmarried woman since his day has proved his statement, happily unwitting of all the philosophies which should prove to her how lonely and comfortless she ought to find herself, and what a hard case hers was, and how, notwithstanding, it behoved her to make some certain amount of sad and patient exertion to vindicate her womanly credit with the world.

[…]

We presume there must be something terribly wrong with that famous windmill, which has borne the assault of so many fiery knights, the thing called Female Education. Since the days of Hannah More[13] – and how much further back beyond that virtuous era who will venture to say? – everybody has broken a spear upon this maiden fortress; yet, judging from the undiminished fervour with which it is still assaulted in the present day, we conclude that no one has succeeded in any measure of reformation. We do not profess to be very learned in the question – the mysteries of a female college have never been penetrated by our profane eyes, though we profess, like most other people, to have seen the product, and to be aware, in a limited way, what kind of persons our young country-women are, and in what manner they manage to fulfil the duties of the after-life, for which in the first place, their education in general does not seem to unfit them. *That* is something in its favour to begin with – but we cannot help being rather doubtful about the value of the report as to the frivolity of female education, when we find the strange inaccuracies and blunders into which its critics fall regarding matters of social usage open to everybody's observation. There is that wise book, for instance, *Friends in Council*, which all proper people quote and admire.[14] Wise books, we are ashamed to confess, inspire us with an instinctive aversion; yet, notwithstanding, we would quote honestly, if the volume were at our hand. There are sundry essays and conversations there touching upon this subject, in one of which the oracle informs us that it is no wonder to find women inaccessible to reason, considering all the homage and false worship with which they are surrounded in society during the first part of their lives, and which is all calculated to persuade them of their own superlative and angelical gifts, and elevation above ordinary fact and information. Is that so? Perhaps if every young girl who shone her little day in polite society, happened to be a great beauty, intoxicating everybody who approached her with that irrestistible charm, it might be partially true; for that men, and women too, fall out of their wits at sight of a pretty face, and are beguiled into all manner of foolishness by its glamour is indisputable; but even then we should decidedly claim it as a necessary condition, that the beauty herself had no young brothers to bring her down to common ground, and only a gracious sire of romance, never worried in the City, nor disturbed by factious opposition in the House. As for all ranks less than the highest, the thing is preposterous and out of the question; and even in the highest, every young girl is not a beauty, and society generously provides its little budget of mortifications for the moral advantage of neophytes. But for the daughter of the professional man, of the merchant, of all the throngs of middle life, to which in reality, all great rules must primarily apply, if there is any truth in them, – what can possibly be more false, we had almost said more absurd? These are not days of euphuism or extravagant compliments. We do not permit the common acquaintances of common society to administer serious flattery to our womankind; and an average young lady of a moderate degree of intelligence, we apprehend, would – so far is the thing out of usage – be much more likely to to consider herself affronted than honoured by the old hyperboles of admiration; and as for home, good lack! what do *Friends in Council* know about it? Fathers who have bills to meet and clients to satisfy; mothers who are straining income and expenditure to a needful junction, and who have all the cares of the house upon their shoulders; brothers who vex the young lady's soul before her time with premature buttons, – are these the kind of surroundings to persuade a woman that she is angelical, and make her giddy with the incense of flattery and admiration? We appeal to everybody who knows anything of common life, and the existence of the family, which is true; and we humbly submit that one might object to take for gospel, without more effectual demonstration, anything else which the *Friends in Council* choose to advance upon female education, or any other of the vexed questions concerning womankind.

Some women writers on the subject are just as guilty of inattention to the real facts of family life, when they speak of adoring fathers or of boys who may do a thousand things not proper for girls:
Where, oh where, are to be found those adorable papas who delight to give their daughters everything they can desire? – those mammas most dutiful, who take every

domestic care off their hands? Are they in Bloomsbury? are they in Belgravia? might we have a chance of finding them in beautiful Edinburgh, or in rich Manchester? And where shall we be able to lay hands upon this ecstatic conception of the boys and brothers, who have learned self-dependence all their lives, are helpful and handy, and may do a thousand things which are not proper for the girls? We should very much like to know; and so, we do not doubt, would a very large number of young ladies still more immediately concerned. For, alas! we are obliged to confess that the greater number of the papas whom we have the personal honour of including in our acquaintance, are apt to hold unjustifiably strong opinions on the subject of milliners' bills – that the majority of the mammas are provokingly disposed to provide for the proper regulation of the future households of their daughters, by advancing these young ladies to an economical participation in domestic difficulties; and as for the boys, did anybody ever know a well-conditioned boy who was good for anything in this life but making mischief? In this holiday season one can speak feelingly – who is it that keeps the house in din and disorder from morning to night – who are the ogres who bring on mamma's headaches, who upset the girls' work-boxes, who lose the books, who mislay the music, who play tricks upon the visitors, who run riot in the unmitigated luxury of total idleness, who are about as helpful as the kittens are, and whom the very littlest of sisters patronise as incapable, who can do nothing for themselves? Oh happy people who have boys at home for the holidays! do you need to pause before answering the question?

And large families, Mrs Oliphant continues, ensure that girls are faced with the realities of running a household and not at all allowed to believe themselves the possessors of angelic qualities. Daughters more than sons have supported their brilliant fathers – from Milton and Sir Thomas More down to Fowell Buxton' – and in the tradesman class it is most frequently daughters who keep the books and make out the bills.

We do not speak abstractly, or in general terms; we say plainly and simply, that whatever theoretical faults there may be in English female education, it turns out women as little apt to fail in the duties of their life as any class of human creatures, male or female, under the sun. We say that it is a mere exploded piece of antique nonsense to assert that society flatters women into foolishness, or permits them to be flattered; and that those who find in the young girls of our families only helpless nosegays of ornament, unqualified to do service either to themselves or other people, are either totally unacquainted with household life, or have a determined 'cast' in their vision, not to be remedied.

Mrs Oliphant concedes that women, mothers and daughters, are sometimes persuaded that what they encounter in print has a special authority even when it runs counter to their own experience. And for this reason she disapproves of the spate of conduct books in Britain and from America which encourage girls to be persistently self-conscious about their sex:

But why, of all classes in the world, our tender young girls, the margin of innocence, and, if you will, ignorance, which we are all heartily glad to believe in, fringing the garment of the sadder world, should be instructed in all the delicate social questions of an artificial life, and put up to every possible emergency of all the relationships between men and women, it seems to us impossible to conceive. Not to say that it is ridiculously unfair in the first instance, for people don't write books for the lads their compeers, instructing them how to arrange their love-affairs, and informing them what the young ladies think of their general conduct. The unfortunate boys have to collect their information on this subject at first hand, or to take the hints of their favourite novels; and we really think it might be a happy experiment to suspend all the talk for a generation, and leave their partners to follow their example.

Mrs Oliphant goes on to consider the situation of married women particularly in the light of recent legislation.[15] *She considers that divorce is an undesirable recourse for women and that 'it must always remain the dreadful alternative of an evil which has such monstrous and unnatural aggravations as to be beyond all limits of possible endurance'. Mrs Oliphant remains conservative about custody provisions:*

But who shall open the terrible complication of the rights of fathers and mothers? What Solomon shall venture to divide between the two that most precious and inalienable of all treasures, the unfortunate child whose very existence stands as a ceaseless protest of nature against their disjunction? From this most painful branch of the question the law retreats, not daring to put in its hand. The present state of affairs is not just – is cruel, frightful, almost intolerable – but national legislation, and all the wisdom of the wise, can find no arbitrary and universal law which could be juster. There is none, let us seek it where we will. Crime itself does not abrogate natural rights and quench natural love; and so long as there are divorced and separated parents, there must be in one way or other, on one side or another, a certain amount of painful and bitter injustice. Women, so far as the law goes, are at present the sufferers, and not the benefited parties; but if the arrangement were reversed, the principle would still be exactly the same. Partition can be made of worldly goods – security obtained for the wages of labour and the gifts of inheritance – but the great gift of God to married people remains undividable – a difficulty which the law shrinks from encountering, and which no human power can make plain. This is not a hardship of legislation, but one of nature. We are very slow to acknowledge the hardships of nature in these days, and still more reluctant to put up with them. All the progress we have really made, and all the additional and fictitious progress which exists in our imagination, prompt us to the false idea that there is a remedy for everything, and that no pain is inevitable. But there *are* pains which are inevitable in spite of philosophy, and conflicting claims to which Solomon himself could do no justice. We are not complete syllogisms, to be kept in balance by intellectual regulations, we human creatures. We are of all things and creatures in the world the most incomplete; and there are conditions of our warfare, for the redress of which, in spite of all the expedients of social economy, every man and woman, thrown by whatever accident out of the course of nature, must be content to wait perhaps for years, perhaps for a life long, perhaps till the consummation of all things.

Mrs Oliphant concludes her article by emphasising her dislike for writing which addresses itself exclusively to women and their wrongs and she warns against lectures to women which 'make their womanhood, instead of a fact of nature, a kind of profession'.

NOTES

1. For Caroline Norton see Somerville, p.131, n.14. When, after their separation, her husband deprived her of her children and tried to attach her earnings, she wrote 'The Separation of Mother and Child by the Law of Custody of Infants Considered' (1837), 'A Plain Letter to the Lord Chancellor on the Infants Custody Bill' (1838) and 'A Letter to the Queen' (1856).

2. This pamphlet was by Barbara Leigh Smith, shortly after Barbara Bodichon (1827-1891). Barbara Bodichon was throughout her life interested in the 'woman question' and worked for the betterment of women in general and for the reform of their education in particular. She became a close friend of George Eliot, immediately recognising her as the author of *Adam Bede*. Her pamphlet had no immediate success, since the 1856-7 campaign for the reform of the property laws relating to married women was unsuccessful, but it remained an influence on the gradual reform of the law on married women's property and the eventual passing of the Married Women's Property Act in 1882 which gave married women the same property rights as unmarried women. Until 1870, however, a husband had complete legal right to his wife's earnings and before 1856 he had this right even if they were separated.

3. Elizabeth Barrett Browning, *Casa Guidi Windows*, 1851, Part II, ll.638-9: 'No help for women sobbing out of sight/Because men made the laws?'

4. Samuel Rogers, 'Human Life', 1819, ll.352-3.

5. *The Hermit* or *Edwin and Angelina* is a ballad by Oliver Goldsmith, included in his *The Viacr of Wakefield*, published 1766. Angelina is wandering in the wilderness lamenting the loss and, she believes, death of her lover Edwin. She chances upon the Hermit's cell and when she explains her sorrow, the Hermit reveals himself as Edwin. Two characters in Gilbert and Sullivan's *Trial by Jury*, 1875, are Edwin and Angelina. Since the opera turns on a breach of promise case, this may not be a coincidence.

6. It is perhaps of interest to remark that this is one of the arguments used against the legality of the new Scottish Parliament.

7. Roland was one of the knights of the Frankish king, Charlemagne (742-814). The last stand of Roland and his fellows at Roncesvalles in the Pyrenees in 778, supposedly, but not historically, against the Saracens, is the subject of the 12th century *Chanson de Roland*. Pierre Terrail, Seigneur de Bayard (c.1473-1524) was known as 'le bon chevalier sans peur et sans reproche' (the good knight, fearless and above reproach).

8. Mrs Oliphant sent her sons to Eton.

9. Richard Savage (d. 1743) is known mainly because of Samuel Johnson's great biography of him which presents a tragic story of ill-treatment and ruined talent. Thomas Chatterton (1752-70) was notorious for the literary fraud of passing off his own poems as the work of a fifteenth-century Bristol poet, Rowley. The poems were, however, talented and Chatterton tragically poisoned himself because of his extreme poverty.

10. One of the more serious productions of Thomas Hood (1799-1845) – published anonymously in *Punch* in 1843. The poem protests against the notorious sweated labour of the seamstress. A woman sits 'in unwomanly rags' stitching a shirt 'in poverty, hunger and dirt'. The appeal is to a middle-class audience with 'mothers and wives': 'It is not linen you're wearing out,/But human creatures' lives.' The poem is as powerful as it is sentimental.

11. The novelist, Susan Edmonstone Ferrier (1782-1854), daughter of an Edinburgh lawyer, was a good friend of Scott. She wrote three novels, *Marriage*, 1818, *The Inheritance*, 1824, and *Destiny*, 1831, all of which are witty accounts of manners and morals and pay attention to both class and national difference. Scott said that as a conversationalist she was 'the least *exigeante*' of any literary lady of his acquaintance.

12. Paul the Apostle to the Corinthians: I Corinthians 7, verse 32 reads 'He [not she] that is unmarried [...] please the Lord'; verse 32 has 'The unmarried woman careth for the things of the Lord, that she may be holy in body and in spirit': Oliphant seems to have confused the two.

13. See Chalmers, p.200, n.9, and Keddie p.221, n.7.

14. Sir Arthur Helps, *Friends in Council*, 1859: a series of essays on the conduct of life.

15. The Infant Custody Act of 1839 made provision for children of under seven to reside with their mother but only if the Lord Chancellor agreed to it and only if the mother was of good character. The Matrimonial Causes Act of 1857 finally took divorce in England completely out of the hands of the Ecclesiastical courts but retained most of the existing inequalities between men and women. Men could divorce their wives for adultery alone but women had to prove the additional aggravation of desertion, cruelty, incest, rape, sodomy or bestiality. There were some minor improvements in the condition of judicially separated or divorced wives but perhaps the most significant difference was that the courts were now empowered to award care of young children to either parent as they saw fit and to guarantee visiting rights. In practice, however, the new Divorce Court was cautious and conservative: it tended to award care of young children (under 14) to the mother provided that she were the innocent party. But a woman judged guilty of adultery continued to be denied both care and access. It was not until the Guardianship Act of 1973 that the mother was given the same legal authority over a child as the father. In Scotland the situation on adultery as grounds for divorce had been different for some time. Since 1560 both the ecclesiastical law and the civil law of Scotland recognised adultery or malicious desertion for four or more years by either husband or wife as sufficient grounds for divorce; it was also much cheaper to obtain a divorce. For further detail about Marriage and Divorce Laws see Lawrence Stone, *The Road to Divorce: England 1530-1987* (Oxford: Oxford University Press, 1990) and Colin S. Gibson, *Dissolving Wedlock* (London: Routledge, 1994).

Isabella Bird Bishop (1831–1904)

Isabella Lucy Bird became one of the most celebrated of Victorian travellers and travel writers, ultimately in 1891 a Fellow of the Royal Scottish Geographical Society and in 1892 the first female Fellow of the Royal Geographical Society. She was the eldest child of the Rev. Edward Bird and his second wife Dora, second daughter of the Rev. Marmaduke Lawson of Boroughbridge. She was born on 15 October 1831 and was brought up in the evangelical tradition of both her parents. Her physical feats and her drive to travel derived paradoxically from the very conditions that one might have imagined would have prevented any such career: she suffered throughout her life from a spinal complaint but faced the problem by living much in the open air and becoming a talented and fearless horsewoman. Her first trip was made in 1854 to a cousin in Prince Edward Island. She recorded the trip, extended to take in Canada and the United States, in *The Englishwoman in America*, published in 1856 by John Murray. From this point until the end of her life, she travelled in improbable places like Korea and China and Japan with an open mind and yet rigid principles, while remaining, of course, secure about many aspects of British superiority.

Isabella from an early age made frequent visits to Scotland and when her father died in 1858, she moved with her mother and only sister, Henrietta, to Edinburgh. Isabella and Henrietta continued to live together after their mother's death and since Henrietta had a cottage at Tobermory on the Island of Mull, Isabella became involved with the welfare, social and spiritual, of the Highland people. She worked with Lady Gordon Cathcart to facilitate crofter emigration to Canada between 1862 and 1866 and argued the cause of the impoverished in magazine articles. Similarly she wrote about the slums and poverty of Edinburgh in *Notes on Old Edinburgh*. By the time her sister died in 1880 she had already visited Australia, New Zealand, the Sandwich Islands, the Rocky Mountains, Japan, the Malay Peninsula, Cairo and the Sinai Peninsula where she contracted typhoid. In the year after her sister's death she married her sister's former medical adviser, Dr John Bishop. He was ten years younger than she, but despite this and her uncertain health, Dr Bishop predeceased his wife by 18 years, dying after a long illness at Cannes in 1886.

Isabella Bird Bishop continued to travel and write. She studied medicine, was an enthusiastic photographer and was baptised to consecrate herself to the missionary cause which she saw as a necessary measure to combat what she described in *A Traveller's Testimony* as 'the desperate needs of the un-Christianised world'. During her travels she founded a number of hospitals, including the John Bishop Memorial Hospital in Kashmir and the Henrietta Bird Hospital for Women near Amritsar in the Punjab; three more hospitals were founded as memorials to her family and husband, one in Korea and two in China. She also founded an orphanage in Japan.

She died in Edinburgh on 7 October 1904 and was buried in the Dean cemetery there. In the following year a memorial clock to her sister's memory was erected in Tobermory in obedience to Isabella Bishop's bequest. As a rest from her travels the Highland experience had continued to offer her isolation, sometimes excessive, and the opportunity for anthropological observation. In December 1880 she wrote to her publisher, John Murray:

The great drawback of Mull in the winter is the irregular and often suspended post, as, for instance, there have been two days within a week in which the postboat has been unable to cross, and almost always when that occurs the gale has been severe enough to prostrate a number of Mull telegraph poles. Thus, amidst howling storms, without letters, newspapers, or telegraph possibilities, the isolation is very trying; but my nerves are so shattered that I need complete rest, and that I have here, with sufficient amount of human interest to make the endurance of solitude wholesome. The Highlanders have some very charming qualities, but in cunning, moral timidity, and plausibility they remind me of savages of rather a low type.

Yet it is clear that in her own way Isabella Bird is attached to her savages of rather a low type from whatever part of the globe.

That Isabella Bird Bishop was an extraordinary woman is too obvious to remark. Yet it perhaps also needs to be said, given current tendencies to debunk various nineteenth-century legends, that her illnesses were far from imaginary and that she wrote some of her work literally lying on her back. Her courage and determination and sympathy were also wholly unsentimental as the sharp and tart comments in the extracts will indicate.

Isabella Bird Bishop, *The Englishwoman in America* (London: John Murray, 1856); *A Revival in America*, by an English Eye-witness (London: James Nisbet & co., 1858); *The Aspects of Religion in the United States of America*, 1859; *Notes on Old Edinburgh*, (Odds and Ends, no.21: 1869); *The Hawaiian Archipelago* (London: John Murray, 1875); *A Lady's Life in the Rocky Mountains* (London: John Murray, 1879; reprinted London: Virago, 1982); *The Golden Chersonese; and the Way Thither* (London: John Murray, 1883); *Unbeaten Tracks in Japan* (London: John Murray, 1885; Tokyo: Edition Synapse & Bristol: Ganesha Pub., 1997); *Journeys in Persia and Kurdistan* (London: John Murray, 1891); *Heathen Claims and Christian Duty* (London: Morgan & Scott, 1894); *Among the Tibetans* (London, 1894); *Japan and the Faith of Christendom* (Exeter & London: Townsend, 1898); *Korea and Her Neighbours* (London: John Murray, 1898); *The Yangtze Valley and Beyond* (London: John Murray, 1898); *Chinese Pictures: Notes on Photographs Made in China* (London: Cassell & co., 1900); *A Traveller's Testimony* (London: The Church Missionary Society, 1905); *Collected Travel Writings*, ed. Olive Checkland (Ganesha Pub., 1997)

Further Reading:

Evelyn Bach, 'A Traveller in Skirts: Quest and Conquest in the Travel Narratives of Isabella Bird', *Canadian Review of Comparative Literature/Revue Canadienne de Litterature Comparée*, vol. 22, no. 3-4, (Sept-Dec, 1995) 587-600

Olive Checkland, *Isabella Bird (1831-1904)* (Aberdeen: Scottish Cultural Press, 1996)

Louise von Glehn Creighton, *Some Famous Women* (London: Longmans, Green and co., 1909)

Anne Gatti, *Isabella Bird Bishop* (London: Hamish Hamilton, 1988)

Mignon Rittenhouse, *Seven Women Explorers* (Philadelphia: Lippincott, 1964)

Anna M. Stoddart, *The Life of Isabella Bird (Mrs Bishop)* (London: John Murray, 1906)

Marion Tinling, *Women into the Unknown: A Sourcebook on Women Explorers and Travellers* (New York: Greenwood Press, 1989)

DNB; *DLB* 166; *HSWW*; Todd 2

From *A Lady's Life in the Rocky Mountains*. Extracts are from the 4th edition, John Murray, 1881.

Isabella Bird's description of her dress shows her perhaps a little short of a sense of the ridiculous, yet she is obviously right when she says that her costume has proved serviceable
November 27, 1879
For the benefit of other lady travellers, I wish to explain that my 'Hawaiian riding dress' is the 'American Lady's Mountain Dress', a half-fitting jacket, a skirt reaching to the ankles, and full Turkish trousers gathered into frills which fall over the boots, – a thoroughly serviceable and feminine costume for mountaineering and other rough travelling in any part of the world. I add this explanation to the prefatory note, together with a rough sketch of the costume, in consequence of an erroneous statement in the *Times* of November 22nd.

The body of the narrative is written as letters to her sister. Like all her travel writing it is packed with both incident and reflection: I have tried in these extracts simply to give something of its flavour.
CHEYENNE, WYOMING, *September 7* [1873]
As night came on the cold intensified, and the stove in the parlour attracted every one. A San Francisco lady, much 'got up' in paint, emerald green velvet, Brussels lace, and diamonds, rattled continuously for the amusement of the company, giving descriptions of persons and scenes in a racy Western twang, without the slightest scruple as to what she said. In a few years Tahoe will be inundated in summer with similar vulgarity, owing to its easiness of access. I sustained the reputation which our countrywomen bear in America by looking a 'perfect guy'; and feeling that I was a salient point for the speaker's next sally, I was relieved when the landlady, a ladylike Englishwoman, asked me to join herself and her family in the bar-room, where we had much talk about the neighbourhood and its wild beasts, especially bears. The forest is full of them, but they seem never to attack people unless when wounded, or much aggravated by dogs, or a young she-bear thinks you are going to molest her young.

I dreamt of bears so vividly that I woke with a furry death-hug at my throat, but feeling quite refreshed. When I mounted my horse after breakfast the sun was high and the air so keen and intoxicating that, giving the animal his head, I galloped up and down hill, feeling completely tireless. Truly, that air is the elixir of life. I had a glorious ride back to Truckee. The road was not as solitary as the day before. In a deep part of the forest the horse snorted and reared, and I saw a cinnamon-coloured bear with two cubs cross the track ahead of me. I tried to keep the horse quiet that the mother might acquit me of any designs upon her lolloping children, but I was glad when the ungainly, long-haired party crossed the river. Then I met a team, the driver of which stopped and said he was glad that I had not gone to Cornelian Bay, it was such a bad trail, and hoped I had enjoyed Tahoe. The driver of another team stopped and asked if I had seen any bears. Then a man heavily armed, a hunter probably, asked me if I were the English tourist who had 'happened on' a 'grizzlie' yesterday. Then I saw a lumberer taking his dinner on a rock in the river, who 'touched his hat' and brought me a draught of ice-cold water, which I could hardly drink owing to the fractiousness of the horse, and gathered me some mountain pinks, which I admired. I mention these little incidents to indicate the habit of respectful courtesy to women which prevails in that region. These men might have been excused for speaking in a somewhat free-and-easy tone to a lady riding alone, and in an unwonted fashion. Womanly dignity and manly respect for women are the salt of any society in this wild West.

[…]

CHEYENNE, WYOMING, *September 8.*

Precisely at 11 p.m. the huge Pacific train, with its heavy bell tolling, thundered up to the door of the Truckee House, and on presenting my ticket at the double door of a 'Silver Palace' car, the slippered steward, whispering low, conducted me to my berth – a luxurious bed three and a half feet wide, with a hair mattress on springs, fine linen sheets, and costly California blankets. The twenty-four inmates of the car were all invisible, asleep behind rich curtains. It was a true Temple of Morpheus. Profound sleep was the object to which everything was dedicated. Four silver lamps hanging from the roof, and burning low, gave a dreamy light. On each side of the centre passage, rich rep curtains, green and crimson, stripped with gold, hung from silver bars running near the roof, and trailed on the soft Axminster carpet. The temperature was carefully kept at 70°. It was 29° outside. Silence and freedom from jolting were secured by double doors and windows, costly and ingenious arrangements of springs and cushions, and a speed limited to eighteen miles an hour.

As I lay down, the gallop under the dark pines, the frosty moon, the forest fires, the flaring lights and roaring din of Truckee faded as dreams fade, and eight hours later a pure, pink dawn divulged a level blasted region, with grey sage brush growing out of a soil encrusted with alkali, and bounded on either side by low glaring ridges. All though that day we travelled under a cloudless sky over solitary glaring plains, and stopped twice at solitary, glaring frame houses, where coarse, greasy meals, infested by lazy flies, were provided at a dollar per head. By evening we were running across the continent on a bee line, and I sat for an hour on the rear platform of the rear car to enjoy the wonderful beauty of the sunset and the atmosphere. Far as one could see in the crystalline air it was nothing but desert. The jagged Humboldt ranges flaming in the sunset, with snow in their clefts, though forty-five miles off, looked within an easy canter. The bright metal track, purpling like all else in the cool distance, was all that linked one with eastern or western civilisation. The next morning, when the steward unceremoniously turned us out of our berths soon after sunrise, we were running down upon the Great Salt Lake, bounded by the white Wahsatch ranges. Along its shores, by means of irrigation, Mormon industry has compelled the ground to yield fine crops of hay and barley; and we passed several cabins, from which, even at that early hour, Mormons, each with two or three wives, were going forth to their day's work. The women were ugly and their shapeless blue dresses hideous. At the Mormon town of Ogden we changed cars, and again traversed dusty plains, white and glaring, varied by muddy streams and rough, arid valleys, now and then narrowing into canyons. By common consent the windows were kept closed to exclude the fine white alkaline dust, which is very irritating to the nostrils. The journey became more and more wearisome as we ascended rapidly over immense plains and wastes of gravel destitute of mountain boundaries, and with only here and there a 'knob' or 'butte' to break the monotony. The wheel marks of the trail to Utah often ran parallel with the track, and bones of oxen were bleaching in the sun, the remains of those 'whose carcasses fell in the wilderness' on the long and drouthy journey. The daybreak of today (Sunday) found us shivering at Fort Laramie, a frontier post dismally situated at a height of 7000 feet. Another 1000 feet over gravelly levels brought us to Sherman, the highest level reached by this railroad. From this point eastward the streams fall into the Atlantic. The ascent of these apparently level plateaus is called 'crossing the Rocky Mountains', but I have seen nothing of the range, except two peaks like teeth lying low on the distant horizon. It became mercilessly cold; some people thought it snowed, but I only saw rolling billows of fog. Lads passed through the cars the whole morning, selling newspapers, novels, cacti, lollypops, pop corn, pea nuts and ivory ornaments, so that, having lost all reckoning of the days, I never knew that it was Sunday till the cars pulled up at the door of the hotel in this detestable place.

The surrounding plains are endless and verdureless. The scanty grasses were long ago turned into sun-cured hay by the fierce summer heats. There is neither tree nor bush, the sky is grey, the earth buff, the air *blae* and windy, and clouds of coarse granite dust sweep across the prairie and smother the settlement. Cheyenne is described as 'a God-forsaken, God-forgotten place'. That it forgets God is written on its face. It owes its existence to the railroad, and has diminished in population, but is a depot for a large amount of the necessaries of life which are distributed through the scantily settled districts within distances of 300 miles by 'freight wagons', each drawn by four horses or mules, or double that number of oxen. At times over 100 wagons, with double that number of teamsters, are in Cheyenne at once. A short time ago it was a perfect pandemonium, mainly inhabited by rowdies and desperadoes, the scum of advancing civilisation; and murders, stabbings, shootings, and pistol affrays were at times events of almost hourly occurrence in its drinking dens. But in the West, when things reach their worst, a sharp and sure remedy is provided. Those settlers who find the state of matters intolerable, organise themselves into a Vigilance Committee. 'Judge Lynch',[1] with a few feet of rope, appears on the scene, the majority crystallises round the supporters of order, warnings are issued to obnoxious people, simply bearing a scrawl of a tree with a man dangling from it, with such words as 'Clear out of this by 6 a.m., or –.' A number of the worst desperadoes are tried by a yet more summary process than a drumhead court-martial, 'strung up', and buried ignominiously. I have been told that 120 ruffians were disposed of in this way here in a single fortnight. Cheyenne is now as safe as Hilo,[2] and the interval between the most desperate lawlessness and the time when United States law, with its corruption and feebleness, comes upon the scene is one of comparative security and good order. Piety is not the *forte* of Cheyenne. The roads resound with atrocious profanity, and the rowdysim of the saloons and bar-rooms is repressed, not extirpated.

A lengthy and, because she is settled, slightly dull, passage deals with Bird Bishop's stay in Estes Park, Colorado. In November she moves on:

DEER VALLEY, *November*

To-night I am in a beautiful place like a Dutch farm – large, warm, bright, clean, with abundance of clean food, and a clean, cold little bedroom to myself. But it is very hard to write, for two free-tongued, noisy Irishwomen, who keep a miners' boarding-house in South Park, and are going to winter quarters in a freight wagon, are telling the most fearful stories of violence, vigilance committees, Lynch law, and 'stringing', that I ever heard. It turns one's blood cold only to think that where I travel in perfect security, only a short time ago men were being shot like skunks. At the mining towns up above this nobody is thought anything of who has not killed a man – i.e. in a certain set. These women had a boarder, only fifteen, who thought he could not be anything till he had shot somebody, and they gave an absurd account of the lad dodging about with a revolver, and not getting up courage enough to insult any one, till at last he hid himself in the stable and shot the first Chinaman who entered. Things up there are just in that initial state which desperadoes love. A man accidentally shoves another in a saloon, or says a rough word at meals, and the challenge, 'first finger on the trigger', warrants either in shooting the other at any subsequent time without the formality of a duel. Nearly all the shooting affrays arise from the most trivial causes in saloons and bar-rooms. The deeper quarrels, arising from jealousy or revenge, are few, and are usually about some woman not worth fighting for. At Alma and Fairplay vigilance committees have lately been formed, and when men act outrageously and make themselves generally obnoxious they receive a letter with a drawing of a tree, a man hanging from it, and a coffin below, on which is written 'Forewarned'. They 'git' in a few hours. When I said I spent last night at Hall's Gulch there was quite a chorus of exclamations. My host there, they all said, would be 'strung' before long. Did I know that a man was 'strung' there yesterday? Had I not seen him hanging? He was on the big tree by the house, they said. Certainly, had I known what a ghastly burden that tree bore, I would have encountered the ice and gloom of the gulch rather than have slept there. They then told me a horrid tale of crime and violence. This man had even shocked the morals of the Alma crowd, and had a notice served on him by the vigilants, which had the desired effect, and he migrated to Hall's Gulch. As the tale runs, the Hall's Gulch miners were resolved either not to have a groggery or to limit the number of such places, and when this ruffian set one up he was 'forewarned'. It seems, however, to have been merely a pretext for getting rid of him, for it was hardly a crime of which even Lynch law could take cognisance. He was overpowered by numbers, and, with circumstances of great horror, was tried and strung on that tree within an hour.[3]

Bird Bishop discusses the issue of drink and potential prohibition; she admits that the districts in which drink is prohibited are almost crime free but points out that the worship of smartness comes close to admiration of cheating:

The truth of the proverbial saying, 'There is no God west of the Missouri', is everywhere manifest. The 'almighty dollar' is the true divinity, and its worship is universal. 'Smartness' is the quality thought most of. The boy who 'gets on' by cheating at his lessons is praised for being a 'smart boy', and his satisfied parents foretell that he will make a 'smart man'. A man who overreaches his neighbour, but who does it so cleverly that the law cannot take hold of him, wins an envied reputation as a 'smart man', and stories of this species of smartness are told admiringly round every stove. Smartness is but the initial stage of swindling, and the clever swindler who evades or defies the weak and often corruptly administered laws of the States excites unmeasured admiration among the masses.[4]

Taking a short cut over the prairie from Deer Valley to Denver she passes through an encampment of the Ute Indians:[5]
about 500 strong, a disorderly and dirty huddle of lodges, ponies, men, squaws, children, skins, bones, and raw meat.

The Americans will never solve the Indian problem till the Indian is extinct. They have treated then after a fashion which has intensified their treachery and 'devilry' as enemies, and as friends reduces them to a degraded pauperism, devoid of the very first elements of civilisation. The only difference between the savage and the civilised Indian is that the latter carries firearms and gets drunk on whisky. The Indian Agency has been a sink of fraud and corruption; it is said that barely thirty per cent of the allowance ever reaches those for whom it is voted; and the complaints of shoddy blankets, damaged flour, and worthless firearms are universal. 'To get rid of the Injuns' is the phrase used everywhere. Even their 'reservations' do not escape seizure practically; for if gold 'breaks out' on them they are 'rushed', and their possessors are either compelled to accept land farther west or are shot off and driven off. One of the surest agents in their destruction is vitriolised whisky. An attempt had recently been made to cleanse the Augean stable of the Indian Department, but it has met with signal failure, the usual result in America of every effort to purify the official atmosphere. Americans specially love superlatives. The phrases 'biggest in the world', 'finest in the world', are on all lips. Unless the President is a strong man they will soon come to boast that their government is composed of the 'biggest scoundrels' in the world.

At the end of her travels Bird Bishop reflects on the need in the settlements she has passed through for her own special brand of feminism:
I have seen a great deal of the roughest class of men both on sea and land during the last two years, and the more important I think the 'mission' of every quiet, refined, self-respecting woman – the more mistaken I think those who would forfeit it by noisy self-assertion, masculinity, or fastness. In all this wild West the influence of woman is second only in its benefits to the influence of religion, and where the last unhappily does not exist the first continually exerts its restraining power. The last morning came. I cleaned up my room and sat at the window watching the red and gold of one of the most glorious of winter sunrises, and the slow lighting-up of one peak after another. I have written that this scenery is not lovable, but I love it.

From *Unbeaten Tracks in Japan: An Account of Travels in the Interior Including Visits to the Aborigines of Yezo and the Shrine of Nikkô,* 1911:

On arrival in Yokohama:
The first thing that impressed me on landing was that there were no loafers, and that all the small, ugly, kindly-looking, shrivelled, bandy-legged, round-shouldered, concave-chested, poor-looking beings in the streets had some affairs of their own to mind. At the top of the landing-steps there was a portable restaurant, a neat and most compact thing, with charcoal stove, cooking and eating utensils complete; but it looked as if it were made by and for dolls, and the mannikin who kept it was not five feet high. At the custom-house we were attended to by minute officials in blue uniforms of European pattern and leather boots; very civil creatures who opened and examined our trunks carefully, and strapped them up again, contrasting pleasingly with the insolent and rapacious officials who perform the same duties at New York.

Outside were about fifty of the now well-known *jin-ri-ki-shas*, and the air was full of a buzz produced by the rapid reiteration of this uncouth word by fifty tongues. This conveyance, as you know, is a feature of Japan, growing in importance every day. It was only invented seven years ago and already there are nearly 23,000 in one city, and men can make so much more by drawing them than by almost any kind of skilled labour, that thousands of fine young men desert agricultural pursuits and flock into the towns to make draught-animals of themselves, though it is said that the average duration of a man's life after he takes to running is only five years, and that the runners fall victims in large numbers to aggravated forms of heart and lung disease. Over tolerably level ground a good runner can trot forty miles a day, at a rate of about four miles an hour. They are registered and taxed at 8s. a year for one carrying two persons, and 4s. for one which carries one only, and there is a regular tariff for time and distance.

The *Kuruma*, or ji-ri-ki-sha,[6] consists of a light perambulator body, an adjustable hood of oiled paper, a velvet or cloth lining and cushion, a well for parcels under the seat, two high slim wheels, and a pair of shafts connected by a bar at the ends. The body is usually lacquered and decorated according to its owner's taste. Some show little except polished brass, others are altogether inlaid with shells known as Venus's ear, and others are gaudily painted with contorted dragons, or groups of peonies, hydrangeas, chrysanthemums, and mythical personages. They cost from £2 upwards. The shafts rest on the ground at a steep incline as you get in – it must require much practice to enable one to mount with ease or dignity – the runner lifts them up, gets into them, gives the body a good tilt backwards, and goes off at a smart trot. They are drawn by one, two, or three men, according to the speed desired by the occupants. When rain comes on, the man puts up the hood, and ties you and it closely up in a covering of oiled paper, in which you are invisible. At night, whether running or standing still, they carry prettily-painted circular paper lanterns 18 inches long. It is most comical to see stout, florid, solid-looking merchants, missionaries, male and female, fashionably-dressed ladies, armed with card cases, Chinese compradores, and Japanese peasant men and women flying along Main Street, which is like the decent respectable High Street of a dozen forgotten country towns in England, in happy unconsciousness of the ludicrousness of their appearance; racing, chasing, crossing each other, their lean, polite, pleasant runners in their great hats shaped like inverted bowls, their incomprehensible blue tights, and their short blue overshirts with badges or characters in white upon them, tearing along, their yellow faces streaming with perspiration, laughing, shouting, and avoiding collisions by a mere shave.

BIRATORI, YEZO, August 24

Bird Bishop devotes a substantial part of her narrative to a description of the way of life of the Ainos of Yezo.[7] *She remarks that she thinks that the most interesting of her travelling experiences has been 'the living for three days and two nights in an Aino hut, and seeing and sharing the daily life of complete savages, who go on with their ordinary occupations just as if I were not among them'. It is impossible to do justice to the detail she provides and so I give her conclusions which have the characteristic mixture of tough-mindedness and sentiment that is her hallmark:*

I expected to have written out my notes on the Ainos in the comparative quiet and comfort of Sraufuto, but [various delays] and the non-arrival of the horses, have compelled me to accept Aino hospitality for another night, which involves living on tea and potatoes, for my stock of food is exhausted. In some respects I am glad to remain longer, as it enables me to go over my stock of words, as well as my notes, with the chief, who is intelligent, and it is a pleasure to find that his statements confirm those which have been made by the young men. The glamour which at first disguises the inherent barrenness of savage life has had time to pass away, and I see it in all its nakedness as a life not much raised above the necessities of animal existence, timid, monotonous, barren of good, dark, dull, 'without hope, and without God in the world'; though at its lowest and worst considerably higher and better than that of many other aboriginal races, and – must I say it? – considerably higher and better than that of thousands of the lapsed masses of our own great cities who are baptized into Christ's name, and are laid at last in holy ground, inasmuch as the Ainos are truthful, and on the whole, chaste, hospitable, honest, reverent, and kind to the aged. Drinking, their great vice, is not, as among us, in antagonism to their religion, but is actually a part of it, and as such would be exceptionally difficult to eradicate.

The early darkness has once again come on, and once again the elders have assembled round the fire in two long lines, with the younger men at the ends, Pipchari [an adopted son of the chief], who yesterday sat in the place of honour and was helped to food first as the newest arrival, taking his place as the youngest at the end of the right-hand row. The birch-bark chips beam with fitful glare, the evening *saké* bowls are filled, the fire-god and the garlanded god receive their libations, the ancient woman, still sitting like a Fate, splits bark, and the younger women knot it, and the log-fire lights up as magnificent a set of venerable heads as painter or sculptor would desire to see, – heads, full of – what? They have no history, their traditions are scarcely worthy of the name, they claim descent from a dog, their houses and persons swarm with vermin, they are sunk in the grossest ignorance, they have no letters or any numbers above a thousand, they are clothed in the bark of trees and the untanned skins of beasts, they worship the bear, the sun, moon, fire, water, and I know not what, they are uncivilisable and altogether irreclaimable savages, yet they are attractive, and in some ways fascinating, and I hope I shall never forget the music of their low, sweet voices, the soft light of their mild, brown eyes, and the wonderful sweetness of their smile.

NOTES

1. The origin of the expression 'Lynch law' is still disputed. Most authorities favour Charles Lynch (1736-96), a Virginia planter who was indemnified by an Act of the Virginia Assembly for having summarily tried, fined, imprisoned or otherwise punished a number of allegedly disruptive Tory Loyalists. Others favour William Lynch of Pittsylvania, Virginia, who in 1780 signed a pact with several other men of Pittsylvania County, Virginia, to track down and punish a band of outlaws. William Lynch later claimed to have been the source of the phrase but his behaviour was less generally known than that of Charles. See *Dictionary of American Biography* (Oxford: Oxford University Press, 1999-). Judge Lynch is the imaginary authority from whom sentences are said to proceed.

2. On Hawaii.

3. 'Public opinion approved this execution, regarding it as a fitting retribution for a series of crimes': I.B.B.'s note.

4. 'MAY 1878. – I am copying this letter in the city of San Francisco, and regretfully add a strong emphasis to what I have written above. The best and most thoughtful among Americans would endorse these remarks with shame and pain.' – I.B.B.

5. The Ute from whom the state of Utah takes its name are Shoshonean speaking native Americans from Colorado and eastern Utah. After the Indian wars (1864-70) most of the Ute were placed in reservations. By the second half of the twentieth century there were about 1,700 in Colorado and 2,660 in Utah.

6. '*Kuruma*, literally a wheel or vehicle, is the word commonly used by the *Ji-ri-ki-sha* men and other Japanese for the "man-power-carriage" [...] From *Kuruma* naturally comes *Kurumaya* for the *kuruma* runner' (I.B.B.'s note). *Ji-ri-ki-sha* is the Chinese word which gives us 'rickshaw'.

7. Yezo is the northern island that we now know as Hokkaido. The Ainos or Ainu have not retained their separateness, although Bird Bishop thought that they might. They are a Caucasoid people and were traditionally distinct from the surrounding Mongoloid peoples. But intermixture with the Japanese has changed them a great deal, particularly they have largely lost the hairiness that Bird Bishop remarks. Their language is not related to any other known language.

Ellen Johnston (1836?–1874?)

Ellen Johnston was known throughout her life as a poet as 'The Factory Girl'. As the following autobiography indicates, she was born in Hamilton where her father was a stone-mason. She began to write when still young and under middle-class patronage (the first edition of her poems has a testimonial by the Rev. George Gilfillan of Dundee) and produced on subscription two editions of her poems in 1867 and 1869. The second edition acknowledges 'the gift of Five Pounds from Her Majesty Queen Victoria, and the grant of Fifty Pounds from the Royal Bounty Fund, by the Right Honourable Benjamin Disraeli, Her Majesty's late Prime Minister, which enabled me to furnish a home and discharge the pecuniary obligations I had unavoidably contracted for my maintenance in Glasgow, while suffering from a delicate constitution and factory life, to which I have long been a victim'. Ellen Johnston's English poetry is often sentimental and technically conservative but the voice of true feeling gleams through the conventionality of its expression. Like Janet Hamilton she celebrated Garibaldi's visit to Britain, comparing him to Wallace who 'purchased Scotland's freedom with the ransom of his life' and hoping that he might visit Dundee where she was then living. Ellen Johnston's poems provoked poetic addresses from other working men and women to which she replied in turn, establishing a culture of cheerful compliment. 'The Last Sark', her most anthologised poem, is radical in feeling and forthright in expression and until recently, when the reclamation of working-class voices has become a widespread project, its fame unfairly relegated her other verse. According to Irving 'this tender-hearted singer was compelled to take refuge in the Barony poorhouse, Glasgow, and died when quite young, soothed by the attention of only a few friends, who knew her career, and sympathised with her troubles no less than with her gifts'. Gustave Klaus has found a record of death of Helen Johnston in the Barony poorhouse in 1874, not 1873, and this is probably the poet.

Both editions of her poems are preceded by an autobiography. I give the whole text of the version in the first edition. The second version omits any reference to her illegitimate child and removes the detail of her persecution by her female fellow workers after her successful court case. Possibly her middle-class supporters suggested that she would achieve a more pleasing image with these omissions. What makes Ellen Johnston's story of her life so moving is that her real sufferings emerge quite clearly in spite of the absence of any suitable discourse to convey them. The abuse by her step father is shrouded in sentimental clichés but her sheer endurance rescues her story from self pity and, given her handicaps in terms of the absence of moral, and educational support, her achievement is remarkable.

Ellen Johnston, *Autobiography, Poems and Songs of Ellen Johnston, the Factory Girl* (Glasgow: William Love, 1867; 2nd ed. 1869)

Further Reading
Florence S. Boos, '"Cauld Engle-Cheek": Working-Class Women Poets in Victorian Scotland', *Victorian Poetry*, 33, no.1 (Spring, 1995) 53-73

H. Gustav Klaus, *Factory Girl: Ellen Johnston and Working-Class Poetry in Victorian Scotland* (Scottish Studies International, 23) (Frankfurt am Main; New York: Peter Lang, 1998)

Julia Swindells, *Victorian Writing and Working Women: The Other Side of Silence* (Minneapolis: University of Minnesota Press, 1985)

Susan Zlotnick, '"A Thousand Times I'd Be a Factory Girl": Dialect, Domesticity, and Working-Class Women's Poetry in Victorian Britain', *Victorian Studies:* vol. 35 no. 1, (Autumn 1991)

DLB 199; *HSWW*; Irving

From *Autobiography, Poems and Songs*, 1867:

I have retained some of the period punctuation and capitalisation which lend a tone to the piece.

AUTOBIOGRAPHY OF ELLEN JOHNSTON, 'THE FACTORY GIRL'

GENTLE READER, – On the suggestion of a friend, and the expressed wishes of some subscribers, I now submit the following brief sketch of my eventful life as an introduction to this long expected and patiently waited for volume of my Poems and Songs.

Like every other autobiographer, I can only relate the events connected with my parentage and infancy from the communicated evidence of witnesses of those events, but upon whose veracity I have full reliance.

I beg also to remind my readers that whatever my actions may have been, whether good, bad, or indifferent, that they were the results of instincts derived from the Creator, through the medium of my parents, and the character formed for me by the unavoidable influence of the TIME and COUNTRY of my BIRTH, and also by the varied conditions of life impressing themselves on my highly susceptible and sympathetic natures – physical, intellectual, and moral.

According to the evidence referred to, my father was James Johnston, second eldest son of James Johnston, canvas-weaver, Lochee, Dundee, where he learned the trade of a stone-mason. After which he removed to Glasgow, where he became acquainted with my mother, Mary Bilsland, second daughter of James Bilsland, residing in Muslin Street, and then well known as the Bridgeton Dyer.

I do not remember hearing my father's age, but my mother at the time of her marriage was only eighteen years old. I was the first and only child of their union, and was born in the Muir Wynd, Hamilton, in 183–, my father at the time being employed as a mason extending the northern wing of the Duke of Hamilton's Palace.

When the Duke was informed that my father was a poet, he familiarly used to call him Lord Byron, and, as I have been told, his Grace also used to take special notice of me when an infant in my mother's arms, as she almost daily walked around his domain.

When I was about seven months old my father's contract at Hamilton Palace was finished, and being of an active disposition, somewhat ambitious, proud, and independent, with some literary and scientific attainments, with a strong desire to become a teacher and publish a volume of his poetical works, he resolved to emigrate, engaged a passage to America for my mother and himself, and got all things ready for the voyage.

But when all the relatives and friends had assembled at the Broomielaw to give the farewell kiss and shake of the hand before going on board, my mother determined not to proceed, pressed me fondly to her bosom, exclaiming – 'I cannot, will not go, my child would die on the way;' and taking an affectionate farewell with my father, he proceeded on the voyage, and my mother fled from the scene and returned to her father's house, where she remained for some years, and supported herself by dressmaking and millinery.

Having given the evidence of others in respect to my parentage and infancy, let me now, gentle reader, state some of my own childhood's recollections, experience, and reflections thereon.

In my childhood, Bridgeton, now incorporated with the city of Glasgow, abounded with green fields and lovely gardens, which have since then been covered over with piles of buildings and tall chimneys. The ground on which the factory of Messrs Scott & Inglis stands was then a lovely garden, where I spent many, many happy hours with 'Black Bess', my doll, and 'Dainty Davie', my dog, with whom I climbed many a knowe and forded many a stream, till one day he left my side to follow a band of music, and we never met again; but for whose loss I deeply mourned, and for three successive nights wept myself asleep, for 'Dainty Davie' was the pride of my heart, for I could not live without something to love, and I loved before I knew the name of the nature or feeling which swelled my bosom.

Perhaps there are few who can take a retrospective view of their past lives, and through their mind's eye gaze on so many strange and mysterious incidents. Yes, gentle reader, I have suffered trials and wrongs that have but rarely fallen to the lot of woman. Mine were not the common trials of every day life, but like those strange romantic ordeals attributed to the imaginary heroines of 'Inglewood Forest'.[1]

Like the Wandering Jew,[2] I have mingled with the gay on the shores of France – I have feasted in the merry halls of England – I have danced on the shamrock soil of Erin's green isle – and I have sung the songs of the brave and the free in the woods and glens of dear old Scotland.

I have waited and watched the sun-set hour to meet my lover, and then with him wander by the banks of sweet winding Clutha [Clyde], when my muse has often been inspired when viewing the proud waving thistle bending to the breeze, or when the calm twilight hour was casting a halo of glory around the enchanting scene; yet in all these wanderings I never enjoyed true happiness.

Like Rasselas,[3] there was a dark history engraven on the tablet of my heart. Yes, dear reader, a dark shadow, as a pall, enshrouded my soul, shutting out life's gay sunshine from my bosom – a shadow which has haunted me like a vampire, but at least for the present must remain the mystery of my life.

Dear reader, I have wandered far away from my childhood's years. Yes, years that passed like a dream, unclouded and clear. Oh that I could recall them; but, alas! they are gone for ever. Still they linger in memory fresh and green as if they were yesterday. I can look back and see the opening chapters of my life – I can see the forms and faces, and hear their voices ringing in my ears – one sweet voice above the rest echoes like a seraph's song; but I dare not linger longer at present with those joyous hours and beloved forms that were then my guardian angels.

In the course of time my mother received some information of my father's death in America, and again married a power-loom tenter[4] when I was about eight years of age, till which time I may truly say that the only heartfelt sorrow I experienced was the loss of 'Dainty Davie'; but, alas! shortly after my mother's second marriage I was dragged, against my own will and the earnest pleadings and remonstrances of my maternal grandfather, from his then happy home to my stepfather's abode, next land to the Cross Keys Tavern, London Road.

HOW I BECAME THE FACTORY GIRL

About two months after my mother's marriage my stepfather having got work in a factory in Bishop Street, Anderston, they removed to North Street, where I spent the two last years of young life's sweet liberty – as it was during that time I found my way to Kelvin Grove, and there spent many happy hours in innocent mirth and glee – but 'time changes a' things'. My stepfather could not bear to see me longer basking in the sunshine of freedom, and therefore took me into the factory where he worked to learn power-loom weaving when about eleven years of age, from which time I became a factory girl; but no language can paint the suffering which I afterwards endured from my tormentor.

Before I was thirteen years of age I had read many of Sir Walter Scott's novels, and fancied I was a heroine of the modern style. I was a self-taught scholar, gifted with a considerable amount of natural knowledge for one of my years, for I had only been nine months at school when I could read the English language and Scottish dialect with almost any classic scholar; I had also read 'Wilson's Tales of the Border'; so that by reading so many love adventures my brain was fired with wild imaginations, and therefore resolved to bear with my own fate, and in the end gain a great victory.

I had also heard many say that I ought to have been an actress, as I had a flow of poetic language and a powerful voice, which was enough to inspire my young soul to follow the profession. In fact, I am one of those beings formed by nature for romance and mystery, and as such had many characters to imitate in the course of a day. In the residence of my stepfather I was a weeping willow, in the factory I was pensive and thoughtful, dreaming of the far off future when I would be hailed as a 'great star'. Then, when mixing with a merry company no one could be more cheerful, for I had learned to conceal my own cares and sorrows, knowing well that 'the mirth maker hath no sympathy with the grief weeper'.

By this time my mother had removed from Anderston to a shop in Tradeston, and my stepfather and myself worked in West Street Factory. When one morning early, in the month of June, I absconded from their house as the fox flies from the hunter's hounds, to the Paisley Canal, into which I was about submerging myself to end my sufferings and sorrow, when I thought I heard like the voice of him I had fixed my girlish love upon. I started and paused for a few moments, and the love of young life again prevailed over that of self-destruction, and I fled from the scene as the half-past five morning factory bells were ringing, towards the house of a poor woman in Rose Street, Hutchesontown, where, after giving her my beautiful earrings to pawn, I was made welcome, and on Monday morning following got work in Brown & M'Nee's factory, Commercial Road. I did not, however, remain long in my new lodgings, for on the Tuesday evening, while threading my way among the crowd at the shows, near the foot of the Saltmarket, and dreaming of the time when I would be an actress, I was laid hold of by my mother's eldest brother, who, after questioning me as to where I had been, and what I was doing, without receiving any satisfaction to his interrogations, compelled me to go with him to my mother, who first questioned me as to the cause of absconding, and then beat me till I felt as if my brain were on fire; but still I kept the secret in my own bosom. But had I only foreseen the wretched misery I was heaping upon my own head – had I heard the dreadful constructions the world was putting on my movements – had I seen the shroud of shame and sorrow I was weaving around myself, I should then have disclosed the mystery of my life, but I remained silent and kept my mother and friends in ignorance of the cause which first disturbed my peace and made me run away from her house for safety and protection.

However, I consented to stay again with my mother for a time, and resolved to avoid my tormentor as much as possible.

Weeks and months thus passed away, but, alas! the sun never shed the golden dawn of peaceful morn again around my mother's hearth. Apart from my home sorrows I had other trials to encounter. Courted for my conversation and company by the most intelligent of the factory workers, who talked to me about poets and poetry, which the girls around me did not understand, consequently they wondered, became jealous and told falsehoods about me. Yet I never fell out with them although I was a living martyr, and suffered all their insults. In fact, life had no charm for me but one, and that was my heart's first love. If a sunshine of pleasure ever fell upon me, it was in his company only for a few short moments, for nothing could efface from my memory the deep grief that pressed me to the earth. I often smiled when my heart was weeping – the gilded mask of merriment made me often appear happy in company when I was only playing the dissembler.

Dear reader, as this is neither the time nor place to give further details of my young eventful life, I will now bring you to my sixteenth year, when I was in the bloom of fair young maidenhood. Permit me, however, to state that during the three previous years of my life, over a part of which I am drawing a veil, I had run away five times from my tormentor, and during one of these elopements spent about six weeks in Airdrie, wandering often by Carron or Calder's beautiful winding banks. Oh! could I then have seen the glorious gems that have sprung up for me on those banks, and heard the poetic strains that have since been sung in my praise, what a balm they would have been to my bleeding heart, as I wandered around the Old Priestrig Pit and listened to its engine thundering the water up from its lowest depth. For days I have wandered the fields between Moodiesburn and Clifton Hill, wooing my sorry muse, then unknown in the world – except to a few, as a child of song – in silence looking forward to the day when the world would know my wrongs and prize my worth; and had it not been for the bright Star of hope which lingered near me and encouraged me onward, beyond doubt I would have been a suicide. 'Tis, however, strange in all my weary wanderings that I have always met with kind-hearted friends, and there were two who befriended me when I was a homeless wanderer in Airdrie. Fifteen years have passed since I saw their tears roll down the youthful cheeks and heard the heavy sigh that exploded from their sympathising hearts. But the best of friends must part, and I parted from them, perhaps never to meet again in this lovely world of sunshine and sorrow.

Dear reader, should your curiosity have been awakened to ask in what form fate had then so hardly dealt with the hapless 'Factory Girl,' this is my answer:– I was falsely accused by those who knew me as a fallen woman, while I was as innocent of the charge as an unborn babe. Oh! how hard to be blamed when the heart is spotless and the conscience clear. For years I submitted to this wrong, resolving to hold my false detractors at defiance.

While struggling under those misrepresentations, my first love also deserted me, but Another soon offered me his heart – without form of legal protection – and in a thoughtless moment I accepted him as my friend and protector, but, to use the words of a departed poet –

> When lovely woman stoops to folly,
> And finds too late that men betray,
> What can soothe her melancholy,
> What can wash her guilt away?

> The only art her guilt to cover,
> To hide her shame from every eye,
> To wring repentance from her lover,
> And sting his bosom, is to die.[5]

I did not, however, feel inclined to die when I could no longer conceal what the world falsely calls a woman's shame. No, on the other hand, I never loved life more dearly and longed for the hour when I would have something to love me – and my wish was realised by becoming the mother of a lovely daughter on the 14th of September, 1852.

No doubt every feeling mother thinks her own child lovely, but mine was surpassing so, and I felt as if I could begin all my past sorrows again if Heaven would only spare me my lovely babe to cheer my bleeding heart, for I never felt bound to earth till then; and as year succeeded year, 'My Mary Achin' grew like the wild daisy – fresh and fair – on the mountain side.[6]

As my circumstances in life changed, I placed my daughter under my mother's care when duty called me forth to turn the poetic gift that nature had given me to a useful and profitable account, for which purpose I commenced with vigorous zeal to write my poetical pieces, and sent them to the weekly newspapers for insertion, until I became extensively known and popular. As an instance, in 1854 the Glasgow Examiner published a song of mine, entitled 'Lord Raglan's Address to the Allied Armies,' which made my name popular throughout Great Britain and Ireland;[7] but as my fame spread my health began to fail, so that I could not work any longer in a factory.

My stepfather was unable longer to work, and my mother was also rendered a suffering object; my child was then but an infant under three years of age, and I, who had been the only support of the family, was informed by my medical adviser that, unless I took a change of air, I would not live three months.

Under these circumstances, what was to be done? I did not then want to die, although I had wished to do so a thousand times before, to relieve me from unmerited slander and oppression.

Many sleepless nights did I pass, thinking what to try to bring relief to the afflicted household – although I did not consider myself in duty bound to struggle against the stern realities of nature, and sacrifice my own young life for those whose sympathies for me had long been seared and withered. Yet, I could not unmoved look upon the pale face of poverty, for their means were entirely exhausted, without hope to lean upon. Neither could I longer continue in the factory without certain death to myself, and I had never learned anything else.

Under those conflicting conditions and feelings, one night as I lay in bed, almost in despair, I prayed fervently that some idea how to act would be revealed to me, when suddenly I remembered that I had a piece of poetry entitled 'An Address to Napier's Dockyard, Langfield, Finnieston,' which a young man had written for me in imitation of copperplate engraving, and that piece I addressed to Robert Napier, Esq., Shandon, Garelochhead, who was then in Paris, where it was forwarded to him. Having written to my employer for my character, which was satisfactory, Mr Napier sent me a note to call at a certain office in Oswald Street, Glasgow, and draw as much money as would set me up in some small business, to see if my health would revive. According to the good old gentleman's instructions, I went as directed, and sought L.10, which was freely given to me; and I believe had I asked double the amount I would have readily received it.

Dear reader, I need not tell you what a godsend those ten pounds were to my distressed family, and kept me out of the factory during five months; after which I resumed work in Messrs Galbraith's Mill, St Rollox, Glasgow, where I continued till July, 1857, when my health again sank; and for change of air I went to Belfast, where I remained two years, during which time I became so notorious for my poetic exploits that the little boys and girls used to run after me to get a sight of 'the little Scotch girl' their fathers and mothers spoke so much about.

In 1859 I left Belfast and went to Manchester, where I worked three months, and then returned again to my native land, much improved in body and mind.

New scenes and systems made a great change in my nature. I became cheerful, and sought the society of mirth makers, so that few would have taken me for the former moving monument of melancholy. I had again resumed work at Galbraith's factory, and all went on well; peace and good-will reigned in our household; the past seemed forgiven and forgotten; and the 'Factory Girl' was a topic of the day for her poetical productions in the public press, but the shadow of death was hovering behind all this gladsome sunshine.

My mother had been an invalid for several years, and, to add to her sorrow, a letter had come from her supposed dead husband, my father, in America, after an absence of twenty years, inquiring for his wife and child; on learning their fate he became maddened with remorse, and, according to report, drank a death-draught from a cup in his own hand, in the village of Cherryfield, State of Maine, North America; and my mother, after becoming aware of the mystery of my life, closed her weary pilgrimage on earth on 25th May, 1861; and disappointed of a promised home and husband, which I was not destined to enjoy, I therefore made up my mind to go to Dundee, where my father's sister resided, whose favourite I was when a child.

Dear reader, were I to give details of my trials, disappointments, joys and sorrows, since I came to 'bonnie Dundee', they would be, with a little embellishment, a romance of real life, sufficient to fill three ordinary volumes. Suffice it here to say, that after myself and child had suffered neglect and destitution for some time, I got work in the Verdant Factory, where the cloth I wove was selected by my master as a sample for others to imitate, until, on the 5th of December, 1863, I was discharged by the foreman without any reason assigned or notice given, in accordance with the rules of the work. Smarting under this treatment, I summoned the foreman into Court for payment of a week's wages, and gained the case. But if I was envied by my sister sex in the Verdant Works for my talent before this affair happened, they hated me with a perfect hatred after I had struggled for and gained my rights. In fact, on account of that simple and just law-suit, I was persecuted beyond description – lies of the most vile and disgusting character were told upon me, till even my poor ignorant deluded sister sex went so far as to assault me on the streets, spit in my face, and even several times dragged the skirts from my dress. Anonymous letters were also sent to all the foremen and tenters not to employ me, so that for the period of four months after I wandered through Dundee a famished and persecuted factory exile.

From the foregoing statements some may think that I am rude, forward, and presumptuous; but permit me to say this much for myself, and those who know me best will confirm my statement, that I am naturally of a warm-hearted and affectionate disposition, always willing, to the extent of my power, to serve my fellow-creatures, and would rather endure an insult that retaliate on an enemy. All my wrongs have been suffered in silence and wept over in secret. It is the favour and fame of the poetic gift bestowed on me by nature's God that has brought on me the envy of the ignorant, for the enlightened classes of both sexes of factory workers love and admire me for my humble poetic effusions, so far as they have been placed before the public, but I merely mention this to clear away any doubt that may possibly arise in the mind of any of my readers.

In conclusion, I am glad to say that the persecution I was doomed to suffer in vindication not only of my own rights, but of the rights of such as might be similarly discharged, passed away, and peace and pleasure restored to my bosom again, by obtaining work at the Chapelshade Factory, at the east end of Dundee, where I wrought for three years and a-half to a true friend. I had not been long in my present situation when I fortunately became a reader of the 'Penny Post', and shortly afterwards contributed some pieces to the 'Poet's Corner', which seemed to cast a mystic spell over many of its readers whose numerous letters reached me from various districts, highly applauding my contributions, and offering me their sympathy, friendship and love; while others, inspired by the muses, responded to me through the same popular medium some of whose productions will be found, along with my own in the present volume.

And now, gentle reader, let me conclude by offering my grateful thanks to the Rev.

George Gilfillan for his testimony in respect to the merits of my poetic productions, to Mr Alex. Campbell, of the 'Penny Post', for his services in promoting their publication, as well as to the subscribers who have so long patiently waited for this volume, which I hope may prove a means of social and intellectual enjoyment to many, and also help to relieve from the incessant toils of a factory life.

NOTES

1. Probably a reference to Elizabeth Helme's tale, *The Farmer of Inglewood Forest* (London: A. K. Newman, 1800).

2. The legendary Jew condemned to wander about the world until Christ's second coming because he told Jesus to go faster while he was carrying the cross to Cavalry.

3. The hero of Samuel Johnson's oriental moral fable, *The History of Rasselas*, 1759.

4. A worker on the frame or tenter for stretching cloth; hence 'to be on tenter-hooks'.

5. The verse is from Oliver Goldsmith's sentimental novel, *The Vicar of Wakefield*, 1766: see also Oliphant, p.239, n.5).

6. 'A Mother's Love' is 'written for Mary Achenvole. Born 14th September. 1852.'

7. Fitzroy James Henry Somerset, 1st Baron Raglan (1788-1855), field marshall, in 1854 became commander in the Crimean War. On 25 October 1854 the indecisive Battle of Balaclava resulted in heavy British losses in part attributable to a misunderstanding between Raglan and the cavalry commander, Lord Lucan, which resulted in the notorious Charge of the Light Brigade.

Constance Frederica Gordon Cumming
(1837–1924)

Constance Gordon Cumming was born on May 26, 1837, the sixth daughter of the large family of Sir William Gordon Cumming, Bart, of Altyre, Morayshire. Sir William was chief of the Clan Comyn or Cumming and her mother was Eliza Maria Campbell of Islay and Shawfield: Constance Gordon Cumming was proud of her distinguished ancestry and speaks in her autobiography of her descent from the Red Comyn, stabbed to death by Robert Bruce in a quarrel in Greyfriars Church in Dumfries. She became a distinguished traveller and author: her travels took her to Asia, Africa, South Sea Islands, America and the British Colonies. In the 1870s she lived in the family of the British Governor of Fiji, Sir Arthur Hamilton Gordon: she writes about her experiences from this privileged position in *At Home in Fiji*. The numerous books that recounted her experiences and impressions were very popular and she was also a regular contributor to journals and magazines. She also sketched and painted watercolours which illustrate her books. She took an active interest in mission work abroad and did some remarkable work in China for the blind. In her old age she settled in Crieff at College House and died there in September 1924 in her 88th year. Gordon Cumming's writing has tended to be overshadowed by that of Isabella Bird Bishop but a long and generous article by Susan Schoenbauer Thurin in the *DLB* somewhat redresses the balance.

Constance Frederica Gordon Cumming, *From the Hebrides to the Himalayas: A Sketch of Eighteen Months' Wanderings in Western Isles and Eastern Highlands* (London: Sampson Low, 1876); *At Home in Fiji* (Edinburgh & London: William Blackwood & Sons, 1881); *A Lady's Cruise in a French Man-of-War* (Edinburgh & London: Blackwood, 1882); *In the Hebrides* (London: Chatto & Windus, 1883) *Fire Fountains: The Kingdom of Hawaii* (Edinburgh & London: Blackwood, 1883); *Granite Crags: An Account of Travels in California* (Edinburgh & London: Blackwood, 1884); *In the Himalayas and on the Indian Plains* (London: Chatto & Windus, 1884); *Via Cornwall to Egypt* (London: Chatto & Windus, 1885); *Wanderings in China* (Edinburgh & London: Blackwood, 1886); *The Last Commandment: A Word to Every Christian* (Church of England Missionary Society, 1889); *Two Happy Years in Ceylon* (Edinburgh & London: Blackwood, 1892); *Memories* (Edinburgh: Blackwood 1904); and others

Further reading:

W. H. D. Adams, *Celebrated Women Travellers* (London: Swan Sonnenschein, 1883)
Dea Birkett, *Spinsters Abroad: Victorian Lady Explorers* (Oxford: Blackwell, 1982)
Dorothy Middleton, *Victorian Lady Travellers* (London: Routledge & Kegan Paul, 1965)
Marion Tinling, ed., *With Women's Eyes: Visitors to the New World, 1775-1918* (Hamden, Conn.: Archon Books, 1993)

DLB, 174; *HSWW*

From *In the Hebrides*, 1883 (the proofs of this volume were read by Isabella Bird Bishop):

Gordon Cumming pays particular attention to those ancient customs that seem to her common to other lands:

In the parish of Avock, in the Black Isles (facing Inverness), is a well called Craiguck, or Craigie Well, probably from the dark crag rising behind it.[1] On the first Sunday in May (old style) all the people from far and near gather here at daybreak – a regular hearty Highland gathering – as merry as a fair, all exchanging kindly greetings and good wishes for the health of the coming year, in good broad Scotch, in Gaelic, or in such pure English as we rarely hear from the poor in any part of Britain, save here, where it is an acquired tongue. The health, of course, is to be secured by a draught of the lucky well. But they must get their drink before the sun rises. Once he climbs the horizon the spell is broken, so, as the last moments draw near, the eager pressing forward for a taste amounts to a downright scramble.

A stranger, whose curiosity induced him to go forth betimes and witness this curious scene, tells how 'some drank out of dishes, some stooped on their knees to drink, the latter being occasionally plunged over head and ears by their companions'. As the first rays of the sun appeared a man was seen coming down the brae in great haste. He was recognised as 'Jock Forsyth', a very honest and pious, but eccentric individual. Scores of voices shouted, 'You are too late, Jock. The sun is rising. Surely you have slept in this morning.'

The new-comer, a middle-aged man, perspiring profusely, and out of breath, nevertheless pressed through the crowd and never stopped till he reached the well. Then, muttering a few inaudible words, he stooped on his knees and took a large draught. Then he rose and said, 'O Lord, Thou knowest that weel would it be for me this day, an' I had stoopit my knees and my heart before Thee in spirit and in truth, as often as I have stoopit them afore this well. But we maun keep the customs of our fathers.' So he stepped aside among the rest and dedicated his offering to the briar bush, which by this time could hardly be seen through the number of shreds which covered it.

For part of the ceremony is that each comer must hang a shred of cloth on a large briar bush, which grows close by the well, as an offering to the healing and luck-conferring waters, forcibly reminding the beholder of those holy wells and bushes in the Emerald Isle, were many coloured rags flutter in the breeze; poor Paddy's votive offering to the blessed St Somebody on behalf of sick parent or child.

Strange, is it not, that this custom should be so widely spread? We find it at Constantinople, where each pilgrim ties a shred torn from his own raiment to the carved windows of saintly tombs; and it is religiously observed by the Mohammedan pilgrims visiting the Mosque of Omar at Jerusalem, beneath the great dome of which lies that huge rock whence Mohammed ascended to heaven, supposed to be the identical rock whereon Abraham did not sacrifice Isaac.[2] This rock is surrounded by a great iron railing, adorned with thousands of rags, tied up by the pilgrims as reminders to the Prophet. Indeed, strips of old cloth seem to be a recognized medium of communication with the spirit-world in all corners of the globe, for in our Eastern wanderings we found many a gaily-decorated shrub in the lonely Himalayan glens and passes, which, in the distance, seemed to be loaded with blossoms, but which on closer approach proved to be laden with bright morsels of rag, the simple offerings of the Hill-men to the spirit of some tree or well.

In Ceylon also, where we spent a lovely moonlight night on the summit of Adam's Peak, the 'Holy Mount' of Buddhists, Sivaites, and Mohammedans, we noted the multitude of rags tied to the iron chains which prevent the roof of the temple, covering the holy footprint, from being blown away. The poor pilgrims believe that a shred of their raiment, thus offered, will surely prevent Buddha from forgetting them and their vows. On these superstitious customs in far-away lands we look with calm indifference, but to find the same practice still lingering among our sturdy Ross-shire Highlanders, is certainly somewhat startling!

From *Fire Fountains: The Kingdom of Hawaii, Its Volcanoes, and the History of Its Missions*, 1883:

Gordon Cumming records a trip to the volcano of Kilauea and the 'firepit' of the Halemaumau crater:
November 2, 1879
I must write a few lines tonight – though the thrilling excitements of the day, and the glory now before me, make it really difficult to do so. For at this very moment there lies before me a vast river of fire – or rather a perfect network of rivers of molten rock, which, having burst from the newly created lake, are now meandering at their own wild will over the bed of the great crater, which, when I arrived here last week, was all cold and ghastly grey. [...] All last night, and the night before, we watched the marvellous scene – fresh rivers bursting up every few minutes from one point or another. First appears a glowing spot of fire in the black lava-bed. Then begins a spouting. Then a pool of molten lava forms, and presently a flow commences, which gradually increases till it becomes a rushing river.

Today I have stood beside rivers of fire – some sluggish, some rushing fully twice as fast as I could possibly run. Roback [the German guide with a Hawaiian wife], being an old sailor, says six knots an hour. I say, faster than the fastest river I know, boiling and turning over huge waves of molten silver – silver on the surface, but revealing the red stream below.

Gordon Cumming describes her progress in the crater with Roback and a young American traveller. She records what is extraordinary in the experience but remarks how quickly one learns to domesticate the amazing:
It is strange how quickly one gets accustomed to new circumstances. When luncheon-time came, it really seemed quite natural to sit on the brink of a fire river, on a raised hummock of lava, and enjoy our sandwiches (and oh, how we prized one orange, divided among the three of us!), while watching the heaving, rushing lava-stream rolling and breaking up in huge half-cooled cakes of surface, to be swallowed and molten afresh in the fire-stream, which flowed within ten feet of us. Roback fished out lumps of very cohesive liquid lava on his stick, and 'made specimens' by embedding copper coins in the hot lava, which in a few moments became solid lumps. Of course the lava thus manipulated does not 'set' properly, and is of no value

whatever as a specimen; so the manufacturer undergoes great heat and exertion to produce a memento infinitely inferior to those so freely offered by nature. But people who visit volcanoes are all supposed to want coins in lava, so they may as well be gratified.

I need scarcely tell you that I preferred to secure specimens of the genuine article, which my kind host is now carefully packing in soft *pulu* fibre, that they may travel safely to England.

We passed the whole long day in the midst of these fiery rivers, and at last turned to leave them with infinite regret. I think my chief feeling tonight is of thankful wonder that we should have returned from such an expedition as safely as from a ramble in English meadows, without so much as a boot singed or a garment damaged.

From 'Across the Yellow Sea', *Blackwood's Magazine* (March 1890) 372-383:

'Mair haste, less speed,' says the good old Scotch proverb. 'The shortest cut may prove the longest way home,' says the English. I proved the truth of both sayings when returning from Peking to Japan, and longing exceedingly to reach Nagasaki, where I hoped to find a large accumulation of letters. I determined to strike out a course for myself, and, instead of returning by mail-steamer all the way to Shanghai, thence taking another mail-steamer across to Nagasaki, I resolved if possible to cross direct, and took passage in one of the small trading vessels which ply between that port and Cheefoo. Many kind friends endeavoured to dissuade me from what seemed to them so great a risk; but as the magnificent steamer Shun Lee, in which I had arrived from Shanghai only a month previously, was then lying a total wreck on a rocky headland at no great distance, I had good reason to maintain that it is not always the Goliaths of the ocean that are most to be relied on.

So, hearing that a small Danish brig, the Thorkild, was to sail the next day, and being especially attracted by her name, which savoured of old Norse mythology and adventure, I applied for a berth, which was at first refused on the ground that she did not carry passengers; but on hearing that the applicant was a lady who had sailed in many waters and knew how to make light of difficulties, the kind-hearted captain, a fair-haired blue-eyed Dane, offered to give up his own cabin to secure my greater comfort, and do all in his power to make my journey pleasant. So that when, in the sunshine of early morning, I embarked in this little vessel of 155 tons, I almost fancied myself on my own yacht starting for a summer's day's cruise.

Slowly we passed the rocky isles which guard the harbour, and the picturesque headland of fine cliffs, known as Cheefoo Bluff, concerning which I had heard sad tales of the hardships there endured, in the bitter cold of the previous winter, by a shipwrecked crew. Then a light fresh breeze sprang up and we sped on our way, expecting a week at the very longest would find us at our destination. The week passed quietly and peacefully, but light head-winds made our progress slow indeed, and sometimes cold wet mists blotted out all the wondrous ultramarine blue of the sea which we call 'yellow', doubtless from the mud washed down by the great rivers, and which discolours the ocean for miles.

Not one sail did we sight in these seven days; but when the mist was most dense, and a brooding silence which we could almost feel seemed to rest upon the waters, a large skeleton junk floated noiselessly past us, its great black ribs looking weird and spirit-like, like one of Gustave Doré's strange fancies.³ There could be little doubt that all her crew had perished, – at all events, no living thing remained on her. Had we struck her in the night we should inevitably have foundered, so we inferred that our good angels had been faithful watchers.

After various threatened disasters on the way, including the fear of being wrecked on the rocky shore of the island of Kuro which almost resulted in the boats being lowered, the 'brave little vessel' sails into Nagasaki harbour. Cumming writes at some length about the fate of Christians and Christianity in Japan from the first visit of the Portuguese in 1541. Christianity was embraced by some Japanese princes: the Prince of Bungo was baptised after 27 years of hesitation, but conflict between the Japanese Buddhist priests and the Jesuits remained bitter, nor was the part played by the Christians in the spread of their religion wholly admirable:

Unhappily the faith was too often spread numerically by force and persecution. Vassals were compelled by their feudal lords to adopt the new creed professed by their masters, the temples so long revered were ruthlessly destroyed, and the priests of Buddha exiled or put to death. Even where the Spanish and Portuguese priests were not directly implicated in these persecutions, they applauded them, – as, for instance, when the Prince of Bungo had burned three thousand Buddhist monasteries and razed the temples to the ground, including one famous for its splendour and its colossal image of Dai Butsu [the Buddha], the Christian priests declared that such ardent zeal was an evident token of faith and charity! As a natural consequence the promulgators of the foreign faith had many bitter foes; and soon after the jealousy of Taiko Sama had been awakened, nine Franciscan and Jesuit missionaries were arrested in Osaka and Kyoto. They were taken to Nagasaki and there impaled, A.D. 1798 – a death of appalling slow agony, which they endured with heroic constancy. Nevertheless, 900 priests contrived to gain a footing in these three cities, and numbered their converts at 1,800,000. Of the priests 124 were Jesuits, the remainder Dominicans, Franciscans, Augustins, and native Japanese. They had churches in all parts of the southern isles, and colleges in which secular knowledge was imparted to willing scholars. In the isle of Amakusa the Jesuits established a college where they instructed the young nobles of Japan in music, Latin, and European science; and the college at Miako numbered 7000 students.

Just as it began to look as though the religion was well established the Shogun Iyéyasu suspected the Christians of plotting to deliver the country into the hands of the Portuguese and a persecution began based on tortures imported from the Inquisition. The co-operation of the Dutch with the persecution of Portuguese Christians ensured the Dutch a monopoly of Japanese trade which they maintained, however, at the cost of their integrity:

So thoroughly was the policy of extermination now carried out, that there was every reason to suppose that Christianity was literally stamped out in Japan. Its very name was whispered in terror. It ranked with such other crimes as murder and arson, sorcery and sedition, and was denounced in company with these, posted in the most conspicuous spots throughout the empire, beside the public roads and ferries, and in all places where men who run may read. It was a crime even to give shelter to one of the evil sect; and rewards were offered to such as should discover them.

One test to be applied to suspected persons was to compel them to trample on a pictured image of the Saviour, which had been cast in copper at Nagasaki, and disseminated for this purpose.

As late as 1829 one woman and six men were crucified at Osaka, because they were known to be obstinate Christians, but things have changed:

Now that religious toleration is apparently the order of the day, the Catholic Mission is carried on by French and Italian priests, under the direction of Monseigneur Marie Joseph Laucaigne, who (according to the custom of the Church of Rome, which bestows the titles of ancient and extinct bishoprics on those whom she sends to labour in heathen lands) is known, not as the Bishop of Nagasaki, but of Apollonie.

The English and American missions are of course plants of very recent growth; and, having no strange resemblances to Buddhism in their teaching and ceremonials, their plain undecorated churches offer little attraction to the native mind, and their progress is necessarily exceedingly slow, being further most seriously retarded by both the example and openly expressed cavillings of the majority of foreigners.

[...]

Today the ships of many nations fly their colours peacefully as they lie anchored in the quiet harbour of Nagasaki, and Christian schools and churches are established on the historic isle of Dessima, where for so many years the Dutch consented in order to secure a monopoly of trade, to live in most dishonourable imprisonment, only allowed to leave the island once a year, for a few hours, by crossing a bridge whereon was engraved the sign of the cross, on which they must of necessity trample as they passed.

Interesting as are these details of the struggles to secure religious toleration, I need hardly say it is by no means a subject which forces itself upon the casual observer. Rather is his attention arrested and captivated by the picturesque aspect of heathendom rampant. Most fascinating to me were the rambles which we took through the old native city, especially when, turning aside from the busy streets of ordinary life (quaint enough, it may be well believed), we found ourselves in one which, like the neighbourhood of Père Lachaise in Paris,[4] is wholly occupied by shops for the sale of flowers, and similar suitable offerings, for the adornment of the multitudinous graves which literally cover the whole hill at the back of the town. On certain festivals each grave in this vast cemetery is adorned by loving hands; pink lotus-blossoms are placed in simple vases and incense-sticks burnt on the little altar before the grave. Some offerings of food are also laid there, in little china cups; and a paper lantern is hung over each tombstone, which is generally an effective piece of stone-carving, and often surrounded by little gardens and shrubs, and enclosed with stone railings and a handsome stone portal, – stone gates, revolving on stone hinges, – suggestive of those discovered by Porter in the giant cities of Bashan, though on a small scale.[5]

At the base of the hill, and at the other side of the town, is a perfect network of temples – Buddhist and Shinto merging one into the other in the most tolerant manner, and producing inextricable confusion in the mind of the spectator, and, I should imagine, of the worshipper also, by the promiscuous use of the emblems sacred to each – such as mirrors of polished metal, paper *goheis*, and strawropes; images of saints, all manner of idols, lotus-blossoms, etc., etc. Each temple is an artistic study; and its surroundings of handsome stone lanterns, fine old trees, curious braziers and fountains, combined with the charming groups of Japanese figures, always coming and going, make up an endless succession of pleasant pictures. Long flights of steep stone steps lead up to the temple, and thence to the innumerable groups of graves, which lie half hidden by tall grasses and brushwood. And looking back hence, you get lovely glimpses of the town, and of the blue harbour and fine hills beyond, all framed by most picturesquely gnarled old fir-trees.

Close to one temple we found the pretty house of a native artist who was painting scrolls on silk, flowers and figures; his family all seemed highly intelligent and artistic. One was an entymologist, who, having visited England, had sent back many cases of insects to a museum there. Others paint lanterns in the form of a parasol, which, when closed, is apparently only a bamboo. In their garden are large tanks, where they raise immense numbers of gold-fish for sale. Passing on thence, we visited the studio of another artist, a real genius, but a type of that too rapid adaptation of foreign ideas which bids fair to quickly wipe out all purely native art. In this man's studio were admirable studies from nature, with all the essentially Japanese characteristics; but latterly he had been devoting his attention to English studies of shipping and rigging, and was producing very foreign-looking pictures in *guache*. He also showed me several volumes of a Japanese 'Guide to Art', all full of English illustrations. Returning from his house we explored most picturesque canals with old bridges; and bought all manner of quaint things in the odd little shops.

Each day offered some new scene of interest. One day we rode across the harbour to explore the old Dutch and Russian cemeteries, which occupy a lovely site on a ferny hill crowned by noble old pines. Several graves are marked by the Greek cross, and in one, which forms a small shrine, is placed a very artistic oil-painting of the Crucifixion. The Japanese graves close by were marked by fresh buds of the pink lotus, sacred to Buddha.

But the favourite afternoon 'ploy' was a boating expedition down the harbour, where ladies and children bathed in one pleasant bay, and gentlemen in another, after which they combined forces for an open-air tea-party; and those who cared for the treasures of the deep ransacked the shores and rocks for fresh wonders. One gentleman – Mr Paul of H.B.M. Consulate – had devoted his attention exclusively to collecting crabs from this one coast; and the beauty and variety of his specimens were really past belief. Every conceivable kind was there: smooth and hairy, sombre and gaudy; so tiny as to be almost microscopic, so large as to measure about three feet across the claws. The Japanese fishermen soon discovered that a pecuniary value attached to the refuse of their dredging nets, and they became careful to preserve all new specimens. And gradually as the collection increased in size and in beauty, their interest and wonder was excited; and when, in 1879, it was lent to the great Nagasaki Exhibition, the native naturalists gazed on it in utter amazement, marvelling to see how great a variety of crustacea could be found on their own shores.

Thus boating, riding, or climbing the steep hill-paths in search of new beauties, the pleasant days slipped away; and now, in more prosaic lands, the memory of the green loveliness of Nagasaki often comes back to me as a haunting vision of delight.

From 'The Offerings of the Dead', *British Quarterly Review* (January 1885), 47-76:

Gordon Cumming discusses ancestor-worship in China. She blames it for various practices of which she disapproves:
For one thing, it is inextricably blended with whatever is understood by the term FUNG [now 'feng'] SHUI, that mysterious, intangible, but omnipotent *something indescribable*, which, like some invisible spirit of evil, stands in the way, and effectually bars every effort in favour of progress and civilisation. It meets the missionary at every turn; it raises infuriated mobs to destroy the house which has been reared a trifle higher than those around it, or to prevent the making of railways and telegraphs, the working of mines, and a thousand other dreaded innovations. It is the mainspring of that ultra-conservatism which, like a mighty resistant breakwater, so stoutly wards off the inflowing tide of all modern inventions, practically declaring the only safe condition of existence to be one of utter inertia, in which nothing old shall be disturbed, and nothing new attempted.

What *Fung Shui* actually is, no one can exactly define, except that it has to do with the good and genial influences which are ever moving gently from the south, and also with the baneful influences which come from the North, and which may possibly be disturbed by any alteration of existing physical surroundings. It seems almost impossible for a foreigner to arrive at any exact understanding of this great overruling belief of the millions of Chinamen; yet no one can be many hours in China ere the term becomes so familiar as to make its solution a matter much desired. Apparently it has especial reference to the repose of the dead, and the influence of the mighty host of disembodied spirits upon the welfare or adversity of their living human successors on this earth.

Since it is the duty of the eldest son to perform the sacrifices necessary to secure the comfort of the dead in the next world, girls are often unwelcome additions to a family:
To this cause also is due the lamentation which too often greets the birth of a baby girl, whereas the birth of a son is the occasion of the utmost rejoicing, and on the yearly feast, known as 'The Boy's Festival', each family which has been so fortunate as to acquire another son during the previous twelvemonth, proclaims its joy by hanging up an immense paper fish, which floats from the roof. But no such welcome awaits the poor little baby girl, whose rearing must involve some outlay, for which her far-seeing parents can count on no return in the Great Hereafter. Even the woman who cannot crush her own maternal instincts so far as to consent to the murder of her new-born child, often wearies of the trouble of tending a baby which is so very unwelcome to its father and all its relations, so the poor little thing is cruelly neglected, and when it becomes sickly and wailing, it costs the unnatural mother few qualms to deposit the useless creature in the nearest loathsome Baby-tower, knowing that her sympathetic neighbours will make no unkind comments on its disappearance.

Thus it is that Ancestor-worship lies at the root of the appalling female infanticide of China – a practice about which there is no concealment. It is fully sanctioned by public opinion, and the Baby-towers for the reception of the bodies of the poor little babies who are not considered worthy of funeral expenses are a hideous and repulsive reality, forcing themselves on the attention of whoever ventures on a quiet walk round the walls of a Chinese city – say, for instance, Ningpo, where the fragrance of the honeysuckle and wild jasmine, which adorn the grey walls, too often mingles with a pestilential breath, which warns us that we have drawn near to one of these loathsome receptacles. From time to time a woman may be seen approaching alone, bearing a small burden wrapped in a bit of old matting; this she thrusts in at the high square opening, which is the only entrance to the tower, and so the unwelcome baby is disposed of.

NOTES

1. Avock is usually now spelled 'Avoch'. The Black Isle, as it is normally called, is not an island at all but a long tapering promontory: there are various stories about how it got its name, none very convincing. The well is now known as 'Clootie (cloth) Well' from the scraps of cloth that are still hung on the bush there.

2. The mosque is generally known as the Dome of the Rock.

3. Doré illustrated Coleridge's 'The Ancient Mariner'.

4. The most famous of Parisian cemeteries.

5. Josias Leslie Porter (1823-1889), graduate of the University of Glasgow, traveller, *Giant Cities of Bashan*, 1865.

Flora Annie Steel (1847 – 1929)

Flora Annie Steel was born Flora Webster at Sudbury Priory, Harrow-on-the-Hill, 2 April 1847, one of eleven children, seven boys and four girls: all, she says in her autobiography, *The Garden of Fidelity*, 'healthy, strong Scottish children, half Lowland, half Highland'. Her father, George Webster, had married Isabella, daughter and heiress of Alexander Macallum, a sugar planter at Cousins Cove, Jamaica. The family was at first prosperous – George Webster had a London house in Palace Yard where Thackeray and the illustrator, George Cruickshank, were among his friends – but when Flora was three 'the financial crisis that had been hanging over the family for years came'. Although the family moved to a tiny villa 'overlooking the cricket field', they still managed to send the boys to Harrow. When Flora was nine the family moved to Scotland, to Burnside, Forfar, when her father was appointed sheriff-clerk of Forfarshire, an appointment which he kept till his death, although the boys continued to board at Harrow. There was little money left over for the girls' schooling: Flora intermittently had a governess or was left to educate herself among the house's abundant books; when she was thirteen she went for six months to her uncle's in Brussels where she went to a 'magnificent school in what had been the Turkish Ambassador's house, where there were thirty-eight pupils and thirty-nine professors'.

At the age of twenty in 1867 Flora, after a written proposal, married Henry William Steel, an Indian Civil Servant, and set out almost immediately for Madras, where being younger than her husband, she was jokingly known as 'Steel's baby bride'. Steel travelled from Madras to Delhi, from there to Lahore and Ludhiana, where she was the only European woman. From there her husband was transferred to Dalhousie. Her first child was still-born, but a daughter born in 1870 survived. Steel was energetic in everything she did – reading, singing, acting and painting and finally, of course, writing. When in 1870 the Steels settled in Kasur, Flora Annie Steel set out to become an expert on India.

She penetrated beyond purdah to come to understand Indian women, and although she often found superstitions risible, she also seems to have understood the feelings that made them credible. She was a great pioneer of education for Indian women and started a schools for girls in Kasur in 1874: she was indeed appointed first inspectress of girls' schools in 1884.

In 1889 the Steels left India and Flora Annie Steel returned to it in her writing, both in her fiction, and non-fiction from travel writing to her cookery book, *The Complete Indian Cook and Housekeeper*, written, some said, by one whose cooking and housekeeping was far from complete. After 1889 Steel returned to India twice – once in 1894 to research her great novel of the Indian mutiny, *On the Face of the Waters*, and finally from the winter of 1897 till May 1898.

From 1900 until 1913 she lived at Talgarth in North Wales, moving from there to Tenbury. In her later life she supported women's suffrage non-militantly. She lived latterly with her daughter and her husband at Springfield, Gloucestershire, where in 12 April 1929 she died.

In all her writing about India, factual and fictional, Steel is both knowledgeable and opinionated, confident about the rightness of her own stance but never merely prejudiced and seldom patronising without also examining her own position.

Flora Annie Steel, *From the Five Rivers* (London: Heinemann, 1893); *The Flower of Forgiveness* (London: Macmillan, 1894); *Tales of the Punjab* (London: Macmillan, 1894); *The Potter's Thumb* (London: Heinemann, 1894); *Red Rowans* (London: Macmillan, 1895); *On the Face of the Waters* (London: Heinemann, 1896); *In the Permanent Way* (London: Heinemann, 1898); *The Hosts of the Lord* (London: Heinemann, 1900); *In the Guardianship of God* (London: Heinemann, 1903); *India* (London: Adam & Charles Black, 1905); *A Book of Mortals* (London: Heinemann, 1905); *A Prince of Dreamers* (London: Heinemann, 1908); *The Gift of the Gods* (London: Heinemann, 1911); *King-Errant* (London: Heinemann, 1912); *The Adventures of Akbar* (London: Heinemann, 1913); *Dramatic History of India* (Bombay: K. & J. Cooper, 1917); *Mistress of Men* (London: Heinemann, 1917); *English Fairy Tales*, Retold by F.A.Steel; illustrated by Arthur Rackham (London: Macmillan & Co, 1918); *The Builder* (London: John Lane, 1928); *The Curse of Eve* (London: John Lane, 1929); *The Garden of Fidelity* (London: Macmillan & Co, 1929); and others

Further Reading:

Daya Patwardhan, *A Star of India, Flora Annie Steel: Her Works and Times*. (Bombay: A. V. Griha Prakashan; Poona, 1963)

Lady Violet Georgiana Powell, *Flora Annie Steel: Novelist of India* (London: Heinemann, 1981)

Nupur Chaudhuri, ed., *Western Women and Imperialism: Complicity and Resistance* (Bloomington: Indiana University Press, 1992)

Mary L. Broe, ed., *Women's Writing in Exile* (Chapel Hill: University of North Carolina Press, 1989)

DNB; *DLB* 153; 156; *HSWW*

From *India*, 1905, with illustrations by Mortimer Menpes:

'The Great Moghuls'
On Akbar the Great (1542-1605):
He is centuries before his time, and the number of laws passed by him within a very few years of his accession at fourteen years of age show a marvellous grasp on what was needed to consolidate his vast empire. Perfect religious freedom, the removal of obnoxious taxation, a whole elaborate system of revenue collection, the prohibition of suttee and female infanticide, the legalisation of remarriage, and the discountenancing of infant betrothal – all this and many another wise law, form a continuous procession of beneficial legislation which, emanating not from a parliament of men, but from the brain of one man only, and that a man whose surroundings were those of Eastern despotism and whose era was that of Queen Elizabeth, is fairly astounding.

'The Women of India'

This is an extremely difficult subject of which to treat fairly, chiefly because it is impossible to swallow wholesale the two opposing estimates of Indian womanhood – the one favoured by most Anglo-Indians and fostered by missionary reports, which represents it as being thoroughly degraded, hopelessly, helplessly depraved, and utterly enslaved; the other – of late so enthusiastically preached by Miss Margaret Noble in her book *The Web of Indian Life* – which asserts that, on the contrary, the ideals of the Indian woman are the highest in the world, and that her conduct is an example, her life free and happy.

Naturally, it is difficult to bring these two absolutely genuine beliefs into line, especially if we adopt the western standpoint and begin by asserting that happiness must hold hands with freedom.

The only thing to be done is to take the assertions bit by bit, and see if they are borne out by facts.

Let us therefore begin with the ideal. In the West we formulate as our ideal woman a human being of equal rights with man; mistress of her own sex, as he is master of his; therefore free to use that sex as she chooses. Mother *in posse*, she has *in esse*, a right to refuse motherhood. She has therefore the right to go down to the grave still withholding from the world its immortality, still denying to it vast possibilities. For it must not be forgotten that to every woman in the world the Angel of the Annunciation brings the divine message, proclaiming that of her, perchance, a saviour shall be born. For the greatest poet, painter, musician, statesman, teacher, remain still amongst those unborn.

In the East this is not so. The ideal there, is of a human being who is not the equal of man; who cannot be so, since the man and the woman together make the perfect human being to whose guardianship is entrusted the immortality of the race. Outside marriage there should be no sex, and not to marry is wilfully to murder the possibility of life.

That is one point of divergence. The next shows even greater cleavage. The Western woman is taught that she has the right to monopolise the whole body and soul of a man. She can demand his love – that mysterious something over and above duty, over and above mere sexual attraction or friendship, which is the sole sanctifier of marriage.

The ideal Eastern woman knows nothing of monopoly or love. The sole sanctifier of her union with a man is the resulting child; the sole tie, the tie of fatherhood and motherhood. Therefore if she has no children, she has two courses open to her: either she must bring a more fortunate handmaiden to her lord, and cherish the children as her own; or she must yield her place in hearth and home, in prayer and offering, give up her spiritual union with her husband, and live apart. Marriage to her, as to her husband, is no personal pleasure: it is a duty to the unborn – a duty which involves self-restraint on both, – on her, since she has voluntarily to give up any personal right in her sex; on the man, because he also has to yield his liberty, since the woman who hands on his immortality is as his mother, and must be treated with absolute respect.

Now there can be no question as to which of these two ideals claims the greatest amount of self-abnegation. Undoubtedly the Eastern.

In other ways also the Eastern outlook on life demands more moral courage.

The Western girl is taught that what is sauce for the goose is sauce for the gander; the eastern girl is taught that this is not so. Her chastity, for instance, is of infinitely greater importance to the home than is the man's, and she accepts the undeniable fact; and by doing so recognises the supreme importance of her own position.

Before passing on to practice, it will be instructive to consider how flatly Western law denies the attitude of the Western woman towards marriage. She proclaims that unless she can find divine love, marriage is no marriage; it asserts that she may love whom she chooses, provided the sexual relationship with her husband remains unimpaired. The husband cannot object to her failure to be to him companion, helpmeet, friend; he cannot even complain if she refuses to be a mother. She may neglect his house, his children, play skittles with his money, his reputation. She stands immune from interference on the rock of her sex; all the rest is mere talk.

This curious antagonism between faith and works makes her position oddly undefined. Like a shuttlecock she bandies, and is bandied over the network of sex which constitutes modern society, claiming a point here, repudiating it there, clinging to the bat of marital faithfulness with one hand, with the other wielding the doctrine of spiritual affinities, until it is no wonder that the Divorce Court is full. Lucky is it that in normally healthy cases love follows on marriage, else we should require more judges, more courts!

To come now to practice. It may be conceded at once that the Indian woman falls further from her ideal than the Western one; but then her ideal is higher. Besides, it is conceivable that were, let us say, some few hundred Eastern mothers-in-law of the uttermost-utmost type to descend on London with an eye to its conversion, as our unmarried Mission ladies do on India, full of sympathy born of their own needs, full of reprobation born of their own ideals, they would find quite as much at which to hold up holy hands of horror as we do – say in Calcutta and Bombay. What is more, were they to go into our country towns and villages, they would find far more at which to cavil than we can in rural India, where life remains singularly pure, singularly simple.

The intolerable indignity of a woman's position generally, prey as she is to familiarities, to coarse words in the streets, to gigglings and screechings in corners, even to her husband's or lover's public endearments, would shock them utterly. For there is nothing of that sort in India. Vice may thrive, but it is silent. Except in the bad-character bazaars, and even there but seldom, there is nothing to suggest sex in an Indian city. The horse-play of hooligans, the open challenge of Tam-o'-Shanter girls, the ticklings and titterings of 'Arry and 'Arriet, are alike unknown.[1] There is outward decency at least, and that is great gain. Then the flaunting abroad of girls claiming attention by their dress, ready to rouse elemental passions in all and sundry – if all and sundry are foolish enough to be so roused, – while they smile, securely amusing themselves, would be terrible.

That is not the woman's portion. If she spends hours over her dress, it must be for the father of her children, to attract him. The drunken husbands, slatternly wives, miserably-neglected children, would all be an offence indeed; while the fact of a bride having often to work hard, instead of being set free from care, would seem real cruelty. Last, but not least, the solitude of home life and the husband's incessant claim on his wife would be great hardships.

To us, on the other hand, it seems horrible to be screened, secluded, shut out from all outside pleasures, and we point out the pettinesses, the quarrelsomeness, which such idleness breeds in the Eastern women.

It is true they are quarrelsome, they are petty, they are idle; indeed, idleness in the women of the towns – for in rural India the women do a lion's share of outdoor work – is responsible for much. I have known a large household of well-to-do native women do nothing at all from year's end to year's end, but talk, eat sweetmeats, and quarrel. Small wonder, then, if they spend their leisure in what their men-folk helplessly call 'the women's law'; that is a code of conduct, etiquette, ceremony, and observance, to comply with all the provisions of a Japanese general. To live as I have done in a Hindu house, especially when the real house-mistress is a masterful and deeply religious widow who is grandmother to the babies and mother to their parents, is no longer to wonder at the absolute terror with which men speak of the *stri achchar*.[2]

There is to be carrot stew for dinner, and the little cosmos licks its lips, until suddenly a child gets the hiccough, and straightway the fiat goes forth: carrot stew is unlucky, it must be pease porridge once more. The latest little bride perchance stumbles on the threshold, and hey presto! such a to do. Red pepper must be burnt, soot smeared, and the whole household propitiate the little brass godlings on the roof with sweetmeats and flowers, lest evil befall high hopes. The wretched husbands in such houses, when they come home or go forth, have to submit to pattings, sprinklings, tying of knots in the hair, and are lucky if they have not to carry concealed about them to court, office, or workshop the most incongruous and sometimes revolting things such as the half-chewed morsel of bread on which baby has cut his last tooth!

For the men of India are – poor souls! – the most henpecked in the world. They – especially the Mohammedans – make a brave show; they may even, should they have some slight knowledge of English, stigmatise their women-folk as 'poor ignorant idiots', but once behind the purdah in the women's apartments, Bob Acres'[3] courage is stable in comparison with theirs. I know no more pitiable object on this earth than an elderly Turk having his beard dyed blue by his female relations! Fatima and Ayesha wink at each other while the other wives look on, and when the farce is over they retire to the cupboard and lock themselves up and give him the key, with strict injunctions to be home punctually and not to look in at the club. Of course there are exceptions, but the general form of Home Rule is feminine despotism veiled by a slavish subserviency in trivial details.

Nothing, however, emphasises the different outlook of the Eastern and the Western women more than the feelings with which, as a bride, the Eastern and the Western girl goes to her husband's home.

The latter, no doubt, puts the husband first in the list of agreeable novelties, but the new house, the new position, the new liberty, run him very close. She has herself chosen everything, the cretonnes, the colour of the bridegroom's wedding tie; she has high hopes of her *cuisine*, of charming dinners when she shall be admired as high priestess; and in these latter days there lurks deep down a vague hope that mother-hood may not come oversoon to interfere with these pleasures. Frankly she goes to the new life as she would go to the theatre, expecting to be interested and amused.

The Eastern bride goes to a restriction of liberty in a cloister; goes self-dedicate to duty. For her there is no new house, no new position, nothing but the extremely doubtful pleasure of a husband whom she has not chosen. No degradation could be deeper to her Western sister than being forced to marry a perfect paladin if she happened to prefer a pawnbroker; but the Indian woman is nine times out of ten quite content with the choice of others. There are indeed few happier households than Indian ones; or rather, one should perhap use the past tense, since the native girl is at last learning to read novels, and ere long will doubtless grasp the fact that love makes the world go round – perhaps by turning people's heads!

It seems a pity; even the purdah is preferable to the titter of the Tam-o'-Shanter girl.

One thing is certain: the Western woman has quite as much to learn from the Eastern woman as the Eastern has from the Western. Were they both to set their minds to the task, they would come near to perfection. Meanwhile they – sisters of our Empire – eye each other, and, woman-like, complain of each other's manners.

Certainly one is free to confess that there are few more ill-mannered creatures on God's earth than a native lady travelling in a first- or second-class railway carriage, who considers her ticket entitles her to smoke, chew pan, suckle her baby, eat sweets, spit, and clean her teeth when and how she chooses.

But all women lose their manners when they are herded together, and so do men. Sex has its benefits.

Go to a Jat or a Sikh village where the women live in *bon camaraderie* with the men, and you will find yourself in a different atmosphere. Dip deeper down into the innermost thoughts of the women, and you will recognise that a good woman is a good woman all the world over.

And in India she is certainly none the less good, because behind all the senseless details, the almost revolting habits, and trivialities of real life, there lies an ideal of what woman should be, which is the highest that the world has ever known.

From *The Garden of Fidelity*, 1929:

Throughout her memoirs Flora Annie Steel is remarkably forthright: although her marriage was clearly a happy one she comments early in her narrative that she has no idea why she married, 'I do not think either of us was in love. I know I was not; I never have been'. She lost her first child, a girl, born dead and bitterly mourned. But with the birth of a daughter when she was twenty-three, she says that 'the whole aspect' of her life changed. In 1871 she joined her husband at his new station, Kasur, a subdivision of the Lahore district.

[Kasur] lay thirty-five miles out on the Firozpur road. We were the only Europeans, as there was neither doctor nor policeman. For some years also there was not even a missionary. But, as we were to live there for long, it was a mercy we took to it at once; there was indeed something delightfully primitive about the only house. It was really the old tomb of some far-away Mahommedan saint, and round the big central dome (some forty feet square) had been added on a slip of a room for a drawing-room, another for a dining-room, with two bedrooms and dressing-rooms tucked away in a corner. But these with their verandah were overwhelmed by that big central dome. It had a queer, little circular parapet at the very top, so that there was a wee platform about five feet in diameter to which access was possible by clambering up notches cut in the five-feet deep masonry of the dome. This perch was, even on a hot-weather evening, cool and pleasant. My husband slept there sometimes while I stayed below to look after baby; the fear lest something untoward should happen if the personal eye is removed being common to most mothers.

Office work went on in the central dome room. It was very quiet, very cool, for the walls were five feet thick. There were but two doors, and the saint under the writing-table gave no trouble.

It was a bit dark, but that was amended by a hanging-lamp, and the echoes rather added to the solemnity of the alien judge who dispensed justice. I can see him now: on the table beside him a tiny Testament in red morocco tooled with gold, and subscribed with his great grandfather's name, 'Thomas Henry Jordan Steel, Mayor of Berwick on Tweed'. And close beside it was the little pot of Ganges water; for in those days strange oaths were permitted, and though holy water was not so binding, there were few Sikhs who would lie on *dharm nal* (by the faith), and none who would swear falsely, his hand on his son's head.

I used often to wonder which of the two holinesses had heard the most travesties of the truth. Personally I think the taking of an oath tends to falsification. One is so anxious to tell everything that events lose their proper proportions. Such at any rate has been my experience. I was once nearly four hours under cross-examination, and I never felt so empty in my life as I did when it was over.

I think, however, that it may be said, in reference to the oft-repeated debate as to whether Indian or English justice suffers most from false evidence, that nowadays, when oaths in England are for the most part deprived of all authority, it is more difficult for the judge to discern anything from the bearing of the witness.

Be that as it may, I loved the old echoing dome, and many a time I have stopped at the doorway tunnelled through the wall to listen to the monotonous echoing drawl as the *sarishtadar* (the head clerk) read over some deposition. It was all so dim, so mysterious, so dignified; the echoes might have reached high heaven.

But there were jokes even here, as when my husband came in with a letter in his hand from one of the clerks which ran thus:

RESPECTED GENTLEMAN – Am unable to attend court to-day. Wife run away with another man. Oh, Lord! How truly magnificent!

We spent that cold weather mostly in camp, my husband an old-fashioned believer in seeing personally as much of his district as possible. I remember well his reply to the remark of a scholastic and captious superior, who had several times commented on a sad lack of schedules and returns. We were cantering through a village, and my husband had just replied cheerfully to a question about a rather difficult problem connected with it.

'You really seem to know a good deal about your district,' was the surprised comment.

'I shoot a good deal, sir,' said my husband coolly. It was not a tactful reply. He should have hinted at hard work; but it was a true one, and there is no manner of doubt that more friendliness, more knowledge, was gained in the old-time camping than in the modern rushes out by motor and subsequent tabulating of returns.

It was glorious weather, and we camped chiefly in the low-lying river or *bajt* land which lay below the old high bank on which Kasur stood. It stretched for fifteen miles of inconceivably green wheat-land down to the real Sutlej river, on the other side of which, some ten miles farther, lay the military station of Firozpur. Of course there was no permanent bridge, so our nearest touch with civilisation was in Lahore.

I think my little daughter provided the first link of my subsequent enchainment to the interests of the village women. A baby is ever a good ambassador, and Fazli, the ayah, was an excellent attaché. So most evenings I held a regular court, and I picked up much more of the language than I should have done otherwise. I likewise did no little doctoring; for, before I married, I had quite made up my mind to it as a profession. Castor oil, grey powder, rhubarb, and ipecacuanha[4] form a very efficient medicine-chest for most infantile ailments. At least so I found.

One ridiculous incident I remember well. We had gone to a village where never before had been seen a *memsahib*. Here the baby was quite out of court beside the fact that I was wearing scarlet stockings; and the women wanted to know if I was the same colour all the way up! Fazli was shocked!

After a period of leave the Steels returned to Kasur.

I was glad we were destined again for Kasur, since I knew and liked both place and people. I have always more rapidly become intimate with Mahommedans than Hindus, and Kasur was an old Pathan settlement. Originally, I suppose, they had come down with the Moghul invaders, but they had remained in the old, high-housed township for centuries. The houses were brick, many storied, purpled by age, set cheek by jowl and windowless; intersected by thread-like, tortuous, evil-smelling alleys. But the people were distinctive; the upper class courteous to a degree, the lower, hangers on of all sorts, all almost passionately fanatical. The ruins of an older, far larger city lay about, but there were still some six thousand houses. Except the garden at the Court House, there was no green about the place. Water was deficient, and when it was brought to the surface by means of deep wells, a skin bag, and oxen, apparently it only succeeded in bringing borate of soda with it! So every attempt at gardening produced the *ak* plant, a species of euphorbia that grows anywhere. But my husband was a lineal descendant of Adam: he had an almost uncanny sympathy with plants. Everything he touched grew, everything he grew flourished, and he knew by instinct when a pot-plant was not thriving. I have seen him say to a Scottish head gardener at a show place, 'There's a wireworm at that geranium'. Indignant denial was met by a swift upturning of the pot – and there was the offender! A big canal crossed the road some ten miles nearer Lahore, and my husband had, even during his previous short tenure of Kasur, applied for a cut to supply the town properly; and when we came back there was fresh, pure water at everyone's disposal. It made all the difference. Gardening was started with a will, and the dusty compound became a wilderness of every kind of flower and fruit. The swimming-bath which had been built by some nabob in the dark ages was also filled, and my husband volunteered to teach me how to swim, for like all West Highlanders I was absolutely ignorant of the art. This he did by pushing me in at an unguarded moment and bidding me swim to the end! Adding that he would pull me out if necessary. It was not so; and three days afterwards I was diving after hairpins from the board, and finding the gravest difficulty in getting to the bottom. We had a trapeze and floating *mussoch* or inflated skin bag. Altogether great fun. One day I saw a pair of glittering eyes in the drain-pipe which fed the bath and thought it was a snake. But it proved to be a wild cat. Crib, the fox terrier, was after it in a moment, and they had a tremendous fight. My husband, stripped as he was, ran for his gun, but before he could get back both animals had fallen into the deep narrow cutting which brought in the water. Luckily the dog fell on top, so was at an advantage, for its enemy proved a most formidable foe – a real lynx cat with small, pointed black ears and semi-retractable claws.

So, what with horses, dogs, fowls, ducks, and his garden, one partner in the concern was supremely happy; but I was by this time mentally in that state of uncertainty about all things in which work seems the only anodyne – the one drug which enables you to present a bold front to your world. Hundreds of Indian wives have felt the *désoeuvrement* which must come with the loss of one's children. Perhaps I was more reasonable than most, for I recognised its inevitableness and deliberately sought a way out.

I began by doctoring the woman and children. I had in a way prepared for this at home; for I had read largely and I had brought out a medicine-chest which contained more than the amateur's castor oil and grey powder and ipecacuanha. Looking back I rather wonder at my own self-confidence or rather cheek, in using quite dangerous drugs. But I really did know something, despite the fact that I had no training – except that given me – oh! so kindly, so ungrudgingly – by medical friends. Why, my dear doctor at Ludhiana had once dumped down half a library on my bed, and said with one of his broad laughs, 'Here, read them yourself – you know quite as well as I do what's the matter.'

And fate was not kind to me, for my first big case in the city was puerperal fever. A mere child, the last wife of a Mahommedan gentleman who had lost all his previous ones. I found her in a little dark closet cooped up with a charcoal fire, all air excluded, being dosed with ginger, honey, and almonds. It required some sheer determination to get her carried on to the roof – it was the hot weather – to rid her of all wraps and quilts, to get the coldest water I could get to her head, the hottest to her feet. But the most appalling thing of all to the spectators was the lime-juice and water for her poor parched lips.

The rest I had to leave to Providence; and Providence was kind. She recovered. Of course it made my reputation. After that, had I chosen to order the painting a patient pea-green it would have been done.

They were very unsophisticated in those days: they knew nothing, and were aware of the fact. Truly a little knowledge is a dangerous thing. Of course there was a native doctor, a sort of dispensary at Kasur; but in those days not one of the women would have gone to him. Indeed, till quite late years the traditions of seclusion, the restrictions of *purdah*, were very strong in this old Pathan town.

Meanwhile other interests cropped up. My husband had of course to inspect schools. I accompanied him, and the execrable English which was being taught to the upper classes decided me on a bi-weekly hour in the garden of the Court House for the most advanced English scholars, mostly lads up to sixteen. These hours proved a great success. I read – mostly stories – and above all I made my class speak. [...] But my experience with these boys showed me the extreme difficulty of educating India on Western lines while the environment remained Eastern. For instance, a nice boy of about thirteen was so conspicuously bad in the little written exercise I used to give out for home work that I asked him the reason why. To my surprise he burst into tears and sobbed, 'My baby is dying'.

And die it did, though I tried my utmost; but the mother was just twelve, and the poor little dear had no vitality. It was just one of those foredoomed babies, one of those children of immature parents for which there is a special name amongst the women, which means the 'forerunner'.

But give an instant's thought to the poor lad who was trying to mix up English grammar with fatherhood? and will there not be a heart-whole condemnation of trying to put new wine into old bottles?

Steel's memoirs continue into her old age and she remains confident of her vigour and abilities until the last, coming finally to feel that she should have taken a more active public role:

I felt, as I have so often felt in my life, that I was not utilising myself as I should. There can be no question of the influence I can exert. What have I done with it? very, very little. It is conceited of me to put this down on paper? I think not. It has been so evident all my life, that I was gifted at my birth with unusual – what shall I call it – charm, vigour, personality, influence, something at any rate which was meant to be useful. So, now that I approach my eighty-third year, there is surely no harm in recognising that I have horribly misused the gift I was given.

Flora Annie Steel's book breaks off abruptly and is closed by a chapter written by her daughter which I give as the final example in this book of these tributes of children, of daughters in particular, to their mothers and as a final example of Steel's characteristic enlivening eccentricity:

Soon after this my father died. Under a very quiet and completely kindly and considerate exterior was the keenest wit, the most penetrating humour and insight. To him my mother was the one entirely right thing in this world, and the loss to her of this background to all her life and activity was immense.

She stayed on at Cheltenham, where her grandson was still at the College. Then came a glorious tour in the Italian Lakes and Venice with my mother, the youngest of us, filling her sketch book with the most delightful things.

Then – my husband retiring from India[5] – she and we settled in one of the most beautiful corners of the Cotswolds. There she wrote *The Builder*, this finishing her series of historical romances of the Moghul Emperors.

Of these she writes:

This book finishes one of the finest chapters in the history of the world, the record of the reigns of the four great Moghul Emperors of India. I have attempted to portray the men themselves and their times, first in *King Errant*, which shows Baber the Knight Errant; secondly, in a *Prince of Dreamers*, which shows Akbar the great Dreamer; thirdly, in *Mistress of Men*, which gives Jehangir, the Compleat Lover, and finally, in the *Builder*, Shah Jehan the Magnificent, how he, perhaps the ablest monarch of them all, failed to keep what he had inherited from his forbears. Thus my task is finished, the story is told.

When this was written, my mother turned to a subject on which she had thought much, and she determined to illustrate her conclusions on the 'Curse of Eve' – oversexed womanhood tempting man as in the old Genesis story.

These are some of her notes – intended for incorporation in her memoirs.

I remember one day going up to speak at some function in London. My train was halted on a viaduct outside the city. Below me lay mean streets, dull interminable. I could see no hint of higher things far as the eye could reach. But they were crammed, literally bubbling over, with children of all sorts and sizes. I suppose it was the dinner interval. Anyhow, the over-population of the world came home to me as it never had before.

The train stopped for perhaps five minutes. In our tangled ways of civilisation some signal had possibly gone wrong. But five minutes was enough. *I saw.*

For years I had pondered over the 'Curse of Eve'. Now, for the first time, the relevancy of the words, 'I will greatly multiply thy conception', became apparent. Alone among animals mankind is the victim of sex. It claims them always, and holds them at all times prisoners in its power.

For days, weeks, months, our humbler fellow-mortals live together peacefully, male and female, undisturbed, forgetful of the dread heirloom of the immortality of the race of which they are the transient possessors, and then, simply, unconsciously, as seed-time and harvest to these, our fellow mortals. They may be but unconscious puppets in the grip of the mighty creative force which uses them for its own ends, but at least they have not, as we have, broken loose from that control and found no other. How has this happened? Why in all the records of primitive man, is there – as Sir James Frazer in the *Golden Bough* put it[6] – 'that deep ingrained dread', that belief that woman is held to be charged with a power dangerous to man? The supposition that the fall of man was the perversion of the seasonal racial instinct to that of an ever possible individual pleasure explains many things – this instinctive dread – in its innumerable manifestations, the sense of sin and shame, so foreign to the whole living world except ourselves.

As the scientist Metchnikoff puts it,[7] 'The sex functions in man are the greatest disharmony in nature.' Now the question is, can we get back and choose the right instead of the wrong way? Can woman find her lost reserve, and man his lost sense of fatherhood?

At any rate, let humanity realise how far it has strayed. And when I came to think of the cause – the clue came suddenly in those idle words I have recorded elsewhere, 'The woman thou hast given me is as jealous as old boots.' That is the clue, 'jealousy', that unfailing attribute of sex, the male of the male, the female of the female; but in the animal world seasonal as sex itself. In the desire to have and to hold, to keep the man from straying, the 'woman's desire was to her husband' – not seasonally but at all times. This may seem to some an idle clue; to others it may seem I have wasted my time, brought nothing worth having to the storehouse of the world, but for myself I have no alternative, what came to me must be given to the world, to the dustheap perhaps, but it will have been given.

These, my mother's last written words on this subject, show the importance she attached to the view that woman's jealousy was the primal cause of that disharmony of the racial instincts which is the root of so many of our social evils.

The *Curse of Eve* was finished in the spring of 1928. For a year my mother had been suffering from the result of a slight abrasion, which, extending its borders, gave her extreme pain and trouble, and for a time crippled her completely. Then suddenly came one of her crises, accesses of vitality, her indomitable will triumphed, and to the astonishment of her medical advisers she became perfectly well and whole. It was then she went to Jamaica to visit the family property, taking her youngest grandson with her. Jamaica welcomed her royally. She toured the island, enjoyed herself extraordinarily. On her return she wrote her experiences and views on the West Indies, and started an animated discussion in the press, which has, I believe, been of distinct value in the cause of Empire Trade.

Then she began work on this *Garden of Fidelity*.

She became much interested in the modern conception of space and time, and read and re-read Professor Eddington's last book. More then ever, she said, she felt the truth of Lewis Nettleship's words, 'There is no room for death'.[8] A short time this spring she spent in her grandson's rooms in Oxford – reading daily at the Bodleian – 'A most plucky attempt to keep term,' wrote the President of his college. Then a reading party for him in Wales, where her old friends welcomed her to the beautiful hills and woods of her sometime Welsh home. There she passed her eighty-second birthday.

Then she turned from her *Garden of Fidelity* to a tale planned long ago, *The Gates of Pearl*, and while telling of those who sought them, suddenly and splendidly passed within them.

NOTES

1. 'Arry and 'Arriet were creations of the humourist E. J. Milliken in *Punch*, 1870-90. See: *''Arry' Ballads*, with 105 pictures. From *Punch* (London: 1893).
2. That is 'the women's law'. I suppose Knox's 'monstrous regimen of women' covers the case!
3. From Sheridan's *The Rivals*, 1775. 'If I can't get a wife without fighting for her […] I'll live a bachelor', he says.
4. An emetic produced from the root of the Brazilian plant, Cephaelis or Uragoga.
5. Steel's daughter married her cousin and had two sons.
6. Sir James George Frazer (1854-1941), British anthropologist, mythologist and writer, is best known for *The Golden Bough*, 1890, which tries to trace the history of man through magic, religion and science. His influence was far reaching and famously extended to the poet, T. S. Eliot.
7. Ilya Ilich Metchnikov (1845-1916), Russian zoologist, is best known for his work on white blood cells. In 1908 he was jointly awarded the Nobel Prize with the German bacteriologist, Paul Ehrlich.
8. Sir Arthur Stanley Eddington (1882-19440), theoretical astronomer and talented populariser of science. Richard Lewis Nettleship (1846-1892), fellow and tutor of Balliol College, wrote on Plato's theory of education, and died of exposure climbing Mont Blanc.

THE ASSOCIATION FOR SCOTTISH LITERARY STUDIES

ANNUAL VOLUMES

Volumes marked * are still available from the address given opposite the title page of this book.